The Japanese
Novel of the
Meiji Period
and the
Ideal of
Individualism

JANET A. WALKER

The Japanese Novel of the Meiji Period and the Ideal of Individualism

PRINCETON UNIVERSITY PRESS
PRINCETON, NEW JERSEY

Contents

Preface vii

PART ONE The Ideal of Individualism and the
Meiji Novel 1

Chapter One Introduction 3

Chapter Two Futabatei's *Ukigumo* (The Floating
Clouds): The First Novel of the Individual 30

Chapter Three Kitamura Tōkoku and the Ideal of the
Inner Life: The Interiorization of the Ideal
of Individualism 62

Chapter Four Katai's *Futon* (The Quilt): The Birth of the
I-Novel 93

PART TWO Shimazaki Tōson and the Ideal of
Individualism 121

Chapter Five The Education of a Meiji Individual 123

Chapter Six *Hakai* (Breaking the Commandment): A
Novel of the Inner Life 156

Chapter Seven *Shinsei* (The New Life): A Novel of
Confession 194

Chapter Eight Shimazaki Tōson's Ideal of the Individual 244

Works Consulted 285

Index 301

Preface

In his famous "Ballad of East and West" (1889), Rudyard Kipling, decrying the popular idea that East and West could never meet, wrote that, on the contrary, the great differences between East and West could be bridged by "two strong men standing face to face."[1] As if in confirmation of his words, meetings between writers and artists of the West and the East were occurring at that very time—peaceful confrontations that were to have profound consequences for both cultures. For already in the 1870s French Impressionist painters, weary of Western representational art, were finding in the brightly colored and asymmetrical Japanese woodblock print an encouragement of their interest in an antirepresentational realism of the moment. Also, by the 1880s and 1890s, writers of the Naturalist and Decadent movements in France had discovered in the woodblock print a technique of nonmoralizing description of the beautiful and the real that they attempted to apply in their literary works.[2] At this same time, the Japanese, convinced of the inferiority of their culture in the face of Western military power, were attempting to reach an understanding of Western technology and Western cultural ideals as well. One of the most important of these was the ideal of individualism. This study treats the discovery of the ideal of individualism by several major literary figures—all but one of them novelists—of the Meiji period (1868-1912).

By *individualism* I mean, very broadly, the idea that the exist-

[1] The lines in question read as follows: "Oh, East is East, and West is West, and never the twain shall meet, / Till Earth and Sky stand presently at God's great Judgment Seat; / But there is neither East nor West, Border, nor Breed, nor Birth, / When two strong men stand face to face, though they come from the ends of the earth!" *Rudyard Kipling's Verse*, Inclusive Edition, 1885-1926, New York, 1928, p. 268.

[2] Earl Miner, *The Japanese Tradition in British and American Literature*, Princeton, 1958, pp. 66-74.

ence, the energy, and the morality of the individual are valuable in their own right and worthy of cultural attention and respect. The idea of individualism, when introduced into Japan beginning in the 1870s, quickly became an ideal with revolutionary implications for Japanese culture, for it symbolized no less than freedom from the strictures of the feudalism of the past. The first Japanese word that expressed the idea, Fukuzawa Yukichi's *dokuritsu* ("independence"), had its origins in the ideal of individuality of John Stuart Mill; developing in the context of the People's Rights movement of the 1870s and 1880s, it signified the achievement of political and social liberty. An individualism of the inner self was proposed in the early 1890s by Kitamura Tōkoku, whose intellectual origins were in Universalist Christianity, Emersonian transcendentalism, and Buddhist mysticism. Another term, *kojinshugi* (literally—"individualism"), was used by the novelist Natsume Sōseki in a lecture given in 1914 and has remained in the modern vocabulary as the most common word for the Western concept. A still broader term that has been used more recently is *kindaiteki jiga* ("modern selfhood"). This term implies political and social modernization, a process by which an individual becomes individualistic and "Western" in his outlook and behavior. Looking back on the development of Japan since the Meiji period, modernization is a process that still has not been completed, and so the expression "the awakening or establishing of the modern self" evokes a spirit of continued vigilance against feudal tendencies.

An intellectual historian dealing with the important contributions to the ideal of individualism in the Meiji period would treat such figures as Nakamura Keiu, the translator of Samuel Smiles's *Self-Help* and an important figure of the Enlightenment movement of the 1870s; Tokutomi Sohō, the editor of the liberal journal, *Kokumin no tomo* (The Nation's Friend), in the 1890s and early 1900s; and Takayama Chogyū, the author of the important essay *Biteki seikatsu o ronzu* (On the Aesthetic Life, 1901). However, this is not a study in intellectual history—rather, it is a study of an ideal of far-reaching implications that became a personal ideal of writers of the Meiji period and, finally, an important theme of their works. Indeed, numerous writers of this age—far more than I have chosen to discuss—were preoccupied with this ideal. The diaries of the novelists Higuchi Ichiyō (1872-1896) and Kunikida Doppo (1871-1908) in the 1890s, and those of the poet Ishikawa Takuboku (1885-1912) in the first decade of the twentieth century, reflect the growth of a modern self in its torments and exaltations. Yet diaries, with the exception of Takuboku's *Rōmaji nikki* (Romaji Diary, 1909), do not present a coherent statement of the author on the idea of the modern self. Of the literary forms of this time, only the novel, with its concern for the individual as a moral being involved in action and growth in time, provides a coherent vision of the individual. Thus, I am omitting from this study Mori Ōgai's short story entitled *Maihime* (The Dancing Girl, 1890), the first fictional work that treats an incident in the life of a modern writer, because the author seems more interested in experimenting with a stylized first-person narrative than he is in presenting his view of the new individual. Furthermore, individualism was not one of the important ideals of the later Ōgai.[3] I omit Natsume Sōseki because, though he was concerned with the Western ideal of individualism, his attitude toward it was at best ambivalent. To clarify the attitude of this major figure would demand a separate study.[4]

The major novelists I discuss are Futabatei Shimei (1864-1909), Tayama Katai (1871-1930), and Shimazaki Tōson (1872-1943)—all of whom were personally sympathetic to the ideal of individualism and creatively involved with it in their works. Futabatei was the first to portray the individual from the inside in

[3] For a translation of *Maihime* see Richard Bowring, "*Maihime* (The Dancing Girl) by Mori Ōgai: Translation and Background," *Monumenta Nipponica* 30 (1975): 151-176.

[4] Such a study is Wha Seon Roske-cho's *Das Japanische Selbstverständnis im Modernisierungsprozess bei Natsume Sōseki*, Wiesbaden, 1973.

a full-length novel; Katai was the author of the first I-novel (*shishōsetsu*), or autobiographical novel. I include a discussion of Fukuzawa Yukichi's ideal of independence to provide the background necessary for an understanding of the complex political climate out of which Futabatei's *Ukigumo* emerged. The discussion of Katai's *Futon* is similarly preceded by an introductory essay on Japanese Naturalism and its most important genre, the I-novel. The discussion of Kitamura Tōkoku, the only non-novelist in the group, is intended as an introduction not only to my treatment of the phenomena that were greatly affected by his ideas—Naturalism and the I-novel—but also the whole second part of this study, for Tōkoku was the most important influence on the ideal of individualism of Shimazaki Tōson. Thus, in some way each of the chapters in Part One leads into the discussion of this author, the novelist who had more confidence than any other of his time in the Western ideal of individualism. The chapters on Fukuzawa's ideal of independence and Tōkoku's ideal of the inner life give insight into the dual ancestry of Tōson's ideal: the samurai ideal of sincerity and the Christian ideal of the inner life. The sections on Romanticism and Naturalism introduce the ideology that underlay Tōson's writing of autobiographical novels, and those on the novels of Futabatei and Katai provide comparisons with Tōson's own novels, and images, of the individual. Finally, the discussion of pre-Meiji images of the individual illuminates Tōson's use of the past, as well as the ways in which he transcended it.

During his fifty-year career as a writer Shimazaki Tōson was one of the most widely read authors in Japan. His position in modern Japanese literature can be properly evaluated if one considers that he was responsible for setting the direction, first, of modern poetry, then, of modern fiction. His complete works—eighteen volumes in the Shinchōsha edition—include several volumes of poetry, short fiction, prose sketches, and personal essays; eight complete novels and one unfinished novel; and several volumes of criticism and letters. Like most writers of the first generation of Meiji, Tōson was exposed to Western culture at an early age; already from his late teens he was reading Western writers in English translation. Tōson's careful study of writers such as Turgenev, Maupassant, Tolstoy, Dostoevsky, Flaubert, Oscar Wilde, Chekhov, Ibsen, Rousseau, and Pascal not only contributed to his own development as a writer but also issued in a series of brief essays that served to introduce these writers to the Japanese reading public. Tōson's oeuvre is known only fragmentarily in the West. Of the novels, an English translation of *Hakai* (Breaking the Commandment, 1906) was published in 1974, Russian and Kazakh translations of the work having existed already since 1931 and 1959, respectively. A translation of *Ie* (The Family, 1911) appeared in 1976, but *Shinsei* (The New Life, 1919) exists so far only in a Chinese translation. Several dissertations in English on Shimazaki Tōson have appeared since 1965, and a monograph-length study by Edwin McClellan, *Two Japanese Novelists: Sōseki and Tōson* (1969), provides a helpful introduction to Tōson's works. Critical discussions in English of modern Japanese literature as a whole, however, have generally ignored Tōson, possibly out of a sense that as a novelist he does not export as well as Kawabata or even Sōseki.[5]

Yet to ignore Tōson is to ignore the role that the Western ideal of individualism, filtered through his life and his works, played in the development of both the modern sensibility and the modern novel in Japan. The present study seeks to draw attention to this major contribution of Tōson, a contribution of insight into the process of the awakening of the modern Japanese self that guarantees him a faithful readership even today when his literary innovations have been all but forgotten. My chapters on Tōson focus on his coming to an awareness of his selfhood in late adolescence, his development of a poetic form to express this selfhood, and finally, his working out of a mature vision of the modern in-

[5] See, for example, the excellent studies of modern Japanese fiction by Masao Miyoshi (*Accomplices of Silence*, Berkeley, 1974) and Makoto Ueda (*Modern Japanese Writers and the Nature of Literature*, Stanford, 1976).

dividual in the two confessional novels written around the close of the Meiji period: *Hakai* and *Shinsei*. The final chapter discusses Tōson's ideal of individualism and his related ideals of love, freedom, and confession, in the context of Meiji fiction.

Japanese names are given in the order in which they appear in the cited work. Generally, in works written in English, Japanese names follow the English order of last name last. In Japanese sources names are given in the traditional order of last name first. The writers Shimazaki Tōson, Natsume Sōseki, Nagai Kafū, and Tayama Katai are referred to not by their family names but, as is customary in Japan, by their pen names: Tōson, Sōseki, Kafū, and Katai, respectively. Where good translations of the novels in question are available, I have quoted from them; otherwise all translations are my own. The footnotes give only the author's name, the title, and the date and place of publication of a particular work. Full references, including translations of foreign titles and characters for Japanese titles and authors, are given under Works Consulted. For the benefit of nonspecialist readers who might wish to find them, I have included in that section also full bibliographical information about literary works, most of them translations from the Japanese, that are discussed but not footnoted in the text.

As any new scholarship rests on the work of earlier scholars, I wish to single out a few people to whose work I am particularly indebted: Jaroslav Prušek, whose great learning and great enthusiasm for the field of East-West literary relations inspired me to research the ideal of individualism in modern Japanese fiction; William Naff, whose fine biography alerted me to the value of Tōson's work; and Edwin McClellan, who was the first Western critic to draw attention to the role that Tōson's confessionalism played in the development of the modern Japanese novel. My special thanks go to Howard Hibbett and Harry Levin, who, as this study evolved over the years, provided continual encouragement and constructive criticism, and to Marleigh Grayer Ryan and Edwin McClellan, who provided valuable suggestions on how to improve the final draft. I am grateful to Rutgers University for a Research Council Summer Fellowship and a semester of leave, which made it possible for me to work full time on this manuscript, and to The Andrew W. Mellon Foundation for a grant in support of its publication. Maureen Donovan of the Gest Oriental Library of Princeton University deserves my thanks for her assistance in obtaining hard-to-find materials, Helen Homiak for her never-ending patience and her expert typing. I wish to thank Marjorie Sherwood of Princeton University Press for the expertise, enthusiasm, and tact that she has demonstrated at all stages in the process of publication of the manuscript. I thank also Virginia Morgan, copy editor, who improved the style of the manuscript in many small ways. Finally, I owe a deep debt of gratitude to my husband, Steve, without whose encouragement years ago this book would never have been written.

J.W.

Highland Park, New Jersey
September 1978

Part One

THE IDEAL OF INDIVIDUALISM AND THE MEIJI NOVEL

CHAPTER ONE

Introduction

Individualism, or the myth of individual freedom associated with the rise of the middle class, could be called the modern myth. In the West, the middle-class individual has been the culture hero since at least the nineteenth century.[1] Carlyle, for example, realized that the middle-class writer or artist, as the avant-garde of his class, was called upon to embody in his life the heroic myth of his culture, which by definition included past heroic myths, and to reinterpret the old myths to suit the needs of his time.[2] In the Meiji period (1868-1912) a similar undertaking began, in a nation that was undergoing economic and cultural changes similar to those that issued in nineteenth-century Western individualism. As the ideal of the free individual slowly penetrated middle-class intellectual circles in Japan, writers began to turn their attention to themselves for the first time, with a seriousness that showed that the ideal of freedom was one of the most inspiring of their age. Through their attempts to define the new individual as they saw him, they succeeded in shifting the focus of their traditional culture to a new type of culture hero—the private individual who is interesting not because of his virtues or heroic exploits in the world but because of his inner uniqueness and the quality of his everyday existence. Yet it is impossible, I feel, to evaluate properly the achievements of Meiji writers in the

---

[1] By culture hero I mean Hippolyte Taine's *personnage régnant*—the individual whose behavior and ideals are considered by a culture to embody the desired or characteristic elements of a particular period. *Philosophie de l'art*, Paris, 1964, p. 64.

[2] Carlyle devotes a chapter of his *On Heroes, Hero Worship, and the Heroic in History* (1841) to the hero as a man of letters, and the nineteenth-century *Bildungsroman* conceived of the sensitive middle-class person as a kind of artist.

realm of their depiction of a new type of individual without a more detailed discussion of the culture heroes that existed in pre-Meiji times.

Culture Heroes of the Japanese Past

Japanese culture, like other cultures, presents not one ideal of the individual but several, each of which is the product of a particular period. The culture hero of a given period inevitably reflects the accession to power or at least the increased dominance of a particular class, as well as the religious ideals of that class. He influences later conceptions of individual heroism depending on the length of time he dominated the culture and the relative importance of tradition in the culture. For example, in Japan a culture hero from the aristocratic period exerted great influence on all later conceptions of the hero. After the decline of the aristocratic culture a new, more dynamic ideal of the individual appeared with the rise to power of the samurai or warrior class. A third ideal, that of the townsman, or *chōnin*, emerged with the development of an urban, merchant culture in the seventeenth century. The townsman ideal combined samurai ethical rigor with an aristocratic love of self-satisfying aesthetic pursuits and sense pleasures, resulting in a dynamic personality type, which at best existed in creative conflict with its surroundings and at worst was divided against itself. Thus, the aristocratic ideal did not die, though its original representatives were early deprived of power. Even the modern individualist culture hero that emerged in the Meiji period under Western influence showed lingering traces of the aristocratic ideal in his preoccupation with his own perceptions and experiences, yet in his concern with moral growth and action he was equally the heir of the samurai.

Aristocratic culture was actually dominant in Japan from about A.D. 700 to 1200, and the sheer length of the aristocratic period, as well as the almost complete isolation and freedom from external challenge that characterized it, probably accounts for the emergence of a culture hero from this era that was to influence all later conceptions of ideal behavior. This was Prince Genji, hero of the eleventh-century romance, *Genji monogatari* (The Tale of Genji). Genji was a man conscious of his place in society, in nature, and in love relationships. For Genji, to live was to be aware of the manifold phenomena, feelings, and processes of the world, to experience the "pathos of things" (*mono no aware*).[3] Genji's existence was based on a felt harmony between individuals and between man and nature, but when the battles of the provincial clans destroyed this harmony in the late twelfth century, initiating a long period of military rule, aesthetic culture was reduced to a system of inherited rituals and practices. Members of the priestly class assumed the burden of preserving the rituals and attitudes of the dying aristocratic culture. The priest Yoshida Kenkō, for example, in his book of essays entitled *Tsurezure-gusa* (Grasses of Idleness, ca. 1332), stressed the importance of planting trees harmoniously around one's house, or of using ancient objects and vocabulary in the proper way.

The Pure Land and Nichiren sects of Buddhism that emerged around the close of the thirteenth century encouraged a dynamic, ethical religious consciousness in the individual. As the military (samurai) class gradually took control of Japan, a new culture hero appeared who joined the virtue of moral responsibility with those of obedience and loyalty to his lord. Later the Zen (meditation) sect of Buddhism, which became especially popular among members of the samurai class in the fourteenth century, advocated the individual's coming to an intuitive awareness of religious truth, an awareness that was to be achieved through strenuous disciplining of the ego. The characteristics of spontaneity and utter selflessness of the Zen enlightened man, and samurai fearlessness and stoicism were united in the renowned samurai cul-

---

[3] For a discussion of the aestheticism of aristocratic culture see Kōsaka Masaaki, "The Status and the Role of the Individual in Japanese Society," in *The Japanese Mind*, ed. Charles A. Moore with the assistance of Aldyth V. Morris, Honolulu, 1967, pp. 245-248, 257-258.

ture hero, Benkei, who is depicted in numerous Nō dramas and in the fifteenth-century epic *Gikeiki* (Chronicle of Yoshitsune). The fact that Benkei cannot be a true culture hero without the presence of his lord, Yoshitsune, attests to the tendency of the Japanese from this time on to see individuals as existing in a network of hierarchical relationships.[4] During the era of intermittent warfare between about 1200 and 1600, then, the individual existed only in terms of his place in the hierarchy; legally, he did not exist at all. Yet Zen, by stressing the individual's personal experiencing of the truth, contributed to Japanese culture a concept of the individual as a free being somehow outside of or transcending the social hierarchy. This paradoxical idea that the individual was socially unfree though experientially free continued to affect Japanese culture even after Westernization began in the late nineteenth century.

In the West, the Renaissance brought about a break with the medieval Christian world. It saw the beginnings of scientific thought, of the idea of society as a secular, abstract unity of individuals, of the capitalist economic system, and of individualism as it is understood in the West: a social system in which the individual is ideally alone in a secularized world, freed from the bonds of the family and tradition. From the thirteenth to the sixteenth centuries in Japan there occurred a great increase in trade with China and Korea, the growth of *za* (trade organizations similar to European guilds), the development of a professional class of merchants, and eventually, in the fifteenth and sixteenth centuries, the growth of towns that were mainly commercial centers. In other words, phenomena occurred similar to those in Europe that eventually destroyed the feudal economic system and led to the formation of unified national states in economic and military competition with one another. Yet Japan, entering a period of peace in 1600, became isolated from the outside world

---

[4] Nakamura Hajime, "Consciousness of the Individual and the Universal Among the Japanese," in Moore, *The Japanese Mind*, p. 182.

after the 1630s, when her new military rulers stopped all trade
with Europeans. Unity and nationhood were achieved through a
forcible continuation of feudal ethics and a freezing of social mobility, while the growth of a merchant economy was purposely
hindered.

The Tokugawa period (1600-1868) was not a heroic age. Like
the earlier Heian period, it was a period of peace; but unlike the
Heian period, it was not one of natural harmony between individuals. In this period it is difficult to find an active culture
hero—a hero who throws himself into the world of action in perfect harmony with a cultural ideal. One possible culture hero of
this time, the *haiku* poet Matsuo Bashō (1644-1694), seems at
first glance to represent merely a continuation of two heroic ideals
of the Middle Ages. His selflessness and acceptance of a monklike
existence of wandering link him to the medieval Zen monk, but
he also embodied the independence and stoicism that were qualities of the warrior. Yet Bashō was not a person of the Middle
Ages, but a person who came to artistic maturity in the merchant
culture of Edo (Tokyo). He had to struggle to attain the older
cultural attitudes of serenity and detachment that appealed to
him—they did not come naturally—and he communicated, in
his writings, a strongly individualized and dynamic sense of self
that was quite different from the medieval monk Kenkō's aristocratic eccentricity.

Those in power during the Tokugawa period, the samurai, did
not appear in literature, probably because in the latter days of
their rule they were no longer living out a heroic ideal. The
samurai of the early feudal period had embodied the ideal of self-
less action directed toward the highest goal of service to his lord.
Now that the battles were over, the ethical goal became work of
chiefly an intellectual and administrative nature for the good of
the collective—the clan government. The samurai had become a
bureaucrat, and the samurai ethic, though it was still being described in Zen-influenced religious terms as late as the early
eighteenth century—for example, in the famous *Hagakure* (Hid-

den under the Leaves)[5]—had become a pragmatic, down-to-earth businessman's ethic. Loyalty was still foremost; otherwise, the ethic stressed the virtues of obedience, uprightness, and consideration for others. A sober, restrained life style was recommended, one that avoided idleness and overindulgence in sex—in other words, activities that had the goal of mere self-satisfaction.

Samurai values were the official values of the Tokugawa period.[6] This was so even though the samurai class was slowly declining in wealth, and probably two-thirds of its members were almost poverty-stricken by the end of the Tokugawa period. The merchant class, which was becoming more and more wealthy, even lending money to samurai, kowtowed to the morality of the samurai class. Rather than attempting to assert the superiority of their value system that emphasized profit over loyalty and diligence, they stressed instead the invaluable labors they performed for the good of the collectivity, and argued that they deserved more respect than their official position at the bottom of the social hierarchy guaranteed them. Every class, whether peasants, artisans, or merchants, was subject to the commandments to work diligently, live frugally, and express obedience to their social superiors, the samurai. Yet as the merchant class gradually increased its financial, if not political power, its own values of pleasure and self-satisfaction began to play a greater role in the culture, in the form of the development of a vast subculture of entertainment.[7] For the Tokugawa rulers any values connected with pleasure were private, and by definition harmful to the stability of the public order. Consequently, they allowed the pursuit of self-satisfaction to take place only within a context that was strictly separated from the approved public contexts of work and family. Symbolic of the rigid separation between political values

---

[5] For a discussion and translation of excerpts from this work see Daisetz T. Suzuki, *Zen and Japanese Culture*, New York, 1959, pp. 70ff.

[6] Robert N. Bellah, *Tokugawa Religion*, Glencoe, 1957, pp. 90-98.

[7] For a discussion of pleasure values or "aesthetic-emotional" values, as Bellah calls them, see *Tokugawa Religion*, pp. 17-18.

(loyalty and obedience) and pleasure values, then, is the emergence of vast pleasure quarters in the major cities, which were set off from other areas of the city by gates and which had their own special customs and rules.

The upsurge of aesthetic and pleasure values in the Tokugawa era can be seen in the appearance, already in the early 1600s, of fictional works called *kana-zōshi* (writings in the *kana* syllabary), which depicted in great detail the life in these pleasure quarters, and generally stressed the attractiveness and excitement of the style of life there.[8] One particular work whose origins were in this tradition but whose level of artistry was much higher than the ordinary *kana-zōshi* captured the energy and lust for enjoyment that were characteristic of the merchant class, and succeeded in creating its first culture hero (in this case, a culture heroine). This was Ihara Saikaku's novel *Kōshoku ichidai onna* (The Life of a Woman Who Loved Love, 1686). The heroine of the novel, called simply *"onna"* ("the woman") by the author, tells her story in the first person. The form of the novel is a burlesqued saint's life—that is, a parody of the patterned narration of the passage from sin to the truth of religion that was so popular in the Muromachi period (1336-1573).

Saikaku's novel, written in a racy, poetic style, tells of the heroine's setting out in the world as a young girl to work and pursue her pleasure, and of her gradual decline in that world to the status of a low-class prostitute. The heroine is from a noble family that had come down in the world several generations before. She starts her activity in the world of work as a servant to a noble family, where she naturally becomes attracted to the life of aestheticism and pleasure that she observes every day, and is soon initiated into it directly. The heroine should be seen as an upwardly mobile person; she longs for the freedom, for the access to fine things and to pleasure that her sex and good looks seem to

[8] Richard Lane, "The Beginnings of the Modern Japanese Novel: *Kana-zōshi*, 1600-1682," *Harvard Journal of Asiatic Studies* 20 (1957): 660-664.

guarantee are within her reach. She attempts to play the role of a female Genji, imbuing the aristocratic life style of pleasure and luxury with the energy and dynamism of her class.

Yet the novel shows that without the guaranteed income of the aristocrat, the pursuit of pleasure can only be done in the brothel. In the pleasure quarter, where looks and talent count more than rank, the possibilities of attaining freedom and wealth seem unlimited. However, mobility can also be downward, as the heroine finds out. The author treats her fall cynically, as if he were saying: "The world is illusory and vain. How, then, can one expect to find success and happiness in it?" Saikaku's world is still the medieval world of the senses and the transitory: *ukiyo*, the floating, ephemeral world.[9] Seen from a Buddhist perspective, it is a world totally without freedom, a free existence being possible in such a context only through an awareness of one's inner spiritual nature. A modern-style *social* world, in which individuals could dream of acting freely in a secularized context, was not depicted in Japanese literature until the early eighteenth century.

As merchant activity, and the middle-class culture developing in the midst of it, became increasingly stifled by the feudal government toward the end of the seventeenth and the beginning of the eighteenth century, a new culture hero emerged in Japan: the middle-class *chōnin* who struggles to win self-satisfaction but is only barely able or totally unable to survive the pressures exerted on him by the morality of family and society. The *chōnin* tried to live according to a morality that suited the samurai, an ethic that demanded much of him but guaranteed him no political power. As Tsuda Sōkichi remarks, "the talents and abilities of an individual were made light of and he was not allowed to work out his own individuality. . . . Further, no room was allowed for an individual to live except by submissively keeping up the order of the

---

[9] For a full discussion of the *ukiyo* of Saikaku see Howard S. Hibbett, *The Floating World in Japanese Fiction*, New York, 1959. The work contains a partial translation of the novel under discussion here.

community."[10] The desire for individual satisfaction was not totally crushed, however. It existed for the wealthier ranks of the *chōnin* in the pursuit of sense pleasures—for this was the mode of self-expression in aristocratic culture that the *chōnin* idealized and the freedom that they wished to attain for themselves. Hedonism in the pleasure quarters was hardly a possibility for the poorer *chōnin*; they attempted to live out their desire for freedom, and for love, in real life, not in the sequestered and ultimately harmless territory of the brothel, and in so doing they threatened the Confucian morality that divided the areas of work and family irrevocably from those of pleasure and freedom.

In the puppet plays of Chikamatsu Monzaemon (1653-1725) that were written and performed between about 1700 and 1720, small tradesmen and low-ranking samurai are depicted as caught in an irreconcilable conflict between *giri*, or obligations toward others, and *ninjō* ("human feelings"), or their own desire for self-satisfaction.[11] In his *Shinjū-ten no Amijima* (The Love Suicides at Amijima, 1721) Jihei the paper merchant cuts a pitiful figure as he fails to solve the dilemmas to which his conflicting desires to love the prostitute Koharu and yet remain loyal to his wife expose him—but he acquires heroic stature when one considers the staggering moral demands made on him. Similarly, the love suicide of Jihei and Koharu at the end of the play takes on heroic dimensions, when one realizes that by killing themselves the unhappy lovers are asserting their freedom, though it costs them their lives. The extent to which the lower-ranking *chōnin* lived a hard-pressed and freedomless existence may be gauged by the fact that, in Chikamatsu's plays at least, the only way for them to gain freedom was to die; in life there was only duty.

[10] Sōkichi Tsuda, *An Inquiry into the Japanese Mind as Mirrored in Literature: The Flowering Period of Common People* [sic] *Literature*, trans. Fukumatsu Matsuda, Tokyo, 1970, p. 227.

[11] Similarly, Schiller created, in a slightly later era, the figure of the rising German bourgeois who must choose between duty (*Pflicht*) and inclination (*Neigung*).

In the West of the same period absolutist governments kept a strong curb on the rise of the middle class, and it is possible to see the heroes of the novels of Le Sage, Smollett, Fielding, and Marivaux as middle-class individuals who, like Chikamatsu's heroes, were oppressed by the morals and politics of a superior class.[12] Yet in the eighteenth century Rousseau provided a justification for the middle-class desire for political power as well as for individual freedom, and novels such as Richardson's *Pamela*, Rousseau's *Julie, ou la nouvelle Héloïse*, and Goethe's *Die Leiden des jungen Werther* marked, for their respective literatures, the beginning of interest in the expression of middle-class individual sentiment in a realistic setting. Furthermore, love was depicted in such novels as a moral force contributing to the growth of the individual. Thus, there existed in European societies at this time two ideas that contributed, according to Ian Watt, to the development of the Western bourgeois novel: that of individualism and that of love as a dynamic moral force.[13]

In Tokugawa Japan, two important aspects of individualism, the desire for social mobility and the desire for self-satisfaction in love, were discouraged by the Confucian moral system and inhibited by the rigidly hierarchical social structure. According to orthodox Confucian morality, love between man and woman was a feeling that had as its goal the satisfaction of sensual desires; it was an antisocial force and therefore an immoral one. The higher qualities of love were not recognized because of the inherent limitations in the Confucian moral vision, with the consequence that the pursuit of love was seen as inimical to man's true goal: the pursuit of knowledge. The Tokugawa government considered love a threat because it feared that too much emphasis on the

---

[12] Nikolai I. Konrad describes what he calls the literature of absolutism in Europe, China, and Japan in the period from the sixteenth to the eighteenth centuries in "The Problem of Realism and the Literatures of the East," in *West-East: Inseparable Twain*, Moscow, 1967, p. 181.

[13] Ian Watt, *The Rise of the Novel*, Berkeley and Los Angeles, 1957, pp. 135-138.

"feminine" sphere of life would weaken the strength of the samurai class. Furthermore, the ideal of love, if it were to spread among the lower classes, would eventually undermine the morality of obedient diligence that the government had been so careful to foster. Obviously, some ideology that recognized the primacy of feeling (*ninjō*) in life, and that valued the role of feeling in the formation of character, was needed before the individual and love could be seen in their true meaning.

A scholar of the Shinto school of learning, Motoori Norinaga (1730-1801), provided this ideology. Norinaga defended the individual's right to express feeling, regardless of its moral nature: "Generally speaking, man, by nature, cannot keep from talking to others about what he has deeply felt. . . . Certainly, neither he himself nor others will profit from such talk, yet it is natural that man cannot help expressing himself."[14] Whereas Confucianists degraded feeling out of a fear of its potential capacity to destroy the moral self in man, Norinaga contended that it was man's nature to feel—and a drive so basic to human nature ought not to be degraded. Norinaga extended his justification of feeling to a defense of literature that expressed feeling, and through his essay entitled *Genji monogatari tama no ogushi* (The Small Jeweled Comb: The Tale of Genji, 1796), began the long process of restoring that novel—in his time condemned by Confucianists as immoral—to its rightful position as the masterpiece of traditional literature. Norinaga's writings not only defended man's natural self against Confucianist charges of immorality; they implied that it was morally superior to the superficial social and moral self created by systems such as Confucianism. All in all, Norinaga's defense of the natural self, and of literature whose aim was to express feeling rather than to instruct, helped to lay the foundation both for the modern validation of the self and for the Meiji literature of the self.

[14] *Isonokami sasamegoto* [My personal view of poetry], 1763, *Motoori Norinaga zenshū*, 6: 489, quoted in Shigeru Matsumoto, *Motoori Norinaga: 1730-1801*, Cambridge, Mass., 1970, p. 48.

Related to the development of theories that validated human feeling was the emergence, in the early nineteenth century, of a kind of fiction known as *ninjō-bon* ("books of love"). These books presented middle-class people in love relationships in a realistic milieu—the pleasure quarters of Edo. Love in Genji's time had been sensual love; in early Tokugawa times it had hardly changed, judging by the way Saikaku depicted it. The love suicides in Chikamatsu's works of a slightly later period were the natural outcome of illicit unions formed on the basis of inclination, carried on in desperation, and doomed to a tragic end. Yet in the *ninjō-bon*, love, for the first time in Japanese literature, was associated with high moral qualities: loyalty, as seen in the lovers' faithfulness to one another, and courage, as seen in their defiance of social norms and their readiness to commit suicide together. In the *ninjō-bon* of Tamenaga Shunsui (1790-1843) written in the 1830s and 1840s, lovers were shown withstanding external obstacles, united by their devotion to one another and their ability to suffer. What was truly unusual about these novels was that heroic moral qualities of devotion and loyalty were now embodied in women, particularly in geisha and prostitutes, for woman had long been degraded by Confucian morality.[15] Yet the *ninjō-bon* and other fictional works were considered low and vulgar; they were not literature, according to the Confucian definition of literature as writing whose aim was to inculcate good morals. Moreover, the *ninjō-bon*, sequestered in the world of pleasure quarters, were unable to depict life realistically. The characters tended to be types, the incidents were strung together, chance was the order that informed the lives of the characters, and there was a tendency toward unrealistic happy endings. All these factors point to the basic impossibility of individual middle-class heroism in the social life of the late Tokugawa period.

[15] For this discussion of the *ninjō-bon*, and of love in the eighteenth- and nineteenth-century Japanese novel, I am indebted to Tsuda Sōkichi, *Bungaku ni arawaretaru kokumin shisō no kenkyū*, vol. 4, part 2, *Heimin bungaku no teisai jidai*, pp. 250ff., and pp. 567-572, respectively.

In summary, the aristocratic hero from the Heian period, Prince Genji, had given Japanese high culture a clear-cut orientation toward values of aesthetic enjoyment and individual expression. The lengthy period of military rule that followed the period of aristocratic rule contributed its own rigorously ethical orientation, stressing the values of self-discipline, courage, and loyalty. The merchant class that emerged in the peaceful years of the early Tokugawa period inherited from the aristocrats the primarily aesthetic values of enjoyment and self-expression, and from the military class the values of self-discipline, loyalty, and stoicism. Since the *chōnin* was a member of a class struggling to gain power, he imbued both kinds of values with his desire to affirm himself and his class in society—that is, with his dynamic sense of selfhood. Yet Tokugawa society denied him this affirmation of self: it degraded the aesthetic-emotional values by segregating them in the off-limits area of the pleasure quarters. Thus, the *chōnin* Jihei's free expression of self in love inevitably flowed into illicit channels, and his devotion to the prostitute Koharu was destined to be ridiculed and chastised by his family and by the society around him. Instead of the freedom to live according to his own morality in society, Chikamatsu gave him freedom in the form of an afterlife with his lover in the Buddhist Pure Land.

At the close of the Tokugawa period, then, self-affirmation was condemned and with it, a whole group of people who lacked the opportunity for self-affirmation. For heroism and moral validity were the property of those firmly entrenched in power: the upper-level samurai. The heroes and heroines of Chikamatsu and Tamenaga Shunsui represented the lower-level samurai, the merchants, and infrequently, the peasants—all those who suffered from a lack of moral validation under the Tokugawa social system. Thus, a new culture hero was making his appearance in the Tokugawa era, one who was depicted in literature as pursuing goals that the official culture defined as immoral. That this individual was depicted also as either resigned to the failure of his ideals or crushed by obstacles in his path is not so significant as the fact that such a culture hero was present. It is precisely this middle-class individual whose desire for freedom and self-expression was thwarted under the Tokugawa that gradually became the culture hero in the Meiji period. The desire to express the individual self that burst forth so violently in the middle-class lyric poetry of the late 1890s, and then in the I-novel (*shishōsetsu*) of the first few years of the twentieth century, was surely a continuation of the late Tokugawa *ninjō-bon*'s interest in the aesthetic-emotional aspect of the individual. Yet it was also the bittersweet fruit of the ideological and political upheavals of the early Meiji period, in particular, of the movement for national and individual independence.

The Early Meiji Ideal of Independence and Its Political Context

On January 3, 1868, the Tokugawa Shogunate was overthrown and a new era, called the Meiji Restoration in reference to the restoration of imperial rule, began. The group of lower- and middle-ranking samurai that had carried out the successful revolution soon demonstrated their desire to lead Japan into the modern world by encouraging the development of modern-style industries, abolishing the feudal system, and actively supporting the dissemination of Western thought. It was during this period of revolutionary change that the concept of the individual as an independent social agent, as a person with a private moral existence and inner life, emerged for the first time in Japanese history. The revolution that began to occur in the sphere of the idea of the individual was shaped from the start by the political realities of the time. The rulers of the Meiji government were aware of the threat posed to Japan by the presence of Western imperialist powers in Asia. After seeing Imperial China fall before the superior military power of the Western nations, they were determined to strengthen the nation so that it would be able to compete with the Western powers. Strengthening the nation meant, first, adopting the technological innovations of the West. However, as the Meiji rulers perceived that it was not only the technology but also the enterprising spirit of the Westerners that had enabled them to conquer the Asian nations, they became increasingly interested in Western ethics.

The movement that was largely responsible for the rapid dissemination of Western thought in the 1870s was the *keimō* ("enlightenment") movement. Founded in 1873, its leaders, many of whom were government officials, envisioned Japan progressing toward a state of civilization (*bunmei*) whose characteristics were unmistakably those of nineteenth-century England or France. Indeed, the group named its movement after the French and English Enlightenment thinkers and their nineteenth-century descendants, the theorists of progress Buckle, Guizot, and Spencer.[16] Though many of the writers stressed the necessity of developing a spirit of initiative and enterprise in the Japanese people, none was so vocal as Fukuzawa Yukichi (1835-1901). In a series of pamphlets written in colloquial style and later gathered into a book entitled *Gakumon no susume* (An Encouragement of Learning, 1872-1876), Fukuzawa described what he called the spirit of independence (*dokuritsu*). Inspired by his reading of Samuel Smiles's *Self-Help* (translated in 1870) and John Stuart Mill's *On Liberty* (translated in 1871), Fukuzawa attacked the Japanese ethical system that for the last two hundred years had promoted inequality and encouraged obedience to a hierarchy, a system that in his opinion had resulted in stagnation and corruption at the top levels of government and frustration among the people. He stressed that the power of the Western nations lay in the ideals of freedom and equality that inspired their people to be responsible for themselves, to take initiative in all walks of life, and to be strong, vigorous citizens ready to defend their nation. Finally, he expressed the hope that once the Japanese pursued the ideal of independence, their nation would be able to "enter the

[16] Carmen Blacker discusses the background and ideals of this movement in *The Japanese Enlightenment: A Study of the Writings of Fukuzawa Yukichi*, Cambridge, 1964, pp. 30-35.

citadel of civilization,"[17] eventually taking its place alongside America and the Western European nations.

Fukuzawa's *Gakumon no susume* had an extremely large readership for that time; it is estimated that one out of every 160 persons in Japan in the 1870s read part or all of it.[18] Fukuzawa's ideals were carried out by men in positions of power, and it is interesting that these men were largely members of a class that had had little or no power under the Tokugawa. Fukuzawa had written that civilization necessarily begins in the middle classes, noting that the great Western contributions to commerce and industry such as the steam engine, the railroad, and the laws of economics, were made by those who, midway between the government and the common people, "lead the world by means of their intellect."[19] The disintegration of the feudal system at the end of the Tokugawa period had eroded the power of the upper-level samurai. Then, after the Meiji Restoration, their lower-level colleagues, along with the merchant and peasant classes, were guaranteed the right to pursue their chosen callings. The energy freed from the hierarchical bondage of the past streamed into the new government as well as into private industry, the military, education, agriculture, and other fields essential to the developing of the country. Thus, the revolution in industry, society, and culture that began in 1868 was indeed directed by a class "midway between the government and the common people"—a class composed of former lower-ranking samurai, some merchants, and a few peasants.

Fukuzawa's ideal of independence, and the ideal of *risshin-shusse* (success and achievement in life) that emerged from the En-

[17] *Fukuzawa Yukichi zenshū*, Tokyo, 1960, 3: 29-62, 70-77, 85-95. For an English translation of *Gakumon no susume* see David A. Dilworth and Umeyo Hirano, trans. and introd., *Fukuzawa Yukichi's "An Encouragement of Learning,"* Tokyo, 1969, especially sects. 1-5, 7, 9, and 10.

[18] Dilworth and Hirano, *Fukuzawa Yukichi's "An Encouragement of Learning,"* p. xi.

[19] *Fukuzawa Yukichi zenshū*, 3: 60.

lightenment movement of the early 1870s must have provided
the people of early Meiji with an almost religiously inspiring
ideal of secular mobility that seemed, for a time at least, to replace the traditional one of social cohesion.[20] The ideal of independence became the ideal of a whole people from the late 1870s,
in the form of the longing for human rights. In section two of
Gakumon no susume, entitled "The Equality of Men," Fukuzawa
had written that all men were equal and that this equality was an
equality in terms of basic human rights. He defined human rights
as "the great moral obligations that give dignity to people's lives,
protect man's property and possessions, and give significance to
his honor and his reputation." Stressing that "it is a basic human
right for man to be able to attain his desires, as long as he does
not obstruct others," Fukuzawa went on to delineate the abuses
the common people had suffered for centuries due to the rulers'
failure to honor their basic human rights. He closed the section
by noting that the common people had allowed themselves to be
abused through ignorance and that "if they wished to avoid a
despotic government, they must promptly devote themselves to
learning, in order to elevate their own talents and virtues to a
position of equality with the government."[21]

The concept of rights (*minken* or *mingi*), then, was needed to
strengthen weak links in the chain of government, in order that
the government itself would become stronger. The idea of a link
becoming strong for its own sake, without the intention of playing its part in the chain, would have shocked Fukuzawa. Yet the
concept of rights implied a view of society that was utterly opposed to the traditional Japanese view. Fukuzawa shared the latter view, which posited a harmonious political entity composed
of government and governed and which thought of government
as, ideally, a contract involving kindness on the part of the rulers
and gratitude on the part of the people. Significantly, the word

[20] Joseph M. Kitagawa, *Religion in Japanese History*, New York, 1966,
p. 189.
[21] *Fukuzawa Yukichi zenshū*, 3: 38, 41.

rights had not existed in the Japanese language before contact
with the West; the word *minken* was coined to translate the terms
Regt (Dutch), *droit* (French), and *right* (English), but it was only
partially comprehensible to the Japanese.[22] The revolutionary
implication of the concept of rights was that it forced attention
away from the notion of an hierarchical bond between unequal
individuals and onto each individual as an independent unit. By
attempting to define the sphere of action and power that was the
individual's own and that had to be defended, legally if necessary,
before others, it assumed and encouraged a state of disharmony or
at least separateness between individuals. The concept of rights
must have seemed threatening to the more conservative Japanese
of the time, for it carried the individual beyond the stable and
familiar areas of class and rank and into morally uncharted territory. For other, less conservative people, however, it must have
symbolized a welcome liberation from the past.

In the 1870s and 1880s people of all classes longed to make the
ideal of independence for each person a reality by bringing about
the recognition of the political rights of the individual. The
movement for the establishment of a representative government
became a channel for the expression of these longings. The Meiji
Charter Oath of 1868 had stipulated that "deliberative assemblies
shall be widely established and all matters decided by public discussion."[23] Yet it was only in 1873 that one of the Meiji leaders,
Itagaki Taisuke, declared himself in opposition to governmental
arbitrariness in choosing its members and establishing policy, by
calling for the establishment of a parliamentary body. His found-
ing of a political society in opposition to the government called
the *Aikoku kōtō* (Public Party of Patriots) sparked the setting up of
local political discussion groups all over Japan. Besides awakening the spirit of political independence among the educated
classes, Itagaki was responsible for forcing the government, in

[22] Blacker, *The Japanese Enlightenment*, p. 105.
[23] Quoted in John K. Fairbank, Edwin O. Reischauer, and Albert M. Craig,
East Asia: The Modern Transformation, Boston, 1965, p. 228.

1875, to promise to set up a national assembly. By 1880, when the Movement for Freedom and People's Rights (*Jiyū minken undō*) had emerged as a powerful opposition force, Itagaki's society claimed to have a membership of 87,000, testifying to the widespread concern for the issue of human rights in all corners and among all classes of Japan.

Fukuzawa Yukichi was in the forefront of those promoting people's rights, as might be expected. In 1878 he published a pamphlet entitled *Tsūzoku minken-ron* (A Simple Account of People's Rights), a work that incorporated the ideas of Mill, Bentham, and Spencer, and in 1879 he called for the establishment of a Diet. When the government, in 1881, actually promised to set up a national assembly by 1890, the People's Rights movement came out in the open and the fervor for the ideal of human rights reached its height. Students at the Western-style higher schools in Tokyo—among them Futabatei Shimei, Kitamura Tōkoku, and Shimazaki Tōson—made plans to serve their country by devoting themselves to the glorious cause of human rights, or by defeating the enemies of Japan, especially Russia and Korea. The quest for personal independence was linked for many to the cause of Japanese independence vis-à-vis foreign powers, and the many political novels that were turned out between 1881 and 1890 satisfied the desires of readers for ways in which to experience vicariously a nameless and fantastic freedom, the longing for which had sprung up in the wake of the crumbling of so much of what had been oppressive to them.

After about 1885 the ideal of independence was either a fantasy to be read about in novels or it was all but identified with the ideal of representative government, an ideal that was not really a goal to be attained by the efforts of those who longed for it but that, it became more and more clear, was a gift that would be bestowed on the people by the Meiji rulers. For while the political parties formed in the early 1880s were agitating openly but futilely from their position of opposition, the government was working to develop a constitution that would reflect its policy of stable government control. Though the Meiji leaders were convinced that popular representation would eventually be a necessity for a strong government, they felt that the first goal was to build a nation that would be able to resist Western powers. Thus they turned for a model mainly to Germany, a newly united nation that was also eager to strengthen itself militarily in order to stand up to older European nations, and whose legal tradition was conservative and absolutist. The chief concern of Itō Hirobumi and the others who worked on the writing of the constitution was that the parliament they created not become a serious threat to the exercise of executive powers of government. In order to justify their own power as rulers in the face of the opposition of the People's Rights movement, they gradually began to emphasize the sacred role of the emperor in the dispensing of power. This in turn was followed by a renewed advocacy of the traditional hierarchical bond between government and governed, and eventually by the resuscitation of the old demand for reverence and obedience on the part of the people.[24]

When one considers that it was largely Fukuzawa Yukichi's ideas on the independence of the individual that were expressed in the political ideals of the People's Rights movement of the late 1870s and 1880s and that moved large numbers of people to a consciousness of the importance of the goal of democratic government, it is significant that Fukuzawa's views on the importance and even the possibility of individual independence changed radically after 1880. From the start Fukuzawa, as a man of samurai origin, had accepted the traditional assumption of the samurai ethic that strength of character, intelligence, and self-assertion were to be cultivated as ideals of service, not of self-aggrandizement.[25] When he advocated independence he cer-

[24] The preceding discussion of the political events of the 1870s and 1880s is indebted to Fairbank, Reischauer, and Craig, East Asia: The Modern Transformation, pp. 278-298.

[25] Furukawa Tesshi, "The Individual in Japanese Ethics," in Moore, The Japanese Mind, p. 237.

tainly did not mean a free-floating, competitive independence of the kind that resulted, in the post-Renaissance West, in the emergence of an isolated, self-centered individual freed from tradition and the family. Yet Fukuzawa's original vision of independence had stressed that, because of man's inherent tendency toward civilization, the cultivation of individual talents and virtues could not help but issue in a peaceful and civilized nation that would interact peacefully with other equal, civilized nations. If the conditions in which this optimistic vision had arisen had continued to operate, doubtless there would have been room in Japan for a development of the individual along these liberal lines.

However, the decade between 1880 and 1890 saw increased imperialist activity on the part of Western nations: the British annexed Upper Burma, ruling the whole country from 1886 on as part of British India; the French established their rule over Cochin China, Cambodia, central Vietnam, and Tongking (1887); and the Germans began to acquire colonies in Africa. Faced with these developments, Fukuzawa realized that the real force that governed relations between nations was competition. "Equality" in such a case meant the ability of a nation to compete militarily with its neighbors; and "peace" meant the ability of a nation to subdue other nations that threatened it. Possibly Fukuzawa's thinking was influenced as well by Darwinian theories of the survival of the fittest, which were gaining currency in Japan in the 1880s.[26] In any case, by the early 1880s Fukuzawa had lost faith in the Japanese people's ability to develop the necessary qualities of independence and civilization in time to meet a possible military challenge by the West. Faced with the reality of

[26] In 1877 Edward S. Morse, a New England naturalist who became the first professor of zoology at Tokyo University, gave a series of three public lectures on Darwinian evolution. These lectures and others on the same topic were published in book form in 1883, and Darwin's *Descent of Man* was translated also in that year. Robert S. Schwantes, "Christianity *versus* Science: A Conflict of Ideas in Meiji Japan," in *Japan*, ed. John A. Harrison, Tucson, 1972, p. 39.

imperialistic politics and their threat to a modernizing nation, Fukuzawa leaned more and more toward the idea that in order to acquire the power to confront other nations the Japanese people needed to rely on the mystical strength of the emperor. In writings of this period he increasingly advocated a return to the ethical attitude of *hōkoku jinchū* (repaying the country with loyalty), an attitude that had underlain the ideal of hierarchical harmony and the, as he himself had called it, subservient behavior of the Japanese people in the Tokugawa period.[27]

The various pronouncements of government policy made public by 1890 reflected the Meiji rulers' decision to proceed slowly with the establishment of representative institutions and the granting of freedoms and rights to the individual. A modern-style army relying on conscription was established by 1873, yet in 1881 an "Admonition to the Military" urged the armed forces to exercise the old samurai virtues of loyalty, bravery, and obedience to the emperor. In the next year the military was made directly responsible to the emperor alone and independent from representative organs of government. The Meiji Charter Oath of 1868 had decreed that learning was to be sought from all over the world; but the Imperial Rescript on Education, promulgated in 1890, indicated that moral education stressing loyalty and obedience to the emperor was to be the most important kind of education for the masses, though a certain amount of Western-style objective knowledge was to be included in the curriculum in order to prepare them to be productive citizens of a modern state. And the final exhortation of the rescript urged reactivation of a traditional attitude of loyalty in the words: "Should emergency arise, offer yourselves courageously to the state."[28] Similarly, the Char-

---

[27] For this discussion of the transformation of Fukuzawa's ideas on independence in the 1880s I am indebted to Albert M. Craig, "Fukuzawa Yukichi: The Philosophical Origins of Meiji Nationalism," in *Political Development in Modern Japan*, ed. Robert E. Ward, Princeton, 1968, especially p. 130.

[28] Quoted in Fairbank, Reischauer, and Craig, *East Asia: The Modern Transformation*, p. 276.

ter Oath had guaranteed religious freedom, but by 1890 the government had forced a religion of chauvinism, under the guise of ethical education, into the school curriculum.

In the area of legal reforms, the legal code adopted in the 1890s for the first time gave the individual the right to own, succeed to, and bequeath property as an individual. Yet the code still recognized the *ie* ("house" or "family") as the legal unit, and consequently, the traditional way of seeing the family—as consisting of a head who had the legal status and various subordinate members with no legal status—continued virtually unchanged. In 1869, as a result of the Charter Oath directive to allow people to follow freely the profession of their choice, class restrictions on professional employment were abolished. Yet strong hierarchical sentiment remained; birth still counted, but wealth and talent enabled a few to gain access to high social ranks. The government bureaucrats, ironically, became the new aristocratic class.[29] Furthermore, the progress that had been made in the development of representative assemblies since 1868 was visible in the composition of the electorate of the lower house of the Diet, the House of Representatives, in 1890: only adult males who paid taxes of fifteen yen or more—about 450,000 people or one percent of the population—voted in the first election. Finally, the constitution promulgated in 1889 severely curtailed the power of the Diet by limiting its function to the checking of proposals initiated by the executive powers.

By the mid-1890s the enthusiasm for human rights of the 1880s had turned into a chauvinistic fervor that centered around the creation of a militarily strong, imperialist Japan. Through indoctrination in the lower schools the government reactivated feudal attitudes of loyalty and obedience to a higher authority in the large majority of the people, justifying its policy on the basis of the need to create a strong, loyal body of citizens that could withstand foreign threats to the nation's independence. The goal

[29] G. B. Sansom, *The Western World and Japan*, New York, 1950, p. 351.

of "national independence through personal independence" that
Fukuzawa had elaborated in his *Gakumon no susume* had also signified the development of a strong nation, but Fukuzawa had
stressed that this goal was only to be achieved through a
strengthening of the rights as well as the duties of the individuals, especially those who had been traditionally neglected and
even degraded by the higher classes. The Meiji leaders chose,
whether wisely or unwisely, to stress national independence at
the expense of personal independence. Through imperialist expansion they offered the subservient masses an opportunity for the
"emotional projection of the self" in the universe that the latter
had lost in their own society.[30] Thus, when Japan won an imperialist war with China in 1895, and when it was also victorious
in its first skirmish with a Western power in 1905, the government's wisdom in making patriots instead of individuals seemed
to have been proven.

    The Meiji rulers' decision to make submissive patriots of the
masses in the 1890s, however politically expedient it seemed, led
to a cleavage between the masses and the intellectuals that was to
have serious consequences for the modern culture that emerged at
this time. For while the majority of people followed the patriotic
doctrines taught to them in school, maintaining almost unchanged the late Tokugawa attitudes of loyalty and obedience
toward the state, those who had attended higher schools, where
Western ideals were dominant, felt drawn to the ideal of independence in its original nineteenth-century European liberal
formulation: individualism based on a free-enterprise system, including free self-expression and the development of an individualist morality. Yet modernizing reforms on the social and political level that would have legitimized the efforts of intellectuals to
cultivate individual freedoms did not take place. The individual

[30] Maruyama Masao, *Gendai seiji no shisō to kōdō*, Tokyo, 1961, 1: 159-160.
An English translation of the essay in question is "Nationalism in Japan: Its
Theoretical Background and Prospects," in *Thought and Behavior in Japanese
Politics*, ed. Ivan Morris, London, 1963.

continued to lack legal status and voting rights, for example, two rights without which he had no social existence as an individual in the Western meaning of the word. In a sense, then, the Western-educated individual lived as a nonperson in a society where to be a person meant to be an emanation of the harmonious entity that was made up of government and governed.[31]

For the Meiji writer the situation was still worse. The continued dominance during the Meiji period of a morality derived from the Tokugawa samurai ethic—a morality that stressed loyalty and obedience, and made service to the country an important priority—weighed heavily on a person whose education in West-

[31] In an essay that attempts to explain the complex relationship between tradition and change in Islam, Manfred Halpern isolates eight forms of encounter between self and other that allow people to deal at the same time with continuity and change. He describes one of them, which he calls "Emanation," as "an intensely passive collaboration at the cost of repressing conflict, a willingness to purchase continuity by implicitly accepting or rejecting change solely at the behest of another, and hence granting mysterious and overwhelming power to the one in exchange for total security to the other." Halpern describes elsewhere what he calls "the pseudo-paradigm of Emanation": an attempt on the part of a culture in the throes of modernization to escape the pains of transformation by returning to an earlier pattern of Emanation. To apply these insights to late Meiji Japan, the government in the 1890s encouraged those Japanese who were not intellectuals to see themselves as emanations of the emperor, a figure whose power was mysterious and overwhelming and to whom they owed absolute, unquestioning loyalty. In Halpern's terms, the Meiji rulers' attempt to hold the majority of their people in a state of enforced emanation was a misguided but understandable attempt to forestall the coming of cultural Incoherence or breakdown that might have led to Transformation, or the liberation of their own source of Emanation. For definitions of Emanation, Incoherence, and Transformation, see "Four Contrasting Repertories of Human Relations in Islam," in L. Carl Brown and Norman Itzkowitz, eds., *Psychological Dimensions of Near Eastern Studies*, Princeton, 1977, especially pp. 64, 83. The concept of the pseudo-paradigm of Emanation was discussed further in a paper entitled "Neither Tradition nor Neo-Traditionalism nor Westernization Can Meet the Challenge of the Modern Age: The Case for the Counter-Tradition of Transformation," given at a conference on The Role of Traditionalism and Neo-Traditionalism in the Modernization Process, Rutgers University, New Brunswick, New Jersey, March 17-18, 1978.

ern-style higher schools had encouraged the development of independent thought and self-reliance. Furthermore, business activity, condemned by the samurai ethic under the Tokugawa, could be justified as a service to the nation,[32] but literature continued to be seen as a frivolous pastime of no utilitarian, let alone moral, value to the nation. Consequently, the Western-educated writer, for whom self-expression was a primary goal, had difficulty justifying his existence not only as a social being but as a person with feelings, longings, and aspirations. Essentially, the Meiji writer who was attracted to the Western ideal of individualism had to face the same problem as the Tokugawa *chōnin*: the lack of validation of the individual socially and in the aesthetic-emotional sphere. The history of Meiji literature, at least that literature that concerns itself with the revelation and discovery of the individual, can be seen as the history of Meiji individuals' attempts to validate the self.

With the decline of the ideal of people's rights in the late 1880s, then, the ideal of independence became dissociated from the political and social sphere and was transformed into an ideal of self-knowledge and self-validation. A Western reader aware of the happy coexistence of private ideals of individualism with liberal economic and political systems, as in the England of the mid-nineteenth century, may find the situation of the Meiji writer depressing. Indeed, because the writers I will discuss in the following pages carried on their enterprise of self-scrutiny and self-revelation in a literary world divorced from the larger society, their writings sometimes suffer from the writer's narrowness of vision. Yet it is surely unrealistic to expect the immediate flourishing of literature with a broad, complex social vision of its time in a country just emerging from feudalism. The literature of

---

[32] Shibusawa Eiichi was largely responsible for making business activities acceptable to former samurai in the early Meiji period. For a discussion of this figure see Johannes Hirschmeier, "Shibusawa Eiichi: Industrial Pioneer," in *The State and Economic Enterprise in Japan*, ed. William W. Lockwood, Princeton, 1965, especially pp. 214-215, 242.

the Meiji period could not depict full-blown individuals engaged in action in a social context, for action presupposes the existence of a morality, and as yet there was no individualist morality in Japan. However, already before 1890 there appeared a work that presented images of the new, Western-educated individual and, implicitly, of that individual's morality, a work that in its turn inspired Meiji people to cultivate their own morality. This was Futabatei Shimei's novel *Ukigumo* (The Floating Clouds).

CHAPTER TWO

Futabatei's *Ukigumo* (The Floating Clouds): The First Novel of the Individual

Ukigumo: *A Novel of the Introvert*

Futabatei Shimei (1864-1909) is usually credited with having written the first modern novel in Japan—the first novel, that is, that uses a modern colloquial language, depicts a character's inner life realistically, and has a coherent plot. For my purposes, however, Futabatei is worthy of attention as the author of the first Japanese novel that places a high enough value on the individual's inner life to depict it expansively and lovingly. Futabatei was born Hasegawa Tatsunosuke in Tokyo in 1864, the son of a low-ranking samurai of the Owari *han* (feudal domain).[1] Like many young men of his class born around the time of the Restoration, Futabatei received an education that included both ethical training in the Confucian classics and practical training in the Western-style subjects of geography, history, and English. As a boy growing up in the politically exciting 1870s, Futabatei's youthful enthusiasm was kindled by the image of a Japanese nation that would be able to perform glorious military deeds. His hero as an adolescent was the samurai hero, Saigō Takamori (1828-1877), who had died leading the last rebellion against the central government, and he dreamed of becoming a general who, like Saigō, would fight to maintain the traditional samurai standards intact. Futabatei advocated a militant attitude toward other nations, especially Russia, which was seen in the 1870s and 1880s as the greatest threat to the nation. He attempted three

---

[1] My discussion of Futabatei's life is based on Marleigh Grayer Ryan, *Japan's First Modern Novel: "Ukigumo" of Futabatei Shimei*, New York, 1967, pp. 3-36.

times to enter a military school, but was rejected each time. Finally, still wishing to play his part in the political future of Japan and still perceiving Russia as the greatest threat to her security, he decided to study Russian.

Once Futabatei entered the *Gaigo Gakkō* (Foreign Language School) in 1881, however, his interest was drawn slowly away from the military sphere. This happened due to a fortuitous set of circumstances. Several native Russians taught at the school, and one of them, Nicholas Gray, made a practice of reading aloud the texts of the Russian novels the students were studying. Futabatei, who had already developed a love for literature, became entranced with the sound of the language, with the way the rhythm of the sentences harmonized with the content. Furthermore, he realized that Russian fiction observed, analyzed, and predicted social phenomena,[2] and that he himself could try to write fiction that would perform the same function for Japanese society. Thus he was able to unite his earlier longing to take part in political life with his newly acquired love of literature. Soon after leaving the school, in January of 1886, Futabatei took the first steps toward beginning his career. He called on Tsubouchi Shōyō (1859-1935), a well-known critic and novelist, who in 1885 had written the first comprehensive theory of the novel in the history of Japanese literature: *Shōsetsu shinzui* (The Essence of the Novel). Basing his remarks on nineteenth-century Western theories of the novel, as well as those of earlier Japanese theorists of the novel such as Motoori Norinaga, Tsubouchi took the position that the function of the novel was to reveal truth about life.

The purpose of the novel was not to teach a narrow morality, he urged, but, by opening man's eyes to the wide world of people and events, to "move the heart and stimulate the imagination." The novel ought to have a tightly constructed and believable plot. Furthermore, it ought to portray characters in depth and build up an impression of everyday reality, and the actual speech

[2] Ibid., p. 20.

of different classes should be rendered realistically. Only when
these demands were fulfilled could the novel attain the status of
an art form and "outdo European novels."[3] It is obvious from
Tsubouchi's remarks what were the faults of the Japanese fiction
of his time: fantastic plots made up of hastily and incoherently
linked episodes; a moralistic tendency to punish vice and reward
virtue that utterly removed the works from any connection with
the reader's experience of the truth of life; and stilted, unnatural
dialogue. However, the worst fault of Japanese fiction, as Tsubouchi saw it, was the inability of writers to depict characters
with any depth to them. Tsubouchi criticized the early nineteenth-century novelist Takizawa Bakin (1767-1848), for example, for creating characters that were mere "ghosts of virtues,"
not real human beings.[4] Indeed, the first translators of Western
novels in the 1870s and 1880s frequently omitted from their
translations passages analyzing the personalities or motivations of
the characters, assuming that the Japanese reader would not be
interested in reading about the inner life.[5] Tsubouchi emphasized
strongly that the goal of fiction was to depict human emotions. In
order to do this, novelists could not just construct a hero to fit a
preconceived ideal, but must portray him as he really was.[6] This
is the directive of Tsubouchi that was most significant for the development of the novel of the individual's inner life, and
Futabatei was the first writer to fulfill it.

Futabatei Shimei wrote *Ukigumo* (The Floating Clouds), the
first Japanese novel to depict a hero in depth, over the years 1886
to 1889. The novel depicts the changes that occur in the relationships between four people over a period of a few weeks in the autumn of one year in the early 1880s. The first change is precipitated by an event that occurs at the beginning of the story:
Bunzō, a young man of twenty-three, has been fired from his

---

[3] Tsubouchi Shōyō, *Shōsetsu shinzui*, in *Nihon gendaibungaku zenshū*, Tokyo,
1962, 4: 161, 151.
[4] Ibid., p. 163.   [5] Ryan, *Japan's First Modern Novel*, p. 99.
[6] Tsubouchi, *Shōsetsu shinzui*, pp. 163, 200-202.

government job. Omasa, the aunt with whom Bunzō has been living since the age of fifteen, reproaches him, disappointed at the thought that her long-cherished plan to marry Bunzō to her daughter, Osei, may fall through. She blames Bunzō for not having followed the example of his colleague, Noboru, in ingratiating himself with his boss. At this point in the novel Osei, who still looks to Bunzō as an elder brother and possible romantic interest, is sympathetic to Bunzō. The entrance of Noboru precipitates another change in the relationships between the characters. Omasa and Osei become attracted to his up-and-coming spirit, and Bunzō sees this as a breach of loyalty, especially on Osei's part. He begins gradually to consider Noboru as an enemy. Finally, when Noboru offers, in front of Osei, to use his influence with the boss to get Bunzō rehired, Bunzō, convinced that Noboru has meant this offer as an insult, barely refrains from punching him in the face. On rethinking the incident, he dimly realizes that he has lost ground with Osei and that it will take an extreme action on his part—an action that will prove his determination and courage—to restore Osei's confidence in him. Yet after pondering the matter fruitlessly for an hour, he returns home only to become infuriated with Noboru again and, losing control of himself, orders Noboru to leave the house.

Bunzō's "extreme action"—not at all the sort he had imagined himself doing—has the effect of alienating both Omasa and Osei. After spending two hours alone in his room thinking over what has happened, Bunzō finally realizes that his only chance to regain the consideration of Omasa, who is now looking with favor on Noboru as a possible husband for Osei, is to accept Noboru's offer. However, he is reluctant to take what he sees as a humiliating step and, for this reason, and because he secretly wishes to test Osei's loyalty, he resolves to let Osei decide whether or not he should ask Noboru for help. Fully expecting she will support him in his decision to stay unemployed rather than ask Noboru for a favor, he is surprised and disappointed when Osei, too, advises him to accept Noboru's offer. By this time Bunzō's relations with Osei have become more complicated, for she is no longer the young girl he had known. As Osei awakens confusedly to feelings of love, she is half-attracted to Noboru, but Bunzō does not see this clearly. He fails to express his own continued interest in her and through lack of understanding of her feelings as well as his own, bungles an attempt to apologize for his rudeness to Noboru.

After this scene Bunzō retreats into himself in humiliation, but while alone he ponders the behavior of Omasa and Osei toward him and finally realizes that he is to blame for the misunderstanding that has arisen between himself and Osei. The next two chapters depict Osei's transformation into a young woman. She develops a real interest in Noboru, then possibly has an affair with him or with someone else. During this time Bunzō is completely out of favor with the two women and considers several times whether or not to move out of their house. In the final chapter, Bunzō, seeing what is happening to Osei, decides to stay on at his relatives' house ostensibly in order to save Osei from ruin. Finally, however, Osei becomes estranged from Noboru for no apparent reason and begins once more to smile at Bunzō. The novel ends as Bunzō, deciding to gamble his whole future on the chance that Osei is once more interested in him, waits in his room for her to return from the public bath.

Ukigumo can be considered a novel of the individual because, though it depicts three characters in addition to Bunzō, only Bunzō is scrutinized at length from the inside; furthermore, the events of the novel are seen largely from his subjective (and distorted) point of view. What makes Futabatei the first writer of modern fiction is his revelation of the inner life of his character. He does this by means of the traditional interior monologue, borrowed from the native dramatic narrative form of the *yose* and made to fit the demands of a more tightly knit narrative, and the Western technique of indirect statement.[7] The former technique is used mainly in the first part of the novel, and its open, extro-

---

[7] Ryan, *Japan's First Modern Novel*, pp. 91-92.

verted, and even humorous style fits the dramatic character of the earlier parts. After chapter eight (out of nineteen chapters) the main action is over, and the characters—particularly Bunzō, but Osei also—retire to closed, introverted places to think over what has happened. Here the technique of third-person indirect statement is used more and more, and its use induces a serious, contemplative mood. Thought, not action, is the heart of the novel: time is slowed down to a leisurely pace and stretched to accommodate the vacillations of Bunzō's mind, rather than rushing forward to meet the demands of physical action. Similarly, Futabatei contracts space in the novel to suit Bunzō's intense but narrow inner life—the most innovative scenes, to the readers of the time, were those where Bunzō cogitates alone in his ten-by-ten-foot room. Bunzō's mentalized action takes place in this room, located symbolically above the rooms of everyday life, while dramatic action occurs on the ground floor. Bunzō is seen, then, as distant both physically and mentally from the other characters in the novel. The result of all this is that Bunzō comes across to the reader as a person with a unique inner life who is literally and painfully separated from other people.

Without the dissemination of logical thinking in Japan, Futabatei would not have been able to see Bunzō as a separate individual.[8] Logical thinking, which made it possible for Japanese to see the individual for the first time as a being with a social and legal existence apart from others, was the basis for the ideals of independence and human rights that were popularized in early Meiji by Fukuzawa Yukichi and the Enlightenment movement. Essentially, logical thinking meant scientific thinking, the rational observation of things with the intent of discovering their laws. It involved a spirit of doubt and experiment that went directly counter to traditional moral modes of thought that stressed the harmonious unity of man and nature. According to Neo-

[8] For a discussion of logical thinking and emotive thinking in Japan, see Nakamura Hajime, "Consciousness of the Individual and the Universal Among the Japanese," in Moore, *The Japanese Mind*.

Confucianism, the philosophical and religious system that influenced all schools of thought during the Tokugawa period, moral principles governed both man and nature and it was on this basis that man and nature were unified. Each thing, including man, had *li*, or an "ideal form or principle that prescribed the norm of its nature." Man's *li* was his *hsing*, or good nature, and consisted of the four virtues of benevolence, righteousness, etiquette, and wisdom. As the mind of Heaven, the underlying principle of unity, expressed itself in man as these virtues, it expressed itself in nature as the four seasons.[9]

Because man's *hsing* had become obscured by his physicality, however, he was no longer aware of his original nature. It was thought that by investigating the *li* of things other than himself, the *li* of all things being essentially identical, man could learn to become aware of his own *hsing* once more. As a consequence of this belief, when traditional Neo-Confucian scholars spoke of the "investigation of things" (*kakubutsu*), they meant, in essence, a discipline of the mind whereby one meditated on the *li* or nature of a particular thing with the objective of not only understanding the thing itself, but also of regaining an awareness of one's own *hsing*. Thus, "investigation of things" was nothing less than a spiritual discipline that led man to recover a lost sense of unity with things. The observation and investigation of objects in their purely physical aspect, without regard to their *li*, was considered to be useless, false learning—yet this was the kind of observation advocated by Western science. Conservative scholars such as Ōhashi Totsuan (1816-1862) criticized Western scientific learning for this reason, noting that "even with hundreds of microscopes," one could never observe principles. Thus, microscopes, and Western learning as a whole, were irrelevant to the true purpose of learning. Indeed, Western-style observation of things was irreverent as well, since it treated natural phenomena as if they

[9] This is the Neo-Confucian metaphysics that was elaborated in the twelfth century by Chu Hsi and that underlay Tokugawa thought. See Blacker, *The Japanese Enlightenment*, pp. 44-45.

were so many dead things, as if they were unrelated to man, and thus destroyed the harmony existing between man and the universe.[10] Futabatei's technique of observation was posited on this new vision of Western science in which harmony between things no longer existed, and in which, as a consequence, one no longer carried out the discipline of observation in order to become aware of moral principles. For the world after the beginning of Meiji, including man himself, had suddenly acquired a depth and mystery that challenged the novelist to discover and reveal it by means of the microscope of analysis.

That readers of the time were shocked by the first use of psychological analysis in *Ukigumo* is evident from the remarks of Tokutomi Roka on his impressions of *Ukigumo* when he read it as a young man: "I was astounded by (Futabatei's) *Ukigumo*. As if I had been dragged for the first time in my life into a room where human beings were being dissected, I was frightened by the sharpness of his pen, which was like a scalpel."[11] His comment recalls the fact that the origins of the realism and Naturalism of late nineteenth-century Europe—the Western literary movements that influenced Japanese novelists after Futabatei—are in Flaubert, whose foundations as a realistic novelist were perhaps laid when, as a child, he observed his father dissecting corpses with his medical students in the amphitheater of his hospital. Though Flaubert was not one of Futabatei's acknowledged influ-

---

[10] For this discussion of the differences between traditional Neo-Confucian learning and the new, scientific learning in reference to the practice of observation, I am indebted to Blacker, pp. 41-50.

[11] Tokutomi Roka (1868-1927) was a widely read author of social or family novels in the early period of realism (the late 1890s and early 1900s). A converted Christian, he visited Tolstoy in Yasnaya Polyana in 1906 and later retired from the literary world to cultivate his spiritual life. His fictional technique is said to have been influenced by Futabatei's translations from Russian literature, which were done in the late 1880s. Tokutomi made this remark about *Ukigumo* in an article written just after he heard that Futabatei had died on the way back from a trip to Russia. See his "Indōyō" (1909), in *Tokutomi Roka shū, Gendai nihonbungaku zenshū*, Tokyo, 1928, 12: 552.

ences, Dostoevsky was—the Dostoevsky who had evolved the dissecting realism of *Crime and Punishment*. Futabatei's appreciation and understanding of Dostoevsky's novels are documented,[12] and it is evident that the self-interrogating interior monologues of parts two and three of *Ukigumo* were influenced by Raskolnikov's monologues in the Dostoevsky novel. Also, though Bunzō is hardly an individual with inner conflicts as destructive as Raskolnikov's, to the readers of the time he must have seemed a man who lacked the comforting, smooth surface of a hero or a villain and, instead of surface qualities, possessed only a rather frightening depth. In effect, what Futabatei had accomplished in *Ukigumo* was to introduce the Japanese reader of his time to a world of the individual that, like Fukuzawa's concept of rights, opened up new and sometimes ominous territory.

In the Meiji period, then, logical thinking replaced the old, Neo-Confucian moral observation done as a spiritual discipline with a secular technique of observation that aimed at revealing

[12] In a brief, informal magazine article written in 1906, entitled "Yo no aidoku sho" (My Favorite Books), Futabatei discussed his favorite Russian writers. He noted that of all Russian writers he liked Dostoevsky the best, and of all his novels, *Crime and Punishment*, and that he especially valued Dostoevsky's psychological analysis of human beings and his interest in the religious. Futabatei's interpretation of *Crime and Punishment*—a novel he saw as communicating a religious message—is interesting from the viewpoint of the idea of individualism. Futabatei wrote: "The basic idea of Raskolnikov was that it was a question of an extreme lack in pride in self if an individual submitted to the authority of the everyday world, his conscience fettered; if there was even the least thing he believed in he must have the courage to act in the way he believed he should, even if he clashed with the authority of the everyday world to his own detriment." Futabatei clearly saw Raskolnikov not as a criminal but as an individual acting according to his own sense of what was necessary. Though he goes on to note that Raskolnikov failed, in that he acted according to logic rather than love, yet the tolerance for individual self-pride and the respect for the rights of the individual conscience that he demonstrates in his analysis of Raskolnikov reminds one of his sympathy for Bunzō in *Ukigumo*, and prove that Futabatei was quite aware of the issue of individualism that was latent in both works. *Futabatei Shimei zenshū*, Tokyo, 1953-1954, 15: 181.

not unity, but multiplicity and depth. It also undermined the Confucian moral system inherited from the Tokugawa period by insisting that natural laws were unrelated to moral principles. The consequence of this was that morality, which had been seen as linked to spiritual or natural laws under Neo-Confucianism, was now liberated. Individuals who were educated in Western logical thinking were thus free to evolve a morality that was based on their own individual laws. As the collapse of the old morality was reflected in the efforts of individuals in the Meiji period to evolve their own morality, it was also reflected in the new way of depicting characters in fiction. Confucian moral philosophy had viewed each individual as a *mei*, or role, to which various virtues, or vices, belonged. According to this view, a person of high class or a person of high status within one class would invariably be depicted as possessing virtues of strength, lower-class characters as possessing virtues of obedience. Those who did not possess virtues inevitably possessed vices. In the pre-Meiji world where people were unified with one another and with nature through their potential awareness of the common *li* that was inherent in all creatures, it was thought that reading about characters who exemplified the Confucian virtues would influence a person to become aware of his own virtues, and thus to become a better person. Correspondingly, reading about characters who exemplified the lack of Confucian virtues would, ideally, have a cautionary effect on the reader. Under the old Confucian moral system, then, the role of fiction was to affirm the world of Confucian values.

Tsubouchi Shōyō's insistence that the novel present characters that were believably and uniquely human contributed greatly to the destruction of the pre-Meiji view of character. Speaking of the eight heroes of the famous Tokugawa novelist Takizawa Bakin's *Hakkenden* (Biography of Eight Dogs, 1814-1841),[13] Tsubouchi

[13] A plot summary of this work may be found in Donald Keene, *World Within Walls: Japanese Literature of the Pre-Modern Era, 1600-1867*, New York, 1976, pp. 427-428.

criticized the author for creating his characters, each of whom represents a specific virtue, with a set moral pattern in mind rather than being guided by his observation of real people. Tsubouchi noted that the reliance on formulas rather than on real life resulted in characters who had no depth and underwent no development.[14] Seen from Tsubouchi's viewpoint, the decision to depict a role rather than a character in the traditional novel accounted for all of its defects, for without a character there was no character development and hence no occasion to depict time in a realistic manner. The absence of meaningful, purposive, human time in the novel in turn led to its episodic and fantastic plot structure and to its unrealistic and unhuman ending.

In the Tokugawa period fiction was not able to transcend these defects; only the characters in Chikamatsu's plays were able to overcome the limitation, in terms of realism, of being identified with a particular role and its specific (and static) virtues. The reason for this was that Chikamatsu depicted his characters as fulfilling several roles—Jihei, for example, is a husband, a father, a son-in-law, a brother, and a merchant. As such, he has specific obligations to fill. Yet Chikamatsu also depicted Jihei as a man in love, as a man who betrays his wife, destroys his family, and commits suicide. Seen from the Confucian point of view these acts are manifestations of selfish desires, and Jihei is thus a vicious man, though from a realistic standpoint Jihei is merely an individual who possesses human feelings that are valid in their own right. Because Chikamatsu depicts these virtues and vices as conflicting in Jihei, the latter achieves a dynamism that is akin to development, and time in the play is human time. In a sense, then, Chikamatsu's Jihei, possessing a depth of character that resulted from the sharp division in him between duty and inclination, prefigured the complex morality of the Meiji character.

Futabatei's Bunzō is not primarily one role, nor several roles, nor even an identity resulting from the conflict between virtue

<hr>

[14] Tsubouchi, *Shōsetsu shinzui*, p. 163.

and vice, but an identity for himself. Presented from the inside rather than from the outside, he gives the impression of being something beyond either a role or a virtue. Bunzō can be said to adhere to certain traditional assumptions about human relations: that there should be harmony among people, chiefly among family members, and that one owes loyalty to the members of one's family no matter what they do. Two further aspects of his morality—his deep respect for and devotion to learning and his belief that it is evil to kowtow before an unworthy superior—seem to stem from the samurai morality of the pre-Meiji era.[15] Indeed, Bunzō's ancestors were samurai. Yet he is not only a samurai in the novel; he is also an individual, and his morality appears as private and individualistic largely because the author depicts his actions and thoughts as springing from an inner center of being. Bunzō's tendency to look inward is a characteristic that does not link him with the old samurai world in which actions were relegated to the category of either virtue or vice, but with a modern world in which the individual's actions are interpreted psychologically. For Bunzō is an introvert: a person who, for better or for worse, acts on the basis of data coming from inside himself.[16]

Futabatei's study of Goncharov's Oblomov, Turgenev's Rudin, and Dostoevsky's Raskolnikov drew him into the world of the introverted person. Yet it was his own ability to observe himself that enabled him to direct his attention to the personality of an imaginary character. It is interesting, then, that Futabatei's friend and mentor, Tsubouchi Shōyō, referred to Futabatei as "timid and introspective—what psychoanalysts call 'introverted,'" Tsubouchi further described Futabatei as a person caught between two conflicting moralities: a Confucian one that

[15] For a discussion of samurai morality in reference to Bunzō in *Ukigumo*, see Ryan, *Japan's First Modern Novel*, pp. 167-171.

[16] C. G. Jung gives a definition of the introvert in *Psychological Types*, Princeton, 1971, pp. 373-407.

demanded allegiance to external norms of behavior and a modern, Western one that made the individual responsible for himself:

> As a writer he was a pure realist but in terms of personal conduct he was a Romantic or idealist. It may have been due to his Confucian training, but he was different from the people who came later. He was correct in his manners, humble, and moderate in speech. He abhorred falsehood, pretense, pride, and frivolity. Consequently he considered his own deceitful words and deeds as the greatest sin, and was always engaged in soul-searching and exposure of his personal weaknesses, censuring himself and speaking ill of himself. He was liable to worry unnecessarily, and was prone to world-weariness and pessimism.[17]

It is probable, then, that Futabatei himself was the model for Bunzō's vacillating nature, and his soul-searching the model for Bunzō's constant examination of conscience. Thus, through Futabatei there passed into Japanese literature the nineteenth-century Western type of the brooding, pessimistic, and introspective hero.

The inner world of the individual, whether or not it was valued in pre-Meiji times, was never depicted in literature before Futabatei's *Ukigumo*. In the novel it is depicted as literally separate both from the world of society at large and from the inner worlds of other individuals. The disparity between Bunzō's inner world and the outer world is shown, for example, in the scene where Bunzō is walking the streets after his quarrel with Noboru, gnashing his teeth and wondering how he can get revenge on his rival. He is obviously completely caught up in his own subjective world at this point and becomes aware of the external world only when he suddenly notices that a policeman is looking at him strangely. He had glared at the policeman, and at the whole world, as if they were Noboru.[18] At such times the author sees the distance between the subjective world of the mind and that of

---

[17] Tsubouchi Shōyō, "Futabatei no koto," in *Kaki no heta*, in *Bungakuteki kaisōshū, Gendai nihonbungaku zenshū*, Tokyo, 1959, 97: 30, 32.

[18] Ryan, *Japan's First Modern Novel*, chap. 9, pp. 287-288.

other people as comic. However, Futabatei depicts Bunzō's estrangement from the world of other people as neurotic and destructive in the scene where Bunzō becomes more and more irritated at Noboru's kidding, finally telling Noboru to leave his aunt's house. It is obvious to the reader that Bunzō is overreacting, taking as an insult what was meant only as a slightly nasty jibe on the part of an extroverted person. Yet the author does not blame Bunzō here. Rather, he presents a clash between two psychic worlds that are naturally opposed to one another: the world of the introvert, whose self exists far inside him, resisting any superficial evaluation, and that of the extrovert, whose self is exposed easily on the surface. It is a matter of incompatibility of personalities: the one remains locked inside himself and is easily attacked, the other ventures forth too easily and can be accused of attacking others. But the scene is painful, both for Bunzō and for the reader who has been seduced into identifying with him.

The introverted Bunzō is a shy, reserved person with a strong sense of loyalty; he is a man of principle also. These characteristics sound like virtues, but Futabatei shows how they can look equally like vices. On being dismissed from his job, Bunzō is put in the position of being dependent on his aunt and uncle. Eventually he becomes dependent on Noboru also, for it is Noboru, the successful bureaucrat, who could probably manage to have him rehired, if Bunzō would only speak up for himself, defend his actions, and kowtow to Noboru. However, just at this point Bunzō's love of principle becomes a stubborn insistence not to toady to an unworthy man (Noboru); his shyness a refusal to defend himself and his interests (in Osei) from encroachment by others; his loyalty a passive hanging onto the affection of his aunt and cousin; and his reserve an unhealthy withdrawal from the world of action. Indeed, from the beginning of the novel when he is dismissed from his job, Bunzō is scarcely depicted as a man of action. As an introvert he had probably always tagged along behind other people, reacting to their actions rather than initiating action himself. When he was protected this did not matter, but

now, when he should act to save himself, he does not, and retreats into a dangerous world of fantasy. This period begins during the excursion to Dangozaka, when Bunzō stays home in self-
pity as Osei goes off with her mother and Noboru.[19] Bunzō
makes the introvert's typical mistake of failing to take into account the demands made on him by the outside world, and thus
his existence becomes airless and narrow. Finally, his small room
with its shabby furniture and its frying pan with the chipped
edge becomes symbolic of the stagnant and dreary consciousness
of its occupant.[20]

Neither Jung's definition of introversion, nor Futabatei's view
of Bunzō as an introvert, indicates that Bunzō is morally wrong.
Rather, Bunzō suffers from a lack of self-knowledge that leads
him to undervalue the demands made on him by others. Then,
too, an excessive amount of self-pride keeps him from looking too
closely at his own motives in his dealings with others. However,
Bunzō's fundamental weakness is his lack of awareness of other
people's inner lives. He continues to see Noboru as his enemy and
dreams of revenge, when Noboru has offered, albeit somewhat
condescendingly, to help him. He continues to see Osei as a
young, powerless girl who is being led astray by Noboru, though
it is clear from the novel that Osei is quite able to manipulate
Bunzō to attain her ends. He sees Omasa likewise in distorted
fashion, as a cold, cruel woman who has mistreated him. Yet
when he retires to his room to think about what she has said to
him and places her words and behavior in the framework of the
events of the several months he has known her, he is able to see
things from her point of view. Bunzō is presented sympathetically as he turns Omasa's behavior and words over and over

[19] Ibid., chap. 7, pp. 259-261.

[20] Bunzō's desire to hang onto his aunt and Osei rather than stand up for his
principles, and his retreat from action into a world of fantasy, can also be interpreted as stemming from a neurotic need for *amae*, or indulgence. See Doi
Takeo, *Amae no kōzō*, Tokyo, 1971. An English translation is *The Anatomy of
Dependence*, Tokyo, 1973.

in his mind, trying to discover their meaning. By the end of his session in his room Bunzō is able to understand her completely to the point of forgetting his own demands on her.

Yet when Bunzō goes out of his room to act he bungles the situation. For example, Bunzō realizes, after reflecting a while, that Omasa must have been disappointed that he lost his job, rather than angry at him, for it meant the failure of her plans to have Osei marry him. Then, moved by Omasa's predicament, he resolves to try to please her, but immediately realizes, after a little further thought, that the only way he could please her would be by getting his job back. To do this, he would have to appeal to Noboru, and the thought of pleading with his rival disgusts him. He decides he cannot bear to sacrifice his pride by speaking to Noboru. To avoid facing the knowledge that by deciding not to speak to Noboru he has in fact given up his plan to regain Omasa's favor, he quickly decides to appeal to Osei. If she too urges him to try to persuade Noboru to get his job back for him, he'll know she is not on his side. Yet he really expects that she will support him in his attitude of lonely pride. Thus, Bunzō's step toward action has ended in an appeal to Osei to justify his nonaction. It is not at all surprising to the reader that Osei, when confronted by Bunzō, urges him to seek Noboru's help. However, when she does so, Bunzō accuses her of disloyalty, failing to understand that for Osei, like himself immersed in her private world of values, his joblessness was a practical problem that required action, not merely something as abstract as sympathy or loyalty. After Osei refuses to confirm Bunzō in his nonaction, he retreats to his room, having once more lost the battle in the world of practicality and action.[21] In this way, Bunzō's resolve to do good, which was the fruit of his sincere attempt to understand another person, has been frittered away by his inability to see action itself as important. This is a consequence of his neurotic introversion.

[21] Ryan, chaps. 11 and 12, pp. 304-316.

At one point in the novel, after Bunzō has made one of several decisions to solve everything by appealing to Osei's loyalty, the author remarks: "If he were patient just a little while longer, everything would work out all right. Poor Bunzō—he was living in a dream."[22] Indeed, the dream ended quickly enough when he actually talked to Osei, for he had taken into account neither her touchiness, which was caused by his own earlier angry treatment of her as well as her growing awareness of her own sexual desire, nor his own unconscious desire for her. Thus, when he began to talk, the failure of communication was complete. Bunzō wanted to apologize to Osei, but

> As he struggled to get out the words, Osei suddenly stood up. He was caught completely off guard and the printed pattern of her obi dancing before his eyes awakened an impulse within him. He seized her sleeve.
> "What are you doing?" Her voice was harsh.
> "I just want to talk to you."
> "I have no time now." She pulled her sleeve free and quickly left the room.[23]

Somehow Bunzō is unable to express to Osei what he wants to tell her. Also, it is clear that even if he could have, he is not taking into account her own desires as an independent and separate person. Indeed, he does not really want to take into account Osei's separateness because he wants so badly to see himself as inseparably united with her and Omasa.

Bunzō's vision of harmony and unity becomes clearer in the last chapter, when he has failed to take any decisive action whatever to change the unsatisfactory situation. He thinks about why, in spite of all the humiliation he has suffered in the Sonoda household, he still remains there. He admits that a certain personal irresoluteness, a certain love for Osei, and a certain shame at admitting that he had bungled his relationship with her all keep him there. Yet what holds him there above all these is his sense of

---

[22] Ibid., chap. 15, p. 328.   [23] Ibid., chap. 15, p. 329.

obligation to the Sonoda family, who are, after all, his relatives, and to a dream of harmony between them. He looks back on the period a few months earlier when the three of them—Bunzō, Omasa, and Osei—had existed in perfect harmony together, each in a distinct relationship to the other that promised future happiness. That was all destroyed, first by Bunzō's losing his job, then by the entrance of Noboru. Since that time, the female members of the household have been scheming, each in her own way, to get what they want; they are no longer working either in harmony with one another or with him.[24] For Bunzō this vision of disharmony is extraordinarily painful. It is as though Bunzō, as the first individual in Japanese fiction, is looking at the situation of being an individual and finding it painful. The vision of past harmony is so strong that any development beyond it seems fraught with difficulty and, ultimately, regrettable. This is the tone of the last chapter, at least. Bunzō never gives up his dream of restoring harmony, for the book ends with him waiting to speak with Osei, hoping to save her from Noboru and thereby to restore the lost harmony. It seems clear, however, that Bunzō will not be able to do this. Osei is pictured, at the end, as more friendly to Bunzō, but there is no reason to suppose that she has decided to return to the former harmony of the family after once venturing abroad. Also, Bunzō's posture of waiting to make a last appeal to Osei is a repetition of an action he had taken before, without it resulting in a restoration of harmony.

Ukigumo can be said to imply an unhappy ending, though it closes as Bunzō is fixed in his dream of a happy future. Yet whether Bunzō succeeds or not in this particular effort to restore a lost harmony, what is important for Futabatei is his dream of the restoration of a harmony and love between individuals that had existed under the hierarchical system of the past. Bunzō is the carrier of the author's dream of recovering a lost unity between individuals, much as Oblomov was the carrier of Goncharov's

[24] Ibid., chap. 19, pp. 349-350.

dream of the restoration of a lost hierarchical harmony, in *Ob-lomov*.[25] Bunzō's worth as a person cannot be measured in the old way, as a carrier of virtues or vices. Rather it is his devotion and loyalty to others that have value for the author. Of all the characters in the novel, Bunzō is the most sympathetic, and it is because of precisely this capacity to dream. As a man of action he is ridiculous; compared to Noboru he is a weakling. Yet as a man with an inner vision, one that, though at times clouded with ignorance, is motivated by love, he is a hero. Even though he will fail to restore either the lost harmony of the Sonoda family or the lost harmony of modern Japan, his dream, made serious by continuous concern and attention, will live on. This, Futabatei seems to be saying, is the value of the inner life: that it allows man to live with hope and dignity and love regardless of what is happening to the world outside.

Bunzō: Japan's New Culture Hero

When we consider Bunzō we should not forget that his clinging to the dream of a restored social harmony is connected to his failure in the world of action. The less he is able to function in the external world the more important his inner world of fantasy becomes for him. Yet Bunzō is not insane. He is an ordinary person. Bunzō is, then, a weak hero, a fact that was noticed by an

[25] In his yearning for a lost harmony between individuals Bunzō shows his kinship to Goncharov's Oblomov, one of the characters after which Futabatei modeled him. One thinks particularly of the chapter entitled "Oblomov's Dream" (pt. 1, chap. 9 in *Oblomov*), in which Oblomov recalls the world of his childhood—a personal Golden Age of peace, harmony, and comfort that he sadly admits is irrecoverable in that form. Bunzō also yearns for the peaceful unity of the family of his childhood, but for him the family is important because its existence gives him the opportunity to demonstrate his devotion and loyalty. For Goncharov the family was rather a locus of comfort and well-being—though for both authors it called up a vision of an old world based on an harmonious hierarchy of classes, a world that was disappearing at the time they wrote their novels.

early reviewer of part one of *Ukigumo* when it appeared in the fall of 1887: "Because the author of *Ukigumo* understands the novel, he purposely makes a mediocre, imperfect man his hero." The critic went on to praise Futabatei's fascinating depiction of his hero's vacillations. Yet later in the same review he appeared to have reservations about the "feminine" character of Bunzō, noting that Futabatei had given the feminine qualities of "timidity, gentleness, indecision, pliancy, agility, modesty" to the male characters, specifically Bunzō.[26] Despite his reservations about Bunzō's "nonmasculine" character, however, this reviewer, and most critics of *Ukigumo*, found the novel innovative in its realism of character and approved of this innovation. However, as it turned out, Bunzō forecast the type of hero that was to dominate a large part of subsequent Japanese fiction of the individual. How did Bunzō, an unlikely candidate for heroism in any traditional sense, become the new culture hero of the Meiji period? In order to answer this question one must consider the fate of samurai values in the 1880s.

The lower-ranking samurai had brought about the overthrow of the Tokugawa government and gained power for themselves by acting according to time-honored ideals of their class: loyalty to their lord and heroic service to the state. In making the revolution, these leaders, who had suffered under the stagnant rule of the Tokugawa from the lack of opportunity to serve their country, wished to create a society in which samurai ideals could truly be fulfilled.[27] Thanks to the preponderance of this class in positions of power in all spheres of Meiji rule, the samurai ideal of service to the nation dominated the early Meiji period. Under the influence of the samurai ideal that stressed the development of a strong, ethically oriented personality that would find its highest expression in concrete patriotic action, a new kind of economic heroism was given validation: Samuel Smiles's *Self-Help*, the

[26] Ishibashi Ningetsu, "*Ukigumo* no homeotoshi," in *Gendai bungakuron taikei*, vol. 1, *Meiji jidai*, Tokyo, 1956, pp. 45-47.

[27] Bellah, *Tokugawa Religion*, p. 19.

Bible of such heroism in early Meiji, was interpreted as a manual
that would inform young men how to serve their country through
their economic efforts. Likewise, Defoe's *Robinson Crusoe*, translated already in 1859, was read as an illustration of how the
virtue of independence, accompanied by those of initiative and
enterprise, could enable a person alone on an island to build a
civilization. Consequently, the culture heroes of early Meiji were
not only samurai heroes in the traditional vein such as Fukuzawa
Yukichi, a tireless educator of his people, or Ōkuma Shigenobu,
a gifted politician. Shibusawa Eiichi, a genial entrepreneur, also
fulfilled brilliantly the samurai ideal of usefulness to the nation.[28]

It is worth emphasizing that *Self-Help* and *Robinson Crusoe* were
acceptable to a reading public influenced by samurai ideals because they presented an ideal of patriotism that, though new,
could be fitted into the old Confucian tradition that stressed loyalty and service to the nation. An aspect of the ideal of individualism that could not easily be fitted into the Confucian heroic
ideal of service to the nation was the longing for undefined and
limitless freedom from political oppression that dominated Japan
in the 1880s, when those interested in the attainment of the ideal
of human rights were anxiously awaiting the promulgation of the
constitution and the holding of the first elections for parliament.
A new sort of novel, the political novel (*seiji-shōsetsu*), sprang up
to express this new longing for a freedom that went beyond patriotism. As Nakamura Mitsuo phrased it, these novels "gave the
most direct expression to the 'vitality' of the society—especially
the youth—which had been roused from the old refuse of the
feudal period by the 'unprecedented upheaval' of the Meiji Restoration, which had been awakened to new ideas and new life."[29]
The political novels, both translations from Western novels and
novels written by the Japanese themselves, spoke for the ideals of

[28] See chap. 1, n. 30, for information on Shibusawa.

[29] Odagiri Hideo, paraphrased by Nakamura Mitsuo in *Nihon no kindai
shōsetsu, Nakamura Mitsuo zenshū*, Tokyo, 1974, 11: 325.

independence and human rights that were the center of the People's Rights movement of the time. Works as diverse and of such varying quality as Schiller's *Wilhelm Tell* (translated as "Tell: Story of Freedom" in 1882) and pamphlets dealing with the sufferings of the Russian Nihilists were received enthusiastically by a wide range of readers.[30]

Among the some 220 political novels written by Japanese on the theme of political liberation in the decade between 1881 and 1890, two in particular present a new type of hero, the patriot speaking out for freedom, and show the mark of their individual author in a way that foreshadows *Ukigumo*. They are *Kajin no kigū* (Strange Encounters with Elegant Ladies, 1885), by Shiba Shirō (pseudonym Tōkai Sanshi, 1852-1922), and *Setchūbai* (Plum Blossoms in the Snow, 1886) by Suehiro Tetchō (1849-1896). The authors of both novels were actively involved in the People's Rights movement and in public life as a whole. Shiba held a post in the government from 1884, was elected to the Diet in 1891, and later, from 1892, headed one of the most famous Japanese newpapers. Tetchō was more of a political thinker. Jailed early in his career as a newspaperman for his advocacy of political parties, he had first-hand experience of the political realities of the day. What is unusual about *Kajin no kigū* is that Shiba Shirō appears in it as himself and tells his own story: how his clan, which had fought the Imperial Army at the time of the Restoration, had been badly treated afterward by the government. Other characters, each one from a land currently suffering under political oppression, tell their stories, but the main emphasis is on the author's ideals of liberation, his sympathy for oppressed countries, and his vision of Japan as the defender of Asia against Western

---

[30] For a detailed discussion of the political novel and its role in the early Meiji period, see Nakamura Mitsuo, *Nihon no kindai shōsetsu*, pp. 320-329; Sansom, *The Western World and Japan*, pp. 397-404; and Horace Z. Feldman, "The Meiji Political Novel: A Brief Survey," *The Far Eastern Quarterly* 9 (May 1950): 245-255.

aggression—ideas that he declaims in a flowery style in between amorous episodes.[31]

Kajin no kigū combined the purposes of entertainment and instruction. In *Setchūbai* these two aims are again united, but here the desire to instruct is much stronger, for the author includes a great deal of concrete analysis of the contemporary Japanese political scene. Tetchō seems to have turned to novel writing when it became impossible for him to express his views in the newspapers, which from 1875 suffered from censorship and harassment at the hands of the government. Through his mouthpiece in the novel, Tetchō spoke out against such harassment, declaring that freedom of speech and freedom of assembly were necessary in order to guarantee an informed public opinion—which in turn was necessary in order for the government and the people to work together to build up a strong nation. It is known that Tetchō in real life advocated the ideal of compromise of all political parties to effect a harmonious working together of the parties and the government, and he put this idea into a speech that the hero of the novel makes at his own wedding party![32] The novels of Shiba and Tetchō, then, can be seen as forerunners of the realistic novel, if only because the authors wrote of their own experiences and expressed their personal convictions in literary form. Before the Restoration it was rare to express one's political opinions in public; that men such as these could do so proved that an era of self-expression had begun.

It is interesting that both Shiba and Tetchō were, in real life, heroic figures on the samurai model: both had clearly defined ethical positions and both served the state, though in their own way, as critics of it. Yet there is a fantastic quality to their novels that differs from their lives as concrete phenomena, a quality that is

[31] A brief plot summary of *Kajin no kigū* may be found in Sansom, *The Western World and Japan*, pp. 412-415.

[32] Yoshio Iwamoto discusses Suehiro Tetchō's views and his novel, *Setchūbai*, in "Suehiro Tetchō: A Meiji Political Novelist," in *Japan's Modern Century*, ed. Edmund Skrzypczak, Tokyo, 1968.

directly related to the fate of the ideal of independence in the 1880s. In retrospect, the ideal of Fukuzawa, though supported by people of all classes through the People's Rights movement, turned out to be an ideal that was not realized—nor, given the situation of Japan as a country just emerging from feudalism, could it have been, at least in the form that the proponents of people's rights envisioned. Thus, while intellectuals in the 1880s were arguing over the advantages and disadvantages of various liberal European political systems, the government was acting pragmatically to bring into being the conservative political system it thought would suit the Japan of that time. The proponents of the ideal of people's rights in the 1880s were aware of the government's intentions; they were aware also that what they were advocating was an ideal, and they knew the difference between ideal and reality. Writers such as Shiba and Tetchō, then, had a dream, a political vision that corresponded to their inner ideal of freedom, and this ideal is what is revealed in their political novels. Because of the lack of realization of this ideal in society, their heroes became mere disembodied mouthpieces for their ideals.

Futabatei's novel of the inner life, *Ukigumo*, appeared, paradoxically, at the end of a decade devoted to politics, to affairs on a grand scale. Yet, in another sense, *Ukigumo* is the natural outcome of the preoccupations of the 1870s and 1880s: the concern for the liberation of the individual and the cultivation of the ideal of independence. However, in *Ukigumo* independence is an ideal that has left the public arena and gone inward, reflecting the failure of the parliamentary movement that was occurring at that very moment. *Ukigumo* is the true descendant of the political novels of the 1880s, for while the heroes of the political novels were fantasies, mere projections of the dynamic ideal of freedom, Bunzō represents the reality of freedom in the Meiji period: his freedom is an inner freedom only. Bunzō's departure from public life to live a mentalized existence in his room is highly significant for the development of the Japanese novel of the individual, then, for it marks the failure of the traditional samurai ideal of heroic moral action. The early Meiji ethical ideal of *risshin-shusse* (rising in the world and making a name for oneself) had signified individual heroic action, whether in government or business, in the service of the state—in other words, Fukuzawa's ideal of developing individual independence in order to bring about national independence. What Futabatei demonstrates in *Ukigumo*, however, is that the sudden expansion of economic and social opportunity of the early Meiji period placed pressure on individuals to abandon the old samurai ideals of loyalty, social harmony, and devotion to learning and hard work—in short, values of service to the state—in the rush to advance on the social ladder. In the figure of Noboru, whose name appropriately means "to rise," Futabatei depicts an extreme example of a samurai who possesses the new virtues demanded by bureaucratic life: competitiveness, ruthlessness, sycophancy, and superficiality. Noboru is a caricature of the samurai ethical ideal and a forecast of its complete disintegration, for, lacking the reverence for the ideal of national independence that was linked with the early Meiji ideal of *risshin-shusse*, Noboru's attempts to succeed in his petty bureaucratic position reveal him to be a *seikō-seinen* ("success-seeking youth").[33] From the example of Noboru, who succeeds in the new style of life centered around the bureaucracy, it is clear that, though the samurai had brought about the Meiji Restoration, ultimately they failed to create a society in which their ideals could be fulfilled.

By contrast, in the character Bunzō, Futabatei has portrayed a person imbued with almost all the true samurai ethical ideals: love of learning, loyalty, desire for social harmony, devotion to

---

[33] The term *seikō-seinen* ("success-seeking youth") was created by Tokutomi Sohō to describe a certain type of late Meiji youth for whom the pursuit of personal success outweighed any patriotic concerns. See his *Taishō seinen to teikoku no zento*, Tokyo, 1916, for a discussion of this phenomenon. Maruyama Masao discusses the difference between *risshin-shusse* and the ideal embodied in the *seikō-seinen* in "Patterns of Individuation," in *Changing Attitudes Toward Modernization*, ed. Marius B. Jansen, Princeton, 1965, pp. 508-510.

principle—yet the corruption of the ethical system, in a time of rapid change, makes it impossible for him to act. For the samurai of the past, the attainment of virtue was useless without the opportunity to manifest it in ethical action. In *Ukigumo* Futabatei portrays a situation in which an individual educated according to samurai ethics is asked to harness his ideals of maintaining high standards and working with devotion for the good of the state to the petty aims of a bureaucracy: carrying out meaningless paper work and serving a petty, ignorant boss. In a situation where action is impossible, virtue becomes useless decoration, and, seen from the samurai point of view, Bunzō becomes a superfluous man. Like the high-principled, educated gentry of the 1840s in Russia who wanted reform but were kept from action and driven to excessive self-absorption by the oppressive atmosphere of tyranny and stagnation in still feudal Russia, Bunzō and members of the samurai class like him can be seen as frustrated by the authoritarian feudal environment of the early Meiji period. As Futabatei created him, Bunzō is a Japanese Oblomov, who, because he does not value his bureaucratic job as a means to manifest his virtues, is not sorry to lose it.[34]

Yet Bunzō is not only a samurai, he is also an individual. Consequently, he has values other than those of his social class. If one looks at him negatively, as a failed samurai, Bunzō conspicuously lacks one of the most important samurai virtues: the desire to do great deeds for the state. Thus, it is not that he is kept from action by the daily minor harassment and pettiness of the bureaucracy, but rather that he lacks interest in action itself. Bunzō does not value action, not even enough to restore the social harmony that is being lost in his very household, a microcosm of Meiji so-

[34] Bunzō has been seen as a Japanese Oblomov and a Japanese "superfluous man" by both Russian and Japanese critics. For a summary of such statements see K. Rekho, "Dostoevskii i yaponskii realisticheskii roman kontsa XIX veka," *Narody Azii i Afriki*, 1 (1972): 123. There is also an insightful discussion of Bunzō in relation to the Russian superfluous hero in Ryan, *Japan's First Modern Novel*, pp. 178-183.

ciety. His spirit is far from that of Saigō Takamori, the hero that the youthful Futabatei admired because of his attempt to restore a lost feudal harmony. Looked at positively, in terms of his own individualized virtues, Bunzō is an authentic introvert whose talent lies in the contemplative rather than in the active realm. Like Goncharov's Oblomov, he was born not to act but to dream, to feel, and to accomplish small unseen miracles in his heart, which for him is the center of the universe. It is the lack of a tradition of introverted literature that prevented Futabatei from making Bunzō's virtues shine forth more clearly—for where Oblomov, even in the midst of his laziness, inspires his friends Stolz and Olga through his virtues, Bunzō only appears to be a failure. For Omasa he is good-for-nothing, for Noboru he is ridiculous, and for Osei he is old-fashioned. The introvert's existence is a bungled one in *Ukigumo*, as it is not in Futabatei's models, the novels of Goncharov, Turgenev, and Dostoevsky. For Bunzō there is no hope of fruitful interaction with the distant world of the others, as there is no hope of reconciliation between the values of the individual and those of Meiji society.

Futabatei's presentation of Bunzō as the new hero of the age, and the appearance of Bunzō's successors, the introverted heroes of the I-novel after the turn of the century, were signs of the decline of the samurai ideal of heroism. Yet the appearance of a hero whose sphere was not action but feeling, and who was unique rather than virtuous, also meant the end of the hold that Confucian moralism had had on fiction. In the Tokugawa era, fiction was written under a manipulative aesthetic; it was used to enforce certain moral attitudes beneficial to the state: obedience, loyalty, selflessness, ethical heroism. Though the novels of Tetchō and Shiba were revolutionary in terms of their expression of the writer's individual opinions, in terms of their purpose they were no different from older novels written to inculcate "correct" attitudes. The hero of *Setchūbai*, for example, is a stereotype of a young man who has great potential for serving his country, and his name, which means "foundation of the country," reveals the author's didactic purpose of providing a model to inspire the young men of Meiji.[35]

In 1885, in his *Essence of the Novel*, Tsubouchi Shōyō had provided the novel with an aesthetic that would replace the old, Confucian manipulative aesthetic. He distinguished between the two types of teaching that a novel can provide, the one a teaching that attempts to manipulate man into "obeying the traditional Confucian principles," and the other a kind of instruction that "goes beyond the limits of (accepted) morality." According to Tsubouchi's vision, the novel was a literary form that would, through the portrayal of life in its wide scope and variety, "instruct people and improve (both) their inner and outer lives."[36] In his emphasis on a contemplative rather than a manipulative aesthetic,[37] Tsubouchi shifted the scrutiny of the novelist to the richness and depth of life that existed outside of the traditional area of ideal and scandalous behavior, of virtue and vice. After Tsubouchi the novel was dedicated to making the individualistic sphere of life—the sphere of aesthetic-emotional values—the center of the novel. Futabatei's *Ukigumo* was the first modern Japanese novel to embody a contemplative aesthetic. In the figure of Bunzō the author presents a person whose individual values are at the center of the world: Bunzō fantasizes, analyzes, dreams, and Bunzō is in love. All of these activities are validated by the author in paragraph after paragraph of analysis that is at times loving, at times irritated or amused, but always respectful. Not since the Heian fictional masterpieces had there been a novel where the character's inner world was respected and where eccentricity (here in the modern form of psychological depth) was admired.

It is not accidental that I mention the Heian fictional masterpieces in connection with Futabatei, for Futabatei and his follow-

---

[35] Iwamoto, "Suehiro Tetchō," pp. 97-99.

[36] Tsubouchi, *Shōsetsu shinzui*, p. 173.

[37] The terms "manipulative" and "contemplative" aesthetic are defined and discussed in reference to Russian literature in Rufus W. Mathewson, Jr., *The Positive Hero in Russian Literature*, New York, 1958, pp. 119ff.

ers, the writers of subjective novels, can be said to have brought
back into the mainstream of Japanese literature the interest in experience, rather than action, and the preoccupation with subjective moral truth that were values of Heian aristocratic
literature—values that had become degraded during centuries of
samurai rule. Furthermore, Tsubouchi's view of the novel as providing knowledge of or insight into life, a knowledge that transcends the accepted limits of morality, and Futabatei's carrying
out of this theory in *Ukigumo* show the influence of Lady
Murasaki's view of fiction. For the author of the *Tale of Genji*, in
her "Fireflies" (*Hotaru*) chapter, defines fiction as a form of literature that, through its portrayal of good and evil—the reality of
life as we know it—points to broad universal truth.[38] Insofar as
they strove to communicate their own broad vision of life, then,
Futabatei and his followers were aristocrats.

Yet Futabatei and the I-novelists that came after him suffered
as aristocrats in a culture that was hostile to aristocratic pursuits.
The aristocrat Genji had pursued truth in the form of aesthetic
knowledge, a kind of knowledge that was held in respect and reverence by his class. He was fortunate in that his rank guaranteed
him the leisure to savor his aesthetic responses to the phenomena
of the world in all their richness and that his society supported his
activities as important cultural concerns, thus confirming him in
his role. However, Futabatei, in his scrutiny of the individual in

[38] Lady Murasaki's remarks, put into the mouth of Genji himself, are in the
nature of a defense of fiction against the charge that it is full of lies. The purpose
of Genji's remarks is to define the specific nature of the truth that fiction portrays. After a long series of arguments he concludes by comparing fiction to
Buddha's parables, which use stories of this world, stories that contain both
good and evil, in order to point to a religious truth that goes beyond the world
of good and evil. Fiction, then, is akin to religious writings in that it teaches a
truth that is broad, universal, and whose meaning is not limited to the factual or
the sense world. Murasaki Shikibu, *Genji monogatari*, ed. Yamagishi Tokuhei,
in *Nihon kotenbungaku taikei*, Tokyo, 1975, 15: 432-433. For a translation of the
relevant passages see Murasaki Shikibu, *The Tale of Genji*, trans. Edward G.
Seidensticker, New York, 1976, 1: 437-438.

Ukigumo, pursued a truth the meaning of which could be recognized and appreciated only by a tiny minority in the culture of his time. For those who responded deeply to the Western ideal of individualism, especially after the movement for people's rights had declined, were separated almost completely from the government leaders in their ideals and aspirations, and from the people as a whole. Further, Futabatei wrote in a society that saw his labor not as work but as a degraded sort of leisure activity. A writer is always a member of the leisured class in this sense, but the lingering influence of the traditional Confucian evaluation of fiction as useless, frivolous, and even harmful, as well as the contemporary emphasis on the importance to the nation of entrepreneurial spirit and business skills, combined to influence the society of early Meiji to view its fiction writers as a class of entertainers whose work had no demonstrable value. It is perhaps because of feelings of uselessness and isolation, as well as because of his unusually high standards, that Futabatei stopped writing fiction after *Ukigumo*, only taking up his novelist's pen again in the more favorable period of the early twentieth century.[39]

As the government increasingly encouraged the cultivation among the masses of a vigorous, warlike, and communal spirit called *Yamato-damashii* ("the spirit of Yamato"—i.e., old Japan), and as the split widened between the popular culture and the cul-

---

[39] After Futabatei finished *Ukigumo* in August of 1889, he immediately took a job in a government office translating English documents. It is quite clear that he took the job in order to earn money enough to support his parents, for translating and writing did not yield a salary that was either adequate or regular. However, personal factors were also involved in his decision to stop writing. Because of his high ideals, Futabatei felt that he had failed in what he had tried to do in *Ukigumo*. Furthermore, he blamed himself for having attempted to earn money by pursuing truth through fiction writing. Finally, he felt alone among literary men of his time because his standards, methods, and models were completely different from theirs. For all these reasons he devoted himself after the completion of *Ukigumo* to the career of translating and newspaper writing, and only tried his hand at fiction again in 1906. See Ryan, *Japan's First Modern Novel*, pp. 137-145.

ture of the intellectuals educated in the Western tradition, an image from the past returned to haunt the Japanese novelist of the self: that of the monk Kenkō, the representative of an aristocratic culture that had been defeated and had gone into exile. Thus, when preoccupation with the inner world, with aesthetic-emotional values, could not move into the center of cultural life, where it had been during the Heian period, it became, as in the Middle Ages, an underground activity. Indeed, the formation, about this time, of the *bundan* ("literary world"), a small coterie of Western-influenced writers, can be seen as an action taken by a cultural minority to protect its culture from outside hostility. Yet there is much truth to the remark of one critic, Itō Sei, that the writers of the *bundan* were runaway slaves—writers who had not achieved freedom but had only escaped temporarily from the political situation that oppressed them.[40] The Meiji *bundan*, then, was a continuation of the Tokugawa brothel: a territory in which aesthetic-emotional activities that were still suspected by the culture as a whole could be pursued in relative freedom. For Futabatei, the ten-by-ten-foot room of Bunzō was the sequestered, isolated place where the individual devoted himself to the scrutiny of the inner life, and the image of small, upstairs rooms where the hero sits alone with his thoughts recurs with great frequency in later subjective novels.

In the midst of these pessimistic reflections on the limitations that hedged in the development of a culture of the individual in Meiji Japan, Futabatei's achievement in reintroducing aesthetic-emotional values, the values of the individual, into a culture that had discredited them for such a long time, should not be underestimated. It is true that the ideal of independence associated with the People's Rights movement suffered a serious defeat around the time *Ukigumo* was written and that, as a consequence, the culture of the individual was not supported politically by a West-

[40] Quoted in Senuma Shigeki, "Kindai bungaku ni okeru ningenshō," in *Kindai nihonbungaku no kōzō*, vol. 1, *Meiji no bungaku*, Tokyo, 1963, p. 67.

ern-style economic liberalism. Thus, one does not find in Futabatei's novel, nor in the later I-novels, the round, fully socialized
characters of Balzac's novels.[41] The fully socialized, vigorous individual was an ideal that, like the ideal of people's rights,
fomented the Meiji individual's desire for self-completion but did
not bring it about. According to Maruyama Masao, in pre-Meiji
Japan the individual had no personal morality.[42] What occurred
with the coming of Western ideals of independence and human
rights was an encouragement of a personal morality in the
Western-educated individuals who were ready to work to attain
it. What is revolutionary in Futabatei Shimei is his sympathy for
the development of such a morality and his depiction of the first
modern Japanese individual with his internal ambivalences and
his everyday humanity.

[41] Senuma Shigeki remarks in this context that "the large size characters with
clear outlines that Hippolyte Taine pointed out in Balzac's works" were not to
be found in Japanese literature of the Meiji period. It was impossible, notes
Senuma, for writers to portray full-blooded characters of this sort at the time
because of the privatistic, asocial life of the middle-class intellectuals who wrote
the enduring literature. Senuma, "Kindai bungaku ni okeru ningenshō,"
pp. 67-68.

[42] Maruyama argues that in Japan, up until 1946, there was no basis on
which private interests could be acknowledged. The concept of the national polity (*kokutai*), the public morality of the Japanese people, based itself on inner
norms of behavior (loyalty, obedience), and since it was not seen as a form but
only as a content, it was impossible for any purely private and personal sphere of
morality to exist apart from it. (This is the morality of "Emanation" as discussed
in chap. 1, n. 31.) When Maruyama says that such a personal morality did not
exist before 1946, he is speaking of the majority of Japanese. A personal morality did come into being in the Meiji period, but only among intellectuals.
Maruyama, *Gendai seiji no shisō to kōdō*, 1: 11-12.

CHAPTER THREE

Kitamura Tōkoku and the Ideal of the Inner Life: The Interiorization of the Ideal of Individualism

Fukuzawa's ideal of independence (*dokuritsu*), the version of the ideal of individualism that had inspired Japanese of the 1870s and 1880s, was deeply colored by traditional samurai moral assumptions. Fukuzawa was himself of samurai origins; born in 1835, he spent the greater part of his adult life in the period before the disenfranchisement and decline of the samurai as a visible class with its own ethical system. It is not surprising, then, that he considered the Western liberal ideal of individualism in a samurai context of ethical service to the state. Not so with the generation of 1868, the generation of Futabatei and the other writers of subjective novels who will be treated in this study. Still children when their traditional privileges as a class (for most of them were samurai) were abolished, they never had the opportunity to live their adult lives as samurai. In the crucial period of their youth they were swept away by the fervor and idealism of the movement for people's rights. More importantly, however, they were exposed to the ideal of individualism directly, in its Western form, through their reading of Mill, Rousseau, Spencer, and Buckle in the Western-style higher schools and through their reading of Western novels and poetry that depicted the individual in his private life and thoughts. Consequently, they tended to perceive the ideal of individualism not as an ethical ideal of action but as a poetic vision of being. Futabatei's Bunzō already forecasts this tendency, for in him the ethical aspect of individualism yields to the aesthetic aspects of reflection, self-analysis, and fantasy.

The early 1890s saw a further development of the trend toward interest in the individual's subjective states of being. Yet looking at the events taking place during this time, one would not think that this period was an auspicious time for the development of an ideal of the individual in Japanese culture. The ideal of popular rights had become the reality of a Diet that represented only one percent of the population. Popular attention had shifted to international affairs, as the government engaged in negotiations with Western powers in the hope of obtaining the abrogation of the hated unequal treaties, and continued its imperialistic forays in Korea. The transformation of the ideal of individualism that took place in the early 1890s was accomplished, then, not by the Japanese people as a whole but by the group most resistant to military ideology and most independent of traditional social organizations: the small middle class of Western-educated intellectuals living in large cities. The large city provided a place where it was possible to be free of the pressures of traditional ideology and the family, as well as access to Western learning and Westerners themselves. Among the latter, Christianity and Christian missionaries were the most important influences on the formation of the new, internalized ideal of individualism; it was the Christian doctrine of the uniqueness of the individual's inner life that indirectly inspired the development of a new ideal of private self-cultivation.

From before the Restoration until well into the 1870s, Christian schools offered the only Western-style higher education. Thus, those seeking to rise in the world of new opportunity created by the Meiji rulers inevitably came in contact with Christian missionaries and with the doctrines of the Christian religion. Significantly, the earliest, the most numerous, and the most enthusiastic of these were of samurai origin. The missionaries, with their strong faith, moral rigor, and above all, their sense of mission, seemed to the young sons of samurai to be embodiments of the virtues of their own class, virtues which were rapidly becoming outmoded in an age of cataclysmic change.[1] Christianity was

[1] John F. Howes, "Japanese Christians and American Missionaries," in *Changing Attitudes Toward Modernization*, pp. 337-349.

attractive to the Japanese of the 1870s, then, not primarily because of its doctrines but because it offered them a heroic ethical system that would support them as they confronted the problems of modernization. However, Christianity was attractive also because it appeared to the Japanese to be the true source of the values of Western civilization as a whole. In this period, the heyday of imitation of things Western, the Meiji leaders, painfully conscious of what they felt was Japan's lack of civilization compared to Western countries, tacitly encouraged the visible growth of Christianity in Japan in order to impress upon the Western powers the fact that Japan was truly a civilized nation. Their hope was that the Westerners would gradually regard Japan as a nation worthy of respect and that eventually steps could be taken to eliminate the treaties that the West had forced on the Japanese as an "unequal" nation. This argument had such power that even Fukuzawa Yukichi, during the height of the treaty controversy in the 1880s, urged that a small number of prominent Japanese leaders adopt the Christian faith specifically in order to impress the Western powers.[2]

Yet Christianity also contributed one of the strands of thought that issued in the People's Rights movement of that time: the visionary belief in the uniqueness of each individual and the equality of all individuals, a belief that implied that freedom was the birthright of every man. Furthermore, many Christians took an active part in the People's Rights movement. The largest number of converts to Christianity in the 1880s were those who became converted while studying at Christian-run schools—those for whom Christianity was merely a religion of the head. Yet of the number of students, both men and women, who were educated at these schools (10,000 by 1889), not a few were influenced by charismatic leaders to develop an internalized, personalized Christianity.

After the promulgation of the Imperial Rescript on Education

---

[2] Schwantes, "Christianity *versus* Science," p. 42.

in 1890, Christian schools were criticized on the basis of their ethical instruction, which with its emphasis on belief in God seemed to the government to be antagonistic to the new official doctrine of emperor worship. As a result they were gradually superseded as trainers of future leaders by government-founded schools. When the government was able to induce the Western nations to revise the unequal treaties, the Western nations lost prestige in the eyes of the Japanese, and Christianity as well. Furthermore, the arrival of anti-Christian thought from the West beginning in the 1880s—the ideas of Spencer, Mill, and especially Darwin—caused Christian intellectuals to doubt the validity of Christian doctrine, and many left the church. Serious divisions occurred also within the church itself, for universalist sects such as the Unitarians that had come to Japan only in the 1880s tended to divert members away from the revivalist or fundamentalist groups already there. As a consequence of all these events, Christianity considered as a church or movement was inevitably weakened; indeed, the growth rate of the church dropped in the 1890s and many adherents fell away.[3] In the midst of a situation of external decline, however, there emerged within the church a new, visionary ideal of spirituality that set itself against orthodoxy and organized religion and stressed the necessity of an inner spiritual life. It was in the context of this movement that Kitamura Tōkoku wrote his works on the inner life.

Kitamura Tōkoku's Ideal of the Inner Life

Kitamura Tōkoku (1868-1894) was the first Japanese to define the inner life of the individual. He was the first, moreover, to stress the necessity for every Japanese to develop his own sense of spiritual selfhood—this time, not in order to build a militarily strong nation but to ensure the harmony of the entire universe.

---

[3] For the history of Christianity in Japan from 1870 to 1910 see Tetsunao Yamamori, *Church Growth in Japan*, South Pasadena, 1974, and Ernest E. Best, *Christian Faith and Cultural Crisis: The Japanese Case*, Leiden, 1966.

His ideal of selfhood developed in the context of orthodox Christian ideals of the spiritual life, but intersected with traditional Eastern ideals of the sage and the enlightened man, to emerge finally, leavened by Emerson's transcendentalist philosophy, as an intellectual and spiritual vision of man in the context of a democracy. His ideal influenced not only writers schooled in Christianity, such as Shimazaki Tōson, but also other writers of subjective fiction who had little or no interest in Christian ideals. Like many of the writers of his generation, Tōkoku was the son of a former samurai. After the defeudalization of the country his father obtained a job in the government bureaucracy, which necessitated his moving from Odawara, his home, to Tokyo. As a consequence Tōkoku, at the age of five, was left in the hands of "my stern grandfather and my grandmother, who didn't concern herself much with my welfare." Tōkoku, who described himself as an "independent, open-hearted, willful, and self-centered" child, naturally resented the restrictions his grandfather placed on his freedom. After his grandfather's death in 1878, Tōkoku lived once more with his parents; the strict regimen of his grandfather was now replaced by that of his mother, a woman of strong mind and nervous temperament who cherished high ambitions for her son.

When Tōkoku entered Taimei Elementary School in 1881 he was able to find some relief from his joyless, overdisciplined home life, for one of the teachers developed a strong affection for him and he found that he was able to gain his teachers' respect through his writing. From his teens Tōkoku alternated between periods of intense ambition and deep melancholy, revealing an idealistic nature that found it difficult to compromise with reality. For example, in 1881, when the progressives had succeeded in forcing the emperor to announce the establishment of a Diet, Tōkoku, stimulated by the idealism of the time, resolved to sacrifice himself for the goal of freedom. When the progressive forces were repressed by the government the next year, however, he succumbed to a severe melancholy that was only broken when he entered the university in 1883. His optimism soon revived after he had begun to live a stable life doing what he enjoyed: reading and studying on his own in the school library. Then he conceived the ambition of becoming a statesman and saving the Orient, sacrificing himself, like Christ, for his people. He wrote that he would obtain his end by "becoming a great philosopher and destroying the new school of 'survival of the fittest' philosophy that was popular in Europe." The following year (1885), after a period in which he fell into despair as he realized the deluded nature of these ambitions, he decided to follow the example of Victor Hugo and "guide the political movements through the power of my clever brush."[4]

It is significant that Tōkoku's first ambitions, like those of Futabatei, were conceived in the politically charged atmosphere surrounding the movement for people's rights. Later, when his ambitions left the political sphere per se, he was still to retain the ideal of ethically serving a body of individuals that politics would call the state but that he would see as "mankind." His essays should be seen, then, as a serious ethical contribution on his part, and his writing of them entailed, almost as he wished, a Christ-like sacrifice. As early as 1885 Tōkoku was aware of the fact that his ideals could not be realized through political action. By 1888 his orientation had undergone a complete change, as can be seen from a letter he wrote in January of that year, in which he spoke of the necessity of fighting the battle of life not with a sword, but with truth, and not with one's own strength but with a strength

[4] The quotations in this and the preceding paragraph are taken from a letter—actually a brief autobiography—that Tōkoku wrote to his future wife, Ishizaka Mina, on August 18, 1887. This letter indicates the insight Tōkoku had into his own inner life and, in particular, into the difficulties encountered by an individual who wished to live freely. *Tōkoku zenshū*, Tokyo, 1964, 3: 162, 168. A biographical sketch of Tōkoku in English is available in Francis Mathy, "Kitamura Tōkoku: The Early Years," *Monumenta Nipponica* 18 (1963): 3-20, and "Kitamura Tōkoku: Final Essays," *Monumenta Nipponica* 20 (1965): 55-63.

derived from God.[5] Two events were responsible for the change: his meeting of his future wife, Mina, and his conversion to Christianity. In the summer of 1887 Tōkoku met Ishizaka Mina, an educated woman three years his senior who was a devout Christian and active in the People's Rights movement. Though he had long been aware of Christian ideas, it was only under the influence of Mina that Tōkoku underwent a conversion experience. He was baptized a Christian several months before he married her in November of 1888. This was an unusually happy time for Tōkoku, for he had married a woman he loved and he had found faith in God.

In 1889 Tōkoku began his literary career with the publication of a poem entitled *Soshū no shi* (The Poem of the Prisoner). The poem shows the influence of Byron's *The Prisoner of Chillon*, which was one of Tōkoku's favorite works, but it differs from Byron's poem in its atmosphere and in its happy ending. From 1889 Tōkoku worked as a translator for Christian missionaries. He became involved with the Quakers and gradually evolved, under their influence, a view of spiritual life that was antiritualistic and unorthodox. But Romantic poetry and the lives of Romantic poets such as Byron continued to inspire him, and in 1891 he wrote a long poem in the vein of *Manfred* entitled *Hōrai-kyoku* (A Tale of Mount Hōrai). By this time Tōkoku had become disillusioned with married life. *Hōrai-kyoku*, a poem that combines Buddhist world-weariness with Byronic exaltation of self, mirrored the tensions in Tōkoku's soul as he struggled to reconcile the demands of reality, in the form of an unhappy marriage, and the demands of his higher self. Significantly, the hero of the poem commits suicide after realizing that he can never regain a love he has lost. It was in 1892 and 1893 that Tōkoku wrote the essays on the inner life that were his major contribution to the spread of the new ideal of individualism in mid- and late-Meiji. In the fall of 1893 he completed a lengthy introduction to the

---

[5] Letter to Ishizaka Mina, January 21, 1888. *Tōkoku zenshū*, 3: 201.

essays of Emerson, a man who had become his new ideal. Yet by the time the essay was published, in April of 1894, Tōkoku was only too aware of his inability to live up to the ideals of his idol. During the next few weeks he lapsed into a state of unremitting melancholy, became unable to sleep or write, and, after once failing to kill himself, succeeded in his second attempt in May of 1894.

There was a great deal of pain in Tōkoku's life. He had little sense of love as a comforting and almost physical force knitting people together. His last months, as well as the intermittent periods in his life when he felt despondent over his inability to put his ideals into practice, must have been difficult for him and all who were close to him to undergo. Yet there was a great love in Tōkoku, a love that was obvious to all who knew him. This love he expressed to the world at large through his vision of the ideal human life. His remarks were always made in criticism of what existed, of what prevented the emergence of true human life. Thus, he spoke in terms of the future, of what could be if only people would realize the truth that lay within them. His words were ultimately convincing because they were beautiful, because his vision itself was beautiful and life-giving. The palpitating, tense beauty, the sense of hidden significance and unlimited possibility in Tōkoku's essays influenced his readers long after they were forced to confront the fact that his ideals had failed him in his own life.

Tōkoku broached the topic of the inner life in detail for the first time in an essay that he published in May of 1892 while he was editor of the Quaker journal, *Heiwa* (Peace). Like Fukuzawa Yukichi, Tōkoku was interested in promoting a spirit of freedom or independence among the Japanese of his day. Yet where Fukuzawa's interest was social and political, his theories influenced by Western social liberalism, Tōkoku's was primarily religious or spiritual. Where Fukuzawa wished to create good, responsible citizens, Tōkoku's desire was to awaken the spiritual selfhood of the individual. Finally, it is worth recalling that Tōkoku as a youth had had the goal of saving the Orient from what he considered the destructive Western doctrine of materialist evolution. This concern lest the ideal of independence taken from the West turn into a materialistic battle for the survival of the fittest in the economic and military spheres shaped Tōkoku's ideal of freedom from the very start. In this first essay on the inner life, entitled *Saigo no shōrisha wa dare zo* (Who Will Be the Final Victor?), Tōkoku noted that "social economics arises from the labor of man; its rule of man is a momentary policy, while that of the absolute is eternal."[6] Thus, the world is governed not, as the materialists claimed, by the economic principle of the survival of the fittest, but by an eternal power, a power Tōkoku called "life" (*seimei*).

As opposed to the spirit of warfare that dominates economic, material life, in the sphere of eternal life there is a spirit of what Tōkoku calls "consistency" (reconciliation). He also calls this spirit "Christ," for Christ's love for man is a force that brings about an ultimate reconciliation of all warring forces. Economic goals being not only temporary but of less value than the eternal goal of harmony, man ought not to run after success (as Futabatei's Noboru and others like him were doing in the atmosphere of opportunity of the late 1880s and early 1890s); rather, he ought to concern himself with the spiritual goal of contributing to the harmony of the universe. As Tōkoku says elsewhere, he does this not by attending church or submitting to baptism—rituals that Tōkoku considered as mechanical, externalized gestures that did not express the individual's true self—but by cultivating his inner life (*naibu seimei*).[7] The concept of the inner life,

---

[6] *Tōkoku zenshū*, 1: 318. For a discussion in English of Tōkoku's important essays on the inner life, see Francis Mathy, "Essays on the Inner Life," *Monumenta Nipponica* 19 (1964): 66-110. I have borrowed Mathy's translations of the titles of the essays.

[7] *Kakujin shinkyūnai no hikyū* (The Heart, A Holy of Holies, September 1892), *Zenshū*, 2: 11.

which was probably suggested to Tōkoku by the "inner light" of the Quakers, is the spiritual energy that is the equivalent, in the individual, of the eternal, harmonious energy on the universal level that Tōkoku called *seimei*.

Tōkoku foresaw that the ideal of independence, if lived out only on the materialistic level of economics, would lead to struggle between individuals, to social and spiritual isolation, and ultimately to disharmony. The ideal of *seimei*, or life, by contrast, gave true freedom in that it directed the sights of the individual toward nonmaterialistic and eternal goals of selfhood and harmony with others. In another essay he links *seimei* to the ideal of freedom, when he implies that the emergence of *seimei* in a particular culture or at a particular period in history is dependent on the presence of what he calls *seishin no jiyū* ("freedom of spirit"). Fukuzawa, in his *Gakumon no susume*, had criticized the morality of traditional Japan for having produced a nation ruled by bullies and supported by slaves, and it is significant that Tōkoku, when looking at the Japanese past for signs of a development of freedom of the spirit, also makes a scathing indictment of it: "The greatest misfortune of the Orient is that, from its beginnings up to the present, it has not known freedom of spirit."[8] In his essay *Naibu seimei ron* (On the Inner Life), Tōkoku wrote that religion, which should have guaranteed man this spirit, exercised a despotic control over man's freedom. Buddhism was against life (*seimei*) due to its spirit of *ensei* ("world-weariness") and its pessimism; the Confucianism of the Tokugawa period was closer to man but its teachings still did not "touch the strings of man's fundamental life (*seimei*)." In fact, the literature of that time, which was strongly affected by Confucian moralism, ridiculed this life (*seimei*), for love, which is in Tōkoku's eyes the gateway to life, was treated as mere lust. However, Tōkoku's strongest criticism of Confucianism was that "its principles do not arise from real

[8] *Seishin no jiyū* (Freedom of Spirit, April 1893), *Zenshū*, 2: 163.

experience, from the inner life (written in English: *innā raifu*),
and consequently they cannot avoid the fallacies of a narrow
positivism."[9]

According to Tōkoku, during the Genroku period (the period
of Saikaku's *onna*) a revolution occurred, for "the common people
were enticed by the idea of freedom." From that time on, writes
Tōkoku, literature was no longer there to preach morality, to
give opportunity for self-indulgence, to be useful, or to entertain,
but rather to express the ideal of freedom. The revolution begun
then has not yet finished; the concern of Meiji literature, therefore, should be with freedom of the spirit in general and, eventually, when social change in this direction has taken place, with
freedom of the individual.[10] As Tōkoku sketches out his idea of
seimei, it is clear that it does involve the political and social
sphere, for it is linked to the freedom of spirit, which exists in
greater or lesser proportions in specific periods and nations. What
Tōkoku is saying, then, is that although Japan in the past discouraged freedom of the spirit, and consequently was against
seimei, with the development of such a spirit in the Tokugawa period and with its continuation in such social movements as the
people's rights agitation, Japan is now moving toward the development of freedom of spirit, and therefore toward life. It is
possible, in fact, to see Tōkoku's own writings as manifestations
of a freedom of the spirit that had emerged in Japan as a result of
the social changes of the 1880s.

In an essay entitled *Kakujin shinkyūnai no hikyū* (The Heart, a
Holy of Holies), which he published in *Heiwa* in September of
1892, Tōkoku writes that Western Protestantism, Puritanism in
particular, was an important milestone in the process of acquisi-
tion of knowledge about man, in that it had brought forth the
ideal of freedom, an ideal that is the basis of the modern age both
in the West and in Japan.[11] To express the concept of "freedom"
Tōkoku used the Japanese word *kokoro*—a word usually having

[9] *Naibu seimei ron* (On the Inner Life, May 1893), *Zenshū*, 2: 238-243.
[10] *Seishin no jiyū*, *Zenshū*, 2: 166-167.   [11] *Zenshū*, 2: 5.

the significance "heart," "mind," "emotions," but which here appears to mean "the validity of individual feeling or morality," and consequently, "the ideal of individual freedom." According to Tōkoku, then, Protestantism, unlike Confucianism, based its morality on the inner life of the individual, and it is clear from this that although he saw the ideal of freedom as having been the main concern of late Tokugawa literature, it was Christianity, with its life-giving idea of *seimei*, that was the impetus behind the development of the ideal of freedom in the Meiji period. Moreover, when he defined the ideal of freedom as the attainment of the Christian ideal of *seimei* (life, eternal life as opposed to materialistic freedom), Tōkoku was describing the process of achieving the inner life (*naibu seimei*) in Christian terms.

According to Tōkoku, in each individual, as in the Temple of Jerusalem, there is a "holy of holies"—an inner sanctum that Tōkoku refers to as the inner *kokoro*. Man usually lives and acts in the outer *kokoro*, a state of material existence that is unfree and therefore without life and hope. In order to be truly free, man must attain the inner *kokoro*, or the inner site of spiritual freedom of the individual. In order to attain the inner *kokoro* one must trust in life (i.e., Christ) and rely on one's own inner strength. The attainment of the inner *kokoro* is thus a mystical process whereby material man is transformed into spiritual man; a regeneration of the individual occurs that Tōkoku describes as a "washing with the waters of Christ." Once the inner *kokoro* is transformed, the individual enters life (*seimei*); he exists in a state of being beyond fear and beyond distinctions of right and wrong, and all that is left in him is the "beauty of nature, and truth."[12]

Tōkoku's reference to the state of having achieved the inner *kokoro* as "beyond the distinctions of right and wrong" and, in a related essay, as equivalent to the Buddhist state of *mushin* or *nirvana* (a state of extinction of the ego),[13] indicates that he saw the

[12] Ibid., pp. 11, 13.
[13] *Shinki myōhen o ronzu* (On Mystical Metamorphoses, September 1892), *Zenshū*, 2: 17.

idea of freedom not only in terms of Christian mysticism but also in terms of traditional Buddhist, specifically Zen, awakening or enlightenment. Furthermore, the pronounced spiritual characteristics of the ideal now make it difficult to see what Tōkoku's ideal could mean to individuals of his time who lacked basic social and human rights. In other words, rather than being intimately connected to democratic political agitation, his ideal now appears to be an ideal that is attainable only by a certain few individuals. Indeed, in an article written before he began his systematic elaboration of the inner life, Tōkoku had sketched the portrait of just such a unique individual: Ninomiya Sontoku (1787-1856), the founder of an agrarian religious movement that had flourished in Tōkoku's home district in the 1800s. Sontoku had led an active life as an administrator-economist, and for his efforts to improve farm production he had been honored posthumously by the government. Yet Tōkoku describes him in quite different terms: "Sontoku was a man who firmly believed in universal good and universal beauty, and in the harmony of men's hearts . . . ; for that reason, his kindly face and smile expressed a subtle truth, and his simple, unsophisticated words were actually able to correct men's hearts. . . . Sontoku was a rare economist; moreover, he possessed a strong belief; he was a great man who, relying on his god-given *inner life* [my italics], worked self-sacrificingly throughout his life."[14] For Tōkoku, Sontoku was a great man because he had relied on his "god-given inner life"; yet the fact remains that Sontoku was a man who had distinguished himself from others and had become famous through his unique talents and energy.

The above description of Tōkoku's ideal man is very similar to the traditional description of a Buddhist or Confucian sage: a man who, having realized his true nature, is able to act in harmony with the entire universe. Tōkoku's remarks that Sontoku's face

[14] *Ninomiya Sontoku Ō* (Ninimiya Sontoku, November 1891), *Zenshū*, 1: 252-253. For further information on Sontoku's idea of farming as religious action, see Bellah, *Tokugawa Religion*, pp. 127-131.

reflected "a subtle truth" and that his words were able to "correct men's hearts" are in that vein. Yet Sontoku also possessed the nineteenth-century, "modern" qualities of enterprise and initiative, as well as the capacity to "look up to Christ" and attain his inner *kokoro*. In his essay on the heart as a holy of holies Tōkoku had asserted that the most important action man can perform is the defining of the inner *kokoro*: "Man must by all means respect his holy of holies; he must make it distinct, he must make it straight, he must make it clear, and he must make it public."[15] It is evident, then, that for Tōkoku, the most important quality of Sontoku was his utter reliance on his inner self, and as such he embodied what was to become Tōkoku's most important ideal: the definition of the self or the inner *kokoro*. Circumstances combined to give Tōkoku the impetus, and the opportunity, to define further his concept of the ideal man. In late 1892 and early 1893 he found himself barely able to support his wife and baby daughter through his writing and translating. Poverty, combined with disillusionment over his marriage, made him more and more insistent in his defense of the ideal of the inner life. Then, in January of 1893, he was able to found his own magazine, *Bungakkai* (Literary World). This magazine, whole issues of which were written and edited by Tōkoku himself, became the mouthpiece for almost all of his later ideas on the inner life.

An attack on his theories by Yamaji Aizan, a leading critic of the materialist school, encouraged Tōkoku to make an impassioned defense not only of his ideals but also of his very existence. In answer to Yamaji's attack, Tōkoku for the first time elaborated his conception of the poet as the ideal man whose cultural mission was to transmit the ideal of the inner life. Yamaji had written an article criticizing the Japanese writers of the past (particularly the writers of *haikai*, such as Bashō) for dwelling overly on nature and for setting up beauty as the highest standard of poetry. According to Yamaji, such writers had failed to develop a spirit of sublimi-

[15] *Zenshū*, 2: 14.

ty, strength, and moral rigor in their writings, and had completely omitted from their works a depiction of those people who had fought for material progress. He urged that the new literature of Meiji depict such people, for it had a duty to benefit mankind. In another article, he wrote that though literature was a kind of enterprise (*jigyō*), if a writer did not contribute to the good of the world, his words, and he himself, were useless.[16]

In his essay published in *Bungakkai* in February of 1893 entitled *Jinsei ni aiwataru towa nan no ii zo* (What Does It Mean "To Benefit Mankind?"), Tōkoku defined the poet as a man who, by acting from his inner self and fighting for truth, becomes an example for ordinary people of one who has attained the ideal of freedom. Because Yamaji had presented the poet as a master of useless, flowery words, Tōkoku made a special point of defending the poet as a true contributor to the good of mankind, and in doing so he indirectly revindicated Futabatei's Bunzō and the useless or "negative" (from a utilitarian viewpoint) heroes of the later I-novels. Tōkoku defended *haikai* and other idealistic poetry on the grounds that it benefited mankind in a limitless, eternal way. Presenting Saigyō, Shakespeare, Wordsworth, and Bakin as "great soldiers," he argued that the fighting these poets had done, "aiming at the infinite mystery of the universe," was superior in value to any ordinary military battle that ended in a material victory.[17]

In an earlier essay, *Shinki myōhen o ronzu* (On Mystical Metamorphoses), Tōkoku had written that "in man there is a divine nature and a human nature; the two are eternal enemies. When the two natures struggle with one another, spirit comes alive."[18] Tōkoku was fascinated by strong individuals whom he saw as engaged in a lifelong struggle of this kind—individuals such as Job and Byron. The poet is likewise a person whose strong human nature has wrestled with the divine; he has an awareness of "spirit," that is, of freedom, and a strong incentive to break out

---

[16] See Mathy, "Kitamura Tōkoku: Essays on the Inner Life," pp. 94-95, for a discussion of Yamaji's articles.

[17] *Zenshū*, 2: 117.   [18] *Zenshū*, 2: 18.

of the material world. Furthermore, he possesses *jōnetsu* ("Romantic ardor"), an impassioned and inspired nature that emanates sublimity, grandeur, and elegance. Yet *jōnetsu* is also "a kind of belief, a kind of religion, a kind of theology,"[19] writes Tōkoku, a religious quality that, when present in literature, inspires man to "leave behind the self and sacrifice oneself for others."[20] The poet also has a longing (*akogare*) for the "other world" (*takai*) of spirit and imagination.[21] Because he has reached this world, by finding his inner spirit of freedom, he is the only person in society who can communicate it to others, and he does this by letting his inner self be awakened or recharged by the limitless, eternal spirit of freedom.[22]

It is no accident that Tōkoku was an admirer of Byron and other Romantic poets in his youth, for in his emphasis on the poet's priestly role as bearer of the vision of freedom and mediator of this vision to the common man, Tōkoku reflects the Romantic vision of the poet as a man closer than most mortals to the gods who, in a moment of inspiration, sees a higher truth and reveals it to mankind through art: the *poeta vates*. Tōkoku's ideal of the poet thus can be called elitist, in that it glorifies the poet's struggle for self-definition and self-expression, leaving to a distant future the question of the self-definition of those ordinary mortals

[19] *Jōnetsu* (Romantic Ardor, September 1893), *Zenshū*, 2: 298-299.

[20] *Netsui* (Romantic Ardor, June 1893), *Zenshū*, 2: 255.

[21] For Tōkoku the "other world" was a state of being where life (*seimei*), freedom, and hope reigned. According to Tōkoku, the poet led people to this other world through the power of his imagination, and through the sublimity, elegance, and grandeur of his inspired words. In a moment of anger against the past, Tōkoku criticized Japanese poets for their lack of imagination, yet later, in *Jinsei ni aiwataru towa nan no ii zo*, he applauded Saigyō and Bashō as writers of poetry that possessed *jōnetsu* (imagination, inspiration, ardor). *Takai ni kansuru kannen* (The Concept of Another World, October 1892), *Zenshū*, 2: 35-44.

[22] Tōkoku calls this awakening of the inner life at the hands of the universal spirit "inspiration" (he uses the English word), and notes that the process of being awakened is like being charged by an electric current. *Naibu seimei ron*, *Zenshū*, 2: 248.

whom his words will inspire. In this sense his ideal of the poet suffers from the difficult situation in which it arose: a situation where a writer had no prestige, and certainly no recognized purpose, and where usefulness and significance of an endeavor were measured by the visible accomplishments of the military man and the entrepreneur. From the writings of Tōkoku, then, there emerges the ambivalent culture hero of the writer whose exalted mission of pursuing and mediating truth to mankind renders him alone and isolated.

Tōkoku's main accomplishment in his essays on the inner life was to provide a philosophy of idealistic humanism that would inspire generations of Japanese after his death. His ideal of personal morality distinguished itself from moralities of the past, and of his time, in that it freed the individual from a strictly social definition of his existence. Fukuzawa Yukichi's ideal of independence had done away with the idea of class divisions, and the inequality resulting therefrom. Tōkoku's ideal of self-definition focused rather on the free, god-given selfhood of the individual and attacked materialism of any sort, whether traditional or Western, that attempted to imprison the individual and his energy in the material sphere. Indeed, it was due to his antipathy toward a materialistic and pessimistic conception of man that Tōkoku was concerned with inculcating the spirit of *jōnetsu* in modern Japanese, reasoning that only *jōnetsu*, with its life-affirming energy and its optimism, would be powerful enough to overcome the traditional spirit of what he called *jakumetsu-shisō* (the spirit of ego-extinction and detachment).[23] Though his own

---

[23] In *Naibu seimei ron* Tōkoku had written that Christianity was life-affirming, whereas Buddhism was against life. (*Zenshū*, 2: 239.) In his essay *Jōnetsu*, he continues to make this distinction between a Western and an Eastern spirit, remarking that the literature of Japan at the present is imbued with pessimistic thoughts of Nirvana or extinction (*jakumetsu-shisō*). Tōkoku expresses about as much anger over the effect that Buddhist fatalism had had on people of the past as Fukuzawa had over the effects of despotic government. *Zenshū*, 2: 301-302.

life was a continued and unresolved conflict between the two,
Tōkoku succeeded, in his essays, in presenting an example of the
optimistic and life-affirming spirit of *jōnetsu* in action. In his last
work, an essay on Emerson, Tōkoku turned away from the artist
ideal and reaffirmed his faith in the ideal of the inner life as an
ideal for all individuals. He singled out ideas of Emerson that he
felt were particularly important for future Japanese: self-reliance,
optimism, and the inner life. After describing Emerson as the
ideal of the "new democratic gentleman," he concluded with the
teaching Emerson had given to the new American people: "Believe in yourself: you can become powerful, you can become
happy, you can go forward with hope, you can take the virtues of
the past for your country and throw out the vices, and thus build
a new republic with new ideals."[24] This was Tōkoku's last message to the Japanese of his time.

Tōkoku's Ideals and Romantic Individualism

Vast social and political changes occurring between Tōkoku's
death in 1894 and 1900 made possible the emergence of a subculture of the individual for the first time in Meiji Japan. The success of negotiations to end the unequal treaties in 1894, followed
by a military victory over China in 1895, led to a spirit of optimism and pride in nationhood among Japanese of all classes.
After the Sino-Japanese War, industrialization increased rapidly,
creating new classes of white- and blue-collar workers in the cities
and encouraging a new morality of success and independence
from the family. As the government continued its policy of aggressive expansionism, there arose a materialistic individualism
of the sort that Futabatei Shimei had forecast already in the late
1880s in the figure of Noboru. As the industrialization of the late
1890s created a steadily rising economic expectancy among the
lower classes, the freer culture and social institutions that

[24] *Emaruson* (Emerson, April 1894), *Zenshū*, 3: 122.

emerged as an indirect consequence of industrialization created in the relatively leisured middle class an intense desire for self-fulfillment and freedom. A popular writer named Takayama Chogyū wrote in his book *New Japan* (1899) that a truly modern era would come, in which an individualist morality and a society based on consciousness of human rights would emerge, led by the youth of the time. Yet such an era had already begun, in the Romantic movement that developed in the early 1890s under the influence of Kitamura Tōkoku.

Tōkoku had founded the main organ of Japanese Romanticism, the journal *Bungakkai* (Literary World), in 1893. Around this magazine there gathered a number of writers in their early twenties who, almost the same age as Tōkoku himself, nevertheless considered themselves his disciples. All of them had attended Christian higher schools in the 1880s and although they had formally broken with Christianity as a religion by the early 1890s, they retained their belief in the Christian spiritual ideals that they had derived from their education and that Tōkoku had interpreted and adapted to Japanese reality in his works: the goodness and divinity of humanity and the existence of a world of freedom and of the spirit that could be reached through the imagination and described or imparted through poetry. The youths who wrote for *Bungakkai* saw it as their mission to fulfill the function of a poet as defined by Tōkoku: to create a literature that would bring imagination and the "other world" of freedom of the spirit into Japanese society. They attempted to do this through their poetic essays and their translations of Western and other poetry.[25] By the late 1890s, however, as the traditionally closed

---

[25] The literary journal *Bungakkai*, published from January of 1893 to January of 1898, was the center of the Japanese Romantic movement (*Romanshugi-ha*), a movement led by Western-educated youth that attempted to create a serious literature expressing a humanitarian view of life that had its source in Western Romantic poets. The German Romantic poets Goethe, Heine, and Schiller had been introduced to the Japanese reading public in a collection called *Omokage* (Likenesses, 1889); the *Bungakkai* was responsible for translating poems by the

economic and social system was forced open by industrialization and the infiltration of Western ideas, middle-class Japanese began to want a kind of vitality and "life" that was far from Tōkoku's spiritualized idea of *seimei*. The new ideal of freedom was found in the realm of the physical and the sensual. Or, to put it somewhat differently, sensuality became the new religion and sensual experience the "other world" of transcendence, and the poetry written by Romantic poets beginning in 1897 described the awakening of the individual in terms of affirmation of the flesh.[26]

The ideal of self-affirmation that appeared in the late 1890s contained an element that the earlier Romantics had not stressed: the link with woman, or love. Kitamura Tōkoku was the source of this ideal, as he had been for the ideal of Romantic self-definition or self-affirmation. Tōkoku coined the word *ren'ai* ("love") to express what he saw as a life-giving relationship between man and woman. In pre-Meiji Japan the proper relationship between the sexes, like that between ruler and ruled, was primarily one of vertical obligation. It followed that the proper feelings between man and wife were generosity on the part of the husband and gratitude on the part of the wife. Tenderness between husband and wife, though it doubtless existed, was not a requirement for marriage from the Confucian standpoint. Furthermore, a relationship other than marriage that was based on a freely chosen attraction between a man and a woman, whether instinctual or spiritual, was considered immoral and threatening to the stability of the social order.

Tōkoku's ideal of love (*ren'ai*) gave validity to the emotional

---

English Romantic poets Wordsworth, Shelley, and Byron. For a complete discussion of the *Bungakkai* and Romanticism see Sasabuchi Tomoichi, *Bungakkai to sono jidai*, 2 vols., Tokyo, 1959.

[26] Nakamura Mitsuo thinks, for example, that the Romantic poets emerging in the late 1890s worked toward "the abolition of the consciousness of sin spoken of by Christianity, and the affirmation of sensual desire." *Meiji bungakushi*, Tokyo, 1963, pp. 148-149.

and spiritual aspects of the relationship between man and woman that had been degraded or, at best, ignored under the Confucianist and Buddhist moralities of the past. In one of his earliest essays, *Ensei shika to josei* (The World-Weary Poet and Woman, February, 1892), Tōkoku wrote that love was the key that unlocked humanity—in other words, the force that gave life (*seimei*) to human beings.[27] Tōkoku saw love, then, as a kind of spiritual energy growing between man and woman that, as it developed, stimulated each of them to self-definition and self-affirmation. In a sense, his ideal was a culmination of the culturally repressed ideal of ennobling passion, as it was expressed (and if not glorified, at least treated sympathetically) by Chikamatsu and the authors of the sentimental *ninjō-bon*. In *Shinjū-ten no Amijima*, for example, love of a prostitute stimulated Jihei to live for once in his life according to the demands of his feelings (*ninjō*) and to take the final step that would guarantee his freedom—the love suicide with Koharu. Similarly, her love for Jihei made Koharu, and even Jihei's wife, Osan, rise to the heights of "life"—Koharu in self-fulfillment in love, Osan in self-sacrifice. According to Chikamatsu, it was wrong to see such a love between man and woman as merely an instinctual attraction, as Confucian morality viewed it. Chikamatsu obviously saw the passion of his lovers as a kind of *jōnetsu* ("Romantic ardor") that, through its heroic sublimity, brought them and those involved with them into the "other world"of transcendent freedom. Thus, the forerunner of love in the Tokugawa era already was an illicit, antisocial love, and one is prepared to see Tōkoku's ideal of love reveal itself, similarly to Western romantic love, as basically antimarriage in its implications.[28]

[27] *Tōkoku zenshū*, 1: 254.

[28] See Denis de Rougemont, *L'Amour et l'occident*, Paris, 1939 and *Les Mythes de l'amour*, Paris, 1967. Maurice Valency, in a study that attempts to give an historical overview of the depiction of love in Western literature, sees the idea of an ennobling and free love between man and woman developing in the Middle Ages as an alternative to a marriage system where little or no choice was al-

Interestingly, Tōkoku's own marriage exposed the failure of *ren'ai* as an ideal of married love. He had written in *"Ka'nen-butsu" o yomite* (On Reading *Ka'nenbutsu*, June, 1892), that spiritual love between man and woman (*ren'ai*) was the beginning of all affection.[29] The revolutionary quality of this pronouncement becomes clear when one considers that in pre-Meiji times it would have read: "Recognition of the debt to one's parents is the beginning of all sense of obligation." In other words, Tōkoku was attempting to replace the ideal of vertical, reciprocal obligation that had been the basis of social relationships in the past with a new, horizontal, egalitarian ideal based on love. The test of the ability of *ren'ai* to provide a basis for a harmonious relationship was Tōkoku's own marriage to the woman he had married for love. When Tōkoku met Mina, she inspired him to convert to Christianity, but not only that—she inspired him to define himself. *Ren'ai* was the key that had opened the gate to life for Tōkoku, but the experience of marriage apparently closed it. For, as Tōkoku explained in *Ensei shika to josei*, the idealist who had hoped to make of love a retreat from the real world by getting married found that love, in teaching him the duties and obligations of marriage, had made him a prisoner of reality. When this happened to Tōkoku himself, he sought a new opportunity to have "life" awakened in himself by falling in love with one of his students.

Tōkoku's own experience with marriage proved that while his ideal of *ren'ai* could initiate a love relationship between a man and a woman, it failed to provide for the "duty" aspects that are needed to sustain a relationship, especially a marriage: forbearance, tolerance, acceptance of the other. In fact, Tōkoku's ideal was an ideal formed in opposition to marriage, for, founded on the insistence on individual freedom, it was against the idea of obligation on principle. Tōkoku's ideal of love had at the outset

lowed. *In Praise of Love: An Introduction to the Love-Poetry of the Renaissance*, New York, 1961, pp. 64-66.

[29] *Zenshū*, 1: 349.

the potential to imprison the lover, but this was not only because it involved marriage but also because it was in an important way an ideal of self-love. Tōkoku had written: "Love is the clear mirror which, as one sacrifices one's self, reveals the 'I' that is oneself."[30] Thus, love, far from implying a rational, conscious commitment to another person, was a way to self-awareness. It was love of the idea of love, of one's own experience of being in love. Possibly Tōkoku's childhood experience of being deprived of parental love had weakened his capacity to love others, and made him particularly vulnerable to the Western ideal of love that promised to make the lover grow spiritually by means of inspiration by another person, yet, paradoxically, would leave him independent of that person's demands. Such a love seemed to guarantee a relationship free of pain and bondage, yet love, when transformed into marriage, an institution of the sense world, caused both anguish and dependency. Tōkoku's experience with marriage and his consequent disillusionment with love caused him to lose most of his earlier enthusiasm for the ideal of *ren'ai*; in fact, he ended by criticizing women for pulling men down into the world of obligation in a way that was typical of traditional Buddhist moralizing.[31]

The ideal of *ren'ai* was perhaps the most popular of all Tōkoku's ideals among the youth of his generation, and, more importantly, it influenced the poetry of two of the greatest Romantic poets of the late 1890s: Shimazaki Tōson (1872-1943) and Yosano Akiko (1878-1942). Passionate love is linked clearly with individual freedom in the Romantic heroine of Shimazaki Tōson's poem entitled *Okume*, one of six poems on women that opened his

---

[30] *Ensei shika to josei, Zenshū*, 1: 260.

[31] Toward the end of *Ensei shika to josei* Tōkoku speaks of marriage as a thing that makes the poet hate society, implying that women, because they are "dominated by the love of man," trap men through marriage and make them their slaves. His remark may be a product of his psychological acuity; yet it demonstrates also the moralistic querulousness of traditional Buddhist criticisms of women. Ibid., p. 262.

famous *Wakana-shū* (Collection of Young Shoots, 1897). In the poem, Okume is motivated by a passion for her lover so strong that she flouts social convention to join him by swimming across a large body of water. Tōson modeled Okume after the Greek lover Leander, and he relates what appealed to him in Leander in this passage written in 1899: "The feeling inherent in the tale of Leander, who swam the Hellespont to get to the house of the maiden Hero, is hardly to be found in a work such as *The Tales of Ise*. Imagine people who are so overwhelmingly in love! . . . How moved I am by Leander, who swam back and forth from shore to shore out of devotion to love."[32] Here Tōson expresses his preference for the modern attitude of daring and courage in love, as exhibited by the Western Romantic poets, over the resigned melancholy of the lovers in his own tradition's *Ise monogatari* (The Tales of Ise), a tenth-century collection of poems and short tales illustrating ideal conduct in a love affair. What is interesting about the poem is that the heroine possesses a Romantic ardor that is idealistic and heroic and entirely untainted by a sense of guilt or sin. Furthermore, the heroine's passion is unchecked by any traditional feelings of filial piety. Since she is unmarried, and thus free of the moral complications that would have been raised by the presence of an angry *jaloux*, she becomes the ideal figure to act out the fantasies of a generation raised on the ideal of self-affirmation in love.

Tōson experienced a personal conflict between his desire to love (i.e., affirm himself in love) and his belief, inherited from both his Confucian and his Christian training, that sensual love was sinful. When he speaks through the persona of the maiden Okume, he seems to be affirming his transcendence of this painful conflict by the sheer violence of his diction:

| Shiri tamawazu ya waga | Do you not know the nature |
| koi wa | of my love? |

[32] Shimazaki Tōson, *Seika yokō*, in *Shimazaki Tōson zenshū*, Tokyo, 1948-1952, 2: 167.

Ooshiki kimi no te ni furete   It is a love which will not stop
Aa kuchibeni o sono kuchi ni   Unless I touch your manly arms
Kimi ni utsusade yamubeki ya   And, oh!, trace my red lips on
                                             your mouth . . .

Kokoro nomi kawa te mo   Is it only my heart?
   ashi mo
Wagami wa subete honoo nari   My hands and feet, my body
Omoi midarete aa koi no   are all ablaze,
Chisuji no kami no nami ni   My thoughts are in a tangle—
   nagaruru   Oh!, the thousand strands
                                                of my hair
                                             Floating on the waves of love
                                                . . .[33]

Tōson's lines are flowing and mellifluous, the phrases marked by
the contrast of clear dark and light vowels and broken only by
exclamations expressing intense feeling. He uses diction invented
by poets in the native *tanka* (thirty-one-syllable lyric) form one
thousand years before. For example, *omoimidareru*, in the second
stanza, means being hopelessly and sinfully (from a Buddhist
standpoint) bound up or tangled in thoughts of love, while the
classical poetic image of *kami* ("hair") evokes a picture of smooth,
long, black hair flowing languidly·on a bed or tangled in passion.
Yet they have been modernized: *omoimidareru* becomes a defiant,
self-affirming absorption in passion and the hair of the heroine is
flowing not on her bed but on the current of a wide, deep body of
water that is carrying her to her lover. Tōson's readers were
shocked by his outspokenness in this collection; yet they read between the lines an assertion of the validity of individual feeling
that they admired and that infected them with the intensity of a
new religion.

   Like the European Romantics, Tōson was able to make of his
own inner conflicts and experiences the material of poetry, and in
doing so he spoke for thousands of his generation who were
struggling to define themselves. Thus, the poems collected in

33 Tōson, *Wakana-shū, Zenshū*, 2: 16.

Wakana-shū were the first successful expressions of the sentiments and values of the first generation to be born and come to adulthood during the Meiji period—the first truly modern generation. They introduced into Japanese poetry a modern tone and subjective style, much as Goethe's lyrical poetry of the 1770s, the *Lyrical Ballads* of 1798, and Lamartine's *Méditations* of 1819 had brought a modern style and a subjective mode of expression into their respective literatures. *Wakana-shū* was followed, in 1901, by the publication of a volume of 399 *tanka* entitled *Midaregami* (Tangled Hair). They were written by the poetess Yosano Akiko (1878-1942) who, with her husband Tekkan, also a poet, had founded in 1900 the leading Romantic magazine of the later period of Romanticism: *Myōjō* (Bright Star). Akiko's poems represented the wing of the Romantic movement that sought its form and style, though not its sentiments, in the literature of the past. For Akiko used the traditional lyric form of the *tanka* and the classical poetic style of the passionate woman poet, though, like Tōson, she wished to communicate her own, modern experience of love.

The passionate women poets, best exemplified in Japanese tradition by Ono no Komachi (fl. ninth century) and Izumi Shikibu (fl. early eleventh century), cultivated a poetic style that was at times witty and intense and at times passionately languorous—a style that expressed their devotion to love and their insistence (in poetry at least) on living an intense, passionate life. Komachi writes in a famous poem that her heart is charring as she waits, in a state of intense passion but in vain, for her lover:

Hito ni awan	On such a night as this
Tsuki no naki ni wa	When the lack of moonlight
Omoiokite	shades your way to me,
Mune hashiribi ni	I wake from sleep my passion blazing,
Kokoro yakeori	My breast a fire raging, exploding flame
	While within me my heart chars.

Izumi Shikibu, waiting for her lover when ill, expresses her feelings in her typical witty yet passionate manner:

Arazaran	This is a world
Kono yo no hoka no	Where I shall shortly be no more:
Omoide ni	If only you
Ima hitotabi no	Would come to visit me
	just once
Au koto mo ga na	For a remembrance in the
	afterlife![34]

Such poems express a strong desire to affirm the self in sensual love, but Akiko's poems add to this a mood of courage and physical daring that is completely modern. For example, among the poems that record moments in her affair with Tekkan, there is one that reads:

Nani to naku	Early evening moon
Kimi ni mataruru	Over the flowering field,
Kokochi shite	I felt somehow
Ideshi hanano no	He was waiting for me
Yūgetsu yo kana	And I came.[35]

One modern element in this *tanka* is that Akiko is free to visit her lover—a freedom denied the earlier passionate poetesses—yet what is truly revolutionary is the strength of feminine will that emerges from the word *"ideshi"* ("I came"). The poem as a whole gives an impression of a woman waiting restlessly for love and longing to follow her feelings in pursuit of it. Another poem depicts the poetess in the act of seducing her lover, whom she represents as an ascetic devoted to poetry:

[34] Komachi's poem is found in the *Kokinwakashū* (Collection of Poems Ancient and Modern), bk. 19: 1030; Izumi's poem is found in the *Goshūishū* (Later Collection of Gleanings), bk. 13: 763. Translations are by Robert H. Brower and Earl Miner, *Japanese Court Poetry*, Stanford, 1961, pp. 206 and 227, respectively.

[35] *Midare-gami, Yosano Akiko zenshū*, Tokyo, 1976, 1: 16. Translated by Sanford Goldstein and Seishi Shinoda, *Tangled Hair: Selected Tanka from "Midaregami" by Akiko Yosano*, Lafayette, 1971, no. 30.

Yawahada no	You do not touch the hot blood
Atsuki chishio ni	Under the soft, fair skin of
	woman—
Fure mo mide	Are you not lonely,
Sabishikarazu ya	You who preach the Way?
Michi o toku kimi.	

Here Akiko affirms the right of individual instinct over the laws of the "religion" of poetry.[36]

It is thanks to Tōkoku's validation of love that these poets of the end of the nineteenth century were able to speak of love in poetry in a context of high seriousness for the first time since the decline of the Heian courtly style of poetry in the mid-sixteenth century. Their poems are a mixture of past and present. Both Tōson and Akiko use an image that expresses the contemporary exaltation of individual feeling at the expense of traditional asceticism: for example, Tōson, in his poem *Otsuta* (the fifth of the five poems on women that open *Wakana-shū*), depicts a young woman seducing a Buddhist ascetic, much as Akiko's young woman had mocked a male ascetic of poetry. Both imitate the passionate experiential flow of the traditional *tanka* that dealt with love, and both use the classical persona of the passionate woman poet. In Tōson's case this was probably due to the fact that as a male poet in an age when the influence of samurai morality lingered on, in the form of a demand for male stoicism and reticence, he found it easier to speak through a passionate persona that had already achieved cultural validation, even if it was not a male persona. Akiko as a woman probably found it easier than Tōson to step into this persona and imbue it with her own modern sensations. Her use of the concise thirty-one-syllable *tanka* form provided her with a direct, concrete, and imagistic poetic

---

[36] Ibid., *Zenshū*, 1: 9. The "way" (*michi*) here refers to the discipline of poetry that some traditional poets in the *tanka* and *haiku* forms undertook as a spiritual discipline. Taking the position of a modern passionate woman poet, for whom poetry was rather a way of expressing passionate feelings, Akiko here expresses her scorn for the male "way" of poetry as an ascetic withdrawal from woman.

vehicle that was superbly capable of expressing the swiftness and intensity of passion. Since Akiko's sentiments and experiences were those of an aristocrat of the senses, she excelled in her use of the aristocratic *tanka* form.

Tōson, by contrast, labored with a longer, more cumbersome, and more complicated poetic form, a new form that had none of the validity conferred by age and tradition. In other poems in *Wakana-shū* he attempted to express complicated moral states in poetry for the first time in the modern period. In general, his poems were less successful as poetry than Akiko's, which were the true expression of an age when the ideal of self-definition was seen primarily as the fulfillment of self through the pursuit of passion. Yet the *tanka* form had limitations, as did the ideal of love as sensation that it expressed. For Akiko was unable to use the *tanka* to express the complex moral implications of passion that she was aware of based on her own experiences. The whole story of Akiko's relationship to her husband, Yosano Tekkan, is too complicated to go into here—suffice it to say that Akiko, bold like the heroines of her many poems, had pursued the man of her choice to Tokyo and lived with him for several months before they were married in October of 1901. However, Tekkan retained his love for his former wife, Takino; he had also fallen in love with Akiko's own friend, Tomiko, and besides having affairs with other women during his married life with Akiko, continued to long for Tomiko after her death in 1909. It is known that Akiko endured agony for years because of her love for Tekkan, her love for Tomiko, and the jealousy that she was unable to prevent herself from feeling. Yet the emotional turmoil that she experienced throughout her poetic career was visible only in occasional suggestive poems such as the following, written in reference to the death of her friend, Tomiko, whom Tekkan had loved:

> That secret
> We sealed in a jar,
> The three of us,

My husband, myself,
And the dead one.[37]

The poem is as enigmatic and suggestive as Komachi's famous
tanka that begins *"Iro miede"*, a poem that expresses a woman's
sadness, hurt, and anger at male fickleness.[38] It has neither time
nor space to go into the question of how to deal with the pain and
suffering that are caused by an individual's free pursuit of self-
fulfillment in love.

Akiko was a true follower of Tōkoku in the sense that her ideal
of love, as expressed in her poetry, was narcissistic and solitary.
Love was the experience that unlocked the gate to life—in
Akiko's terms, sensual freedom; but about the moral consequences of love her poems, like Tōkoku's essays, were silent. Tōson's poetry is interesting from the viewpoint that, after the first
few poems on women in *Wakana-shū*, he attempted to deal with
the moral conflicts caused by the individual's desire to love and to
define himself. His interest in the moral aspects of self-definition
led him to use a longer poetic line and a longer poetic form, until
finally, in 1906, he turned away from poetry altogether, finding
the proper vehicle for his exploration of moral states in the novel.
The example of Tōson suggests that as long as it was a question,
during a short period around the end of the 1890s, of expressing
in literature the sheer exuberance of passion, a short poetic form
with roots in, or at least links to, tradition, sufficed; but as the
new age brought with it a demand for scrutiny of the moral existence of the individual, new forms were required. Akiko in her
poems spoke as an unusual person and as a poet—as Tōkoku had
spoken. By contrast, Tōson's poems began to give expression to

[37] Quoted in Goldstein and Shinoda, *Tangled Hair*, p. 14.
[38] The poem, which is found in the *Kokinwakashū*, bk. 15: 797, reads: "Iro
miede / Utsurou mono wa / Yo no naka no / Hito no kokoro no / Hana ni zo
arikeru." ("A thing which fades, its color invisible, is the flower of the heart of
man in this world of the senses.") For a detailed interpretation of the poem see
Brower and Miner, *Japanese Court Poetry*, pp. 204-205.

the moral conflicts of the ordinary middle-class person who became the new culture hero of the Meiji period. Yet the first vehicle for the expression of the sentiments and values of this hero was the I-novel that emerged under the auspices of the Naturalist movement in the early 1900s.

CHAPTER FOUR

Katai's *Futon* (The Quilt): The Birth of the I-Novel

Naturalism and the Development of the I-Novel

In the years between 1900 and 1905, as in the years immediately following Tōkoku's death, the political and social situation in Japan underwent important changes that influenced the role the individual was to play in modern culture. The signing of a treaty of alliance with Britain in 1902 seemed to indicate that Japan was to be counted among the world powers; the defeat of Russia in 1905—and the consequent winning of Korea as a protectorate—brought Japan further glory and international recognition. Yet along with the jubilant feeling of success brought about by the victory came a feeling of uncertainty, for the goal of equality with the West that had been set by the early Meiji leaders had been reached, yet there was no new goal in sight. The government, which had become more and more dependent on the military during the late 1890s, began to use the goal of nationalism to fill the void. Starting in the early 1900s, it introduced into elementary textbooks a philosophy called *kokutai* ("national polity"), which stressed the divine and incorruptible nature of the Japanese state. Whereas Fukuzawa and his followers had urged the development of qualities of independence, both in the state and in the individuals who composed it, this philosophy stressed the forging of an harmonious entity made up of people, emperor, and nation that rested ultimately on the unquestioning loyalty of the citizens.

Meanwhile, the urban intellectuals who were exposed to liberal democratic ideals in the higher schools and in their jobs in the Westernized sector of government offices, banks, and universities, began to see the definition of the individual's role in modern society as the most important task of the day. Tōkoku's ideal of the inner life had an important influence on the youth of this time, as is clear from the fact that middle-class youth began to experience and define the self in numerous ways. The cultural type of the *seikō-seinen* ("success-seeking youth") of the late 1890s was now joined, for example, by the so-called *hammon-seinen* ("anguished youth"), youth for whom neither self-serving economic success nor self-sacrifice for the nation was an adequate path.[1] Various philosophies arose to satisfy the demands of those seeking to cultivate the self. A philosophy of individualism that stressed that the satisfaction of instinct, rather than adherence to a moral code, meant happiness for the individual—as propounded by Takayama Chogyū in his *Biteki seikatsu o ronzu* (On the Aesthetic Life, 1901)—attracted many. Others read the works of Nietzsche, the main influence (along with Carlyle) on Chogyū, for his philosophy of the superman. Still others were attracted to Christian mysticism, as lived and described by Tsunajima Ryōsen.[2] Yet the ideas that had the greatest influence on the ideal of the individual as it appears in the I-novel were those of the Naturalist movement (*Shizenshugi-ha*). For it was Naturalism that, following the path set by Tōkoku, finally succeeded in forcing a break with the traditional moral system and laying the foundations for an individualist morality.

Because of the wide gap between the Western-educated elite and the masses, Japanese intellectuals around the turn of the twentieth century lacked a clear identity: they had broken away from the morality of chauvinism and loyalty of their fellow coun-

[1] Tokutomi Sohō identified the *seikō-seinen* and the *hammon-seinen* as two contrasting types of youths who were caught up in the pursuit of self that characterized the late 1890s and early 1900s, in an article in *Kokumin Shimbun* (The Nation's Newspaper), September 25, 1904.

[2] In the early 1900s Tsunajima Ryōsen, a baptized member of the Congregational church, had a series of mystical visions of God. The essays he wrote describing these experiences had an important influence on youth for the next decade. See Kōsaka Masaaki, *Japanese Thought in the Meiji Era*, Tokyo, 1969, pp. 299-321, for a discussion of both Takayama Chogyū and Tsunajima Ryōsen.

trymen, yet they were not, and never could be, Westerners as long as they lived in Japanese society. Naturalism, which emerged just after 1900, was the philosophical and literary movement that sketched out a modern way of looking at things that, when adhered to or believed in, became a basis for their identity in the chaotic and uncertain period between 1900 and 1910. It should be no surprise that Japanese intellectuals took Naturalism as a kind of doctrine, which, far from being confined to literature, had important implications for life as a whole. Indeed, Zola himself had seen Naturalism in broad terms, as a new way of thinking and, more importantly, of viewing the world. In 1880 he had defined Naturalism in the following way: "Naturalism is the return to nature; it is that operation the scientists made the day they decided to start with the study of bodies and phenomena, to base their work on experiment, and to proceed by means of analysis."[3] He went on to characterize Naturalism as a development of the human spirit whose main efforts had begun in the eighteenth century, with Diderot and Rousseau, but that, due to the accompanying social upheaval of the French Revolution, had become the movement of the contemporary mind in France. As proof of this he discussed writers of the nineteenth century who used the methods of Naturalism. Stendhal and Balzac were the originators of a new formula for the novel, which demanded that nature and man be observed from life, using a method of dissection and analysis. To this formula Flaubert had added the perfection of form, the Goncourt brothers the perfection of language, with the result that the novel, once a trivial form, could now take its place, along with science, as the master of the world and of nature.[4]

As French Naturalism had influenced the breakthrough into modern times of Norway, Denmark, and Sweden in the 1870s and 1880s, the Japanese Naturalist movement had much to do

[3] Emile Zola, "Le Naturalisme au Théâtre," in *Le Roman expérimental, Oeuvres Complètes*, Paris, 1928, 41: 95.
[4] Ibid., pp. 93-103.

with the breakthrough into modernity, or with the development of an ideology that would separate the culture from the evils of the past. This was in large part the ideology of science, and Zola's interpretation of Naturalism as the triumph of the scientific method that swept away the old order, can be applied at least partially to the Naturalism that emerged in Japan around 1900. Yet the main contribution of Japanese Naturalism to the development of a modern culture was its strengthening of two attitudes already existing in Japanese culture: the attitude of objectivity and the respect for and interest in man.[5] Zola had defined Naturalism in literature as "the acceptance and depiction of what is,"[6] and had praised writers who based themselves on real phenomena and on experience. One of the two leading Naturalist writers of Japan, Shimazaki Tōson, discovered the modern attitude of objectivity while reading Rousseau's *Confessions* at the age of twenty-two, in 1894; he wrote later that reading Rousseau at that time had taught him how to look at nature directly and had clarified for him the modern (scientific?) way of looking at things that he and his peers would have to follow.[7] The idea that the novel was the form that best depicted reality had been expressed already by Tsubouchi Shōyō in 1885. Yet it was the introduction around 1900 of Western scientific methods as well as novels written in the objective manner—those of the Goncourt brothers, Zola, Flaubert, and Maupassant—that made Zola's idea of the novel as the form that best "painted what is" dominant among Japanese intellectuals.

The other important element that Japanese Naturalism emphasized was the validity, and the importance, of man. As Tōkoku had pointed out in his essays on the inner life, traditional Japanese thought systems had undervalued man, Buddhism by

<hr>

[5] My view of the role played by Naturalism in the modernization of Japanese culture has been shaped by Kōsaka, *Japanese Thought in the Meiji Era*, pp. 392-430.

[6] Zola, "Le Naturalisme au Théâtre," p. 95.

[7] Tōson, "Rūsō no '*Zange*'-chū ni miidashitaru jiko," *Zenshū*, 14: 14-15.

advocating a negation of the self and Confucianism by ignoring the individual's ability to contribute to the moral system. Christianity, which emphasized the necessity for individual spiritual selfhood, provided a basis for the development of the idea of the individual in the 1890s and early 1900s, but it was the religion of only a tiny minority of Japanese. Furthermore, the Christian ideal of otherworldly spirituality, though it was understood by Tōkoku and described eloquently in his writings, had little appeal for an age oriented toward sensual freedom. It remained for Naturalism to provide a justification for selfhood in secular, concrete terms that would be understandable to people on the basis of their experience. Science had enabled Naturalism to do this in its French context, and the Naturalists of Europe had followed Zola's directions in their depictions of "a shred of existence," "a single page of human history," and in their "official records" of a hundred different varieties.[8] That Japanese Naturalists understood the relevance of the scientific method of research to the writing of novels is evident in Tōson's comment, in his article on reading Rousseau's *Confessions*, that the *Confessions* were the record of a human being, as well as in the appearance, after the turn of the century, of numerous fictional works exploring or researching particular milieux. It was due to the influence of Naturalism that the depiction in literature of a particular individual in his social context came to acquire high value, and that the kind of novel Futabatei had attempted to write in the 1880s now truly came into its own for the first time.

It must be remembered at this point that the Japanese individuals who attempted to carry out the ideological and literary revolution of Naturalism were scarcely removed from the old moral and aesthetic systems themselves. They were still affected, in other words, by the Buddhist view of life as ephemeral, of human action as subject to fate, of human personality as basically an illusion, and of human existence as a recurrent, changeless and there-

[8] Zola, "Le Naturalisme au Théâtre," p. 102.

fore unchangeable pattern of events. The influence of Confucianism lingered in their minds in the assumption that their greatest energy should be spent in serving a narrowly defined and unchanging collective. They existed between two worlds, one a declining world and the other a new Western world of which they had inadequate understanding and virtually no experience. For example, Japanese intellectuals of this time often did not understand the implications of the fact that the Western world of positivist, liberal, and scientific thought was the outcome of centuries of intellectual and social development, when they attempted to integrate such ideas into their own philosophical system. The phenomenon of Japanese Naturalism should be seen, then, not as the wholesale importation of nineteenth-century Western liberal ideals but rather as the attempt of certain Western-educated individuals to change their own and others' thinking along the lines of Western liberalism. The contribution of Western Naturalism to the development of individualism at this time was that through its emphasis on the truthful scrutiny of man, it served the function of pushing the attention of Japanese forward toward the problematic sphere of the individual that had been revealed as new territory by the writings of Tōkoku.

The People's Rights movement, and the Naturalist movement that was in some ways a continuation of it, helped to bring to the consciousness of modern Japanese certain forms of oppression that the past continued to exercise on the individual. Naturalism made Japanese aware that the tyranny of Buddhism and Confucianism—which saw the individual in terms of idealistic, abstract, and absolute qualities—had degraded the concrete, individual life. Yet the government's attempt to restore by force a dead, synthetic conception of the unity of man, the divine, and the state made the climate unfavorable to the working out of a new, objective way of thinking about man.[9] Furthermore, the

[9] This "synthetic" conception of the unity of man, the divine, and the state is the *kokutai* philosophy mentioned earlier. For a fuller discussion see Fairbank, Reischauer, and Craig, *East Asia: The Modern Transformation*, pp. 531-538.

regressive political climate of the early 1900s discouraged agitation for political reforms that were based on the assumption of the validity of each individual. Such movements that did arise, for example, were banned or harassed, and the execution of eleven Socialist anarchists in 1911 after an unsuccessful attempt to assassinate the emperor made it clear that political freedom of the individual was not a goal to be achieved in late Meiji. Given the discouraging climate for freedom of thought and political action, middle-class intellectuals tended to concentrate their attention on one particular aspect of the oppression exercised by traditional idealistic thought: the sacrifice of the sensual self in the service of an abstract ideal. In this the Japanese Naturalists have often been considered the logical followers of the Romantics—for as the Romantic poems of Shimazaki Tōson and Yosano Akiko presented individuals attempting to define themselves through the assertion of their will toward sensual freedom, the Naturalist novels often presented the sexual awakening of their protagonists.

Zola had defined Naturalism in literature as "the return to nature and to man" and "the acceptance and depiction of what is." The Japanese version of Naturalism in literature focused on nature and man and, like European Naturalism, which rebelled against idealistic classical aesthetic norms, it accepted and painted what was. As Zola had done, Japanese Naturalists took Rousseau as one of the prime Naturalists, but their interest in Rousseau stemmed not so much from their reading of Zola's *Le Naturalisme au Théâtre* as from their own intuition of what Naturalism was. For when Tōson spoke of Rousseau's *Confessions* having taught him how to look at nature directly, he meant by *nature* the life of an individual as it is, with no attempt to conceal unflattering details. *Nature* referred, more specifically, to the sexual experiences recounted in the *Confessions*, and to the fact that Rousseau could describe, in an attitude of freedom and outspokenness, subjects that traditionally had demanded an attitude of reticence or even shame in Japan. Finally, *nature* probably referred to the atmosphere of aesthetic freedom and sensual spontaneity that is found in the pages of the first six books—in particular, in the episodes describing Rousseau on his travels or living with Mme. de Warens at their idyllic Les Charmettes. In other words, Tōson and other Naturalists tended to interpret the English word *nature* in terms of their own word *shizen*, which means "as it is," according to its own nature, i.e., naturally, spontaneously, and—in the sense of "not following laws outside itself"—irrationally.

The Naturalists, then, understood the concept of nature largely in terms of their own tradition: as a state of utter spontaneity, freedom, and irrationality. Similarly, their idea of the self was a spontaneous self that, like nature, followed its own laws. The spontaneous self had historically asserted itself against moral and social law; it had often been cultivated in rebellion against the demand made of the individual to subordinate himself to the group. Confucianism in particular had attempted to force socialization on this self, by requiring the individual to wear a mask for the benefit of others, but the spontaneous or unsocialized self insisted on being for itself alone. The strength of this spontaneous self in Japanese tradition can be gauged by the fact that numerous ways of cultivating the self existed in the realm of aesthetic-emotional values: the enjoyment of sensual experience; the act of perceiving; the experience of *satori*, or the mystical affirmation of the void in one's own physical body; and the act of suicide as an expression of both one's privacy and one's highest freedom. The spontaneous self had been particularly repressed under the Confucian morality of the Tokugawa period, as was demonstrated by the banning of ways of cultivating that self from the mainstream of Tokugawa culture. It was this self that, with the decline of Confucian morality in the 1890s and early 1900s, emerged again in the individualist culture of the intellectuals. Thus, even Kitamura Tōkoku's equation of the inner sphere of individual freedom with *mushin*, a Buddhist mystical term for the void that is experienced in the state of *satori*, reveals his influence by a tradition that saw self-cultivation as asocial and largely experiential.

Naturalist writers, then, saw the self largely as spontaneous, irrational, and unsocialized. Their stress on the instinctual, sensual self stemmed both from their enthusiasm for theories of the aesthetic life (such as that of Takayama Chogyū) and from their reading of novels by Zola and Maupassant that depicted the instinctual self. However, the new morality of pleasure that the Romantics and Naturalists evolved in order to replace an idealistic and rigidly repressive samurai ethic resulted in denying the individual any idealism, and hence any freedom. The self escaped the limitations of reason only to find itself imprisoned in sensation. The Naturalist novelist depicted an individual who exists in an aesthetic, amoral universe, for the repressive political situation and the influence of a tradition that saw the self as unsocialized made it difficult for the writer to see his characters as social beings in the way that the novels of Zola and Flaubert presented them. Furthermore, the Naturalist novelist, finding it difficult to see a character as a socialized self, logically turned to himself as a subject for his novels; but since it was difficult for him to gain perspective on his feelings and actions, he often depicted them as unorganized data in the flow of subjective experience. In the Naturalist novel, narration often turned into lyricism, and the objectivity of the novel form was discarded in favor of the subjectivity of a poem. Finally, since the Naturalist writer was not able to see his character in relationship to society, he was unable to depict him as possessing true social freedom but only the freedom of the irrational self. As a consequence, the Naturalist character was depicted as existing in an abstract situation of freedom where he pursued the limited truth of his own sensual awakening, separated completely from the realms of society and history.

Naturalism as an actual literary movement lasted from about 1900 to 1911, but its period of dominance of the literary world lasted only from about 1906 to 1911. Japanese Naturalism produced a kind of novel that, taking its inspiration from the French Naturalists Zola and Maupassant but influenced as well by Turgenev, Ibsen, Hauptmann, and Tolstoy, attempted to de-

scribe, in objective and unsentimental terms, an individual or individuals in a particular social situation or milieu. Some of these
novels, which dealt with the milieux of the family, the school,
and the brothel, attempted to describe the decline of an individual in terms of the effects of heredity and environment, but all
paid close attention to the important Naturalist theme of the sensual awakening of the individual. It is noteworthy that this
Zolaesque form of novel tended, like the pre-Meiji novels, to suffer from an overcomplicated plot and a sentimental fatalism,
qualities that interfered with the objective point of view attempted by the authors. None of them has survived as literature,
and their fate was to be a transitional form between the pre-Meiji
novel and the Naturalist novel form that developed around
1907.[10] This was the I-novel (*shishōsetsu*), a novel form of the
experiential, sensual self that many critics consider to be the typical product of Japanese Naturalism. The *shishōsetsu* form relies
heavily on the author's life, the details of his daily life as well as
his *Weltanschauung*. Like the Zolaesque novel, it possesses the
Naturalist interest in truth, but its truth is the subjective truth of
experience. Sensual awakening is also a theme of the I-novel, yet
the self is seen not objectively, as involved in history or society,
but subjectively, as the self that follows its own laws. In this lyrical rather than objective novel form, complexity of plot yields to
diarylike recording of events, and unity of plot gives way to unity
of experience.[11]

[10] For a discussion of the Zolaesque Naturalist novels see Yoshida Seiichi,
Shizenshugi no kenkyū, Tokyo, 1955, 1: 10-16, 145-200. The work, in two volumes, is useful for an understanding of Naturalism in Japan in general.

[11] Two articles in English on the I-novel are Howard S. Hibbett, "The Por-
trait of the Artist in Japanese Fiction," *The Far Eastern Quarterly* 14 (May 1955):
347-354, and Kinya Tsuruta, "Akutagawa Ryūnosuke and I-Novelists,"
Monumenta Nipponica 25 (1970): 13-27. Important articles in Japanese on the
I-novel are Kume Masao, "Shishōsetsu to shinkyōshōsetsu," in *Gendai bungaku-
ron taikei*, vol. 3, *Taishō jidai*, Tokyo, 1956, pp. 286-293; Kobayashi Hideo,
"Shishōsetsu ron," in *Kobayashi Hideo zenshū*, Tokyo, 1968, 3: 119-145; and Ara
Masahito, "Shishōsetsu ron," *Bungakkai* 6 (September 1952): 23-30.

The chief characteristic of the genre, then, is its subjectivity, both of content and of point of view, and this is what distinguished it from the Zolaesque Naturalist novels, as well as from anything else written up to that point in the modern period. The term *shishōsetsu* is, generically speaking, a shoddy one, for the only formal characteristic is the identification of the author with the hero. In this sense, the *shishōsetsu* appears to be an heir of the traditional genre of the *zuihitsu* ("random notes"), an essaylike genre in which the author's subjectivity was the focus and history, society, and action were absorbed in the memories and reflections of the organizing "I."[12] The term *shishōsetsu* was actually first used in reference to the Naturalist novels written in the early 1900s, in 1923 or 1924, after the I-novel had come to be recognized as a distinct novel form. The I-novel may be any length, from the five-or-six-page "novels" of Shiga Naoya to his masterpiece in the genre, *An'ya kōro* (Long Journey in the Dark Night, 1921-1937), which runs to almost five hundred pages. Furthermore, the *shishōsetsu* may be narrated in the first or third person, and many of the more famous examples are in the third person. The form at times almost dispenses with plot, and sometimes with other characters as well, and the hero (the "I" or "he") is usually the only person whose viewpoint is represented in the work. Finally, time in the I-novel focuses on the eternal present of the experiencing self.

The I-novel can be said to have arisen as Japanese writers who cultivated the self experienced what Ralph Freedman has called "the growing tension of the age between inner and outer experience,"[13] the tension between their awareness of the burden of individuality and the insensitivity to these values on the part of the culture around them. The remark was made in the context of Freedman's description of a novel form that arose in the 1890s in

---

[12] See Yoshida Seiichi's definition and discussion of the *zuihitsu* form in its Japanese and Western manifestations, in *Zuihitsu nyūmon*, Tokyo, 1961.

[13] Ralph Freedman, *The Lyrical Novel*, Princeton, 1966, p. 41.

Europe, a form that I see as analogous to the I-novel. Freedman defines what he calls the "lyrical novel" as a novel that explores the poetic self of the hero and, excluding the greater world outside him, often presents other characters as "personae for the self."[14] The analogy with Freedman's novel form is that both forms emerged in response to the writer's need to redefine his existence at a time of cultural breakdown around the beginning of the twentieth century; the actual self explored was quite different. However, the *shishōsetsu* is even more analogous to a form of confessional novel that developed in Europe from the end of the eighteenth century: the small autobiographical novel form that Joachim Merlant calls the *"roman personnel"* and Jean Hytier the *"roman de l'individu."*[15] This was a novel form that explored the world (Hytier prefers to use the word *métaphysique*) of the individual rather than the individual in relation to the social world or in the context of history. Like the term *shishōsetsu*, the two terms are formally vague, for the only characteristic that unites the various examples of such novels is their exclusive concern with either the mental, emotional, or spiritual existence or experience of the individual—an individual who may or may not be the author himself. Chateaubriand's *René* (1802), for example, is a poetic, fragmentary novel that explores the hero's *mal du siècle*; Senancour's *Obermann* (1804) is a loosely connected series of reflections or essays in diary form; Constant's *Adolphe* (1810) and Sainte-Beuve's *Volupté* (1832) are novelistic, structured analyses of the course of a *grande passion* and its effect on the hero. Finally, Alfred de Musset's *La Confession d'un enfant du siècle* (1836) is a novel that treats the hero's experiences according to a pattern of sin, followed by *examen de conscience*, confession, and rebirth.

Merlant sees the *roman personnel* as a form that originated, around the time of the French Revolution, as the individual felt an increasingly strong need to defend himself against the de-

---

[14] Ibid., pp. 1-2.

[15] Joachim Merlant, *Le Roman personnel de Rousseau à Fromentin*, Paris, 1905, and Jean Hytier, *Le Roman de l'individu*, Paris, 1928.

mands of society. The individual had, in effect, to defend his right to exist as a private person, and his concerns in this novel were to discover an inner self that was morally and spiritually strong.[16] This generalization is applicable to the *shishōsetsu* as well. Then, too, the relationship of the *roman personnel* to the I-novel is one of direct influence, for Rousseau, the main figure behind the development of the European form, was an important influence on at least one writer of *shishōsetsu*, Shimazaki Tōson.

The response of Japanese writers at the turn of the twentieth century to the confessional, subjective literature of Rousseau and the English Romantic poets presents an analogy to the response of French writers in the early decades of the nineteenth century to Rousseau. Nagai Kafū (1879-1959), one of the great modern writers who began his career under the aegis of Naturalism, made some perceptive observations on this subject. In 1916 he discussed his method as a writer: "To begin with, the kind of thing I am doing—as a writer of fiction, writing a tale (*monogatari*), and putting together, just as they are, events that involved me—was done by various people in the West from the beginning of the nineteenth century. The *roman personnel* was born and has not yet become obsolete."[17] The importance of Kafū's remarks, which show his customary perspicacity on differences and similarities between East and West, lies in his sketching of a worldwide tradition of subjective fiction of which the modern Japanese subjective novel is a part. Given Kafū's insights into the relationship between the overthrowing of the feudal system of government and the blossoming of individual self-expression in his own country, it is likely that he perceived an analogy as well between the *roman personnel* and the new Japanese subjective novel as products of an age when feudalism was giving way to a political system that permitted the expression of individual sentiments. Yet Kafū wrote often, and with eloquence, of the failure of individualism in a nation that had not sufficiently rid itself of the evils of

[16] Merlant, *Le Roman personnel*, pp. xxii-xxv.
[17] Nagai Kafū, "Yahazu-gusa," *Kafū zenshū*, Tokyo, 1964, 14: 248-249.

feudalism, and it is in this context that one should understand his remark that the genre of the *roman personnel* is not yet obsolete.[18] Kafū doubtless realized that writers of his time needed the subjective novel in order to explore the new culture of individualism that had come into being in the wake of the decline of feudalism. The fact that the subjective novel or I-novel occupies a special, honored place in Japanese letters even today is proof that writers continue to feel this need, and that the cultural task of defining the self that began in the Meiji period has still not been completed.

Katai's Futon *(The Quilt): The First I-Novel*

Tōkoku's writings on the inner life had indicated the direction the modern Japanese individual should take. Yet it was the liter-

[18] After spending five years in America and France in his twenties, Kafū returned home in 1908 with an acute consciousness of what was truly Japanese and what was truly Western. His years spent abroad made him decry the vulgar, superficially Westernized culture of the Meiji period, and express nostalgia for the past. Yet often, too, he expressed anger that the freedoms of Western culture were only superficially understood, and inadequately realized, in his country. One such passage is the following: "I feel that the importation of Western culture in modern times has stopped at the surface, and that the Japanese people have taken not at all kindly to the deeper content of Western ideas. . . . In the atmosphere that surrounds Japan, even with the constitutional government she has now, there is something that is unchanged from the feudal past, something indescribably Oriental and despotic, such that even if you change the external forms, the natural features and the climate and all the invisible things will continue to bear malice toward the freedom of human will and the liberation of human thought." "*Reishō ni tsukite*" (On *Sneers*, 1910), *Zenshū*, 13: 42. Similarly, in *Reishō (Sneers*, 1910), Kafū lamented the traditional repression of love in Japan in favor of patriotism and honor; in "Shinkichōsha" (Diary of a Person Recently Returned from Abroad, 1909) he revealed an admiration of Western individualism and a distaste for the Meiji pseudo-individualism that was a product of cultural disharmony and confusion; and in "Yatate no chibifude" (Notes from My Humble Inkhorn, 1914) he criticized the Meiji period for its inferior democracy and for its maintaining of all that was worst in feudalism. *Reishō* and "Shinkichōsha" are found in *Zenshū*, vol. 4, and "Yatate no chibifude" in vol. 14.

ary and philosophical movement of Naturalism that provided
Japanese who desired it with the basis on which to build an individualist morality, in that it placed the individual in the center of
life, it legitimized the desires of the sensual and experiential self,
and it gave the individual a method of objective scrutiny to use in
his pursuit of the truth of the self. Several short novels appeared
in the first decade or so of the twentieth century that treated the
individual in this new context, novels in a brief, often fragmentary form that was ideally suited to the goal of exploration of the
problem of individualism. Among them were Shimazaki Tōson's
Hakai (Breaking the Commandment, 1906), Futabatei Shimei's
Heibon (Mediocrity, 1907), Tokuda Shūsei's *Kabi* (Mold, 1911),
and Natsume Sōseki's *Michikusa* (Grass by the Wayside, 1915).
Not all of these are considered to be in the *shishōsetsu* genre, but
all of them share to a great degree the Naturalist ideology that
holds that man is the center of life and that the novel is the proper
vehicle for the most rigorous search for truth. The best known of
these, and the novel considered to be the first and the most typical I-novel, is *Futon* (The Quilt).[19]

Futon was published in 1907 by Tayama Katai (1871-1930),
the novelist who, along with Shimazaki Tōson, was the prime
shaper of Japanese Naturalism. It was a novel that shocked its
readers not only because its contents were scandalous but also because the sexual feelings and experiences described in it were
clearly and unmistakably those of the author himself.[20] At the
time Katai wrote *Futon*, self-revelation was still frowned upon in
society. By confessing such private details of his life, even
through the distancing mechanism of fiction, Katai was in effect
challenging the old morality that considered public expression of
the self to be immoral. At the same time, *Futon* can be seen the-

[19] *Futon* is available in a German translation. See Oscar Benl, *Flüchtiges Leben*,
Berlin-Schoeneberg, 1942, pp. 186-283.

[20] Since Katai's audience was the relatively small public of his confreres who
belonged, as he did, to the *bundan*, it would have been able to identify the
events and the emotions described in the novel as being linked to Katai. In this
sense, the I-novel was a *roman à clef*.

matically as a Naturalist novel that treats the sensual awakening
of the individual. Yet in *Futon* it is more than a question of sexual
awakening, it is a matter of the awakening of an individual conscience. For the awakening of sexual feelings toward a person not
his wife creates a conflict in the hero that precipitates his birth as
an individual. He is suddenly faced with the choice of either satisfying his desires for the girl who is his student or renouncing his
desires in the interests of maintaining his outward respectability.

The situation is an ancient one, yet the way it is presented in
Futon is entirely new. A person living in pre-Meiji times, before
the introduction of the Western idea of an individualist morality,
had the task of merely adhering to established morality, which
meant that he could do as his desires directed him as long as he
did not lose face. He acted in accordance with a moral system that
allowed for human weakness and merely stipulated that it not be
revealed publicly. However, the hero of *Futon* no longer has the
opportunity of satisfying his sexual desire and his desire for respectability at the same time, and this is not only because society
has changed but also because he himself has changed internally;
an individual conscience has awakened in him that forces him to
make a choice between self-satisfaction and self-suppression. No
matter which decision he makes, he will be unhappy, because he
lives at a time when traditional and modern ethics overlap. His
sense of freedom is exacerbated by the conflicting demands that
he himself makes on himself, but one thing is clear: he must
choose. Indeed, *Futon* is the first Japanese novel that poses the
problem of individual moral choice. It is also the first Japanese
novel that shows the suffering such freedom entails, and it is because this suffering is deeply felt by the reader, despite the melodramatic plot, that *Futon* was considered from the start to be a
groundbreaking modern work.

Briefly, the plot is this: Takenaka Tokio, a writer of some fame
who is approaching middle age, takes into his home as a pupil a
Western-educated girl named Yoshiko. When it becomes apparent that he is falling in love with her, his wife makes him move

the girl to the house of a relative. Tokio's feelings are confused and ambivalent at this point: he is tempted to seduce Yoshiko but holds back out of a mixture of his sense of duty, as her teacher, and plain cowardice. One and a half years pass. Suddenly Tokio hears that she has acquired a boyfriend, and he is plunged into jealousy and self-reproach. Tokio finds himself in an even more uncomfortable position when, ironically, Yoshiko and her boyfriend ask him to defend their love against the certain opposition of Yoshiko's parents. The boyfriend, Tanaka, brings the matter to a head by leaving school and coming to Tokyo to join Yoshiko and to look for work to support them after they marry.

At this point, Tokio writes to Yoshiko's father and reveals the situation to him. The meeting that follows between the father, Tokio, and Yoshiko is a masterpiece in its analysis of the age-old conflict between the young and the old. The father lays down the conditions that the two young people will have to meet before they can marry, conditions that are tantamount to forbidding them to see one another. Tanaka refuses to accept them. It is during this scene that Tokio finally takes his revenge on the two young people for having, as he sees it, deprived him of his sensual happiness with Yoshiko. Yoshiko had always sworn to him that her love for Tanaka was pure, and Tokio had helped them, though insincerely, on this basis. Now, seized by a sudden suspicion that Tanaka's tenacity and his insistence on his right to Yoshiko rests on the fact that he has possessed her physically, Tokio asks to see their love letters. When Yoshiko reveals that she has destroyed them, Tokio is convinced that his suspicions were correct and takes pleasure in seeing her in a state of humiliation. Shortly after, Yoshiko confesses in a humble letter to Tokio that she had indeed lied to him about the nature of her relationship to Tanaka. Yet by this time she has accompanied her father home in dishonor, her chances for marriage ruined. Tokio finds himself once more in the midst of his desolate life, after she goes, and in the last scene (a scene that caused a minor scandal) he is shown pressing his face against her quilt in self-pity and despair.

Whereas in the usual I-novel only the hero's point of view is represented or only the hero acts morally, in this novel three of the characters are depicted as moral beings.[21] The choices they make, in the conflict situation provided by the author, are an important means toward understanding late Meiji individualism. For Tokio, the hero, the moral choice seems straightforward: it is a choice between satisfying his desire for Yoshiko and fulfilling his socially respected role as protector of the young. From the beginning, where we see Tokio as a weak-willed, sentimental person looking back with regret and anger at his missed opportunity to seduce Yoshiko, it is obvious that Tokio's internalized sense of control is stronger than his desire for sensual pleasure. Yet the situation is more complicated, for there exists a third alternative besides the two choices mentioned, and that is the one Tokio chooses, though he appears to be unconscious of his choice. While he *seems* to make the second choice, that of acting as protector of the young, he in fact makes the third choice: that of avoiding acting on his desires. Tokio's internalized guilt at having individual desires makes him condemn them and try to repress them. Thus, though he appears to make the choice of renouncing Yoshiko, the desires he tries to repress are too strong for him and they are expressed unconsciously, in spite of his moral censor, in his jealousy of Tanaka and in his eagerness to humiliate Yoshiko, who had yielded to her desires. His *avoidance* of free expression of his sensual desires allows him to maintain not only an air of outward respectability, but one of moral superiority as well. Yet in the end he clutches Yoshiko's quilt as the symbol of his lost sensual selfhood, for he knows that he had chosen in his inner heart to do what the young people did, and that he had allowed fear and cowardice to keep him from self-expression.

[21] It is a paradox to me that *Futon* is considered the quintessential I-novel, when it has a clearly outlined plot or story and presents other characters than the author with insight and understanding. Probably its historical position as the first novel of the genre guaranteed it the position it still holds today as the most important I-novel.

That Katai saw Tokio's moral conflict as modern is obvious from the fact that he compares Tokio indirectly to two heroes of Western works he would have considered modern, i.e., Naturalistic, in their orientation toward life. In his unhappiness of encroaching middle age and in his marriage to a woman who is old-fashioned, uneducated, and knows nothing about her husband's emotional life, Tokio is similar to Johannes Volkrath of Hauptmann's drama, *Einsame Menschen* (1891). In that play, too, the subject is the conflict in a man between his attraction to a modern, educated woman and his duty toward his simple, uneducated wife. Volkrath, unable to solve the conflict, commits suicide in true Naturalistic manner. The other hero to whom the author compares Tokio is Turgenev's Chulkaturin, the hero of *The Diary of a Superfluous Man* (1850). Since the reference occurs in a climactic scene, one in which Tokio wallows in self-pity and anger at having missed his opportunity to seduce Yoshiko, it has an important meaning for the novel as a whole. Tokio is reminiscing on his life:

> He'd already learned in past years that his courage always broke down just when he was about to take the one step which would put him in the midst of fate. Over and over again he experienced the humiliating pain and loneliness of one who was just outside the circle. It was that way with his literary career, and it was that way in his social life. When he imagined that it would be that way in love, even in love, a sense of his own lack of self-respect and the unfairness of fate lodged deeply in his heart. He thought of himself as Turgenev's "superfluous man," and recalled the fleeting and useless life of that hero.[22]

It is interesting that the particular heroes that Tokio compares himself with are people who are left behind by life, who somehow

---

[22] Tayama Katai, *Futon*, in *Tayama Katai shū, Gendai nihonbungaku zenshū*, Tokyo, 1955, 9: 36. Turgenev's Chulkaturin, like Katai's Tokio, loses his loved one to another man. While Tokio uses psychological warfare to combat Yoshiko's boyfriend, Chulkaturin fights a duel with his rival, which he loses. What most clearly links the two characters, however, is their masochistic brooding and introspection.

are unable to make decisions or act to achieve their desires, and who take refuge in self-pity or suicide. From the mention of these two Western heroes early in the novel, it is evident that Tokio, when confronted with the moral dilemma, will make the choice of self-control rather than self-liberation.

While a moral infringement is usually thought of by society and organized religion as a sin, it may be a step toward self-knowledge in terms of its meaning for the individual. In this sense, Tokio lacks the courage to sin, but possesses only the courage to watch and accuse others. His is the knowledge of sin (potential freedom) in himself, a knowledge that, because it does not lead to action (actual freedom) results in hypocrisy. Yet Tokio suffers a great deal from his internal conflicts, and through this suffering he gains knowledge. He has both gained and lost something at the end of the novel. Though Tokio does not act to fulfill his desires, the choice is there; and where there is choice, there is moral consciousness and individuality.

Compared to Tokio, Yoshiko dares more—she dares to act. The crux of the novel is whether she and Tanaka have slept together or not. If they are innocent of physical love, they are to be sympathized with, Tokio's role of protector is justified, and tradition (in the form of Yoshiko's unbending father) is in the wrong. If they are not innocent, they are sinful (especially Yoshiko, because punishment for moral offenses is greater for a woman), Tokio becomes a fool in his own eyes for believing in their innocence, and the stern father, along with tradition, is proved right. If an individual can be said to possess moral consciousness when he has internalized a sense of sin, Yoshiko is a person with moral consciousness. Yet the further demand made of a moral individual, that he take responsibility for his acts, is not met by Yoshiko. While in the anonymity of the big city she can accept responsibility for her behavior; but once her father comes to Tokyo to see her, bringing with him the traditional values of the family and rural life, her citified, individualistic values break down. In the end, "no longer capable of thinking clearly,

Yoshiko submitted to the power of custom . . . and went home with her father."[23] Once she was back in the provinces, morality became a matter of saving face before others. The author implies, then, that in the future, Yoshiko's family rather than Yoshiko herself will bear the main burden of her behavior, for they will lose face. In Yoshiko's case, traditional morality wins out.

Katai characterizes Yoshiko as a "modern" or "Meiji" girl, a girl who knew independence unheard-of for women in traditional society, a girl who was educated and taught to develop her own life, and, what is especially relevant for the story, a girl whose sexual life was her own affair. Yoshiko's parents were devout Christians, and they had sent Yoshiko to a Christian school for girls. Christian schools in the Meiji period were noted for their freedom—for example, girls at Yoshiko's school were allowed to read novels of the period such as Ozaki Kōyō's *Konjiki yasha* (The Gold Demon, 1898), a melodramatic novel about unrequited passion, whereas girls of more traditional upbringing were prohibited from reading novels at all. Later, after Yoshiko leaves the school and comes to Tokyo to be Tokio's disciple, she allows men to come to her room and stays out late; on one occasion she takes a trip of several days alone with Tanaka. It must be admitted that Yoshiko's behavior, seen through Tokio's suspicious eyes, seems furtive and evasive. It is even understandable that she conceals from Tokio her real relations with Tanaka, seeing him as her guardian or father. Yet a real change in her morality would be indicated by her living openly with Tanaka. Like Tokio, then, she conceals her individual desires and her behavior in the hopes of maintaining social approval.

Tokio and Yoshiko are similar in that they both have desires, the satisfying of which conflicts with social morality. Yet Yoshiko's case is more upsetting for the reader than Tokio's. Being young, she is less aware of the implications of her behavior; she makes a tragic miscalculation in assuming that she possesses

[23] Ibid., p. 56.

more of the modern spirit of independence and freedom than she actually is capable of living out. In the end she realizes her mistake when she says to Tokio: "When it comes down to it, I am a woman with an old-fashioned heart and I don't have the power to live out the new ideas."[24] It is much easier for Tokio, being older and educated according to the traditional morality of saving face, to cover up his deviation in thought from that morality; for Tokio, hypocrisy is a natural form of existence, though of course it does not make him happy. But for Yoshiko the choice is between daring self-expression and submissive self-concealment. Once she allowed the old morality to define and judge her behavior, as she did by going home with her father, she was lost.

In contrast to Tokio and Yoshiko, who are trapped in the old morality, Tanaka is presented as a modern youth, one who has learned to use the new morality of individualism to his own advantage. He has picked up from the Christian school, in which he is training to become a minister at the beginning of the story, an appearance of smooth piety and unctuousness that allows him to seem to please his elders while actually rebelling against them. He has certain features of the *seikō-seinen* depicted in Futabatei's *Ukigumo* in the figure of Noboru—the bureaucrat, the new man who makes his way, alone and aggressive, through the world. Tanaka seems to take advantage of the individualist morality of Yoshiko to get his way, in that he plays up to her promiscuity, then tries to force her father to let him marry her. Yoshiko's father, at least, is convinced of this, and considers Tanaka a fortune hunter. Yet Tanaka, too, loses out in the end. Not only does he not acquire Yoshiko (and her money), but he has lost the favor of his family by leaving school against their wishes, and is thus left with nothing at the end of the story but feelings of bitterness and angry frustration. It is possible, however, that just that combination of energy, frustration, goal orientation (as seen in his

[24] Ibid., p. 55.

single-minded pursuit of Yoshiko), and anger will enable him to make his way in the competitive society of the future.

In the course of the novel, both Tokio and Yoshiko attempt to live according to a morality that defines as good that which satisfies the individual. Yet they both demonstrate that the appearance of this morality in a person causes conflict and suffering, since the new individualist ethic clashes with a previously internalized morality that demands that the individual save his (and also another's) face. It is not as easy for Tokio to seduce Yoshiko as he would like to think, nor is it as easy for Yoshiko to deceive both Tokio and her father as she expects it will be. Katai's novel implies that when the individual tries to go against traditional morality, he exposes himself to confusion, suffering, and tension. His view of the possibility of individual satisfaction is pessimistic, since he presents all three of his characters as sad, defeated, or frustrated at the end of *Futon*. Yoshiko accepts her dishonor and defeat, having failed to be an individual responsible for her behavior. Tanaka is at least free from crippling self-condemnation, but his behavior tends toward the unscrupulous and immoral. Between these two extremes, there remains as an example of individualist morality only the mediocre, superfluous figure of Tokio, the hypocrite who is afraid to act out his desire but who survives, and even saves face.

With the appearance of *Futon*, the path of the Naturalist novel was determined. In fulfillment of the directives of Tsubouchi Shōyō of some twenty years before, the novel would present morally believable characters and reveal the inner psychological life of man. Even more, following the directives of Kitamura Tōkoku, it would attempt to depict the self-definition of the individual and thus to inspire others to cultivate their inner life. For this is what Katai was doing as he presented his three characters struggling to define themselves. Thus, the I-novel can be seen as marking the entrance into Japanese culture of a modern morality based on the individual, and *Futon* can be seen as the first in a hypothetical series of steps that the Japanese novel took toward the goal of full revelation of the individual.[25] Yet these steps were difficult for the Japanese novel to take, as a comparison with the French *roman personnel* will make clear. The *roman personnel* of the nineteenth century had behind it a solid tradition of moral introspection, an interest in human motives and states of mind that was expressed in early novels such as *La Princesse de Clèves* (1678), as well as in the genre of moral reflections that developed contemporaneously with the French novel. Furthermore, the individual was given moral seriousness in Rousseau's *Confessions*, for here the thoughts and emotions, if not the actions, of one individual—in short, his moral sensibility—were defended against the external mores of a corrupt society. Symbolically, too, the individual was considered important enough for his inner experiences to occupy a whole book.

The ideal of the *schöne Seele* as elaborated by Schiller and others provided the basis for the European defense of the individual's inner morality, and for the appearance of the individual moral self in more public forms of literature—for example, the social novel—after the period of the *roman personnel*. Furthermore, the ideal of the individual was firmly linked with the rise to power of the bourgeois class in Europe, so that the individual was not only an inner man but also a person with a distinct social existence. By comparison, the I-novel of the early twentieth century in Japan scrutinized an individual that had only recently begun to be defined as separate from the social body around him. There was no tradition of moral introspection, and no long-standing philoso-

---

[25] It is evident that the goal of complete revelation of the inner self has been only one of several goals of the Japanese novel in general since Futabatei's *Ukigumo*. Yet if one links the novel to the spread of the ideal of individualism, both in its social and political manifestations and in the less obvious internal transformations, as I do here, one cannot help remarking the strength and endurance of the tradition of the subjective novel, and the progressive depth of revelation of the inner self that it has attained, between *Ukigumo* and, say, Ōe Kenzaburō's *Kojinteki na taiken* (A Personal Matter, 1964).

phy, defended in literature as well as legally, that stressed the importance of the individual's taking responsibility for his own actions. The Buddhist mode of seeing the individual inherited from the past stressed that man was a creature only fleetingly encased in a body, his true destiny being to overcome life in the physical body altogether. Rather than emphasizing the liberating aspect of karma—the individual's capacity to take responsibility for his past actions and his consequent power to affect his future through present actions—it stressed the interpretation of karma as fate, an external force to which the individual can only submit. The Confucian morality that dominated the Tokugawa period, on the other hand, forced the individual to look outward to the social group, demanding that he save face before the group but allowing him no freedom, and thus no opportunity to take responsibility for himself. The literature of the time went along with this view. The *onna* of Saikaku's *Life of an Amorous Woman*, for example, was depicted from the outside, and thus was seen as paying lip service to her own downfall. She was unable to internalize responsibility for the sinfulness incurred by her contact with the world, for she had no free will. From this example it is clear that the Japanese individual had to have the freedom to disobey social and moral laws in fulfillment of his own desires before he could become a morally serious character.

The lingering influence of these two thought systems clearly placed obstacles in the path of the development of an individualist morality in the late Meiji period. However, Naturalism, and particularly the method of objective analysis that became popular under its auspices, forced the writer of subjective novels to look into himself deeply and to report truthfully what he found there. Whether the contents of the mind that he discovered were good or evil by traditional moral standards was irrelevant—the habit of looking carefully at the inner self had, in the long run, the beneficial effect of making the writer more aware of his inner self, and more conscious of his responsibility for its contents. When he transferred the technique of self-scrutiny to his characters, in the form of objective analysis of their psychic states, he introduced a method of moral introspection that became the basis for the development of a psychologically realistic novel form in Japan.

Futabatei Shimei had used this technique, especially in the later chapters of *Ukigumo*, and though Tokutomi Roka likened such analysis to the dissection of a corpse, Bunzō was revealed, on dissection, to be quite harmless. The progress that the technique underwent due to the influence of the Naturalist movement can be seen in *Futon*, where the character that Katai reveals is clearly an ugly sort of hypocrite, who is self-pitying and cruel besides. The following passage of analysis of Tokio's fantasies shocked Katai's readers as much if not more than Futabatei's analysis of Bunzō had shocked Tokutomi Roka:

> At that time he used to meet a pretty teacher on the way to work each morning, and meeting her became increasingly his only pleasure. He imagined all kinds of things in connection with this woman: What if a love affair were to develop and he were to take her to some little *machiai* near Kagurazaki where, hidden from the eyes of others, they could be happy? Or what if he were to take walks with her in the suburbs, unbeknownst to his wife? No, not only that—since his wife was pregnant at the time, what if she were to die in a difficult childbirth and he could then marry the woman? He walked along, thinking coolly how he would bring her into his house.[26]

The fact that the human mind could entertain evil thoughts was not a surprise to Meiji intellectuals. Rather, it was the fact that such thoughts could be recorded and presented as the individual's identity, and the record itself taken as a kind of truth about man, that shocked and disturbed them. For the technique of objective analysis revealed an image of man as complex, morally undefined, and, what was most frightening, responsible for his thoughts and deeds.

The passages in which the hero's self-pity and pessimism are

[26] *Tayama Katai shū*, p. 32. A *machiai* is a house of assignation.

expressed in long interior monologues are clearly the important parts of the novel, since they, rather than the scenes in which characters interact with one another, are what remain in the mind of the reader. This fact has led critics to refer to *Futon* as a confession of the author. Indeed, we must not forget that the events narrated in *Futon* were barely disguised events in Katai's own life, and that, as a consequence, it is possible to consider Tokio as really Katai himself: a man who was aware that he suffered from moral restrictions on his behavior but who had no idea how these restrictions could be eliminated. Judging from the work, Katai's sense of the individual was strong enough for him to be conscious of his feelings, yet he lacked an ideal of action or change that would have allowed his individuality to impinge on society. The result was pessimism and self-pity on the author's part, moods that pervade the novel and interfere with the objective portrayal of the characters and events, just as the sentimentality and fatalism of the author had hindered the objectivity of the early Naturalist novels. Thus, *Futon* exists as an expression of the author's unconscious rebellion against the strictures of society that he has himself experienced. Since the rebellion is unconscious and only the suffering caused by oppression is conscious, the novel fails to depict the sensual awakening of an individual and becomes instead a statement of the author's suffering.

In a sense, then, Katai used *Futon* as a way of relieving himself of the pressures of an old, inhuman moral system without becoming consciously rebellious in his suffering. A similar kind of unconscious rebellion is seen in the character Tokio. The latter is conscious of his suffering at wanting Yoshiko but being unable to obtain her; his suffering is intensified when the youth Tanaka snatches her away from him. At no time, however, do we see him contemplating a rebellion against the part of him that prevents him from acting. It is as if he is not even conscious of a rebellious voice within him. Yet the rebellious desire is there, and because it is unconscious, it is expressed in a way that is not overseen by Tokio's moral self. Firstly, Tokio, who is an unconscious or invisible rebel himself, turns against the visible rebels: the young couple who dare to defy their elders. Consequently, instead of becoming an individual who defies custom and tradition, Tokio turns into a supporter of tradition. Secondly, Tokio's unconscious rebellion turns into cruelty toward Yoshiko. It is he, after all, who notifies Yoshiko's father of what is going on between the young lovers, and in doing so he obtains a kind of revenge against her—as if he blamed her for having refused him, when it was *he* who was too cowardly to approach her. Later, when Yoshiko informs him that she has burned Tanaka's letters to her, Tokio gets a grim satisfaction from scolding her, as if it is up to him to punish her for her moral infringement. Yet in the end Tokio is left, like the author, with nothing but self-pity and hopelessness toward the future: the fruits of his failure to rebel against an intolerable situation.

Yet Tokio becomes a sympathetic character in the end—not because of his actions, which are disquieting, but because of his capacity for moral suffering. Yoshiko is also a sympathetic character, in spite of her failure, for she dared to live the way she wanted and she, too, suffered in the end. Only Tanaka is not a sympathetic character, because, though he acts, he lacks the capacity to suffer. Suffering in *Futon* is a positive characteristic, because it somehow implies growth or learning, both of which take the individual into the future. Yet Katai does not show us the future. At the end of the novel Yoshiko is at home, her individuality presumably buried under the weight of her parents' morality, and Tokio clutches her quilt as a remnant of his past dreams of happiness. Since Katai has no confidence that an individualist morality will eventually be possible, there is no ideal in the novel by which one could justify the characters' suffering. Katai has merely taken them out of the safety and innocence of the old moral world without fully bringing them into the new. Innocence has been lost but experience has not yet proved its greater worth for the individual. It is no wonder, then, that the past, though enclosing, still offers the individual a certain comfort.

Part Two

SHIMAZAKI TŌSON AND THE IDEAL OF INDIVIDUALISM

CHAPTER FIVE

The Education of a Meiji Individual

The Naturalist movement of the early twentieth century had made possible a break with the old heroic morality of the samurai class. Yet Naturalism was in turn an outgrowth of the general cultural ideal of self-definition that, first elaborated in Fukuzawa's writings on independence in the 1870s, was given a deeper interpretation in Futabatei's *Ukigumo* in the late 1880s, Tōkoku's essays on the inner life in the early 1890s, and Katai's *Futon* in the first decade of the twentieth century. Consequently, by 1907, the year of *Futon*'s appearance, there existed what can be called a culture of the individual among the urban, Western-educated middle class, a culture that was given expression in numerous brief novels about the self that were later given the name "I-novel." The confrontation with the self was the partial aim of the work of most of the great writers of the time, but it was Shimazaki Tōson who made perhaps the greatest contribution to the new culture of the individual. For Tōson was the most serious disciple of Kitamura Tōkoku. Through his poetry of the late 1890s he played an important role in shaping the Romantic image of the individual and, though he claimed he was not a Naturalist but an individualist,[1] he wrote a series of autobiographical novels that demonstrates the Naturalist interest in the pursuit of the truth of the individual—a series of novels that was unique in the Meiji period and even later, in its delineation of the development of a human life in time.

---

[1] Kataoka Ryōichi records that Tōson said this to his good friend, Oda Masanobu, in his *Kindai nihon no sakka to sakuhin*, Tokyo, 1954, p. 427. Tōson probably meant to distinguish himself from those writing in the Zolaesque style, with this remark, for it is quite clear that as a novelist he owed a great deal to the Naturalist movement of the early twentieth century.

Part one of this study considered each work or each literary figure as an important step in the acculturation of the ideal of individualism in Meiji Japan, as well as in the development of a novel of the individual. Part two will consider the ideal of individualism as it was interpreted and expressed in the life and literary works of one important researcher into the truth of the individual. A biographical method will inevitably predominate in the discussion of his formative years, but biographical details from any stage in his life will be brought in if they seem to shed light on Tōson's struggles with the problems of individualist morality that have been isolated so far: independence from the family and past morality, self-expression through literature, love, and specifically ethical problems such as sin and guilt. It will become clear to the reader that Tōson was involved in all the historical movements connected with the ideal of individualism that were discussed in part one: the People's Rights movement, Meiji Christianity, and Romanticism and Naturalism. As a child and youth his participation in the process of assimilation of the ideal of individualism was necessarily largely passive, though after he began his literary career, in the early 1890s, he began also to influence the way the ideal was understood by his compatriots. Finally, in two particular works, he contributed his mature vision of the modern individual: *Hakai* (Breaking the Commandment, 1906) and *Shinsei* (The New Life, 1919). Though the latter novel was written in the Taishō period (1912-1926), it is a work that is in many ways a culmination of the Meiji Naturalist movement. It is also a work that is permeated by the optimistic spirit of the mid-Meiji period, and by the particular optimism of Tōson, the writer who captured the Meiji spirit better than any other writer.

The Childhood and Youth of a Meiji Individual

Shimazaki Tōson was born Shimazaki Haruki (Tōson is his pen name) in 1872, in the mountain village of Magome in Shinano

Province (present-day Nagano Prefecture).[2] Though Magome was located in one of the poorest and most isolated areas of Japan, the Shimazaki family enjoyed a certain prosperity and prestige as the most prominent family in the village. At the time of the Restoration Tōson's father, Masaki, was a landowner and village headman (*shōya*); in addition to this hereditary position he held also the hereditary position of *honjin*, or keeper of the post station. Though the family was not strictly of samurai origin, nevertheless they considered themselves, in terms of culture and status, to be samurai rather than peasants, and the Shimazaki household was marked by the typically samurai atmosphere of moral rigor and devotion to learning and public affairs. Clearly, the Restoration occurring in Tokyo made itself felt directly in this small village far from the capital only through the transfer of power, and for those in power the change was great. With the defeudalization that followed the Restoration Masaki lost his rank and function as *honjin*; shortly after, his post of *shōya* was eliminated and a new local administrator was appointed by the central government. Yet while Tōson's father suffered personally from his loss of status, as well as income, Tōson's life went on much as before. As he described it later in *Osanaki hi* (My Childhood Days, 1913), the first nine years of his life were spent in an atmosphere similar to that of an isolated European village before the Industrial Revolution. Tōson's mother wove her own cloth and sewed the family clothes, as well as prepared food from wild and cultivated plants; and master and man lived a closely intertwined existence in the culturally isolated world of the village.

Tōson was the youngest of seven children. When he was seven his elder brother Hideo, thirteen years his senior, was elected village headman, after which he married and came to live with his

[2] For the biographical details of Tōson's life I am indebted primarily to Senuma Shigeki, *Hyōden. Shimazaki Tōson*, Tokyo, 1959, and secondarily to William E. Naff, "Shimazaki Tōson: A Critical Biography," Ph.D. Univ. of Washington, 1965.

bride in Tōson's father's house. There was another brother slightly older than Tōson (Tomoya) who was his constant playmate. Otherwise, the people with whom the young boy spent his days were his mother, his grandmother, in whose bed he frequently slept at night, and his own personal nursemaid, O-maki. A manservant connected with the family, Daisuke, made him sandals and, as Tōson put it, "thought of me as his own son or grandson."[3] Tōson's mother, aside from teaching him classical poetry, apparently made little impression on him, but his relationship with his father was complex and crucial to his development. Masaki was a largely self-educated man for whom the samurai ideal of public service was a stern and demanding duty. He opened a school in the village and instructed many of the village children, as well as his sons Haruki (Tōson) and Tomoya, in the Confucian classics; after the Restoration in 1868 he wrote several memorials to the emperor protesting the policies of the new government; finally, he wrote various literary works, including an autobiography. For the young Tōson, Masaki was a stern and unapproachable figure. He writes in *Osanaki hi* that he tried to avoid contact with his father as much as he could, only coming before him to recite from memory passages from the Confucian classics.[4] Yet Masaki had discerned in his youngest child a love of learning that distinguished him from his other children, and often spoke of Tōson as his spiritual heir.

During the first six years of Tōson's life his father was often away from home looking for employment. These were years of bitterness and disillusionment for Masaki, who had lost the basis for his very existence when defeudalization occurred. Growing depressed over the hopelessness of his situation, he gradually succumbed to paranoia and, after setting fire to a Buddhist temple, was confined to a cell where he died soon after, hopelessly insane, in 1886. It was only much later, when he was in his forties, that

---

[3] *Osanaki hi*, in *Bifū* (Gentle Breezes), *Zenshū*, 10: 374.
[4] Ibid., pp. 383-384.

Tōson was able to understand the sufferings his father had undergone as a member of the transition generation, and it is significant that Tōson's last completed novel, *Yoake-mae* (Before the Dawn, 1935), a three-volume work that some consider his greatest novel, was to deal with his father's generation. Meanwhile, the same Restoration that had destroyed Masaki opened a new world of opportunity to his youngest son, for already before Masaki's death it had been decided that Tōson should be sent to Tokyo to acquire a Western-style education. Emotionally, the journey to Tokyo was an unimaginable distance; the villagers gave Tōson the sort of leave-taking that one would get if one were going across the sea, for in a sense, Tokyo was the "America" of rural Japanese aspiring to lead a modern life. The actual journey took one week. Since no railroads existed as yet, Tōson had to travel the first part of the journey on foot. Then, after crossing several steep mountain passes, he arrived at a town where he could get a coach bound for Tokyo.[5] All in all, this journey took Tōson out of the world of his father and of the past, and his village became the "old country" over which he became nostalgic in later years, but to which he never returned to stay.

After arriving in Tokyo in 1881 at the age of nine, Tōson lived first with his sister Sono (sixteen years his senior) and her husband, then with a family only recently arrived from Tōson's home area, the Yoshimuras. After much discussion his father reluctantly agreed to let Tōson learn English, and it was this step, taken at the age of twelve, that separated the son from the father's culture more irrevocably than had the physical journey to Tokyo. In 1887 Tōson entered the Meiji Gakuin (Meiji College), a liberal arts college newly founded by American and Scottish Presbyterians, and this signified another important step away from the past. The Meiji Gakuin had been chosen by Tōson's family because of its reputation for giving good instruction in English, but besides its secular, Western-style learning, the school dissemi-

---

[5] Tōson describes this journey in *Osanaki hi*, pp. 391-393.

nated an atmosphere of idealism and moral rigor that was typical of Christian-run higher schools in the 1880s. The teachers maintained high moral standards and demanded equally disciplined behavior from their students. Moreover, the fact that the students at the Meiji Gakuin were being trained to play their part in the future building up of the nation lent the school an atmosphere of idealistic patriotism. Yet the strict mood of self-discipline was attenuated by the intense spirit of Christian fellowship that was expressed regularly in the numerous social activities of the school.

Tōson apparently spent his first year at the Meiji Gakuin enjoying the wholesome and idealistic atmosphere, in particular the social life with his fellow students, both male and female. He enjoyed singing hymns with his friends and attending the weekly literary meetings held jointly with the girls from the affiliated Meiji Jogakkō (Meiji Girl's School). He apparently viewed the girls with a mixture of awe and passion for, in an autobiographical novel describing his years at the school, he wrote that "as he heard the youthful girl students reciting poetry and singing in English, he forgot what was around him. He felt as if a joyous happiness were waiting for him wherever he turned."[6] Influenced no doubt by the spirit of idealism and patriotism that informed the school, as well as by the atmosphere of freedom that dominated the 1880s due to the People's Rights movement, he cherished for a while the ideal of becoming a politician or a scientist. Yet probably the most important event that occurred during Tōson's first year at the Meiji Gakuin was his meeting with Kimura Yūji, one of the most outstanding Japanese Christians of the time. He lived for a short time as a boarder in this man's home and was baptized by him in June of 1888, at the age of sixteen. For many students at Christian-run schools in the 1880s, conversion to Christianity meant little more than an intellectual acceptance of its ideas or ethics, as studying English meant the acceptance of the need to acquire a practical skill that was impor-

---

[6] *Sakura no mi no juku-suru toki* (When the Cherries Ripen, 1918) *Zenshū*, 4: 258.

tant in the modern world of Meiji.[7] For Tōson, however, conversion was rather a voluntary acceptance of a certain atmosphere of free fellowship that was especially appealing to a boy away from his parents, of a spiritual, poetic mood induced by the daily singing of hymns, and above all, of the love and concern offered him by Kimura Yūji, a man whom Tōson later described as like a father.[8]

Tōson himself writes of the period after his baptism: "Since there were a lot of missionaries at our school I had many opportunities to hear about nature and religion. Because of this I was tormented by the Christian view of the world and the cosmos. From that time on, solemn, Puritanical religious ideas and wild, free, artistic ideas often fought with one another in my childish head."[9] This passage, written almost thirty years after the actual experiences, conveys little of the specific nature of the torment that Tōson underwent; it does indicate, however, that Tōson's conversion to Christianity had sparked internal conflicts and tensions. The specific incident that set off the conflicts seems to have been Tōson's platonic love for the dean of the Meiji Jogakkō, a woman five years his senior. Apparently late in 1888, a fellow student reprimanded Tōson for his allegedly improper conduct with this teacher—conduct which seems to have consisted of nothing more than a silent but impassioned adoration—and succeeded in plunging the youth into an abyss of guilt and self-hatred. The torment caused by this incident, coupled with his failure, at the end of his second year, of the entrance examinations to the University of Tokyo (and consequently the failure of any

[7] Mutsuro Sugii has coined the term *chokunyū-gata* ("pattern of straight entrance") to describe a conversion to Christianity that is merely an intellectual acceptance of Christianity as ideals or as an ethical system. See Yamamori, *Church Growth in Japan*, p. 57.

[8] In 1927, Tōson had a stone memorial tablet set up in Komoro, where he taught from 1899 to 1905 at a school run by Kimura. On it was a reference to Kimura as "our father." Itō Kazuo, *Shimazaki Tōson kenkyū*, Tokyo, 1969, p. 305.

[9] "Meiji Gakuin no gakusō" (The Meiji Gakuin), *Zenshū*, 14: 93.

hopes he might have had for a political career), effectively destroyed the image that Tōson had of himself. He became a virtual recluse for the remainder of his years at the Meiji Gakuin. It seems, then, that the encounter with Christian morality, in the form in which it existed at the Meiji Gakuin, was responsible for forcing Tōson to define himself—to be reborn not as a Christian, as he had been in the ritual of baptism, but as an individual.

The Calvinist atmosphere of the Meiji Gakuin, with its belief in the utter irreconcilability of good and evil, clearly accentuated the gravity of what was undoubtedly a minor offense. Consequently it must have seemed to the youthful Tōson that one could either be good or evil, and that since he was unable to be good, he must therefore be evil. For a seventeen-year-old boy living away from home and not intimate with anyone to whom he could have revealed his suffering, this judgment of his behavior, and of himself, must have seemed overwhelmingly final. Tōson's inability to confront and resolve the moral dilemma aroused by the condemnation of his peer caused him intense emotional suffering. The remonstrances to behave properly (i.e., to maintain his integrity, or "face" before the outside world) that had been the substance of his moral training at the hands of his father had not prepared him to deal with sin. They had told him only what he should do, not how to proceed when he had done something wrong. Tōson's sense of self at this time was still a childish one in which there was no division into good and evil; his idea of God was a figure of about fifty who combined the features of a "familiar teacher and an awesome father" and who possessed the "simplicity of Abraham and the solemnity of Moses."[10] He could no more approach this father-God to ask for forgiveness than he could his own father or Kimura Yūji. Furthermore, the Christ of the New Testament, whose role in becoming man was to reconcile the sinful, "fallen" man to God and thus to overcome the division of the world into good and evil, had no real religious significance for

---

[10] *Sakura no mi no juku-suru toki, Zenshū*, 4: 387.

Tōson, who considered Christ to be merely a poetic personality like Shakespeare or Goethe.[11] Nor could Tōson confess his sin and ask the Buddha Amida for forgiveness, for he had had no training in Buddhism.

Tōson's sin involved an internalized consciousness of having done evil that was far out of proportion to the actual offense. It is clear, then, that the importance of his "crime" was largely subjective. As the adolescent hero in Hermann Hesse's *Demian* (1919) confronted evil, with the result that his inner sense of self became stronger, so Tōson's confrontation of sin eventually ended in a greater consciousness of, and pride in, self. Yet for the time being his ego was not strong enough to encounter the inner world of sin and guilt. In order to lighten such a burden either insight or grace was needed, but Tōson was of a slow, long-suffering temperament and not inclined to self-analysis. While he waited, in a profound state of misery and self-disillusionment, for a stimulus from the outside to bring relief from his torment, he was comforted by his reading of English literature, especially the poetry of Wordsworth. However, grace of a more dramatic nature came in the form of a lecture Tōson heard at a Christian summer camp that he attended in the summer of 1890. Speaking on the subject of the differences between Greek and Christian ethics, the noted Christian philosopher Ōnishi Hajime argued that Greek morality referred completely to this world, and that the Greek idea of happiness was one of the human world alone. In contrast, the Christian idea of morality had introduced the idea of sin; but this idea had entered its ethical system because Christians felt inside themselves the need of escaping from the real world that oppressed them.[12]

---

[11] Sasabuchi notes that Tōson considered Christ as the "manifestation of the appearance of truth" rather than the son of God or the savior. Christ was a man of wisdom like Saigyō, Bashō, Dante, and Shakespeare, and the difference between Christ and these figures was merely one of degree. *Bungakkai to sono jidai*, 2: 835.

[12] This lecture is quoted in part in Sasabuchi, *Bungakkai*, 2: 824-825.

Tōson might have been able to conclude from this lecture that
sin, rather than a distressing burden, was the expression of a valid
desire of the individual to go beyond the world as given, and thus
was linked to positive ideals of freedom and growth. Instead,
Tōson saw his melancholy in a new way, as stemming from the
conflict between his desire as a Christian to leave behind the real
world, and his inability to do so. Thus, he thought that if only he
could somehow get beyond the "real world" of sexual feelings to
the "other world" of Christian purity (a world he could only
imagine as the pure, elegant atmosphere of his school), his problem would be solved and his melancholy would disappear. Tōson
had filled three notebooks with translations into Japanese of John
Morley's *English Men of Letters*, a collection of biographical and
critical essays on English writers of the eighteenth and nineteenth
centuries. When he returned home from the summer camp he
tore them up and burned them, hoping thereby to destroy in
himself any inclination toward the sensual world of literature. He
also tried to throw himself into an atmosphere of pure Christian
evangelism through intensive hymn singing and Bible reading.
Tōson's attempts to lead a pure life yielded him a needed relief
from the torture of seeing himself as evil, but the relief was only
temporary. Tōson had merely attempted to pretend that he was
still a child existing in a pure world of good; his torment was
bound to continue as long as he did not consciously acknowledge
the significance of his sexual self, and thus of evil.

Years later, Tōson described his tormented feelings of this period: "Why did God create such a strange world? Why did he
make things in it beautiful or, in particular, why did he make
ugly things? Why did he put hawks beside sparrows, wolves beside lambs, snakes beside frogs, weasels beside chickens? Why
did he doom even God's peaceful church to an eternal secret feud,
and why did he make the rich elders and poor deacons quarrel
with one another?"[13] Tōson's words imply that he was gradually
beginning to accept not only the duality inherent in life as a

[13] *Sakura no mi no juku-suru toki, Zenshū*, 4: 314.

whole, but the particular dualities in his own life as well. For a time he had hoped that by putting thoughts of sex and literature behind him he could escape from the torments of the real world, but as he saw the inevitability of that world, he took as his ideal a literary man who not only had not escaped the real world but had managed to exist in it without debilitating moral conflicts. This was the Romantic poet, Byron, of whom Tōson wrote:

'Do not commit adultery, do not violate a virgin, do not steal your brother's wife'—these and others were all commandments of the God Jahveh. This God could not possibly have approved of the life of Byron. When the English poet traveled to Italy, hadn't Venetian mothers of marriageable daughters closed their windows before this good-looking, debauched man? But hadn't Byron's poems, the poems of a man who had suffered many things, charmed him? What was this charm? Though his conduct was loathesome enough to pucker the faces of the pastors, how could one say that his art was not beautiful?—He couldn't help thinking such thoughts.[14]

Tōson knew that Byron's behavior was evil in terms of the Christian morality he had accepted up to that time—indeed, his disgust is evident in this passage. Yet he was strongly attracted to Byron's poetry, and his attraction to the poetry—which was, after all, the expression of the broad-minded geniality of the man—made him open up to the charm of Byron himself, in spite of his evil deeds. It appears that Tōson was slowly becoming aware of the possibility of an individualist morality that could include both good and evil and nevertheless be accepted by the world—not only tolerated but considered the high and worthwhile expression of a genial humaneness.

During his last two years at the Meiji Gakuin, Tōson was reading Wordsworth, Burns, Shakespeare, Matthew Arnold, Byron, and Milton in the original, and Goethe and Dante in English translation.[15] He headed one of the many literary groups at the

[14] Ibid., p. 314.

[15] For a discussion of Tōson's reading of Western writers at this time, see Sasabuchi, 2: 734-755.

school, and wrote his first stories and poems for this group. In fact, Tōson's independent reading and his efforts at writing were his most important educational experiences during these last years at the Meiji Gakuin. However, Tōson's writing at this point in his life was not done in conscious preparation for a career; rather, it was done in fulfillment of an intense inner need to define and express himself. Thus, when Iwamoto Yoshiharu, the director of the Meiji Gakuin, discouraged Tōson from writing what he considered effusive and self-serving literature, it became clear to Tōson that the Calvinist morality of the school was hostile not only to his sexuality but also to his basic desire for self-expression. Consequently, Wordsworth and Byron were at this point in his career not so much poetic models for Tōson as examples of men who, through their poetry, had created their own moral worlds and then existed in them, regardless of the opinions of a narrow moralism.

After Tōson graduated from the Meiji Gakuin in the spring of 1891, he worked in the store run by his foster parents, the Yoshimuras, for a summer, making the dull, hard work bearable by reading Hippolyte Taine's *History of English Literature* in the few spare moments during the day. Apparently his foster father intended eventually to make Tōson his partner in the business, and even cherished plans to have him marry his daughter, but Tōson was not interested in a future as a businessman. He already had experienced vague stirrings of an ambition to become a writer—at that time a vocation with a precarious future—and had appealed to Iwamoto Yoshiharu, his former principal and head of a literary magazine called *Jogaku Zasshi* (Magazine for the Education of Women), for work. While doing small translation jobs from English for the magazine, he began teaching classes in English literature at the Meiji Jogakkō, the girl's college affiliated with his former school, in the fall of 1892. His life at this point was still very much under the influence of the solemn, idealistic atmosphere of the Meiji Gakuin. Thus, an observer of Tōson and other graduates of the Meiji Gakuin who were teach-

EDUCATION 135

ing at the school noted that: "When the Meiji Gakuin graduates Togawa, Baba, and Shimazaki enter their classrooms, they first lay their books on the desk; then, after offering a solemn prayer, they begin their lectures."[16] Even Tōson's lectures showed the influence of his religious training, for one of his students wrote in her diary that Tōson used English literary works primarily to inculcate high moral standards in his students.[17] At this time he was still involved with the Presbyterian church, finding a refuge from his loneliness, as he had at school, in its varied social activities. Yet the most significant contact that Tōson had during this period of his life was that with Kitamura Tōkoku and the other graduates of the Meiji Gakuin who formed an intellectual circle under his leadership.

Tōson had first become acquainted with Tōkoku when he read the latter's essay, *Ensei shika to josei*, shortly after it appeared in late February of 1892 in *Jogaku Zasshi*. He remarked at the time that he was impressed that anyone could speak out his thoughts so boldly.[18] When he actually met Tōkoku in March or April of the same year he soon developed a feeling akin to reverence toward this man whom he considered his teacher. The lasting influence of Tōkoku on Tōson as a man and as a writer can be judged by looking at Tōson's poetry and novels, but it seems clear that Tōkoku's immediate influence on Tōson was to encourage the latter to make the break that he had already begun to make with past morality—both the Confucianism of his childhood and the narrow Presbyterian morality of his adolescence—and to find his own self and his own path in life. For example, in his novel *Haru*

[16] This comment is recorded in Sasabuchi, 2: 833.

[17] One remark from the diary of Satō Sukeko, the student with whom Tōson fell in love, presents Tōson as a teacher who saw it as his task to inculcate virtue in the future mothers of the Japanese nation. See Senuma, *Hyōden. Shimazaki Tōson*, p. 98, for excerpts from her diary.

[18] Quoted in Itō, *Shimazaki Tōson kenkyū*, p. 321. See Itō's interpretation of Tōkoku's significance for Tōson, on pp. 320-327. For another view of Tōkoku's relationship to Tōson see Odagiri Hideo, *Kitamura Tōkoku ron*, Tokyo, 1970, pp. 221-232.

(Spring, 1908), Tōson wrote that Tōkoku's struggle and death had stimulated himself and the others in the *Bungakkai* circle to "push forward to achieve that which each of us had decided to aspire to."[19] That he felt that Tōkoku had inspired him to achieve the goal of becoming a writer Tōson himself made clear years later when he wrote: "The first things I wrote were poems, and my steps were in the dark—but before I could put what was inside me into words I needed considerable courage and patience. What encouraged me was the experience at Sendai where I, through a little work, was able to secure my body and soul, and the death of Tōkoku, who deliberately became a springboard to the age that was to come."[20] Tōson's stay at Sendai came in 1896-1897, and Tōkoku's death in 1894, but the meaning of his remark becomes clear when one considers that in 1892 Tōson had just turned down an offer of a steady job running the Yoshimura store in order to risk his future in the uncertain profession of a writer. Tōkoku's example, as an older brother or father who lived the precarious life of a writer, and later his death as a sacrifice to the next generation, provided Tōson with a model of a person who lived a modern life according to individual goals, a model of courage and moral daring who would risk the future, and life itself, in order to define himself.

During the first period of his friendship with Tōkoku, and under the influence of his spiritual ideals, Tōson's attention was pulled away from the sexual torments that he had suffered intermittently since his second year at the Meiji Gakuin. He devoted himself enthusiastically to his work as a teacher and translator, and enjoyed the discussions with Tōkoku and the other members of his circle. Yet early in 1893, when he had been teaching at the girl's school scarcely five months, an event occurred which again threw Tōson completely off balance: he fell in love with one of his students, a girl named Satō Sukeko. Their love was a hopeless one from the start, for there was no possibility of Tōson's marrying

[19] *Haru* (Spring, 1908), *Zenshū*, 4: 178.
[20] *Sōshun* (Early Spring), cited in Itō, *Shimazaki Tōson kenkyū*, p. 327.

the girl, who was engaged to be married as soon as she graduated. Furthermore, Sukeko was from a wealthy family whereas Tōson was poor. Tōson's love for Sukeko was a true *amor de lonh* ("love from afar"), and its significance lay not in the object of love but in the subject—in Tōson's transformation through love.[21] For the incident with Sukeko, like the incident with the woman dean five years before, forced Tōson to redefine his position vis-à-vis Christian morality. Love for a woman once again placed him in a seemingly insoluble situation: one part of his self was convinced, following Tōkoku's ideal of *ren'ai*, that love between man and woman ought to be platonic; yet another part of him, which was equally strong, yearned for a sexual expression of this love. For a while Tōson continued to preach to his students of the virtues of chastity, but the hypocrisy of his situation soon overwhelmed him and he resigned from the school. While at a younger age Tōson had been able to deny his rebellion against the oppressive Calvinism of the school by escaping temporarily into a childish world of purity and self-denial, at the age of twenty-one it was no longer possible for him to deny the sexual aspect of his nature. His leaving behind the school (and the morality that was tormenting him) meant not that he was escaping from an impossible situation but rather that he was in active rebellion against that morality. It is probably true that Tōson had no way, at this point, of justifying his rebellion to himself; he merely acted out of the obscure conviction that it was necessary for his moral survival, and therefore valid, for him to leave the school.

It was Tōson's travels around Japan from January to November

---

[21] Tōson's youthful love for the unapproachable Sukeko had all the intensity, and the pain, of a first love. I use the expression *amor de lonh* to describe it—an expression from Jaufré Rudel's poem "Lanquan li jorn son loc en may" that characterizes his celebrated love for the distant countess of Tripoli—to suggest that the discovery by Tōson and his generation of spiritual love for woman was akin to that of the eleventh- and twelfth-century troubadours. See Frederick Goldin, *Lyrics of the Troubadours and Trouvères*, Garden City, 1973, pp. 100-107.

of 1893 that guaranteed him the independence and freedom from the school atmosphere, as well as the experience of life, that he needed to come to a consciousness of his own morality for the first time. Tōson traveled mainly between Tokyo and Kyoto, at times by train but often, like the religious pilgrims of the Middle Ages such as Saigyō (1118-1190), on foot. Tōson saw himself, imitating Saigyō and Bashō, as a *tabi-bito*, or spiritual traveler; as he took on the costume of the ascetic traveler, the sensual torment of the past months melted away. It was during this time that Tōson discovered his natural heritage, both visually and through his reading of Bashō's poems and prose writings on nature. Yet he also read from the Book of Romans, and was possibly inspired by Paul's message of a new life to be attained in Christ, a new life that was beyond the old law of sin.

In a situation of physical and moral freedom for the first time in years, Tōson was likely to have interpreted this new life in terms of his most immediate needs: as the liberation of the imprisoned sensual self. An important event in his new life of sensual freedom, then, was his brief affair, on his travels near Kyoto, with a friend of one of his Tokyo literary colleagues, a woman four years his senior named Hirose Yoshiko. Whatever else it may have meant to him, Tōson's passionate affair with this woman signified the completion of a struggle for self-affirmation that had begun when Tōson first fell in love at the age of sixteen. At that time the arousal of his feelings of love for the woman dean, followed by the abrupt condemnation of them by one of his peers, had resulted in Tōson's attempt to deny his sexuality altogether by fleeing backward in time to a childish existence that contained no passion. When he fell in love with Sukeko at the age of twenty he experienced an even more intense platonic love—Tōkoku's *ren'ai*—than he had at age sixteen, but his sexual longing was also more intense than it had been in his youth. Yet, as in his adolescence, the morality of the Meiji Gakuin forbade the very existence of such a longing. Tōson's flight from the Meiji Jogakkō in 1893, then, demonstrated his determination not to remain any longer in an atmosphere where he would be forced to see his sexuality as evil. Though he had to renounce *ren'ai* in his experience of sexual love, Tōson's love affair with Hirose Yoshiko had the positive effect of affirming and validating the sexuality that he had had to deny during his years as both student and teacher at the Meiji Gakuin.

Tōson apparently resisted an offer of marriage from Yoshiko, and returned to Tokyo to take up his career as a writer. Even before his *Wanderjahre* began he had written consistently for the *Jogaku Zasshi*, in 1892 translating Shakespeare's "Venus and Adonis" and one chapter of the Chinese novel *Hung Lou Meng* (Dream of the Red Chamber, ca. 1760). He had also published an essay on Wordsworth's "To the Cuckoo," a translation of a chapter from *The Tale of Genji*, and various biographical articles on famous Western figures. Finally, while he was away on his travels during the major part of 1893, Tōkoku and others had founded the magazine *Bungakkai*, and in it, in 1894, appeared his first major literary effort, a tragedy in six acts entitled *Biwa hōshi* (The Biwa Priest). The work was obviously inspired by Tōkoku's *Hōrai-kyoku*, published in 1891. In it Tōson wrote of the ghost of a Korean girl who falls hopelessly in love with a man unworthy of her, and an atmosphere of sadness and melancholy is provided by the narrator, a roving lute player who sees their love as reflecting the fateful ways of the universe. It is tempting to see in the hopeless love of the Korean maiden a reflection, albeit fancifully disguised, of Tōson's own hopeless love for Sukeko, and the mood of disillusionment and resignation that hovers over the work seems typical of Tōson's attitude toward life after the failure of his relationship with her.

The Birth of a Poet

While the years between 1888 and 1894 were years filled with conflict and tension and marked by depression, they were also years in which Tōson was gradually developing a view of life—

call it a morality—that would satisfy his particular needs. At this point I would like to review briefly the developments of these years, for it is important to understand how they laid the foundation for Tōson's first coherent vision of man, a vision which emerged in his poetry of the late 1890s. All in all, these crucial years saw Tōson move from a strict adherence to Christian morality as he had been taught it to a shocked confrontation with it, then, during his travels of 1893, toward an inquiry into traditional Japanese attitudes toward man and nature. The morality taught by the Meiji Gakuin, when tested in the incident of Tōson's encounter with the older woman in 1888, had proved to be rigid and suppressive of something that the adolescent Tōson would be likely to have seen as sexuality. In truth, it threatened Tōson's natural vitality, the spring of his life that welled up not only in sexuality but also in creativity. He knew he had to rid himself of the burden of this morality because it had divided him into two selves, one hating the other.

The worst thing about the reprimand Tōson received at the Meiji Gakuin was that it shattered his idea of himself as essentially innocent. For underneath the protective sheath of social morality there had existed in Tōson a soft, childlike self that resisted moral strictures: the unsocialized experiential self of the Naturalists. This self the native Shinto religion had seen as essentially innocent or "clean," "sin" being not a moral failing but an external blemish that could be washed away by purification. In pre-Meiji times an individual who had sinned stood at the mercy of patriarchal Conficianism, which, in the case of a samurai, demanded death as the only means of wiping away dishonor. At the opposite pole from Confucianism was matriarchal Shinto, which allowed the individual to return to a state of nature, i.e., innocence, through making an obeisance to nature in the form of purification by water. Submission to nature healed the rift in the unity of self and nature caused by sin, and the individual was magically restored to his original state of innocence. Tōson's Christian training had taught him only to condemn this self, and nature as well; there was no way, as far as he knew, to give it value. Yet as a Japanese Tōson had access to a native tradition that valued the self, seeing it as essentially innocent rather than as evil. Wishing to recover this essential innocence, Tōson turned away from the Christian God and toward the traditional Shinto God, Nature, for a solution to his moral and spiritual torment.[22]

It is significant that just at a time when he was most in need of a kind of grace that would remove his burden of sin, Tōson had an unusual experience in nature. It occurred just after the close of the summer camp in 1890, when he was about to return to Tokyo. He had walked alone to the foot of Mt. Gotenzan and was just recalling the many days of emotional turmoil he had recently undergone, as well as the walks in nature he had taken to soothe his troubled soul, when

> Suddenly something unexpectedly beautiful opened up before Sutekichi's (Tōson's) eyes. The color of the sky was already beginning to change. Never since his birth had he seen the beauty of the setting sun to such an extent. Wishing to share the miracle, Sutekichi ran to where his friend Suge was, but by the time he had fetched him and they stood on the top of the mountain, the color of the sky had changed. The sky was now scarlet like a sea of flame. A startlingly vast world that he had not been aware of until that day flashed before him. And he awoke to existence. As he and his friend retraced the lonely evening path to the dormitory, a feeling of indescribable happiness filled Sutekichi's breast.[23]

Tōson's first action after returning home from the camp had been to give up his literary efforts and devote himself to leading a pure

[22] Sasabuchi Tomoichi, one of the foremost interpreters of Tōson's relationship to Christianity, sees Tōson as having been involved in a dualistic battle between flesh and spirit since his late adolescence—a battle that was initiated by his conflict with Christian morality. Though Tōson acknowledged the priority of the spirit, he could not deny the reality of the flesh. Consequently his desire was not to be saved from the flesh but for a world in which it would be possible to unify flesh and spirit. This he found in traditional pantheism, which saw God, man, and nature as one. *Bungakkai to sono jidai*, 2: 827, 835.

[23] *Sakura no mi no juku-suru toki, Zenshū*, 4: 291.

life. Under the influence of the Christian moralism of the Meiji Gakuin, he still believed that "innocence" meant a life of consciously willed or even forced moral purity; he was only dimly aware at this point of the restorative powers of nature, and of the unconscious, life-giving vitality of his self. Yet, as is proved by his retelling of this incident years later, Tōson had had an intuition already in 1890 that true innocence would be restored to him not by a conscious decision to be innocent, but by a kind of grace that was typically Japanese: the healing of the soul through an experience of a unity of the vital self with nature.[24] Significantly, it was about this time also that Tōson looked to Byron as a man who, in spite of his many crimes, remained, like nature, essentially innocent.

After his graduation from the Meiji Gakuin in 1891, Tōson slowly gained distance from the harsh, dualistic Calvinist morality that had oppressed him. Correspondingly, he became more and more aware of the morality of his native Japanese tradition, and from this point on he interpreted Christian ideas that appealed to him in those terms. Paul's "new life" became for him a restoration or healing of his vital, sensual being, and took on as well the modernist implications of sensual freedom. During the ten or so months he spent traveling around his native land Tōson came in contact with nature, with his vital self, and with his sensuality. Nature in the form of mountains, rivers, and flowers became visible and tangible, divine reality to him. As he read the nature *haiku* of Bashō, the Japanese literary past, the maternal heritage that had been kept from him throughout his years of Christian education, now became his. Tōson's rediscovery of nature had originally been stimulated by his reading of Words-

[24] In traditional Japanese religion there was an attitude that stressed harmony rather than duality, innocence rather than sin—an attitude that derived from the indigenous Japanese religion, Shinto, but was influenced by Buddhism in the direction of pantheism. Such an attitude informed the poems of Saigyō and Bashō (both of whom were Buddhist monks with a strong sensitivity to the divinity of nature). See Sasabuchi, 2: 838.

worth's poems years before, at the Meiji Gakuin. The poems he began to write in the early 1890s showed the influence of Wordsworth, and Shakespeare as well. In fact, Tōson might have had in mind the passage in *As You Like It* where Shakespeare depicts his characters experiencing pastoral happiness in the Forest of Arden, when he wrote the following lines:

Ware wa iwa ni nemuri	I'll sleep on a rock,
Kusa ni fushi	I'll lie down on the grass,
Mizudori o tomo to shite	I'll lower my fishing rod
Tsuri o taruru nomi	with the water-bird, my friend.
Hitotsu no kusa ni sekkyō ari	In one blade of grass there can be a sermon,
Hitotsu no iwa ni mo sambika arubeshi.	In one rock a hymn![25]

Yet in other poems written during these years Tōson began to speak of nature with an attitude of reverence that a Christian, especially a Presbyterian missionary teaching at the Meiji Gakuin, would have reserved for God alone. For Tōson, divinity increasingly became a vital force that coursed through all things, as his ancestors, the Japanese poets Saigyō and Bashō, had depicted it.[26]

[25] These lines are from Tōson's confessional prose poem, *Aien* (A Sad Fate, 1894). Quoted in Senuma, *Hyōden. Shimazaki Tōson*, p. 111. The specific lines in *As You Like It* that he alluded to in the last two lines of the quoted passage are: "And this our life, exempt from public haunt, / Finds tongues in trees, books in the running brooks, / Sermons in stones, and good in everything" (Act II, Scene i, ll. 15-17).

[26] William R. LaFleur argues convincingly that Buddhism, when it came to Japan, was forced to accommodate itself to the indigenous religion of Shinto, which saw God (*kami*) in all things, by giving nature a higher soteric value than it had had in either India or China. According to LaFleur, Saigyō, the great nature poet of the Middle Ages, was the poet responsible for validating nature as the divine, in his numerous poems. It is significant, then, that Tōson admired Saigyō, and his descendant, Bashō, in his formative period. See "Saigyō and the Buddhist Value of Nature," *History of Religions* 13, no. 2 (November 1973): 93-128 and vol. 13, no. 3 (February 1974): 227-248.

Tōson returned from his travels in late 1893 with a strengthened sense of self, a deeper knowledge of his Japanese past, and the beginnings of an awareness of his place in the world of nature. He was immediately beset by difficulties that severely tested this new sense of self, for Tōson found himself faced with the responsibility of supporting his family, who had now moved to Tokyo from Magome. He continued to earn small amounts of money for a while by writing and translating for *Bungakkai* but when these small sums proved insufficient, he was forced, in the spring of 1894, to ask for his old job at the Meiji Jogakkō. There he was teaching when he heard the news of Tōkoku's suicide in May of 1894. As if this was not enough, in the same month Tōson's eldest brother, Hideo, was sentenced to prison for fraud in connection with a business deal he had undertaken in order to restore the family fortunes.[27] Tōkoku's suicide removed from his side not only a friend but also a person who had inspired Tōson to live his life according to his own inner morality. The arrival of his family from the country, and the subsequent imprisonment of Hideo, meant that Tōson would have to become the chief means of support for the family, and this development threatened the career and life goals he had set for himself. Tōson was still in a state of emotional shock when he learned, the following summer, that his former love, Sukeko, now married after her graduation from the Meiji Jogakkō, had died in pregnancy. Like Tōkoku's death, the death of his first love had no practical effects on his prospects; rather it signified the disappearance of an ideal without which life for a time seemed unbearable. What saved Tōson from despair during this period was his reading of Rousseau's *Confessions* in August of 1894.

The Japanese writers who created the first modern literature in the Meiji period typically discovered themselves as individuals

[27] Tōson's eldest brother, Hideo, became involved in four schemes to restore the family fortune between the late 1880s and the early years of the twentieth century. An honest but gullible person, he was twice imprisoned when his partners implicated him in fraudulent activities.

through their reading of Western literature. Futabatei had discovered in the novels of Turgenev, but also of Dostoevsky and Goncharov, the kind of self he was seeking to portray. In a very real sense, he could not have done it had he not had as a model a novel that was the reflection of a diffuse, rich personality, for there was no such novel of personality or individuality in earlier Japanese literature. Similarly, in an essay entitled "Rūsō no *'Zange'*-chū ni miidashitaru jiko" (The Self That I Discovered in Rousseau's *Confessions*, 1909), Tōson wrote, looking back at his feelings in 1894: "That period was a time of great difficulty for me, and I was pessimistic. I got hold of Rousseau's book by chance, and as I was reading it enthusiastically, I had the feeling that my self (*jibun*), an entity of which I had been unaware up to that time, was being drawn out."[28] Tōson may have meant by this that as he read Rousseau's pages, which were permeated by the aura of Rousseau's personality, he was jolted into an awareness of his own self that existed, like Rousseau's, in the past and in the present, in the form of experiences, memories, and reflections. At the same time, the sheer number of pages devoted to the exploration and remembrance of the self must have convinced Tōson of the reality and validity of Rousseau's life—and, insofar as he found his self in those pages, of his own.

As Tōson was evolving a view of life based on the unity of man with nature in the late 1880s and early 1890s, Byron had been an important inspiration, for Byron's life, like nature itself, was one that transcended an ordinary, patriarchal morality based on principles of duality. Above all, Byron presented an example of a modern kind of affirmation of self at the most vital levels of sensuality and creativity: a youthful Dionysian model of self-affirmation that meant more to Tōson at this point in his life than Tōkoku's Apollonian models of Dante, Goethe, and Bashō. For Tōson was seeing nature more and more the way the Naturalist movement would see it after 1900: as a vital principle of life and

[28] *Zenshū*, 14: 14.

the free expression of sensuality. Thus, when he wrote that Rousseau's *Confessions* taught him to see nature directly, he probably meant that Rousseau taught him to see his life as the expression of vital energies that, though labeled good or evil by Christian morality as he knew it, were nevertheless valid. In this sense Rousseau's significance to Tōson was comparable to that of Byron at an earlier period.

In the period of his life when he was coming under the influence of Tōkoku's grand ideals of freedom on the metaphysical level, Tōson was attracted to Byron's Faustian daring, as exemplified by his *Manfred*. Now, faced with daily threats not only to his image of himself but also to his expression of self in his chosen vocation, Tōson was attracted to Rousseau's more practical heroism: "Reading Rousseau's *Confessions* I didn't have the feeling that I was reading the biography of a so-called swashbuckling hero (*eiyūgōketsu*). His *Confessions* are, in the last analysis, the record of the life of a weak human being who fails and becomes discouraged, just like us. More than any other great man, he gives us the feeling that he is our uncle, and close to us. His life can be seen as a self-discipline that we can attain to."[29] The image of Rousseau as a model of moral self-discipline would doubtless have surprised critics of Rousseau's libertinism such as Irving Babbitt. Yet it is precisely Rousseau's steady scrutiny of himself in all his weaknesses and at times of discouragement that Tōson sees as essentially moral in its motivation, that he sees as something modern. Moreover, Tōson praises this stance in preference to the life of the *eiyūgōketsu*, a hero of popular fiction who proves himself in adventure after fantastic adventure but who lacks any inner life. Rousseau seemed worthy of respect to Tōson because he lived according to his inner needs, and suffered from his own disappointments. Thus, it was the informal, weak Rousseau of the *Confessions* rather than the famous author of the *Contrat social* that became the inspiration for Tōson. Indeed, this fact is

[29] Ibid., p. 15.

an indication that for him, as well as for Futabatei, the inner man had replaced the exalted and distant hero as the culture hero of modern literature, much as the Werther or René type had replaced the idealized romance heroes of the medieval and Renaissance West.[30]

In Europe Rousseau's influence had rested on his frankness in exposing his deeds and thoughts to the public, even if the *Confessions* were only published posthumously. In Japan the *Confessions* made a deep impression on Japanese for the same reason, for a traditional posture of reticence, accompanied by feelings of shame, about baring one's self in public continued to dominate the culture. Formerly a writer spoke only as a representative of a social body or a literary or philosophical tradition, not as a representative of himself. Thus, Tōson doubtless admired Rousseau's frankness, but he admired his self-pride as well, for behind the pride in self he saw demonstrated in Rousseau's confessions of his intimate experiences, he detected what he thought was Rousseau's conviction that he was essentially innocent. Indeed, the Rousseau of the *Confessions* frequently insists on the essential innocence of his soul that will outweigh any evil he may commit and that, as he expresses it in the introduction, will ultimately support him at Judgment Day. Yet Rousseau's insistence that he is innocent in spite of what he has done betrays a need to defend himself not only against the criticisms of the external morality of the Calvinist church but also against his own internalized feelings of self-blame and even self-hatred.[31] Tōson was himself in a similar situation vis-à-vis Confucian morality and the Calvinist morality of the Meiji Gakuin, and it is possible that he found Rous-

---

[30] Taine had divided Western culture into eras, each with its *personnage régnant*: "in Greece, the naked young nobleman who was accomplished in every athletic skill; in the Middle Ages, the ecstatic monk and the lovelorn knight; in the seventeenth century, the perfect courtier; in our day, a Faust or Werther, insatiable and sad." *Philosophie de l'art*, p. 64.

[31] This idea has been expressed by Jean Starobinski in his essay on Rousseau in *L'oeil vivant*, Paris, 1961, pp. 97-104.

seau's tone of self-defense, with its underlying guilt feelings, particularly sympathetic for that reason.

The ideal of independence, which rested on respect of the culture for the individual as well as on the individual's respect for himself, was not yet realized in Japanese society as a whole, nor even in the society within a society of Western-educated intellectuals. Tōson, then, like others of his elite group, continually came up against the restrictions on individual development posed first of all by the family, then by the morality of self-submission enforced by the Meiji government. Rousseau was valuable as a model for Tōson because he had found a way of standing before the world in his essential nature or, as Tōkoku would have said, of "manifesting his inner *kokoro*." This way was confession. It has been suggested that Rousseau unconsciously used confession as a means of gaining a needed source of punishment for his "sin" of acting according to a morality that was not commonly accepted.[32] For Tōson, who had early in his adult life conceived of sin without any idea of forgiveness, the idea of confession to a public could have been attractive because it was a way of revealing actions and feelings about which he was ambivalent. It is possible that as Tōson increasingly defined himself, often in opposition to traditional morality and the institutions that maintained it, he developed guilt feelings over his betrayal of both the community and its commonly agreed upon morality. The idea of confession to the public probably appealed to Tōson, then, because it offered him an opportunity to escape from his solitariness as well as an opportunity to reestablish unity with that humanity of the past from which his "sin" of self-definition had separated him. As will become clear in *Hakai* and *Shinsei*, the only two confessional novels that Tōson wrote, public confession exposed him to a purgative judgment that made it possible for him to begin to live all over again, in a new state of innocence. Thus, confession became

[32] Eugene Goodheart, *The Cult of the Ego*, Chicago, 1968, pp. 22-23.

the internal grace provided by the vital self that restored Tōson to unity with nature and with his essential innocence.[33]

Tōson's fortunes suddenly changed for the better in September of 1896 when he was offered an appointment as teacher of Japanese composition at a Christian-founded secondary school in the city of Sendai in Northern Japan. This job, which he acquired through the efforts of his former teacher and pastor, Kimura Yūji, guaranteed Tōson enough income to contribute to the support of his family. At the same time it enabled him to gain distance from the family and the personal sorrows that engulfed him. Perhaps most importantly, it brought him an opportunity to define himself in fresh surroundings, to build a new life on his own. Tōson read widely in the school library, concentrating especially on the poems of Goethe and Heine, and began to write a series of poems that were later gathered into a collection and published in 1897 under the title *Wakana-shū* (Collection of Young Shoots). Considered by many critics to be the first successful collection of modern-style poetry in Japanese, *Wakana-shū* spoke for the feelings of a whole generation of Meiji youths intoxicated by the ideal of self-expression. Yet the title has a personal significance: traditionally young shoots were the first green plants eaten after a winter diet of preserved vegetables, and their appearance in early spring thus implies a transition to the vitality of spring after the hardships and deprivations of winter. Tōson used this image to express the hope for the future that had arisen in him as

---

[33] Japanese Buddhism provided its adherents with various ways of gaining spiritual peace and relief from their sins through confession. For a discussion of such rituals see Heinrich Dumoulin, "The Consciousness of Guilt and the Practice of Confession in Japanese Buddhism," in *Studies in Mysticism and Religion Presented to Gershom G. Scholem*, Jerusalem, 1967. Tōson was not a Buddhist, though he might have had some familiarity with such practices of confession. His idea of confession was more likely a combination of Rousseau's public self-revelation through words and the traditional Shinto private and wordless ritual of purification of self through the experience of unity with nature.

he became able to express himself successfully in poetry after a
long "winter" of frustration.

The influence of Rousseau, and of the opportunity to live his
own life in Sendai, is clearly visible in the confidence with which
Tōson was able, in *Wakana-shū*, to confess his emotional sufferings before an unknown public. Yet Tōson was ambivalent about
confession at first, for he began the collection with five poems
using a female persona, as if he lacked the confidence to express
himself directly. In these poems women symbolized Tōson's
highest and most extreme aspiration to freedom of self-expression; their free acts became symbols of that which was not permitted to a man, self-expression for Tōson being an ideal that
only in the most extreme situations could be translated into reality. However, most of the other poems in the collection are written in a male persona, and some of them seem to be autobiographical. For example, the poem entitled *Betsuri* (Parting), as
the headnote indicates, is spoken by a man who climbs a mountain to watch the house of his lover, a married woman, from afar.
Here Tōson seems to be writing of his own unhappy love for an
unattainable married woman—possibly his student Sukeko. In
the second and third stanzas the man says:

Kiyoki koi to ya katashigai	Rather than yearning alone
Ware nomi mono o omou yori	In a pure, one-sided love,
Koi wa afurete nigoru to mo	I would like to overwhelm and
Kimi ni namida o kakemashi o	muddy you with my love,
	And drench you with my tears.
Hitozuma kouru kanashisa o	If only you had pity on me
Kimi ga nasake ni shirimoseba	Loving a married woman—
Semete wa ware o	I would be happy if you
tsumibito to	at least
Yobitamau koso ureshikere	Called me a sinner.[34]

The narrator is clearly suffering from the torment of an unrecipro-
cated love, for apparently the woman is either unaware of his love

[34] *Zenshū*, 2: 81-82.

or indifferent to the violence of it. The man wishes to express this violence in order to make the woman acknowledge it as valid and to gain her compassion. Her ignorance, or her impassivity in the face of his passion, frustrates him, and his love festers fatefully inside of him. Not a great work, the poem is interesting because it suggests that as soon as Tōson became aware, through an experience that tempered his idealism about love, of the limits to individual desire and of the sorrow that results from this awareness, he gave up the idealized and aesthetic female persona of his first poems. Yet his use of a male persona shows the influence also of the poets suffering in love as depicted in early poems of Goethe and Heine, as well as the figure of Rousseau suffering in love that occurs often in his *Confessions*. The poem *Betsuri*, unskillful though it is, already projects the mature personality of Tōson in its evocation of brooding, tormented feelings that, frustrated in life, seek expression in confession.

In *Nōfu* (The Farmer), a poem of some eight hundred lines that he published in his collection *Natsukusa* (Summer Grasses, 1898), Tōson continued his exploration of that which, through his experience of suffering in love and his reading of Western poets, he had learned to see as the male world of suffering in love. In the poem the farmer, in love with a girl in his village, goes reluctantly off to war, only to find, on his return, that the girl has died. In the climactic section of the poem entitled "Shin'ya" (Midnight), the farmer, overcome by his sorrow, expresses the desire to leave behind his existence by becoming a wanderer:

Toki ni wa oya mo harakara mo
Ie mo takara mo sutehatete
Yo no azakeri to mi no haji o
Omou itoma no araba koso
Sugari todomuru mono araba
Keotosu made mo yaburiide
Yukue mo shirazu kurokumo
    no
Kaze ni midarete mayou goto

Sometimes I wish to leave behind
My parents, my brothers and
    sisters, my home, and my
    possessions,
Without caring for the world's
    scorn and my own shame.
Breaking out even if I have to kick
    down what holds me back,
I want to be a black cloud that

Mata wa izayou ōbune no
Umi ni nagarete otsuru goto
Mata wa aki naku karigane no
Hitori misora ni toberu goto
Mi wa yorube naku uraburete
Michi naki nobe ni wakeirite
Aruwa mi ni sou hikari naku
Tōki urabe ni samayoite
Shiru hito mo naki hanagusa ni
Umore haten to omou nari

Wanders drifting on the wind,
   not knowing its destination,
Or a ship that drifts on the sea,
Or a wailing goose flying alone in
   the wide sky.
Ragged and friendless I'll make
   my way through the pathless
   fields,
Or, wandering to a distant shore
   with nothing to light my way,
I'll die, burying myself,
   unnoticed, beneath the
   flowers.[35]

This stanza is followed by one in which the farmer dreams of gaining solace from his sorrow by becoming a monk, and another in which he dreams of being reunited with his sweetheart in the dark world of death. The interest of the section lies in the variation of the hero's sentiments: first sorrow creates anger and a desire for independence, but this independence ends in world-weariness and a desire for death. Then the farmer wishes to become a monk, and, finally, he desires to be reunited with his love after death. Tōson's hero seems to waver between a Western mood of anger at his fate and an Eastern mood of world-weariness, referring to Tōkoku's differentiation between a Western life-loving and an Eastern life-hating mentality. In part he reminds one of the solitary Romantic wanderer who cannot be happy in society or in love, and is most himself in a state of aloneness in nature—Chateaubriand's René, Byron's Childe Harold, the hero of Schubert's song-cycle Die Winterreise, and, of course, Rousseau. Yet, as the later two stanzas imply, he is also the traditional Japanese tabi-bito ("wanderer") in the vein of Saigyō and Bashō who forsakes the world to find enlightenment in nature, and the traditional lover of the Tokugawa period who finds happiness with his love only in death.

[35] Ibid., p. 262.

Tōson's tendency to write poetry that was both dramatic and narrative was already noticeable in his first published work, *Biwa hōshi*, a lengthy drama in verse; even in the five poems on women that begin *Wakana-shū* the heroines speak in dramatic fashion, as if to an audience, and their words imply, if they do not actually tell, a story. In *Nōfu* Tōson continues these two tendencies: the poem is arranged in dramatic scenes, and the characters speak as if to an audience. Furthermore, the poem is a narrative that, besides the farmer's story, tells the stories of several other people in the village. In *Nōfu*, then, Tōson was already experimenting with a long form in which to delineate indirectly his feelings and experiences as well as events outside himself, for the poem transcends the purely subjective focus of lyric poetry. Confession occurs in the poem in a way that also foreshadows Tōson's later works. Tōson admired Rousseau's avuncular, intimate tone as he spoke of his feelings and experiences in the *Confessions*—yet his use of generalizing images such as the cloud, the ship, and the goose in the quoted passage tends toward epic distance rather than avuncular intimacy. In another passage the farmer says:

Nani o kokoro no hashira to shi	What shall I make the support of
Nani o wagami no yado to sen	my heart, what my shelter?
Shinobu to suredo yo no tsuki	I try to bear (my anguish), but
no	When I see the shadow of the
Sora yuku kage o miru toki wa	moon
Yorozu no utsuru kokochi shite	That passes in the sky,
Namida nagarete todomarazu	My feelings are reflected in it a
	thousandfold
	And I cannot hold back my
	tears.[36]

Here the manner of describing emotional torment is again distant rather than intimate, revealing Tōson's innate reserve as a person brought up under Confucian morality.

At the end of the poem the farmer, after lamenting his sorrow

[36] Ibid., p. 261.

for several stanzas, suddenly hears the crow of a cock announcing the coming of a new day. Immediately his sorrow falls from him and his inner vitality, which was dammed up by grief, begins to flow again:

Ima wa midori no ki no kage ni	Now in the shade of the green
Ka no chie no ha no oishigeri	trees
Ikeru ushio wa nagarekite	The rich leaves are luxuriant;
Yūbe no yume o araitsutsu	While living currents begin to
Ugokeru mushi wa su o idete	flow
Kusa no shigemi ni haimeguri	And wash away the dreams of last
Chikara afururu sugata koso	night,
Ge ni konogoro no natsu nare	Insects stir and leave their nests,
ya	Crawling about in the thick
	grass—
	A sight overflowing with vitality!
	These are truly the days of
	summer![37]

Tōson's technique here is to relive poetically, without analyzing them, the painful feelings and experiences connected with a certain incident. Eventually the hero's torment builds up to a natural breaking point, when under the influence of a natural phenomenon (the crowing of the cock) the emotional tension is suddenly dispersed and life or vitality, seen in its broadest dimension as human and natural energy, rises and flows freely again. As he had used spring as the vitality that replaced the death of winter in *Wakana-shū*, here Tōson relies on summer and daylight, the rebirth of life and the senses, to symbolize the yielding of dry emotions to life.

It is likely that a combination of his reading of Western Romantic poetry and his awareness of his own native tradition's attitudes toward nature influenced Tōson, already from the time of his experience at the summer camp in 1890, to see the achievement of self-awareness, or spiritual rebirth, as a kind of grace worked by nature. By the time he wrote *Nōfu*, then, Tōson

[37] Ibid., p. 269.

was already evolving a myth of human existence that, basing itself on experiences of his youth and mediated both by traditional
Japanese religious views of man and by the writings of Paul,
saw human suffering as an awareness thrust upon man by life. According to this myth, contradictions such as that between spirit
and flesh (or what traditional morality labels sin) are inevitable
and must be endured, but suffering is relieved finally, and
miraculously, by a recovery of new life, or of the season and spirit
of youth.

Thus, the farmer, in *Nōfu*, innocent and whole at the beginning of the poem, is separated from his true self by his experience
of sorrow at losing his love. However, after he has endured his
grief for the time natural to him, as the day breaks, the nature
external to him but linked to his inner self through its divine
vitality suddenly endows him with a new life. In *Nōfu* Tōson
evolved a plot pattern that he was to use in his first novel, *Hakai*,
eight years later. Not only *Hakai* but also *Shinsei*, written in
1918-1919, is related to his period as a Romantic poet, for these
novels can be seen, in the context of *Nōfu*, as expanded poetic
statements that, like *Nōfu*, tell of the hero's loss of innocence, his
suffering, and his emergence, with the help of nature, into a new
life. The act of confession that is the equivalent of innocence-
restoring grace is here only latent in the lyric form of the poem. It
is in his two confessional novels that Tōson makes confession into
a device that enables his hero to take direct moral responsibility
for his selfhood.

CHAPTER SIX

Hakai (Breaking the Commandment): A Novel of the Inner Life

In 1904 Tōson's collected poems (*Tōson shishū*) appeared, and in a famous preface to the work Tōson discussed the meaning of his poetry in the context of the late 1890s. He wrote that he saw his poems as typical of a period that had seen the awakening of youthful imagination; it was a time when youths opened up a new life with the new words of their poems, and when youths like himself spoke of their "sorrows and anxieties" in their poems. In fact, Tōson justified the expression of his own youthful torments and joys in terms that show the influence of Rousseau's *Confessions*: "If one thinks a thing, one should say it—one should say it without holding back."[1] Yet even as he wrote these words Tōson was looking at his poetry as a thing of the past, for after the publication of *Rakubaishū* (Collection of Fallen Plums) in 1901, he wrote no more poetry. Between the years 1899 and 1906 Tōson attempted to evolve a new form of self-expression that would treat the individual not only in the limited lyrical world of his emotions and experiences but also in his relation to the world at large. In a series of experiments in a form of prose sketch that left no room for what he had come to see as the naive confessionalism of his youth, Tōson explored the relationship between man and nature, gradually evolving a human-centered, religious view of man as basically himself in nature rather than in the world of society. During these same years, he continued his own struggle for self-definition, as he began to write a work that would describe his new ideal of the individual. The novel that emerged from this period of struggle in 1906, *Hakai* (Breaking the Command-

---

[1] *Tōson shishū, Zenshū*, 2: 3.

ment), was for Tōson, like *Wakana-shū*, both a personal victory of self-expression and a mature statement on his views of the individual and his inner life.

Toward a New Vision of the Individual

In July of 1897 Tōson resigned from his teaching position in Sendai and returned to Tokyo, where he at first took up residence with the family of his brother Hideo. Tōson was now twenty-five years old, the author of numerous essays and of the collection of lyrical poems (*Wakana-shū*) that was soon to be published. At this point in his life, his first literary success achieved, Tōson drifted for a year, taking piano lessons at a music school and reading widely with no particular literary purpose. He had a brief affair with one of the teachers at the music school, Tachibana Itoe, and contact with her was to last for several years. Tōson's future took another important turn in April of 1899 when he was offered, again under the auspices of his former teacher, Kimura Yūji, a job teaching Japanese and English at a school run by Kimura in Komoro, a town of eight or nine thousand in the Japanese Alps about one hundred miles northwest of Tokyo. Before leaving for Komoro, Tōson married Hata Fuyuko, a recent graduate of Meiji Jogakkō and daughter of a wealthy fish-net merchant from Hokkaido. When they arrived in Komoro, the couple moved into a small thatched house on the edge of the Komoro pleasure quarter, where they rented adjacent land and grew vegetables to supplement Tōson's meager earnings.[2] Though his life in Komoro was a constant struggle for physical and moral survival, Tōson seemed to be happy to be back in the mountains—they not only reminded him of his youth in Magome, but also symbolized a return to the youthful selfhood that he idealized increasingly as he grew further and further away from it. As the

---

[2] For a detailed description of all aspects of Tōson's life in Komoro see Hayashi Isamu, *Komoru naru kojō no hotori: Shimazaki Tōson to Komoro*, Komoro, 1967.

year in Sendai, a provincial city far from urban Tokyo, had provided him with the isolation, the peace, and the confidence in his
selfhood to bring forth his first good poems, now the life in
Komoro gave him the discipline and the challenge necessary to
launch his next important literary effort. He stayed in Komoro
for six years, only returning to Tokyo when, having almost completed his first novel, he felt ready to emerge a second time in the
literary world.

Already in *Nōfu* Tōson had turned away from the Rousseauian
stance of direct and lengthy confession that had inspired him in
Wakana-shū, allowing the farmer to express his feelings only in
the objectified world of a dramatic narrative. Then, as Tōson
neared thirty, toward the end of the century, he probably felt he
was past the age when he could rely on a persona of direct confession. In addition, Tōson was doubtless influenced by the change
in the literary world around the turn of the century toward realism, toward a search for a more objective truth than a confession
of feeling would permit. Thus, after a period when he enthusiastically trusted in the truth that ensued from direct confession of
feeling, Tōson began to see this truth as too subjective and as ultimately limited and superficial. It is not that he lost the desire to
depict his experiences. Rather, putting the self temporarily in the
background, he searched for a truth that went beyond the limits
of his subjectivity. In his youth he had encountered a writer who
had described his experiences but, instead of putting his self in
the forefront, had succeeded in universalizing and poeticizing his
experiences. Significantly, this was a writer of Tōson's own native
tradition, the *haiku* poet Bashō, and Tōson's turning to him at
this point in his life demonstrates that he saw the modern self as
developing not only out of contact with the West but also out of a
long tradition of self-cultivation in Japan.

Tōson wrote later that what had impressed him as he studied
Bashō during his years in Komoro, and even earlier, was that
Bashō had "created a pattern for his own life, he had achieved the

goal of making his life art."[3] Tōson probably meant that Bashō
had succeeded in subduing his naive, confessing self, and in dis-
tilling the essence of his experiences, his travels, his moments of
illumination, and his feelings about life in concise travel diaries
and poems. In other words, Bashō had attained a kind of objectivity in dealing with the self that Tōson greatly admired at this
point in his career as a writer. In the last of the nine pieces in his
collection *Hitohabune* (Little Leaf Boat, 1898), Tōson had tried
his hand at a diarylike prose form that was obviously modeled
after Bashō's travel diaries. Here he concentrated on making the
experiences he wrote about universal, as if they could have happened to anyone; he used "I," but only as a persona that had
merged with that of the traveler, as in Bashō's diaries:

The clear Hirose River flows along the outskirts of Sendai. On the
riverbank, where autumn is reflected morning and evening in the
deep current of the river, is an inn and rustic teahouse known as the
Ikkentei. Having explored the red leaves, we climbed to an eight-
mat room on the second floor of this inn to rest our feet. We were
both at ease with one another where an occasional sake was concerned, so we said to one another: "Make yourself comfortable" and
"Cross your legs." Though he didn't seem to be the type, my friend
got drunk after two or three cups of sake from the capital. I say "sake
from the capital," but it was really local sake—it was the color of tea.
While my friend lay stretched out, giving off an odor of sake, I leaned
against the railing watching autumn on the river.[4]

[3] "Bashō no isshō" (Life of Bashō, 1913), *Zenshū*, 14: 123. For a discussion of
the influence of Bashō on Tōson see also Yoshida Seiichi, *Gendai bungaku to
koten*, Tokyo, 1962, pp. 43-59.

[4] *Kisotani nikki* (Diary of the Kiso River Valley), *Zenshū*, 2: 175. Tōson's passage may be an allusion to Bashō's travel diary *Sarashina kikō* (A Visit to
Sarashina, 1688), in which Bashō, on a trip to view the autumn moon, stays
overnight in a rustic lodging. He and his companions view the moon, drinking
sake out of rough, large cups that seem to Bashō to typify the charm of the
country as opposed to the city. For a translation see Bashō, *The Narrow Road to*

There follows a description of sounds and sights, and the passage ends with the "I" returning home and finding a telegram from Tokyo that informs him that his mother has just fallen sick. This was the telegram that, in real life, had been sent to Tōson in 1896 to announce that his mother had fallen ill. Aside from a few such places where autobiography intrudes, the twenty-or-so-page work flows like a Bashō travel diary: the traveler goes to a place, experiences things there, and narrates what he saw and experienced in a detached and laconic manner. The things observed are distinctly in the foreground. No subjective "I" unifies them into a sentimental picture, and the last line of the quoted passage, which reads like the last line of a *haiku* in its evocation of the mood of autumn, artistically completes the generalized picture the author has sketched.

In 1900 and 1901, while he was teaching at Komoro, Tōson continued his efforts to evolve a type of prose that would enable him to describe his experiences more objectively. In his free time he wandered about the town of Komoro and the surrounding countryside, observing and conversing with people at their work. He also paid close attention to the fluctuations of natural phenomena, to which his reading of Ruskin's essays on clouds (in his *Modern Painters*) had made him more attentive. He took walks frequently with two artist friends, Maruyama Banka and Miyake Katsumi, carrying a sketch book in which he made careful notations that he later converted into longer prose sketches. For Tōson was taking part in the literary exercise of *shasei* ("sketching from life") that was an important development around the turn of the century. *Shaseibun*, or pieces sketched from life, were short, *haiku*-like prose pieces that continued the *haiku*'s interest in natural phenomena but whose technique of observation was derived not from the Neo-Confucian investigation of things but from Western science and Western Impressionist painting. Signifi-

---

the North and Other Travel Sketches, trans. Nobuyuki Yuasa, Baltimore, 1966, pp. 91-95.

cantly, the *shasei* movement developed under the influence of the *haiku* poet Masaoka Shiki (1867-1903).[5] In 1897 Shiki had written an essay, *Haijin Buson* (The Haiku Poet Buson), which, forecasting the rage for Western scientific objectivity that dominated the early 1900s, attacked the vagueness and subjectivity of Bashō, until then considered the greatest *haiku* poet, and praised the objectivity of the *haiku* of Yosa Buson (1715-1783). Shiki favored a purely objective style that is exemplified by this *haiku* of his: "Tsuki ichi-rin / hoshi mukazu sora / midori kana" ("One full moon, stars numberless, the sky dark green"). Here the things are described with little sense of their relationship to the observer. There is a quiet coldness hovering about the images, and the emphasis on numbers ("one," "numberless") and color ("dark green") gives an acute sense of the particular. Shiki's *haiku* clearly rests upon a scientific view of the universe that holds that the world of nature exists separate from man, that there is no God or divine harmony uniting man and nature, and that all phenomena are of equal value in that they are all capable of being observed through the camera of the eye.

A *haiku* by Bashō shows quite a different world view: "Hito-ie ni / yujō mo netari / tsuki to hagi" ("In the same house courtesans slept too—moon and bushclover"). While Bashō has also mentioned several phenomena, as is customary in a *haiku*, it is evident that his relationship to them is more important than Shiki's to his objects. The *haiku* treats a particular experience of Bashō that he recorded in his most famous travel diary, *Oku no hosomichi* (Narrow Road to the Interior, 1691). At a certain out-of-the-way place he had slept overnight in an inn where two traveling courtesans were also sleeping. Overhearing their conversation through the thin walls, he had felt compassion for their hard life and had written the *haiku* directly out of his experience of unity with them, and with nature (the moon and the white

[5] See Yoshida Seiichi's discussion of the *shasei* movement of the 1890s in *Zuihitsu nyūmon*, pp. 28ff.

bushclover). The *haiku* has a personal and serene atmosphere about it that does not appear sentimental unless one, like Shiki, lives according to a view of life that assumes the separateness of man from things and things from things. Bashō's view of the universe is clearly one that posits a unity between man and nature, for things are not purely physical but contain moral principles (*li*) that ensure their intelligibility to man. For Bashō, the artist is not a camera but a human being for whom perception is a moral and spiritual act, and for whom art is a means of revealing the unity between man and nature.

When Tōson was experimenting with the discipline of *shasei* in 1900 and 1901, he was well aware of Shiki's manifesto on the objective *haiku*. Around this time he was also steeping himself in the works of Balzac, Maupassant, Zola, Flaubert, the Goncourt brothers, Turgenev, and Ibsen. His reading of these writers, and of Darwin's *Origin of the Species*, introduced him to the tough, skeptical view of life that was beginning to dominate Japanese culture after 1900 in the wake of Naturalism. Yet Tōson clearly chose a method of objectivity that was firmly rooted in the Japanese tradition, particularly in the *haiku* of Bashō and in the *zuihitsu* ("random notes") of the late tenth-century poetess Sei Shōnagon. He wrote in an essay entitled "Shasei," for example, that when he tried to practice *shasei* he had often become too analytical and had lost the "it-ness" of the thing. He finally decided that "unless there is vitality in the description, one is not reflecting life."[6] In other words, *shasei* must aim at capturing a truth that transcends mere scientific investigation; observation must be human, and must involve an active respect for the living quality of the thing observed.

Another short essay entitled "Inshōshugi to sakubutsu" (Impressionism and the Literary Work) sheds further light on Tōson's method of *shasei*. In this essay Tōson analyzed the technique of the Western Impressionist painters Monet and Sisley, charac-

---

[6] "Shasei" (Sketching from Life, 1909), *Zenshū*, 14: 38.

terizing it as a simple and concise observation of things. The structure of an impressionist work was one made up of many carefully observed details rather than dominated by an idea or an incident. He then went on to speak of an Impressionist novel and listed Turgenev, Chekhov, and Maupassant as Impressionist prose writers. Yet earlier in the essay he had written that "Goncourt and Whistler liked Japanese painting. If they had had a translation of *The Pillow Book* . . . with what enthusiasm they would have read it! It is astonishing that deep in the past there existed a woman who had perceptions like Sei Shōnagon."[7] It is clear that Tōson saw that Western Impressionism was the Western equivalent of the *shasei* method. His remark to the effect that the impressionist method could be used as the basis of a novel form (as in the novels of Turgenev, Chekhov, and Maupassant) is also important, for it was just at this time that Tōson was working to evolve a novel form. It is in this context, in fact, that his comment about Sei Shōnagon can be interpreted. Tōson brings up Sei Shōnagon, the author of the tenth-century impressionistic work, *The Pillow Book*, in order to show that the Japanese, long before the Europeans, had evolved an impressionist method. His mention of Sei is a way of saying that if he adopts an impressionist method in his novels, he will be following a native tradition and will not be a mere imitator of the West.[8]

The results of Tōson's efforts at *shasei* can be seen in the sixty-five sketches of the people and landscape of Komoro that he wrote during his years there and published in 1912 under the title

[7] "Inshōshugi to sakubutsu" (Impressionism and the Literary Work, 1909), *Zenshū*, 14: 35-36.

[8] Sei Shōnagon's *Pillow Book* (Makura no sōshi), which was written in the last decade of the tenth century, is a compilation in the *zuihitsu* ("random notes") form of sketches, observations, and perceptions of court life. It is not a novel the way Turgenev's works are novels—that is, there is no plot that unifies the whole work. Rather, the perceiving sensibility of the author unifies the impressionistic details. The form of the sketches that Tōson was doing in the early years of the twentieth century is close to that of Sei's sketches in *The Pillow Book*, as it is also close to that of Turgenev's *A Sportsman's Sketches*.

Chikumagawa no suketchi (Sketches of the Chikuma River). Though
the work lacks any political emphasis, it is similar in format to
Turgenev's *Zapiski Okhotnika* (A Sportsman's Sketches, 1852),
which Tōson was reading in the early years of the twentieth century: random observations of the people and landscape of a particular rural area are unified by an observer who describes the
actions, sometimes telling a story, but leaves the reader to draw
the conclusions. The following is an example from a sketch called
"Barley Fields":

> The green fields are filled with the boiling glare of the sun. The
> trees planted here and there at the edges of the fields are covered with
> fresh new leaves. Mingled with the cries of skylarks and sparrows, the
> penetrating voice of a reed warbler can be heard. . . .
>
> On the grass at the edge of a rice field, his mud-covered legs out-
> stretched, lies a man sleeping flat on his back, apparently exhausted
> from his work in the fields. The heads of the green barley are begin-
> ning to ripen into yellow leaves, and the white flowers of the *daikon*
> (white radish) are blooming riotously. I pass between a stone fence
> and a grassy embankment and walk down a narrow path made of
> pebbles. I soon come out into a barley field near Yoramachi.
>
> A young hawk is flying over my head. Choosing a spot where grass
> is growing, and breathing the smell of earth, I stretch out on my
> stomach. When a moisture-bearing breeze blows in my direction, the
> barley heads rub against one another making a whispering noise.
> Nearby is the sound of a farmer's hoe cutting. . . . When I strain my
> ears I can hear a trickle of water falling toward the floor of the valley.
> In that sound I try to imagine sand flowing along. I listen to the
> sound for a long time. But, unlike the fieldmouse, I can't bear to stay
> alone for long in the grass. The bright sky, clouding over and becom-
> ing a milky color, exhausts me. For me, nature is a thing I can't bear
> to keep my gaze fixed on . . . somehow I want to get away from it and
> go home.[9]

In some of the other sketches there is conversation, but in all the
sketches the things heard, seen, and smelled are particularized

[9] *Chikumagawa no suketchi* (Sketches of the Chikuma River, 1912), *Zenshū*, 3:
315-316.

phenomena existing in a flow of experience of the conscious "I." The "I" is alert to many things, a fact that indicates indirectly his enthusiasm for life in all its manifestations, whether good, bad, beautiful, or ugly. The "I" does not force his emotional reactions on the reader—the one obvious expression of emotion is not heavy-handed but humorous, as the "I," possibly parodying Bashō's reverent attitude toward nature, admits that he personally can stand only so much of it. Yet there is a unity between the "I" and the observed objects that results from his keenness of observation and his equal devotion to each thing.

After a first period of enthusiasm for Rousseau's egoism and direct confession, the natural classicism of a nation long trained in reserve and reticence about personal matters reasserted itself in Tōson, and he sought his models in writers of his own tradition: Bashō and the Heian impressionist writer Sei Shōnagon. During the years 1898-1901 he seemed to be most interested in their technique of objectivity, yet behind technique there inevitably lies a world view. It is not surprising, then, that behind Bashō's detachment lay a religious view of unity and harmony of the cosmos that appealed to Tōson just as much as the literary technique of detached observation. Yet Tōson's choice of Bashō in particular as a model in this period of his literary career, and of the *shaseibun* ("sketch from life") as a literary form, has an even more important significance, for not only was Tōson adhering to tradition by practicing *shasei*, he was also choosing to treat a subject that had played an extremely important role in Japanese tradition as well as in his own life: nature. Still more importantly, his decision to practice *shasei* rather than devote himself to the Zolaesque social novel implies that he had decided, whether consciously or unconsciously, to depict the individual's inner life in its relation to nature rather than his social self in relation to society.[10] Modern

---

[10] During the years Tōson was experimenting with *shasei* he was also trying his hand at several short stories in the Western realist-naturalist vein. In 1901, for example, he wrote the short story *Kyūshujin* (Former Master), a work that, inspired by *Madame Bovary* but based on details in the lives of people he knew in

Japanese of Tōson's time suffered from a loss of identity that stemmed from their suddenly being uprooted from the matrix of traditional culture: the network of relationships that linked them with other individuals and with the universe around them. Tōson's achievement in the sketches he made in the first few years of the twentieth century was to discover his physical location in the universe of nature and to find words to describe the new, modern relationship between man and the world outside himself—in short, to discover a new meaning in man's relationship to nature.

Traditional Japanese literature had seen the depiction of man and his relationship to nature as primarily the province of poetry. Religion provided a basis on which to establish a link between man and nature and, more importantly, gave man's existence a meaning. In the earliest poetry Shinto, through its animist doctrine of the existence of the divine spirit in all things, provided a basis for poets to speak of man and nature as parts of a unified cosmos. Later, Buddhism compared man's existence to the fleet-

---

Komoro, told the story of a citified woman who, unhappily married to a man much older than herself and dissatisfied with country life, has an affair with a local dentist. This work, when it appeared in the November 1902 issue of the journal *Shin Shōsetsu* (New Fiction), caused the issue to be seized by the police because of its alleged immorality. In the next few years before the appearance of *Hakai* Tōson published *Wara zōri* (Straw Sandals, 1902), *Oyaji* (The Father, 1903), *Rōjo* (The Old Maid, 1904), *Suisaigaka* (The Water-color Artist, 1904), and *Tsugaru kaikyō* (The Straits of Tsugaru, 1904). All of these works are stories, not novels, and all use the impressionist method of Maupassant's stories. Several are based on incidents in the lives of people Tōson knew—and consequently are *documents humains*. Several have Zolaesque themes: adultery (*Kyūshūjin*), heredity (*Rōjo*), and the animality of passion (*Wara zōri* and *Oyaji*). In these stories, his first attempts at fiction, Tōson experimented with point of view, dialogue, and narrative technique itself. If Tōson was a Naturalist at any time in his career, it was in these years when he followed Zola and Maupassant. Yet this fiction depicts man as a creature with animal instincts living in society, while Tōson's *shasei* show man as a creature of divine instincts living in nature. The fiction Tōson wrote at this point in his career (before *Hakai*) is not typical of his later fiction, in that it presents a Zolaesque view of man as a creature of instinct. It is for this reason that I consider it only in a footnote.

ing ephemerality of nature, and with the coming of the Zen sect
in the late Middle Ages poetry was able to speak of man's experience of mystical unity with nature. In the late seventeenth century Bashō carried on the tradition of depicting the experience of
mystical unity between man and nature in his *haiku* and travel
diaries, but his personality came more into the foreground as a
compassionate observer of whatever he saw, be it nature or people. The novel in traditional Japan generally had a social orientation. Only in Lady Murasaki's *Tale of Genji* (early eleventh century) does one find an emphasis on the link between man and nature, and here, as in the poetry of the time, man's life is compared to natural transformations in its changeability and ephemerality.

When man's life is linked with nature, it takes on a profound
religious meaning. Such is the case in *The Tale of Genji*, but in
later great works of fiction, where man is not linked with nature,
he loses his depth and significance. The novels of the late-
seventeenth-century writer Saikaku, for example, place man in
the world of the city, not of nature. Moreover, the city is a mere
pictorial scene with little depth, for the characters have no deep
emotional or spiritual relationship with the places described.
Though Saikaku's characters exist in a world dominated by the
Buddhist idea of transience, here the idea of transience has lost its
earlier religious meaning and man's existence is cheapened. Nature description in Saikaku's novels, the few times that it occurs,
is external and picturesque rather than deeply felt. Nature becomes a pretty stage set totally divorced from the people who are
playing their roles on the stage of *ukiyo*, or the floating world of
sense pleasures. Man's relationship to other men is one of manip-
ulation, and is based on cynicism and a lack of a significant feeling of unity. Finally, the sense of inner spiritual freedom that
emerges in literature that depicts the individual in nature is totally lacking here.

Though Futabatei Shimei was a masterful depictor of the
internal man, he delineated man as essentially a social being and

thus followed Saikaku, though broadening and deepening his observation. Like Saikaku's view of man, his view of man in *Ukigumo* is generally comic or intellectual rather than spiritual. Not surprisingly, Futabatei's awareness of the link between man and nature is superficial. In his translation of Turgenev's *Aibiki* (The Rendezvous), he found words to communicate another writer's conception of man and his relationship to nature faithfully and brilliantly—indeed, it was the passages of nature description that were perceived as new when *Aibiki* appeared. In his own novels, however, he pays almost no attention to man's place in nature, one of the few exceptions being the following passage:

> The cool moon rose, outlining the leaves of ten slim bamboo trees which stood in the corner of the garden. There was not a single cloud and its powerful, radiant, white light lit up the face of the sky. . . . At first the bamboo fence between the houses held back the moonbeams and they extended only halfway across the garden. As the moon rose in the sky, the moonbeams crept up to the verandah and poured into the room. The water in the miniature garden there shimmered in the light; the windbell glittered and tinkled. Then the moonlight silhouetted the two young people and stole the brightness of the single lamp in the room. Finally it climbed up the wall.[11]

In *Ukigumo* nature is urban; as in Saikaku, it is a scene that is a mere backdrop for the action of the characters, which the author considers much more important. Futabatei's description shows the influence of Western scientific observation in its careful attention to the location of the moonbeams in relation to the houses and garden, yet the parallelism in the sentence "The water in the miniature garden . . . shimmered in the light; the windbell glittered and tinkled" reveals Futabatei's adherence to the Tokugawa novel's method of nature description, derived from classical Chinese poetry, which presented details in two grammatically parallel phrases. The details in Futabatei's description are carefully chosen, but they lack a relation to the characters that would

---

[11] Ryan, *Japan's First Modern Novel*, p. 217.

give them meaning. Finally, the moon is personified, and this has the effect of making the whole passage retroactively comical.

The practitioners of the *shasei* method in the late 1890s and early 1900s turned their complete attention to nature, with the result that they virtually excluded man. As a contemporary critic of *shasei* put it: "*Shaseibun* originally referred to [the technique of] *shasei* in *haiku*, and was a method used chiefly by *haijin* [writers of *haiku*]. But the beauty celebrated by *haiku* was basically of a natural kind; if there were human beings [in a *haiku*], *haiku* paid attention only to their surface beauty, exactly as it did for natural objects. Consequently, . . . when *shaseibun* moved outside the realm of *haiku*, . . . its investigation of human beings was superficial, limited to what one could get by taking pencil and sketchbook and walking about on the streets."[12] Thus, most *shaseibun* failed to deal with the inner person at all, treating man in the typical *haiku* way as a person under an umbrella in the autumn rain. There was also a strong tendency in the *shasei* method toward a nonliterary, purely naturalistic observation of unrelated details, and Shiki's own *shaseibun* suffered from this defect, as another critic pointed out: "A description from life (*shasei*) in words, using a painter's method without altering it, seizes the outline and surface of the object but does not penetrate deeply into its interior. . . . In that sense, the *shaseibun* initiated by Shiki are in general superficial, painterly, vacant, and lacking in climax; they are not suitable for penetration of the depths of psychic life, nor for reproducing thoughts."[13] Shiki's *shaseibun* lacked a coherent vision of the world, a personal presence that would make the details observed more than the random observations of a logbook. The traditional form of the *zuihitsu*, of which the "impressionistic" *Pillow Book* was an example, had as its unifying point the personality of the author. However, in Shiki's eagerness to restore objectivity to the *shaseibun*, the natural de-

---

[12] Takahama Kyoshi, "Shaseibun no yurai to sono igi," in *Gendai bungakuron taikei*, vol. 2, *Shizenshugi to hanshizenshugi*, Tokyo, 1955, p. 326.
[13] Yoshida, *Zuihitsu nyūmon*, p. 34.

scendant of the *zuihitsu*, he had stripped it of any unifying element, and thus of the moral vision of the world that is necessary in order for a work to qualify as art.

It is not difficult to understand why Tōson would have rejected Shiki's sort of *shaseibun*, which saw only a cerebral connection between man and nature, in favor of the travel diaries of the early modern writer, Bashō. Bashō was the last writer before the Meiji period to treat man in connection with nature and thus the last Japanese figure to believe in the possibility of a spiritual unity between them. Furthermore, Bashō was clearly already a modern person in that he had to struggle to attain this unity—and it was probably on this basis that Tōson was able to identify with him. Yet Tōson went not only to the Japanese past. Already as he was writing his *shaseibun* and in the following years when he was actively preparing to write his first novel, he was gradually becoming attracted to the works of a contemporary European writer who was concerned with the significance of man's life and with his relationship to nature: Leo Tolstoy. As far back as 1892 Tōson had read Tolstoy's "Labor," and the influence of that story, as well as that of Tolstoy's interest in the worker, the farmer, the merchant, and the craftsman, can be seen in Tōson's careful observation of people of all classes, with respect to their innate dignity, in *Chikumagawa no suketchi* and in *Nōfu*. Tolstoy's technique of description made a deep and lasting impression on Tōson, and he wrote, in reference to *Chikumagawa no suketchi*, that "I was attracted to the truthful descriptions [of 'Labor'] and sometimes when I started off toward the plateau upstream by the Chikuma River, I pictured before my eyes all the various characters in that work."[14] Tōson was clearly impressed by Tolstoy's realism as a technique, but one can discern in this remark also his excitement at the vastness of Tolstoy's vision.

Already in the 1890s Tōson had read Tolstoy's novels *The Cossacks*, *Boyhood*, and *Youth*. In April of 1903 he read *What is Art?*

---

[14] Tōson, *Chikumagawa no suketchi: Okugaki* (Postscript to Chikuma River Sketches), quoted in Itō, *Shimazaki Tōson kenkyū*, p. 269.

and, at some time during the next year, *Resurrection*. Also, in January of 1904, just before he started writing *Hakai*, Tōson read Dmitri Merezhkowski's *Tolstoi as Man and Artist* (1902), a work that, differentiating Tolstoy the writer of epics from Dostoevsky the writer of tragedies, probably influenced Tōson to view Tolstoy as a creator of vast works where the individual's egoism is balanced or at times even overwhelmed by nature and life.[15] Tolstoyan ideas were also being disseminated through the Christian Socialist movement (*Kirisutokyō shakaishugi undō*) in the late 1890s and early 1900s: namely, that man was linked to other men, of whatever class, through a humanitarian love and respect for their selfhood, and that the personal life had to be cultivated before the reconstruction of society could take place. These are ideas that Tōson would naturally have been exposed to as a person living in Komoro, a minor center of Christian Socialist activity.[16] Tōson's reading of Tolstoy in the crucial years just before he began to write *Hakai* provided him with an example of a modern writer who, like his master Tōkoku, insisted on the spiritual self-definition of each individual. Tolstoy thus continued Bashō's, and Rousseau's, concern for the inner self and, like them, often depicted the individual as truly himself only when united with nature. It is not surprising that it is Tolstoy's humanitarianism that, filtered through Tōson's own experiences, is the spirit that informs *Hakai*.

Hakai: *The Discovery of the Inner Life*

Tōson began writing *Hakai* probably in April of 1904 and completed it in late November of 1905. It was published by the au-

[15] In a letter he wrote on January 23, 1904, to Tayama Katai, who was supplying him with the latest Western books that were unavailable in Komoro, Tōson spoke enthusiastically of the Merezhkowski book as an important guide to the study of modern literature (Tolstoy and Dostoevsky). *Tōson zenshū*, Tokyo, 1966-1971, 17: 77.

[16] For a discussion of the movement of Christian Socialism and its relationship to Tōson, and to *Hakai*, see Itō, *Shimazaki Tōson kenkyū*, pp. 421-438.

thor himself in the spring of 1906 with funds borrowed from his father-in-law, and Tōson is reported to have pushed a cart containing the first few hundred copies through the streets of Kanda, an area of Tokyo noted for its numerous bookstores, to deliver them to a publisher he thought would be willing to sell the novel. The publication of *Hakai* made Tōson an immediate success, with the result that he was able to move his family into a decent house for the first time in his life. Critics praised the daring social theme of the novel, as well as its progressive, humanitarian viewpoint, and hailed it as a groundbreaking formal achievement: the first Japanese novel to rival European novels in its combination of coherent plot, depth of characterization, and social scrutiny.[17] *Hakai* dealt with a member of the despised *eta* caste, a group of people whose livelihood was gained through work traditionally considered unclean by the Buddhist religion: tanning, herding, and slaughtering. In 1871 the word *eta* was officially abolished and the former *eta* were referred to euphemistically as *shinheimin* ("new commoners"). But discrimination did not cease—in fact, it worsened, as *eta* were crowded out of their old professions yet not permitted to enter new ones. At the time Tōson wrote his novel, *eta* persecution was at its height in certain areas, and the Christian Socialists had made the improvement of the condition of the *eta* one of their primary goals.[18]

An important limitation on the freedom of the *eta* caste was the fact that they were forbidden to attend higher schools—and since graduation from a higher school was the passport to a bureau-

[17] In his study of the development of realism in Japan, Nakamura Mitsuo notes that "our novel, through *Hakai*, took an important step in the internalization of the influence of modern European literature," adding that "Tōson followed the orthodox pattern of the modern Western novel in reproducing social events in the world of feelings." *Fūzoku shōsetsu ron: kindai riarizumu hihan* (1950), in *Nakamura Mitsuo zenshū*, 7: 538-539.

[18] For a discussion of the *eta* in general, and of their condition at the time that Tōson was writing *Hakai*, see George De Vos and Hiroshi Wagatsuma, *Japan's Invisible Race*, rev. ed., Berkeley and Los Angeles, 1972, especially sects. 1, 2, 4, and 6.

cratic job in the new Meiji world, the inability of the *eta* to attend
the higher schools deprived them of the opportunity to rise in
society. Segawa Ushimatsu, the twenty-three-year-old hero of
Hakai, is an *eta* who, by passing as an ordinary Japanese, has
managed to graduate from a higher school and get a job as a
teacher in a mountain village without anyone finding out that he
is an *eta*. Years before, Ushimatsu's father, eager to see his son
attain the worldly success and status that he had never been able
to achieve as an *eta*, had made him swear an oath that he would
never reveal his origins. At the beginning of the novel
Ushimatsu, a successful teacher beloved by his pupils, has managed to forget he is an *eta*. Then he is drawn to the books of Inoko
Rentarō, an *eta* who, after being educated like Ushimatsu, had
publicly revealed his origins and is now working actively for the
betterment of the *eta* caste. When Ushimatsu reads Inoko's *Confessions*, he becomes aware for the first time in his adult life that he
is indeed an *eta* and begins to question the honesty of his secrecy.

Ushimatsu is particularly moved by Inoko's *Confessions*, for in
them he discovers a man who is proud of his origins and his selfhood and makes a point of being honest toward the world. Reading Inoko's angry criticisms of Japanese society for allowing in-
justices to be perpetrated on *eta* people, he recalls the personal
pain he had felt as a child when other children had thrown stones
at him and called him ugly names—pain that he had succeeded in
repressing until that moment. Ushimatsu admires Inoko's honesty and pride, but at the same time he cannot forget his father's
admonition. When his father dies suddenly, Ushimatsu is
thrown into a painful dilemma: in a sense, he is now free from his
father's direct retribution should he decide to reveal his origins.
However, his father's death has placed the responsibility for deciding what to do squarely on his shoulders, and it is a responsibility he is not yet ready to assume. He knows that he has everything worldly to gain by not revealing his secret, while revealing
it would mean becoming a true outcast like Inoko. He is pulled,
then, between guilt and fear. After meeting Inoko in person he is

drawn to him out of admiration and respect. Time after time he is tempted to tell Inoko his secret, yet time after time he remains silent. Eventually he sinks into a state of shame, cowardice, and fear of discovery that is the same as if he had committed a crime.

When, about halfway through the novel, someone finds out his secret and spreads the rumor around the village, Ushimatsu still does not act, but only buries himself in his room in despair. As the rumors increase, he sells Inoko's books to avoid being implicated in the latter's *eta*hood—yet his awareness of his cowardice and lack of honor drives him almost to suicide. The climax of the novel occurs when Inoko, who has been supporting a local liberal candidate in the upcoming election for the Diet, reveals publicly in a speech to the townspeople the dishonesty of the rival candidate, who had secretly married a rich *eta* girl from a nearby town in order to finance his campaign. It is only when Inoko is murdered by this man's hired thugs after the speech that Ushimatsu is moved to reveal his origins. The final scenes show him confessing humbly before his class of schoolchildren and being dismissed from his teaching job; at the last moment he accepts a job offered to him by a local *eta* who has decided to migrate to the freer country of America and buy a cattle ranch in Texas. A girl, Oshio, whom he has grown to love for her humble and tender qualities, joins him in spite of his outcast status. At the end of the novel it is clear that by confessing, Ushimatsu has in some way won himself, and his mental and moral suffering is replaced by a feeling of peace and a vision of a new life.

The above is merely a summary of the main thread of the action: Ushimatsu's development away from cowardice and toward self-pride. It should be noted that *Hakai* also contains beautiful, concise descriptions of the mountainous Shinshū area and its people, descriptions that were in several cases taken directly from the sketches Tōson had done in Komoro. It also gives sharply detailed descriptions of the lives of several members of a farming family (Oshio's family), of the family of a Buddhist priest, of an *eta* community, and of teachers and administrators of a small-town school. In addition, the novel is in some measure a satire on self-satisfied school administrators of the early Meiji period who put the ideal of progress above any humanitarian considerations. Finally, it is also a critique of the corruption of local politics on the eve of a parliamentary election; Ushimatsu's story is woven into this subplot by Tōson's making the corrupt political candidate the one who found out Ushimatsu's secret and then revealed it. Thus, it is not surprising that *Hakai* has consistently been evaluated by some critics, from the time it appeared, as a social novel: a novel that criticizes the abuses of society and, in particular, speaks out for the rights of the oppressed *eta* caste.[19] Yet others have consistently noted that the theme of *eta* oppression cannot be the central theme of the novel, for Ushimatsu pursues not freedom for the *eta* caste as a whole but rather his own liberation.[20] Again, if one takes *Hakai* as a novel that depicts the longing for social freedom, its ending is pessimistic: Ushimatsu is forced to yield to centuries of prejudice against his people and to accept the fact that there is no place for him in Japanese society. However, when reading the ending one does not in fact have the impression that Ushimatsu has failed but rather that he has won something very precious: a new life. This is due to the fact that Tōson was merely using the situation of the *eta* as a means of exploring a problem that was much nearer to his heart: the problem of self-definition.

Much as his *Wakana-shū* had inspired those young people of the day who yearned to define themselves, *Hakai*, appearing as it did at a time when Christian Socialism spoke out for the right to freedom of all people, seemed to Western-educated Japanese a call for the awakening of the individual. In *Hakai*, Tōson wrote of what later scholars have referred to as *kindaiteki jiga e no*

[19] Among these critics are Hirano Ken, *Shimazaki Tōson*, Tokyo, 1960, pp. 30-32, 41-43 and Kataoka Ryōichi, *Shizenshugi kenkyū*, Tokyo, 1957, pp. 68-70.

[20] Such critics include Wada Kingo, *Shizenshugi bungaku*, Tokyo, 1966, pp. 115-116, 124.

mezame, "the awakening to modern selfhood"—an ideal of political, social, and moral selfhood that has been called the guiding spirit of the Meiji period, and of the modern period as a whole.[21] Yet Tōson viewed what was a vast cultural undertaking of his time through the vision of the inner life of Kitamura Tōkoku, and through his own experience of awakening to selfhood under the influence of Tōkoku, Rousseau, Tolstoy, and Dostoevsky. At times Tōson even used the word "inner life" (*naibu seimei*) as if in allegiance to Tōkoku, and it is the latter's concept of the modern self that, mediated by Tōson's own experiences, underlies *Hakai*. When one looks closely at *Hakai*, it becomes clear that what Ushimatsu awakens to at the beginning of the novel is not the need for social freedom in the sense of the right to vote or the right to education, but the need for a sense of self that he can be proud of and that he can show to others without fear. He is attracted to Inoko Rentarō because, though Inoko is a member of a socially oppressed class, he possesses this pride in self and honesty toward others. In other words, Inoko is a man who has defined his inner *kokoro* and has manifested it before others, though it has cost him material benefits.

The idea that the act of confession is a manifestation of selfhood and an expression of honesty is introduced when Ushimatsu reads Inoko's *Confessions*. (Possibly Tōson is communicating here his own inspiration at reading Rousseau's *Confessions*, years earlier when he was twenty-two.) It is with his reading of the *Confessions* that Ushimatsu awakens to his true selfhood as an *eta*, and that the idea of eventually revealing his origins first occurs to him. As

---

[21] Nakamura Mitsuo discusses the ideal of *kindaiteki jiga e no mezame* in "Nihon no kindaika to bungaku," *Zenshū*, 8: 458-475. For further discussion of the *kindaiteki jiga* see Senuma Shigeki, *Kindai nihonbungaku no naritachi*, Tokyo, 1962, pp. 6-18; Oketani Shūshō, "Kindaiteki jiga to kojinshugi," *Kokubungaku Kaishaku to Kanshō*, 36 (1971, no. 7): 16-23; Okamura Kazuo, "Kindaiteki jiga o meguru kansō," *Koten to Gendai* (1968, no. 7): 8-14; and Kenneth L. C. Strong, "Downgrading the 'Kindai Jiga,'" *Nihon bunka kenkyū kokusai kaigi—gijiroku*, Tokyo, 1973, 1: 178-183.

Tōkoku had written that the struggle to define the inner *kokoro* was a battle between the human and the divine self, Ushimatsu's struggle to define himself can be seen as a battle between his desire for a purely material freedom (freedom of the outer *kokoro*) in the form of material success and worldly happiness, and spiritual freedom of the inner *kokoro*. Ushimatsu's father clearly had desired the former: in order to prevent anyone finding out about his relationship with Ushimatsu he had accepted the lonely, deprived life of a herder of bulls far up on the slopes and distant from any human settlement. He had also demanded that Ushimatsu subscribe to his idea of freedom by making him swear an oath that he would renounce his true selfhood in order to attain material success. Inoko equally clearly represented the latter ideal: the man who in his self-pride and openness is the incarnation of the modern freedom of spirit (*seishin no jiyū*) that Tōkoku had described.

The struggle between the two figures for Ushimatsu's allegiance takes a dramatic turn when Ushimatsu receives word that his father has been gored to death by one of his bulls. That Ushimatsu feels a struggle between the two ideals raging within him is indicated by his thought that an internal revolution (*kokoro no naka no kakumei*) had occurred in him[22] due to his contact with Inoko's works. At this point, however, he is still sad and even resentful at the loss of innocence he suffered when he recalled he was an *eta*. Thus his energies are concentrated on recovering a lost paradise, however fantastic, rather than on fighting for a new, real one. However, Tōson's decision to have the father die is already a sign that the father's side will ultimately lose the battle. This fact is made perfectly clear in a remarkable scene where Ushimatsu and Inoko watch silently while the bull that gored the father is slaughtered.[23] As the bull is ritually destroyed, one has the feeling that the materialistic spirit of the father, as embodied

---

[22] *Hakai* (Breaking the Commandment, *Zenshū* (1948-1952), 3: 83 (chap. 7). I have indicated the chapter numbers for the benefit of those who use a different edition of *Hakai*.

[23] *Zenshū*, 3: 125-130 (chap. 10).

in the gross physicality of the bull, yields to the superior spiritual power of Inoko, who then replaces him as Ushimatsu's father. After the bull is taken away Ushimatsu internalizes the two figures: he feels more and more drawn toward making a revelation of his identity to Inoko, yet the fear and cowardice stemming from his attachment to worldly benefits also increase.

One passage in chapter nine gives unusual insight into Tōson's idea of the inner life as it develops in Ushimatsu. Ushimatsu has just been asking himself why he has failed to tell Inoko his secret, and, thinking about the situation a bit, he realizes that his conscience will not, in the long run, permit him to hide the truth from his mentor. He also discovers that he really longs to tell Inoko his secret:

> A rising spirit of youth also gave a strong stimulus to Ushimatsu's feelings. For example, Ushimatsu was like young grass sprouting beneath the snow. Though his heart longed for spring, it was completely closed up by doubts and fears, and the life within him (*naka no inochi*) was unable to grow. Was there anything strange in the snow's melting, warmed by the sun? Was there anything odd in youth's going forward, dedicating its respect to its mentor? The more he saw him, the more he heard him speak, the more Ushimatsu was inspired by Rentarō and the more he could not help admiring his freedom of spirit (*seishin no jiyū*). He must tell him, he must tell him—surely that was his path! The vital force of youth in him urged Ushimatsu on.[24]

This passage describes a point in Ushimatsu's evolution where, as a result of the battle in him between the divine and the human, the spiritual and the worldly, the inner *kokoro* has begun to emerge. Tōson describes this inner life in terms that are partly Tōkoku's and partly his own. He sees Ushimatsu's inner life as a youthful spirit of idealistic dedication to a worthy master, but he also sees it as a plant that wishes to grow but is temporarily blocked by the winter—that is, in terms similar to his use of

[24] Ibid., p. 119 (chap. 9).

seasons as symbols of relative states of emotional freedom in
Wakana-shū. The coming of spring will melt the selfhood whose
expression is blocked, and Inoko is compared to the sun that will
eventually melt the snow covering the self. Inoko is seen here as
the grace of God that, in Tōkoku's essays, is the instrument that
brings about the definition of the inner *kokoro*. However, Tōson
sees the will of Ushimatsu, the inner life that is temporarily frozen, as a natural thing that, when warmed by the radiance of
Inoko's more powerful self, will once again bloom with vitality,
youthfulness, and courage. Considering the natural terms according to which Tōson defines Ushimatsu's inner self, and the significance of spring (Inoko) in his struggle, one can interpret this
passage as a forecast of the rebirth, i.e., the coming of "spring,"
or grace, that ends the novel. Furthermore, in it is evidence of the
faith in the natural vitality of the self that Tōson's youthful experiences in nature had given him.

As the novel progresses tension builds up in Ushimatsu, and
he lives a life increasingly marked by a secret anguish, with only
the austere mountain scenery and his rare encounters with the girl
Oshio providing him any consolation. His internal struggle
reaches a climax in chapter eighteen, when he comes into the staff
room at school one day to find his colleagues engrossed in a discussion of Inoko. When he hears one of them call him a dreamer
and a madman, he loses his temper and defends his teacher even
though he knows he is betraying his affiliation with the *eta* caste
by doing so. Interestingly, he describes Inoko here in terms that
recall Tōkoku's description of the artist who wages a battle for
truth on a battlefield of the spirit—as a man "battling with the
world" and a man who "went to the battlefield resolved to die."
He also stresses Inoko's utter courage and honesty, and hearing
him, his friend Ginnosuke remarks that "he had the feeling that
he was coming in touch with Ushimatsu's inner life (*naibu seimei*),
which was more youthful, stronger, and more vital than it had
been in a long while."[25]

[25] Ibid., p. 235 (chap. 18).

It seems clear, then, that at this moment Ushimatsu's inner *kokoro* has been defined and manifested in defense of the freedom of the self. Yet this instance of courage akin to Inoko's is matched and almost canceled out by his final attempt, in chapter nineteen, to escape the struggle for selfhood, for here Ushimatsu considers suicide. It is only the example of Inoko, who makes the ultimate sacrifice of dying in pursuit of the truth of his self, that moves Ushimatsu to confess his true origins. His act of confession, first before his pupils, then in front of his colleagues and Oshio, is an insistence on honesty whatever the consequences to himself. After this, his final struggle, Ushimatsu achieves the peace of the warrior who has fought well for the truth, and won.

Tōson had gone far beyond Tōkoku, and far back in Japanese tradition, in his attempts to discover a new, modern relationship between man and nature. It would be surprising, then, if this novel that deals with the unfolding of the inner self did not treat the relationship of that self to nature. Indeed, nature plays an extremely important role in Ushimatsu's drama, for nature scenes are the important structural foci of the novel. The narrative flows along, interrupted at certain strategic points by moments in which a lyrical expansion of feeling takes place and in which the character's emotional states are revealed. Scenes of nature description are places where the Romantic self of Tōson's poems emerges in its utmost sincerity. Finally, nature scenes in *Hakai* are barometers of the spiritual changes Ushimatsu undergoes in the course of the novel. The first such scene occurs in chapter four, at a point where Ushimatsu has become conscious that he is an *eta* but wishes to avoid any change in his life that would stem from this awareness. As he takes a walk in the countryside along fields where peasants are harvesting their crops, he feels "life reawakening in him."[26] Some action intervenes, after which Ushimatsu reflects upon his past life before he knew he was an *eta*. In his present state of mind, in which he wants to avoid going forward

[26] Ibid., p. 45 (chap. 4).

and facing the consequences of his *eta*hood, that time of his life seems to him to be a world of innocence and unawareness that is irrecoverable.

As he returns home later that evening, Ushimatsu walks through a countryside reflected in the rays of the setting sun, and the author remarks, recording his thoughts: "If only one could enjoy the beauty of such a scene to the full, free of care and mental suffering, what a time of bliss youth would be! The more painful Ushimatsu's inward conflict, the deeper his sense of such beauty, of external nature as a living force permeating his very being."[27] Here Tōson distinguishes between three types of relationships between Ushimatsu and nature: the first is a pure, innocent, and unconscious one that is only possible between nature and a child. This is the one that Ushimatsu has lost, and despairs of ever regaining. The second is the Romantic relationship, in which the tormented individual sees in nature only his own painful, and beautiful torment. This is the one that Ushimatsu finds himself in, to his chagrin. The third is a mysterious one in which nature, through its vitality, energy, and divinity, rouses the individual from his self-involvement and despair, the nature that can be enjoyed only by a person who has defined his inner *kokoro*. That Ushimatsu suddenly awakes, in the midst of nature, to an awareness of his right to live, even if he is an *eta*, is a sign that the third relationship will be possible for him.

The next time Ushimatsu finds himself in nature is after his father's death (chapter seven). As he walks the path to the high mountain village to attend the funeral, at first he is overcome by despair, and the muddy waters of the Chikuma River, along with the austere mountain landscape, reflect and heighten this despair. Then, as Ushimatsu gradually walks higher and higher, gaining distance from the towns below him, he begins to feel refreshed by the high mountains as they come into view. As before, Ushimatsu associates the town with the social world in which he

[27] Tōson Shimazaki, *The Broken Commandment*, trans. Kenneth Strong, Tokyo, 1974, p. 45 (chap. 4).

would be degraded if people knew his secret, but nature is a place where his higher, spiritual self is validated, and thus he is at peace. On the journey home he takes a walk with his idol, Inoko Rentarō. With Inoko, a man who has defined himself and is fearless, he achieves a rare mood of self-forgetfulness and feels that he is innocent once more. Yet because Inoko's presence reminds him of the self he is concealing and degrading, his joy in nature is spoiled: "Nature could console, but only for the briefest moment, for with every step he took toward Nezu his awareness of what he was, of himself as an *eta*, an outcast, . . . weighed more heavily upon his spirit."[28] Here nature is again identified with Ushimatsu's pure, asocial self; the enjoyment of it or rather the experience of unity with it is seen as even less likely to occur than in chapter four, because Ushimatsu's awareness of his torment is more acute. By the time he takes his next walk with Inoko (chapter eight) he has decided to tell *him* at least the secret of his origins. With this resolve in mind and in a feeling of unity with the honesty and courage of his mentor, he is able to experience the pure exaltation of gazing on the impenetrable peaks, though in the end he fails after all to reveal his secret.

When Ushimatsu spends several days in the mountains after his father's funeral (chapter eleven), walking daily in the fields and hills, he feels the "tide of youth" surge in his veins, yet he also sees that his energy is somehow blocked. At this point it does not occur to him that defining and revealing his self would be the means to set it free, and, significantly, nature refuses or is unable to give him an answer to the dilemma that he experiences so strongly: "Nature brought comfort, inspiration; but which turning to take at the crossroads—this she could tell no man. To Ushimatsu's question, the fields, the hills, the valleys gave no answer."[29] Here Ushimatsu is clearly close to finding an answer to his dilemma, for he can pose the question consciously and only needs a stimulus to make him answer it with action. However,

---

[28] Ibid., p. 78 (chap. 7).   [29] Ibid., p. 121 (chap. 11).

this stimulus must be given by human beings, not by nature. The help that Ushimatsu needs comes in a strange way, for others find out his secret and begin to pursue him. At one point, on a cold December day, he sinks to the depths of self-pity and despair as he walks along the banks of the frozen Chikuma River (chapter nineteen). In a state of fear that his secret will be revealed and his life ruined, he considers drowning himself in the river. Nature corresponds to his gloomy thoughts: the river is tight and frozen, like Ushimatsu, possessing in its deadly cold water the power to drown; and the landscape in general conveys the unbearable harshness of the Shinshū winter. Inoko forces Ushimatsu to re-solve his dilemma: the shock of his death jolts Ushimatsu out of his preoccupation with death and stimulates him to consider the meaning of his mentor's sacrifice and the ideals that brought it about. Ushimatsu decides to follow Inoko's example of honesty and pride in self and, once he has confessed his secret in that spirit, he attains a new relationship to nature (chapter twenty-three). As Ushimatsu walks on the snow behind the sledge that carries Inoko's ashes, the author remarks: "This world of snow, whispering beneath each step he took—at long last it was *his*. . . ."[30] It is clear, then, that nature, which represented an inno-cence of spirit and a vitality of self that Ushimatsu had lost while he concealed his true self, has now been regained by his revealing it.

Tōson's depiction of the process of awakening to selfhood shows the influence of Tōkoku's description of the definition of the inner *kokoro*; woven into it is Tōson's own faith in the soteric power of nature as well as Tolstoy's view that the highest destiny of man is his spiritual cultivation of self. Rousseau's influence is also present in the form of the hero's turning to confession as an act of self-validation. Yet the influence of Dostoevsky's *Crime and Punishment* is also present in *Hakai*, and in a very concrete way: Tōson was reading this novel in English translation as he was

[30] Ibid., p. 244 (chap. 23).

planning *Hakai*, and he admitted in an interview that he had taken the general structure of *Hakai* from Dostoevsky's novel.[31] What Tōson probably meant by this was that he had patterned his novel after *Crime and Punishment*'s structure of crime followed by suffering and culminating in confession and rebirth, for Ushimatsu's "crime" of self-definition is followed by great moral suffering, which in turn ends in confession and rebirth.[32] Admittedly the crime in *Hakai* is hardly the sort of crime that Raskolnikov commits. Yet Tōson's following of the pattern of *Crime and Punishment* suggests that he must have seen Ushimatsu's turning his back on his past, as well as his refusal to be an individual, as in some measure a crime against society and against the self, respectively, a crime that had to be followed by punishment in the form of an internal moral suffering that is similar in nature to Raskolnikov's.

Since Tōson had great faith in the regenerative nature of the process of self-definition, he probably saw in Dostoevsky's novel a kindred vision of man, in that Dostoevsky seemed to allow for the rebirth even of a person who had murdered in order to define himself. Then, too, Tōson was attracted to the ideal of new life as depicted in the Book of Romans, and Dostoevsky stresses this view also, through the figure of Sonya and the story of Lazarus. It is due possibly to his reading of and adherence to the same New Testament ideas that Tōson's narrative describes the new life of Ushimatsu in terms similar to those that describe Raskolnikov's rebirth in the Dostoevsky novel. For example, while reading Inoko's *Confessions* Ushimatsu felt that he was drawn toward a "new world" (*atarashii sekai*). Similarly, Inoko notes in his *Confes-*

---

[31] Mentioned in Itō Kazuo, *Shimazaki Tōson jiten*, Tokyo, 1972, p. 296. Many critics have noted also that Tōson modeled his characters after those in the Dostoevsky novel.

[32] Itō Kazuo's imaginative interpretation of *Hakai*, in his *Shimazaki Tōson kenkyū*, stresses the hero's undergoing a Christian process of sin and guilt, followed by confession. He sees Inoko Rentarō as the Christ-figure who brings about Ushimatsu's salvation. See pp. 366-386.

sions how his discovery that he was an *eta* led to his entering a new life (*atarashii seishō*). In chapter twenty, Ushimatsu, when deciding to confess, "felt the approach of a new dawn" (*atarashii akatsuki no chikazuita koto o shitta*). Finally, as he prepares to leave the town, the temple bell tolls, telling of departure but also of "the dawn of a new life" (*akesometa issei no akebono*).[33]

Similarly, ideas of new life and regeneration occur in *Crime and Punishment*, particularly in the second half, as the process of crime gives way to the suffering that will end in rebirth. Sonya's reading of the story of Lazarus, with its message of rebirth, comes in part IV, iv. In part VI, iii, Porfiry Petrovich, knowing that Raskolnikov is the murderer, says to him: "Plunge straight into life (*zhizn'*) without deliberation. Don't be uneasy—it will carry you direct to the shore and set you on your feet." In epilogue two, after Raskolnikov's illness and his dream of the horrifying rationalist Apocalypse, the narrator notes that gradually "life took the place of logic" (*vmesto dialektiki nastupila zhizn'*) and foresees that as he struggled, a "new life" (*novaya zhizn'*) would gradually come to Raskolnikov. Finally, at the end of the novel the narrator notes that: "This is the story of the gradual renewal of a man, the story of his gradual regeneration, of his slow progress from one world to another."[34] The words "regeneration" (*pererozhdenie*) and "progress from one world to another" (*perekhod iz odnogo mira v drugoi*) recall Tōson's mention of a "new world" and a "new life." The reader is meant to understand that Raskolnikov will eventually experience a rebirth to innocence, a rebirth that will come not by the grace of God but through the intercession of a human being, Sonya, much as Ushimatsu's rebirth was mediated by Inoko Rentarō. For both writers, however, the following verse from the New Testament seems to be a motto for the process described: ". . . the new spiritual principle of life 'in' Christ Jesus lifts me out of the old vicious circle of sin and death (Romans

[33] *Zenshū*, 3: 13 (chap. 1); 257 (chap. 20); 291 (chap. 23).

[34] Fyodor Dostoevsky, *Crime and Punishment*, trans. Jessie Coulson, ed. George Gibian, New York, 1975, pp. 388, 464-465.

8:1)."[35] For both Dostoevsky and Tōson, however, the "new spiritual principle of life" is seen in vitalistic terms, and as existing in the heart of the individual himself.

Tōson's reading of works of Tōkoku, Rousseau, Bashō, Tolstoy, and Dostoevsky while he was preparing to write his first novel helped him to perfect a realistic technique of description and to evolve a humanistic moral vision that suited his temperament. Yet the evolution of a technique and a vision, and even the taking of a structural plan for the novel from Dostoevsky's *Crime and Punishment*, would not in themselves make a novel. To write a lengthy fictional narrative Tōson needed actions and feelings centered around a hero and around a problem that would develop in time and eventually be solved. When Tōson began to write *Hakai* early in 1904 he looked to his own life, both past and present, for this hero and this problem, and the struggles of his inner self provided him with the raw material that he shaped into *Hakai*. Tōson first looked back on the torments he suffered in the early 1890s, a period when he was attempting to fulfill his goals of becoming a writer and an individual. If one takes the transformation of Ushimatsu that is achieved through the influence of Inoko Rentarō as a fictional projection of Tōson's transformation at that time by the ideals and personality of Kitamura Tōkoku, still deeper levels of meaning in *Hakai* will become apparent.

For example, Ushimatsu's situation, at the beginning of the novel, of being asleep to his true self is similar to Tōson's just before he met Tōkoku. The reading of Inoko's *Confessions* introduces Ushimatsu to the liberating, transcendent world of the self, much as Tōkoku's essays on the inner life—but also, at a later date, Rousseau's *Confessions*—had awakened Tōson to the possibility of a life lived according to his own goals. Then, too, the symbolic battle in *Hakai* between Ushimatsu's father and Inoko for Ushimatsu's allegiance is paralleled by Tōson's experience, in

---

[35] *The New Testament in Modern English*, trans. J. B. Phillips, New York, 1958, p. 331.

his early twenties, of being torn between his father's attitude of self-submission and the modern individualism of Tōkoku. When one becomes aware of the fact that Tōson's father was an opponent of Christianity, it is logical to assume that Tōson felt guilt about turning away from the ways of his father when he was converted to Christianity and also later when he came under the influence of Tōkoku.[36] This betrayal, then, is perhaps the model for Ushimatsu's "crime" of turning his back on his father's way of life, in *Hakai*. Also, Tōson's gradual coming to a consciousness of himself in the period after Tōkoku's death is probably the process that underlies Ushimatsu's rebirth at the close of *Hakai*. As Tōkoku had the effect of encouraging Tōson to define himself and to become a writer, so Inoko encouraged Ushimatsu to be proud of himself and honest toward the world. Tōkoku's death in 1894 was in some measure a sacrifice—as Tōson put it, Tōkoku was a springboard for those to come—and likewise, Inoko's death is a Christlike sacrifice of self that for Ushimatsu, attains the significance of a moral and spiritual lesson. Finally, Tōkoku's influence on Tōson can be seen in his works, beginning in 1897, that were documents of self-expression, just as Inoko's major influence on Ushimatsu is his leading him toward a path of honesty through confession.

Tōson's novel *Hakai*, set in 1891, was in a sense a tribute to the idealism, and the pain, of that period in his development as an individual and as a writer. Yet the novel emerged even more clearly from Tōson's struggles to define himself in the isolated town of Komoro in the years between 1899 and 1905. Numerous aspects of his life in Komoro threatened to undermine Tōson's

---

[36] In one of his books Tōson's father, a staunch adherent of *Kokugaku* (National Learning), had written that Christianity was not the orthodox way. Itō, *Shimazaki Tōson kenkyū*, pp. 378-379. When one considers that he agreed only with reluctance to let Tōson learn English in 1881, one wonders how he would have felt if he had known that Tōson converted to Christianity in 1888. Like Ushimatsu's father in *Hakai*, he died before he could see his son turn his back on the orthodox way.

goal of living according to his own modern, individualist morality. One source of torment was his isolation from his literary
friends and the literary world of Tokyo, for Tōson feared that a
prolonged stay in the provinces, where there was not much intellectual stimulus, might delay the entrance onto the literary scene
that he desired so intensely. Indeed, two of Tōson's friends from
the Meiji Gakuin and later from the *Bungakkai* group centered
around Kitamura Tōkoku—Baba Kochō and Togawa Shūkotsu—had, like Tōson, accepted jobs as teachers in rural schools.
Now, several years later, they had been unable to get anywhere as
writers and were filled with a sense of depression and aliena-
tion.[37] Tōson clearly felt that the same fate might overtake him if
he did not make the most of these important years. His good
friend Tayama Katai, who visited him and sent him copies of the
latest Western literary works during his years in Komoro, wrote
of Tōson's life at this time: "The way I imagine it, the several
years Tōson spent in Komoro were characterized by, on one hand,
a collision between art and life, and on the other, a scarcely en-
durable loneliness. I had the distinct feeling that he was gazing
steadily and silently at himself and at human beings, appearing
calm on the outside but inwardly in turmoil."[38] The turmoil that
Katai speaks of is a possible model for the turmoil that Tōson
depicts in his character Ushimatsu, and the loneliness as well.
However, far more violent for Tōson was the clash between art
and life, for he must have felt intensely alienated as an intellectual and writer living in a provincial town where people either
engaged in commercial activity or worked the land. Where those
around him seemed engrossed in work that only maintained life,
Tōson saw himself as a seeker of truth. He had to fight continu-

[37] Tōson described the depressing fate of these two friends later in a story
entitled *Namiki* (A Row of Trees), published in 1907. One of them, Baba
Kochō, complained publicly in a rebuttal that Tōson had used details of his life
in an unflattering way.

[38] Tayama Katai, *Tōkyō no sanjūnen*, *Bungakuteki kaisōshū*, *Gendai nihonbungaku zenshū*, Tokyo, 1959, 97: 339.

ally to defend this pursuit of truth against the financial demands of his family in Tokyo, the exhausting teaching schedule that left him little time to write, the indifference of his own wife, who was engrossed in care of the house and children and understood nothing of his work, and the poverty that haunted him and his family at every moment. Interestingly, none of this torment comes through in the serene and objective *shaseibun* that Tōson wrote during this time, but it is certainly this atmosphere that permeates a good portion of *Hakai*.

Tokutomi Sohō, the editor of the influential liberal journal *Kokumin no tomo* (The Nation's Friend), had written an article already in 1893 describing the effects of the traditional family system on young men attempting to make their way in the Meiji world. In this article, entitled "Family Tyranny," Tokutomi painted a bleak picture of young and ambitious men who were stifled in their desire to make a name for themselves by lazy, dependent relatives, and advocated the development of a system of individualism to replace the family system that sacrificed young people to their elders.[39] Tōson's struggle to gain independence from his family can be seen in the context of this modern problem that had been brought out in Tokutomi's article. Since 1893, when his mother moved permanently to Tokyo, Tōson had borne partial responsibility for her support (until her death in 1896) as well as that of the families of at least one of his older brothers. Furthermore, it seems that his relatives indirectly exerted pressure on Tōson, as the youngest son and the one with the brightest future, to aid in restoring the family fortunes. It was partly with the idea of escaping from family control over his future that Tōson had accepted the job far from Tokyo, for teaching at least kept him in contact with literature and reading, though it paid badly. However, by not bowing to tradition and taking a better-paying job in Tokyo so that he could contribute to the build-

[39] Kenneth B. Pyle, *The New Generation in Meiji Japan*, Stanford, 1969, p. 135.

ing up of the family fortunes, Tōson was subjecting himself to feelings of guilt over having somehow abandoned his family. It was a conflict of loyalty of this sort, then, that tormented Tōson during the years in Komoro, as well as his intellectual isolation.

The years in Komoro were the most crucial of Tōson's life in terms of his winning of his spiritual freedom. They were also the most crucial years in terms of his development as a writer. For Tōson these two goals had been closely linked from the beginning of his self-awareness as an adolescent, and the search for truth as a writer had later combined with his search for the inner self, in works that were to some extent confessional. There is an earnestness about his work during this period that contrasts greatly with that of earlier periods in his life. The writing of *Wakana-shū* was difficult, and it followed upon years of frustration, yet in the mid-1890s Tōson was young, he felt that self-expression was his right, and the confession of his sufferings in *Wakana-shū* was unburdened by thoughts of the future. Now, in the period of preparation for *Hakai*, Tōson was thirty, past the God-given period of youth. It was up to him to make his way alone, and it is doubtful whether young men his age of generations past had had quite the same feeling of aloneness in their struggles. Yet his ego was stronger now than it had been in his adolescence or even in his twenties. Also, Tōson gained valuable moral support for his decision to lead the life of an individual and to write a novel that revealed an individual's truth from his reading of Western novels, as well as from his literary colleagues such as Katai.

During his years in Komoro Tōson's conflict with the family was brought to a head, in a way that he would never have imagined. In the spring of 1905, as Tōson's heavy teaching schedule made it almost impossible for him to continue work on his novel, he borrowed money for publishing expenses from his father-in-law and, resigning from his teaching position, moved to Tokyo with his wife and three children, where he was able to work full time on *Hakai*. It was clear that for Tōson the work on *Hakai* was a life-and-death matter—he felt that he had to finish the novel at any cost, or he would have a future neither as an author nor as an independent individual. However, because of Tōson's severe curtailing of expenses in order to finish his novel, within one year of his arrival in Tokyo his three small daughters died, their resistance to disease weakened by an inadequate diet.[40] Thus, Tōson's choice to define himself rather than support his family had resulted in the sacrifice of his three daughters. That he saw their deaths this way is indicated by his calling the last ten chapters of the first edition of *Ie* (The Family, 1911), the novel that deals with his years in Komoro, "Sacrifices."

Tōson's placing of his work over the welfare of his family in this crucial situation has often been criticized, and the remarks of the I-novelist Shiga Naoya are among the most severe: "Someone wrote that twenty some years ago, when Shimazaki Tōson was writing *Hakai*, determined to finish his work no matter what sacrifice it entailed, he cut his expenses to the minimum with the result that his family became undernourished and his daughters died one after the other. When I saw this I became extremely angry. I wanted to ask, 'Was *Hakai* a literary work of the same value as these children?' That several daughters died for it is a serious matter. It seemed to me to involve something more than whether Tōson could have written *Hakai* otherwise."[41] Shiga is right in insisting that one cannot morally make the argument that if Tōson had not made the necessary sacrifices, he could not have written *Hakai* and hence that those sacrifices were somehow justified. Tōson himself surely did not consider the sacrifices to be justified. Also, one cannot try to exonerate Tōson by stressing that the deaths of his three children could have been avoided had his older brothers been able to give him financial help, since he probably would not have accepted money from them, out of a fear of losing his spiritual freedom. Furthermore, he consciously used

[40] See Senuma, *Hyōden. Shimazaki Tōson*, p. 172, for information on the illnesses of Tōson's daughters.

[41] Shiga Naoya, "Kuniko" (1927), *Shiga Naoya shū, Gendai nihonbungaku zenshū*, Tokyo, 1959, 20: 353.

the money he borrowed from his own wife's father not for his children but for his publishing expenses.

The responsibility for the sacrifices incurred by finishing *Hakai*, then, rests squarely on Tōson. It must not be thought, however, that his decision to finish his novel at all costs was taken without pain and suffering and some awareness that his family might suffer because of it. Surely he must have realized that his choice meant less food for the family, though he could not have imagined that his children would eventually die partly due to the deprivations they suffered at this time. Tōson made the decision to go ahead with his writing, not to hurt his family, but because he saw his writing as an activity that was closely linked with his will to live as an individual. To give up the writing would have been to give in to the forces of everyday life that were inimical or indifferent to the truth that he pursued in that writing. When it came to a choice between living for himself and his work or for others, Tōson chose the path of self-definition. Doubtless there was egoism mixed up in this desire, as well as a sincere desire for self-expression. In any case, Tōson undoubtedly realized from this experience that the self-definition Tōkoku had written of so eloquently was full of pitfalls when one tried to put it into practice in real life. He also must have realized that the new life of the self was in fact often built on the suffering of others. Rather than praising Tōson's action or condemning it, it is better to see it as a manifestation of his strong feeling of duty toward himself, a feeling that had developed in him gradually since his contact with Tōkoku and that, for better or for worse, is a sign that the process of the awakening to modern selfhood was going on in him at the time he was writing *Hakai*.

Before he was thirty Tōson had probably thought of himself as a young person struggling against the family, as represented by his mother and his older brothers. However, when his own daughters, who depended on him as he had depended on his parents, died after the completion of *Hakai*, Tōson must have realized for the first time what it was like to be one of the selfish elders who sacrificed their young for their own purposes. One could speculate that he was for a time repulsed by the excess of his individualism, much as he had been in the late 1890s and early 1900s after the publication of the effusive *Wakana-shū*. One could speculate also that Tōson might have found Dostoevsky's *Crime and Punishment* meaningful at this point in his life precisely because it depicted a person who, like himself, had turned radically away from the morality of his parents through his devotion to a process of self-definition that involved him in a secret crime: the neglect of his loved ones. Possibly Tōson even identified with Raskolnikov, who had suffered extreme mental torment because of a crime he could not consciously acknowledge, and possibly, because of his suffering, he was moved also by Dostoevsky's view of man that held out rebirth even to the criminal. Yet these are, at basis, idle speculations. The important thing is that it was Tōson's own experience of the guilt of one who had turned his back on the past in order to adopt an individualist morality that enabled him to create the first character in modern fiction who communicated a sense of deeply lived personal experience.[42] *Hakai*, then, even more than *Ukigumo* or *Futon*, is the first novel of the inner life in modern Japanese literature. The hero of *Hakai*, *because* he is a reflection of the Tōson of those years, is the first hero of modern Japanese fiction to become conscious of and take responsibility for his selfhood.

[42] Edwin McClellan sees the sense of personal history and personal sincerity as Tōson's contribution to the development of the modern Japanese novel. See "Tōson and the Autobiographical Novel," in *Tradition and Modernization in Japanese Culture*, ed. Donald H. Shively, Princeton, 1971, pp. 366-378.

CHAPTER SEVEN

Shinsei (The New Life): A Novel of Confession

After the publication of *Hakai* in 1906 Tōson continued to write novels that, influenced by the Naturalist demand for truthful scrutiny of the individual's life, were autobiographical in their basic intention. *Haru* (Spring, 1908) was followed by *Ie* (The Family, 1911), and Tōson became increasingly recognized as one of the leading novelists of his day. Then, after a period of several years in which he wrote no major novel, his lengthy novel *Shinsei* (The New Life) appeared in 1919. *Shinsei* occupies a special place in Tōson's oeuvre, for it delineates what was probably the most painful personal crisis in his life. It is Tōson's most mature treatment of the individual who is emerging from the influence of a feudal morality, and, like his early poems and the novels that followed them, it deals with the important Meiji theme of the struggle for self-definition. Along with *Hakai* it is the novel of Tōson's that communicates the author's most intense sympathy for the hero's struggle—though, unlike *Hakai*, *Shinsei* is a barely fictionalized record of particular events in Tōson's own life. Both novels present the hero's life in terms of a now familiar pattern of sin followed by moral suffering and growth, and culminating in confession and a "new life." *Shinsei* is unlike *Hakai*, however, in that it focuses not on sin but on the resurrection that follows it, a resurrection that comes about through the hero's love of a woman. Finally, *Shinsei*, written when Tōson was in his late forties, ended a period of almost thirty years of concern for the Meiji ideal of individualism, and in it Tōson gave what was to be the last in a series of personal interpretations of that ideal.

The Events Leading up to the Publication of Shinsei

As an acute critic of literature who had seen many possible fictional forms in his wide reading of Western and Eastern literature, Tōson must have recognized what was successful and what was not in his first novel, *Hakai*. Possibly Tōson discovered that he had a particular genius for autobiography only after he had thought over the strengths of *Hakai*: the richness of his observation of the details of everyday life, a richness that was infused with the powerful sense of his own personality emerging lyrically through the character of the hero, Ushimatsu. In any case, Tōson began about this time to devote his talents of observation to a relentless self-exposure. This meant that he turned his gaze away from society and social issues and concentrated on his own life and that of his immediate family or peer group. In the process his own life became history, and his pursuit of the truth became an exercise in capturing the significance of this personal history as it unfolded in time. For Tōson's thoughts after *Hakai* wandered over the events of several periods in his life: his experiences with the *Bungakkai* group in the early 1890s, his years as a struggling novelist in Komoro and Tokyo from about 1899 to 1910, his adolescent experiences at the Meiji Gakuin, the moral crises of his early forties, and finally, in his last completed novel, the life of his father in the turbulent years before and immediately after the Meiji Restoration.

In *Hakai* Ushimatsu was surrounded by a world of people with whom he interacted, even though the significant moments of his existence were those in which he experienced his selfhood in nature and in the company of Inoko. In *Haru* and his later novels, with the exception of the last completed one, *Yoake-mae*, Tōson's image of the individual is that of a person alone, surrounded only by his immediate social group (usually the family) and cut off almost completely from the outside world of historical and political realities. Though Tōson's novel *Ie* describes the events of his fam-

ily life from 1898 to 1910, it does not even mention the Russo-
Japanese War of 1904-1905, surely the most important event in
Japanese history of the time and, judging by other accounts, an
event that caused Tōson extreme personal anguish.[1] Nor does any
other historically important event impinge on the sequestered
family life of the Shimazaki family, which, however, has no lack
of tensions and controversies. Such narrowness of vision or viewpoint may be the result of Tōson's decision to devote himself to a
sphere of life limited enough to allow him scope for indirect lyrical expression, but it is also related to the general narrowing of
vision of the literary world as a whole after the Russo-Japanese
War. Katai's *Futon* appeared in 1907, signaling the beginning of
the dominance of the author-centered I-novel, and though Tōson's *Haru*, written in 1907 and 1908, was not directly influenced by *Futon* (it was begun before the appearance of Katai's
novel), it nevertheless reflects the general tendency of the writers
influenced by Naturalism to observe and record only the aspects
of life that they knew intimately, i.e., their own lives.

Tōson's fictional method after *Hakai*, then, relied less on in-
vention and more on observation and recalling of what actually
had happened. Thus, Tōson no longer had to rely on another author's plot, as he had done in writing *Hakai*; furthermore, invented dialogue could be replaced by recalled dialogue or narration in indirect statement by the author. The important role of
the author's memory and vision of the events of his life meant
that *Haru* and the novels that came after it were subjective
novels, depending for their movement and action more on the
fluctuations of the emotions of one character and on the flow of

---

[1] According to Tayama Katai, who volunteered as a war correspondent early
in 1904, at the outbreak of the Russo-Japanese War, Tōson had come up to
Tokyo from Komoro in the hope of becoming a war correspondent, but he arrived after Katai and his group had already left for the front. Katai writes that
Tōson then returned home and began the opening chapters of *Hakai* in the spirit
of a war correspondent. *Tōkyō no sanjūnen*, p. 341.

his experience than on a structured story line.[2] The emphasis of these novels was on the development of one character, Tōson (usually given the name Kishimoto Sutekichi), over a limited period of time. By the end of each novel, Kishimoto's life progressed to a certain point, a point of significance that was assigned by Tōson to the myriad, unstructured events of his own life. Furthermore, Kishimoto's progress was seen as a spiritual growth according to a pattern of sin followed by moral suffering and ending in rebirth that was already given in *Hakai*—an interpretive structuring of the development of the individual that went far beyond the limited objectives of the I-novel of the time. In *Haru*, for example, one episode is linked to the next in terms of its representation of one stage in the coming of spring, or new life, after the long winter of suffering. As Tōson looked back at the episodes in his life in the period of his involvement with Kitamura Tōkoku that were discouraging and seemingly without hope, he saw them, as in *Wakana-shū*, as the winter that would inevitably be overcome by spring, even if, as in this case, spring or new life comes only beyond the confines of the novel.

By 1911, after the publication of *Ie*, Tōson had reached a new peak of popularity. The long years of struggle to define himself as an individual and as a writer had resulted in two novels (*Haru* and *Ie*) that were innovative expansions of the fragmentary Naturalist I-novel form.[3] Furthermore, Tōson had acquired a relatively

---

[2] In a conversation of 1907 Tōson discussed the radical change in his novelistic method that had occurred between *Hakai* and *Haru*, emphasizing his new reliance on a structure that responded to the changing demands of his subjectivity: "When I began to write *Hakai* the structure was exactly determined from the start; it was thoroughly mapped out how I would write this and how I would write that. With *Haru* I completely stopped working out a structure and, having only vaguely in mind that I would try to paint such and such sort of character, I wrote the work without making any sort of plan." "*Haru* to *Ryūdōkai*," *Zenshū*, 17: 323.

[3] *Haru* is the first novel in Tōson's series of autobiographical novels. The second, *Ie*, is a novel in which the character that represents Tōson, here given the

small but faithful group of followers among the middle-class readers of Tokyo. He was now earning enough through his novels, essays, and criticism to live above the poverty level, though he was still not free of the burden of supporting his brother Hideo's family as well as his own. Yet in the next two years personal problems were to shatter the life he had labored to build up, and almost ruin his reputation. The difficulties of Tō-son's life that precipitated the moral crisis described in *Shinsei* actually began with the sudden death, in childbirth, of Tōson's wife in the summer of 1910, while he was still at work on *Ie*. The death of his wife plunged Tōson into a long period of loneliness and misery, a period that was fallow literarily as well.

It is typical of Tōson's attitude toward truthfulness in art that he would present his marriage realistically in one of his novels. That novel is *Ie*, and the twelve-year marriage of Sankichi (Tōson) and Oyuki (Tōson's wife, Fuyuko) is that of Tōson and his wife in all major respects. The description of Tōson's marriage in *Ie* reveals that it was clouded almost throughout by Tōson's jealousy and suspicion of his wife, for it seems that day-to-day contact with a woman destroyed the illusions about women that Tōson had formed in the period of his youth, under the influence of Romanticism. In his youthful poems written in the late 1890s Tōson had depicted with admiration the passion of Okume, a maiden who swam across a large body of water to join her lover in defiance of her parents. However, when Tōson, soon after he and Fuyuko were married, discovered a love letter Fuyuko had just written to a man she had loved before her marriage to him, he

---

name Koizumi Sankichi, does not monopolize the narrative point of view, as he does in *Haru* and in all the other novels of the series. *Ie* is the only one of the series in which Tōson consciously depicts a social group—the family. In its scope and in its preoccupation with a family it reminds of Thomas Mann's *Buddenbrooks* rather than of Zola's novels, though, interestingly, *Ie* is considered by numerous critics to be the masterpiece of Japanese Naturalism in its Zolaesque form. For an English translation see Tōson Shimazaki, *The Family*, trans. and introd. by Cecilia Segawa Seigle, Tokyo, 1976.

became intensely jealous, and even considered divorcing her—though he himself continued, not without guilt feelings, to visit his old love, Tachibana Itoe. It seems, then, that when Tōson found in his own wife an Okume who had a will to love regardless of morality, his pride was injured and his jealousy and hatred were aroused.

It is possible that the incident of what he saw as his wife's infidelity, and his own, reawakened the moral torment Tōson had suffered as a youth at the Meiji Gakuin when he had been forced to see himself as guilty of an immoral passion. In any case, Tōson's overserious reaction to this incident showed that it had touched an open wound. Probably a Victorian morality that exalted love and denied sexuality between man and woman was, in Tōson, superimposed on a Confucian conception of sexuality as valid but inferior, and love as nonexistent. Furthermore, an idealism stemming from his Christian education had caused Tōson to be ashamed of his own sexuality and naive in his expectations of women—he apparently expected a purity in women equal to his own shyness and restraint, a purity that would confirm the validity of his own reverence for women. The realization that women had wills, as well as active interest in sexuality, destroyed his idealistic faith in women. Though his marriage was satisfactory from a Confucian standpoint, in that he and Fuyuko had seven children, Tōson continued to yearn for a communion of souls. Yet the very relationship of marriage, with its basis in everyday life and the rearing of children, tended to draw emphasis away from intellectual or spiritual companionship. In fact, Tōson was quite aware that his wife was not interested in his work, and from this point of view also the marriage was a disappointment for him.

If Tōson had been more conscious of his need for a spiritual or intellectual companion, he would have chosen a wife for himself, as his mentor Tōkoku had done. Instead, Tōson had Iwamoto Yoshiharu, the former principal of the Meiji Gakuin and Fuyuko's principal at the Meiji Jogakkō, arrange a marriage for him. Tōson's wife had been a good student at the Meiji Jogakkō, but she was hardly the sort of person with whom he could have enjoyed spiritual or intellectual companionship. The daughter of a wealthy merchant family, she had been raised to expect a high standard of living as well as freedom of behavior. Like Katai's Yoshiko, the apprentice writer in *Futon*, she was an example of the new Meiji woman who, educated to develop a consciousness of self, demanded more of life than had her feminine ancestors. Doubtless Fuyuko was disillusioned at finding herself, after her marriage, imprisoned in a monotonous and exhausting routine of childrearing and housework in a remote mountain village. Then, too, Tōson's seriousness, reticence, and shyness with women probably made him difficult to live with. His moralistic attempts to shame her, and his morose jealousy on discovering her affection for another man, doubtless made the marriage difficult for her to bear. As portrayed in *Ie*, however, she seemed to overcome her shame and went on to live what she considered a happy enough life with Tōson. Yet she continued to maintain a moral independence from Tōson that was incomprehensible to him and that he bitterly resented.[4]

The novel *Ie* ends with Sankichi (Tōson) and Oyuki (Fuyuko) somewhat reconciled to one another, united temporarily as they face the difficulties of life. In Tōson's actual life, however, those moments of reconciliation occurred only a short while before his wife died in giving birth to their seventh child. After Fuyuko's death, besides the psychological adjustment, Tōson was faced with the immediate practical problem of what to do with the four young children she had left behind. He decided to put the baby

---

[4] In preparing to write his novel on domestic life (*Ie*) Tōson was once again inspired by Tolstoy, but this time the Tolstoy who was avidly concerned with family life. It is indicative of Tōson's mood, however, that he wrote *Ie* with *The Kreutzer Sonata* (1889), not *Family Happiness* (1859) on his desk. For *The Kreutzer Sonata* is the story of a man driven mad by suspicion of his wife's infidelity, a man who will not grant his wife moral independence from himself. See Senuma, *Hyōden, Shimazaki Tōson*, p. 202.

girl and his youngest son in other homes; his two older sons he
kept with him. During this time he was supporting the families
of both of his elder brothers. At first his second eldest brother
Hirosuke's two daughters looked after the children, but after the
elder of them was married in 1912, Tōson was virtually alone in
the house with the younger one, Komako (1893-). It was in the
bleak mood of sorrow and emptiness that Tōson experienced after
his wife's death that he turned to this girl, his niece, for companionship and affection. After a while it became clear that she was
pregnant, and Tōson, terrified that the affair would be found out,
left for France.

Tōson departed for France in April of 1913 without anyone but
Komako and one friend, Nakazawa Rinsen, knowing the precise
reason for his going. In order to finance the trip, Tōson had sold
the rights to all his works written up to that time and had arranged with the *Asahi Shimbun*, a leading Tokyo newspaper, to
write articles on his travels in Europe. With this money he intended to support not only himself and his own children but the
wives and children of his two older brothers as well. A few weeks
after his ship had left Kōbe, Tōson finally wrote a letter to his
brother Hirosuke, explaining the reason for his quick departure.
His son by Komako was born four months after he had left for
France, and was immediately sent to be brought up in the country. No one else in his family knew about Tōson's relationship
with Komako besides his brother, and he had escaped a confrontation with the family by leaving the country. Nevertheless,
Tōson was unable to rid himself of feelings of guilt at having
abandoned Komako. His stay, first in Paris, then, after war broke
out, in Limoges, was colored by this painful memory. Yet the
years in France were also a time of intellectual enrichment and
growth, as Tōson attended the latest plays, read the latest literary
works, and took an active part in cultural life.[5] Finally, he be-

---

[5] Tōson's journals from his years spent in Paris were published in the *Asahi
Shimbun* and later collected under the title *Heiwa no Pari* (Paris in Peacetime,
1915) and *Sensō to Pari* (Wartime Paris, 1915). *Zenshū*, vol. 12.

came aware of the uniqueness, and the value, of Japanese culture as he lived in the midst of French culture; it was at this point in his life that he resolved to study in depth the period in which his father had lived, the important period just before and after the Meiji Restoration. In effect, Tōson was already planning the research that would issue in his last, and possibly greatest, novel, *Yoake-mae* (Before the Dawn).

Tōson had originally planned to settle permanently in France, but as the war continued and it became increasingly difficult for him to support himself and the two families at home with his earnings, he decided to return to Japan. His involvement with Japanese history while in France apparently also convinced him that he still had an important task to perform in the field of literature: the revelation of the meaning of the Restoration in Japanese history and culture. Furthermore, the guilt that he felt over his action three years earlier demanded relief, a relief he could only achieve by confronting Komako. Tōson arrived home in July of 1916. In 1917 and 1918 he serialized in a magazine an autobiographical novel about his years at the Meiji Gakuin, *Sakura no mi no juku-suru toki* (When the Cherries Ripen), and wrote several stories for children. To complicate matters, he resumed his affair with Komako after his return from France. The two met clandestinely at first, but soon it became obvious what was going on, and Tōson's brother Hirosuke forbade his daughter to see Tōson. Neither Tōson nor Komako could break off the relationship, which had become a hopeless continuation of a love that had no future. Finally, shortly after the death of Komako's mother in April of 1918, Tōson began to write *Shinsei*, serializing it in the *Asahi Shimbun*. He considered the confession that he made in *Shinsei* his form of expiation for the crime he had committed six years earlier. Indeed, proof of his sincerity on this point is the fact that he wrote the novel, "sweating hot and cold sweat," as he put it—in misery and fear of what would happen when people read what he had done, but nevertheless in a do-or-die spirit.[6]

---

[6] Itō, *Shimazaki Tōson kenkyū*, p. 630.

It is reported that when Tayama Katai read installment number thirteen of *Shinsei*, the one that includes the words: "Setsuko confessed to Kishimoto in a low voice that she was going to become a mother," he expected at any moment to hear the news that Tōson had committed suicide.[7] This attitude, expressed by a writer who had himself revealed none-too-flattering details of his personal life in his novel *Futon*, demonstrates why Tōson had reason to be fearful as he determinedly released the installments of his novel one after another to the newspaper. Yet as Tōson neared the end of part one, it became clear that the general response to his confession was favorable, and he adopted a more confident tone in part two. The publication of *Shinsei* had the effect of ending Tōson's affair with Komako, for Hirosuke, out of fear of further scandal, sent Komako off to Taiwan to live with the family of Tōson's eldest brother, Hideo. In the long run, Tōson's decision to publish a confession of his sins in *Shinsei* impressed his readers, for after the minor scandal caused by the appearance of part one had worn off, his reputation, far from being ruined, actually improved. A collection of his complete works was made in 1922, from which he gained enough money to live moderately well for the first time in his life. In the 1920s he published two more collections of short stories, and he remarried in 1928. His epic trilogy on the life of his father, *Yoake-mae*, was finished in 1935, after which Tōson spent the remaining years of his life in relative solitude and disciplined writing. By the time of his death, in 1943, he was recognized, along with Natsume Sōseki and Mori Ōgai, as one of the great writers of the Meiji period.

Shinsei: *A Novel of an Individual's Rebirth through Love*

Shinsei, though certainly not one of the greatest of Tōson's novels in literary terms, merits consideration because it is probably the

---

[7] Reported in Hirano Ken, *Shimazaki Tōson*, p. 53. Hirano remarks, however, that far from intending to commit suicide, Tōson, while writing *Shinsei*, carried out his act of confession "with the persistent animal strength of a man who wanted to survive."

most personal statement of a writer who is interesting because of his personality. *Shinsei* is interesting also because in it the author discusses in detail thoughts and feelings he had when undergoing conflicts raised by his desire to lead the moral life of an individual; thus the novel has given later generations a vivid sense of what it was like to be a person caught between two cultures, as intellectuals were in the Meiji period. Furthermore, *Shinsei* is the best example of Tōson's innovations in the realm of autobiographical fiction of his time. Possessing 495 pages to *Hakai*'s 291, it focuses only on one individual; yet because the period of time covered is much longer than in *Hakai*, it gives an impression of epic grandeur. Like *Hakai*, *Shinsei* is narrated in the third person by an observer. In this novel, as in his other novels of the autobiographical series, Tōson looks back on events that took place in the past. Yet here he does not take advantage of his knowledge of the outcome of the events to structure them in a finished fictional pattern, as he did in *Hakai*. Or, rather, he does not narrate the events according to a fictional structure that sees time progressing toward a known end, but carefully preserves the illusion that he is narrating the events just as they occur.[8] The narrative is divided up into such events, each one the length of a newspaper installment (one to two pages), and one event follows another, giving the illusion that they are happening as they would in a day or a sequence of days. Thus, Kishimoto's reflective periods, in which the moral crisis unfolds and develops, are interspersed, as they would be in normal life, with visits from

[8] In part two of *Shinsei* Tōson narrates events of the present, and what in part one was a *technique* of narrating events just as they occurred, without foreknowledge, becomes in part two a necessity, for Tōson, as he wrote part two, did not actually know what would be the outcome of the action he was narrating: namely, his affair with Komako. His revelation of what had happened so far actually helped to shape future events, for it was because Tōson confessed in the newspaper that he had resumed the affair with Komako that his brother decided to end the affair by sending her to Taiwan. Then this event, which had been caused by Tōson's narration of earlier events, was in turn narrated by Tōson in his next installment in the newspaper.

friends, scenes where he plays with his children, walks through
the streets of Paris, descriptions of political events, descriptions
of people he met and talked with, and descriptions of scenery.
Finally, actual conversations, poems, and letters are included to
give the novel the air of a *document humain*.

The episodes in *Shinsei* depicting the moral problem that is of
particular interest to this study are scattered among prosaic
episodes, the way emotional high points would normally alter-
nate with prosaic moments in a person's life. Allowing for this
aspect of the structure of the novel, then, the plot of *Shinsei* is as
follows. Part one starts out with a presentation of Kishimoto's life
during the bleak period after his wife's death. In the midst of a
despair and loneliness that he does not attempt to remedy by remarrying, Kishimoto becomes involved in a sexual relationship
with his own niece, Setsuko (Komako in real life), who is alone
with him in the house. When Kishimoto hears from Setsuko that
she is pregnant with his child, his first reaction is to close himself
up in his study on the second floor of the house, as if to escape the
burden of his situation. He is eager to break out of the paralyzing
sorrow brought on by his wife's death, however, and when a
friend suggests that he go abroad for a while, he decides to go,
brushing aside the question of his responsibility toward Setsuko.
Kishimoto passes three lonely years in France, years that are intel-
lectually rich but years in which he is unable to find rest from the
guilt that is pursuing him. Finally he decides to return to Japan
and confront his action of three years before.

Part two begins with his return. Kishimoto is unsure how
many of the family know about his affair with Setsuko—he had
told only his elder brother Yoshio (Hirosuke in real life), Setsuko's father, in a letter written after his departure from Japan. The
child that had resulted from the affair had been given away to be
brought up in the country. On his return, Kishimoto lives for a
while with Yoshio and his wife, the wife's mother, Setsuko, and
his own two sons. It is only after his return that Kishimoto
notices how Setsuko has suffered on his account. Rather be-

latedly, he assumes responsibility for her welfare and hires her to do secretarial work for him. He is eventually rewarded for his efforts as he sees her recover her former good spirits. Yet their relationship soon becomes complicated due to Setsuko's odd position in her family. Setsuko's family had treated her badly in Kishimoto's absence, and now, after his return, he is still the only person she can rely on for support and affection. Kishimoto at first feels only pity for her, but gradually finds that he is again attracted to her. They resume the affair. Kishimoto begins to love Setsuko for the first time, but then realizes that his love is hopeless for he can never marry her. He gradually becomes depressed by the hopelessness of the affair, but finds that he is incapable of breaking it off. Finally he decides to remove the unbearable falsehood from his life by confessing everything in a novel. When episode thirteen of his confessional novel appears in the newspaper, Yoshio disowns Kishimoto and forbids him to see Setsuko again. She is sent to live with Kishimoto's eldest brother in Taiwan, and the novel ends with Kishimoto resigned to losing Setsuko but feeling that he has regained his self-respect by confessing the story of their affair.

When retold in the external terms of the events of a plot, the story of *Shinsei* is undoubtedly melodramatic, and apparently fit only for the cheap novel or the newspaper scandal sheet. Yet, in writing *Shinsei*, Tōson was clearly not interested in delineating the external events of his crisis but rather the process of inner moral transformation that lay concealed beneath their scandalous surface.[9] As in *Hakai*, the steps in the hero's transformation and the places where the hero is presented in the midst of his thoughts

[9] Such was the case also with the English Romantic writer William Hazlitt, who wrote a confessional work entitled *Liber Amoris* (1823), which described his frustrated love for the daughter of his landlord. Interestingly, both Hazlitt and Tōson were about forty when the events occurred, and both used the writing of their books as a way of discovering the meaning of the experience, and of love in general. Both works, when published, provoked a scandal but also elicited admiration for the authors' honesty about painful human matters.

and feelings are the important foci of the novel. Since Tōson's method of analysis and atmosphere of subjectivity are unlike those of any Western writer of subjective fiction that I know of, in the interests of presenting a new and unusual method of self-revelation to the Western reader who will have no other chance—since *Shinsei* is not translated—to see it, I will trace in detail the steps of the moral transformation that occurs in *Shinsei*.

The novel *Shinsei* begins, *in medias res*, with a letter from a friend of Kishimoto's who has left the city to live in nature. Kishimoto reads this letter just as he is becoming depressed about his moral stagnation, for he has been living a life of solitariness, boredom, and psychic death since his wife died three years before. He is forty-one years old and approaching middle age: "He sometimes compared himself to his friend Nakano. His friend had a composure which was lively and relaxed, while his own was the silence of death. In the midst of that dead silence, he waited for a storm which would attack him violently." The image of the storm expresses Kishimoto's ambivalent feelings toward the future: on one hand, the "crime" toward which he is pushed by his unconscious desires will "attack" him; on the other hand, it will paradoxically bring relief. In the meantime, however, the moral offense that he commits is conceived of only as something that has been thrust on him by an external force, as is seen in the following remarks of Kishimoto when Setsuko reveals her pregnancy: "The storm had finally come into the room which he compared to a Trappist cell, and to the monk in that cell."[10]

The moral struggle that Kishimoto undergoes in the course of the novel is generally held to be unclear and vague, due to the narrator's reticence, and even concealment of Kishimoto's feelings,[11] and it is true that the narrator often does not analyze

[10] Tōson, *Shinsei*, pt. 1, *Zenshū*, 6: 13 (chap. 5); 42 (chap. 15). I have indicated the chapter numbers of *Shinsei* for the benefit of those who use a different edition.

[11] For example, Edwin McClellan writes of *Shinsei*: "It is the kind of a novel that demands, by the very nature of its content, a ruthless and articulate exami-

Kishimoto's feelings intensively. Yet he does go back in time to discuss problems in the life of Kishimoto that, since they come up again and again, I conclude are put in deliberately to provide a context in which the moral crisis might be interpreted. One of these references is to Kishimoto's relationship to women and, in particular, to his wife. In the months of bleakness before Setsuko's revelation, Kishimoto had brooded about his past relationship with his wife, Sonoko (Fuyuko in real life):

> He thought over the months and days he had spent with Sonoko.
>
> 'Father, trust me—trust me—.' She had said this, crying, her face buried in his arm. The sound of her voice remained distinctly in his ears.
>
> Twelve years had gone by before Kishimoto listened to these words. Sonoko had not been like the daughter of a wealthy family at all; she could put up with hardships, she liked to work, and she had a character which made her husband happy in many ways, but she had come to him as a bride who had committed an indiscretion, a fact which had aroused fierce jealousy in him. It was too late before Kishimoto realized that he had looked too harshly on her. It had taken twelve years for him and his wife to gradually open their hearts to one another. And when he finally thought about the words she had spoken to him that time, she was already dead.
>
> •   •   •   •   •   •
>
> Without really intending to, Kishimoto had become the kind of person who couldn't bear to listen to talk of his remarrying. Celibacy for him was a kind of revenge against women. He had even come to be afraid of loving, so deeply had the experience of love hurt him.[12]

---

nation of the state of mind of the characters involved. . . . When judged in the light of what we presume to have been Tōson's primary intention of writing it—that is, to write a 'confessional' novel—it is an obvious failure." *Two Japanese Novelists: Sōseki and Tōson*, Chicago, 1969, pp. 123-125. Yet the same critic later made a fairer evaluation of Tōson's sincerity in the context of his times, and praised Tōson's "emotional commitment" and his "seriousness of intention." See McClellan, "Tōson and the Autobiographical Novel," especially p. 66.

[12] *Zenshū*, 6: 30-31 (chap. 8).

Alongside the painful memories of his wife and his active resentment of her "infidelity," there exists in Kishimoto a desire to turn his back on the world, like the monk in *Tsurezure-gusa* (*Grasses of Idleness*), as he puts it, and taking his children with him, go away somewhere, away from his stagnant and unproductive situation. In short, he longs for a new life.

It is against this background that Setsuko tells Kishimoto of her pregnancy, and unleashes the storm he had unconsciously been longing for. Her announcement has the expected result of making him conscious of the crime he has committed, but its main effect is to make him fearful of the shame that would ensue should it be discovered. (In this he is like Ushimatsu in *Hakai*, for whom the awareness of his *eta*hood meant first, fear of discovery, and only later consciousness of his responsibility to himself.) The revelation also elicits in Kishimoto further memories of his past relationship with his wife, memories that give more insight into the moral problem at the heart of the novel. Kishimoto thinks back on a fireworks festival that had taken place a few years before his wife's death, when she was still in good health. Something had apparently loosened up in their relationship at that time:

> Kishimoto's warm treatment of his wife resulted in her rewarding him with similar treatment. . . . He who for a long time had been overzealous about guiding his wife morally, learned, about that time, how to make her happy. He discovered that his wife was one of those women who want from a man not awkward admiration but passionate love.
> From that time on Kishimoto's body seemed to come alive. . . . He learned about aspects of his wife that he hadn't known existed.[13]

Yet precisely when he had begun to learn how to love, his wife had died, leaving him in a state of loneliness and deprivation. Part of the desire to take revenge on women by becoming a veritable monk and not remarrying is surely linked to an unconscious

[13] Ibid., p. 41 (chap. 14).

feeling of resentment against his wife for dying and leaving him in a state of emotional and sexual deprivation. It is also possible that at her death the strong feelings of jealousy and anger he had felt when he discovered Sonoko's alleged infidelity reasserted themselves, and contributed to a generalized hatred of women.

Thus, when Kishimoto hears that Setsuko is pregnant, he does not feel particularly sorry for her, because she, like all women, means very little to him. His main thought is for his own reputation should the news become public. Because he is so little aware of his own feelings, it is no wonder that the shock of Setsuko's revelation causes him to turn inward in self-pity rather than outward in compassion for Setsuko. He is dominated by a coldness and objectivity toward others at this point in his life, an attitude that is due at least in part to his forced deprivation and isolation. As the narrator notes:

> In many situations Kishimoto was cold toward women. The fact that he faced many tempting situations as a bystander was not because he forcibly restrained himself, but rather stemmed from his innate scorn for women. . . . Kishimoto had gotten himself into a situation in which he would have to suffer together with his niece. It was not that he had chosen *her* from among many women. Setsuko was like young grass pushing itself up gently from beneath a stone. She was a girl who had neither loved nor been loved. She had possessed nothing that particularly tempted Kishimoto's feelings. All she had had was a sort of girlishness, a way of looking to her uncle for help, of relying on him. What an irony of life![14]

Kishimoto finds himself entangled in a fateful situation with a woman he did not consciously seek out, and whom he does not even love. His niece had had nothing to tempt him with, and yet he fell into a trap that could have tragic consequences for him. The ambiguity of his relationship to Setsuko will become more clear later, as Kishimoto learns from the experience. At this point all he can think of is escaping from the situation, for the affair had occurred just when he wanted to begin a new life, alone.

[14] Ibid., p. 42 (chap. 15).

Kishimoto decides to take the advice of a friend who urges him to submit himself to new stimuli, and leaves for France, intending to stay forever. He has felt threatened by the approaching birth of his child by Setsuko, and after seeing friends and relatives for the last time, he feels like the man in the Buddhist parable who left behind the "burning house," a metaphor for worldly involvements and suffering.[15] Now he assumes the symbolic guise of the exile, the traveler, the monk—the person outside of normal involvements with other people and with life. In part, it is a self-condemned exile, taken up to atone for his guilt, as he notes later. Kishimoto's self-imposed exile recalls Tōson's self-imposed isolation after he had become involved with the older woman at the Meiji Gakuin, and his self-inflicted exile when he was unable to suppress his feelings for his student Sukeko, at the Meiji Jogakkō. Each time, Tōson had adopted the solitary life of a wandering monk (marked by poverty, if not by celibacy) as a punishment for what he saw as his immorality. However, such a self-imposed exile is a much more serious matter for a person of Tōson's (Kishimoto's) age. Kishimoto cannot exile himself permanently from the problem caused by his action, because the problem he now faces due to his involvement with Setsuko is linked to too many of the lingering psychological attitudes that have caused him trouble in the past. He is at a point in his life where he will have to face it, even in exile.

To a certain extent, then, Kishimoto intends the journey to be one of penance. The narrator says: "At the very least, he wanted to atone for his immorality by taking on the burden of suffering."[16] During his stay abroad, he feels the weight of the burden of guilt, which manifests itself in feelings of boredom, aimlessness, and fatigue. As the narrator writes of this period, "the more he tried to bury it, the more the crime came alive in the depths of his heart."[17] Kishimoto reaches the depths of despair and for-

[15] Ibid., p. 95 (chap. 43).
[16] Ibid., pp. 73-74 (chap. 31).
[17] Ibid., p. 127 (chap. 62).

lornness one spring, when he realizes that he is unable to find
peace even in the beautiful spring weather:

> Though he cherished the thought of resurrection, the days when
> his feelings were strangely unquiet continued for Kishimoto. It was
> not that he had wished for luxury in coming on this journey. He had
> only wanted rest for his soul. There was nothing that was more neces-
> sary to him. . . .
> Whether he stayed in his apartment or walked the stone streets of
> Paris, was all the same to Kishimoto, since he could not find rest.
> When days like that came, he would aimlessly go to parks, stand in
> front of shops and look at their windows, sit down in strange
> restaurants—just because there was no other way to pass the time.
> Sometimes he did this for days in a row.[18]

In a sense, Kishimoto is atoning for his "crime" through the
listlessness he suffers—a continuous loss of vital energy that is his
unconscious heart's way of punishing him for not facing his guilt
consciously.

During the time in Paris Kishimoto receives letters regularly
from Setsuko. Each time they come, he feels as if the wound has
opened up again. Against his will, he is forced to think about
Setsuko and her life:

> It was only Setsuko's letters that he threw away or tore up. Kishimoto
> didn't leave them around where he could see them. . . . He wished
> that she would forget him, and think about herself—she still had a
> long future before her. On account of feelings like these, Kishimoto
> decided to avoid writing to Setsuko if he could help it, and to direct
> to Yoshio any replies he had to make to her letters. But just as he
> would think that she had to a good extent forgotten him, another
> letter would arrive from her, increasing his irritation. The number of
> letters she had written since he had left Kōbe lay in his heart like a
> question. She wrote that she, who had been followed without a day of
> relief by a dark cloud, had gradually become free of it. Somehow she
> was a different person. Even though she was burdened with such an
> injury, she knew no regret. He wondered at the fact that a woman

[18] Ibid., pp. 142-143 (chap. 72).

like Setsuko, born with a girlish heart, was able to reveal her girlish feelings to someone like himself, who was much older than she, and whose mustache had half turned white. Every time he thought of this, he reminded himself that she was the mother of a boy. Again he reminded himself how deep were the roots of the bond between man and woman, a bond he had thought was so easy to leave behind and forget. There were some points in her letters that he could not fathom unless he let his thoughts go that far.

· · · · · ·

Whenever he thought of Setsuko so far away, he felt the deep sadness of his guilt. But that was not all—he began to feel an unspeakable fear as well.[19]

It is obvious that Kishimoto had not loved Setsuko earlier. In fact, what had irritated him at that time was his involvement in an affair that reflected none of his conscious will. Though Kishimoto still feels no love for her, Setsuko's repeated efforts to communicate with him force him to become aware of her and of how he stands in relation to her. Kishimoto is amazed at her courage in facing the future without regret. He sees that she seems to have a strong attachment to him, a devotion she demonstrates by continually writing to him even though he does not write back. The fear he now feels, along with the heightened sense of the crime he has committed against her, is the fear of involvement, for she is turning out to be a stronger personality than he had imagined. He had seen her previously only as an object of his pity, but now, as a person who demands his love, she threatens the solitary security that he is used to and unconsciously wants to maintain.

The change that now begins to occur in Kishimoto's feelings toward Setsuko marks the beginning of his moral transformation. At the time of the disastrous relationship with his niece, Kishimoto was living a solitary and unhappy life, suffering from the loss of his wife more than he was aware. The revelation of Setsuko

[19] Ibid., pp. 167-168 (chap. 87).

that she was pregnant seemed threatening to him not only because she was related to him, and he could be legally prosecuted for his behavior if it were known; her revelation also forced Kishimoto to see himself as lustful and exploitive, and this was a vision of himself that he could not bear. He fled to France hoping, among other things, to wipe away this image of himself. The images of the bachelor and the monk—supposedly images of freedom and detachment—were actually images assumed out of fear. Viewed from this perspective, then, Kishimoto's escape to France was a cowardly act. By going to France, he had left Setsuko to bear the blame for their action completely alone, and at the mercy of her family. Yet, what could he have done had he stayed there? The problem is not simply one of cowardice but is complicated by a practical consideration—namely, that Kishimoto could never have married his niece and solved the problem in such a simple manner.

A second alternative would have been to simply hush up the affair and proceed as if nothing had happened. This was a common traditional way of dealing with such in-family scandals, but it was unsuited to a man such as Kishimoto. The fact that his feelings were in torment and he had thought of suicide after he heard that she was pregnant showed that Kishimoto felt some guilt toward Setsuko. Furthermore, the sense of human rights was ingrained enough in him for him to realize that he had committed a crime against another human being. Yet he was obviously unable to confront the idea of taking full moral responsibility for his action, and so he fled. The scandalous situation depicted in *Shinsei*, then, turns out to be a moral and spiritual problem, due to the very fact that a practical solution—in this case, a marriage between the two—is impossible. The question of what the crime means to Kishimoto as a human being thus takes precedence over the view of his action as a problem that can be either hushed up or dealt with practically. The escape to France allows the problem to develop into what it really is: a psychological and moral dilemma that has deep roots in the heart of Kishimoto. There, in a state of isolation and detachment guaranteed by his distance from the situation, the problem works itself out naturally, with time.

The question is, then, what does this attachment to Setsuko, which has occurred without his really willing it, mean to Kishimoto? Is it a horrible trap, as the narrator refers to it? Will this attachment to Setsuko drag him down into the dirt, or does it have in it regenerative possibilities? The one thing that Kishimoto had not counted on is Setsuko's contribution to the situation. From the last passage quoted, it is obvious that he is beginning to realize that she herself is a person, that she has changed through this incident, and that she can have an effect on him. Unconsciously, he is beginning to see that she alone, of all the people he knows, cares enough about him to write to him frequently, and it is because he begins to care for her that he eventually decides to return to Japan and confront the moral dilemma head-on. Here it is possible that Tōson, following the plot of Dostoevsky's *Crime and Punishment*, is presenting Setsuko in the role of the Sonya figure who forgives or rather cancels crimes against her through her love. Sonya was a victim, yet she somehow did not accept the idea of herself as a victim, and thus remained free of the stigma of crime. Likewise, Setsuko considers neither her own action nor Kishimoto's as a crime, and thus she feels no remorse. Consequently, she frees Kishimoto from the feeling that he has utterly ruined her, for there is still some life in her, and therefore there is room to expiate for the one who committed the crime against her. As Sonya persuaded Raskolnikov to confess and led him part of the way toward a spiritual resurrection, Setsuko's love cancels out the crime of Kishimoto and leads him to a new life that is free of guilt.[20]

After the outbreak of World War I, Kishimoto moves with a

[20] It is difficult to assert that *Crime and Punishment* was directly influencing *Shinsei*, as it influenced *Hakai*. Yet Tōson's choice, in this novel as well as in *Hakai*, of a plot that follows the pattern of sin or guilt followed by suffering, confession, and rebirth, is doubtless linked to his initial influence, in Komoro, by the religious and humanistic view of life of Dostoevsky and of *Crime and Punishment* in particular.

friend to a village near Limoges, in Haute Vienne, where he attains mental peace for the first time since he left Japan. The realizations that Kishimoto comes to in Haute Vienne can be seen within a context that Tōson himself gives us. While in the provinces Kishimoto spends long hours sitting in the local Roman Catholic church. He thinks of the novelist Joris Karl Huysmans's joining of the Catholic church and entrance into the religious life, and considers doing the same, since the spirit of Catholicism that he absorbs in the village church gives him a long-needed peace.[21] It seems clear that Kishimoto's interest in the Catholic church at this point stems from his intuition that religion would overcome his moral stagnation, for the Tōson who is behind Kishimoto had experienced the bankruptcy of emotion and spirituality of the Naturalist world view, just as Huysmans had in the 1890s.[22] The period just after he had finished his Naturalist novel *Ie* was one of horrible boredom, monotony, and restlessness for Tōson; he often read the poems of Baudelaire at this time.[23] Then, too, it seems

[21] *Zenshū*, 6: 194-195 (chap. 103). Joris Karl Huysmans (1848-1907) is best known as the author of the novel *A Rebours* (Against Nature, 1884), which presents, in the character Des Esseintes, the quintessential Decadent: the man who out of boredom and world-weariness pursues ever more artificial and bizarre sensations and experiences. Though Huysmans's use of symbols, his aestheticism, and his lyricism link him to the Decadent poets Baudelaire, Verlaine, and Mallarmé, his detailed documentation and his objective style demonstrate unequivocally his indebtedness to the Naturalist novelist Zola.

[22] During the last ten or so years of the nineteenth century, powerful antipositivist forces in France were proclaiming the "banque-route de la science," and the movement of Naturalism, which was based on scientific positivism, underwent a decline. Finding that neither positivism nor aestheticism satisfied his spiritual needs, Huysmans in the 1890s and early 1900s took an active part in the occult and religious movements that sprang up in the wake of the decline of Naturalism. In a series of spiritual autobiographies—*Là-bas* (1891), *En route* (1895), and *L'Oblat* (1903)—Huysmans, using the persona of Durtal, told in detail the story of his conversion to Catholicism. It is possible that Tōson, in reading these works, was influenced by the detailed, third-person mode of autobiographical narrative that Huysmans employed.

[23] Tayama Katai describes the years after the death of Tōson's wife when he spent most of his time alone in his study on the second floor of his house, in his

that Tōson, during the bleak period described at the beginning of
Shinsei, was coming to some of the same realizations that the
French Decadents, from Baudelaire to Huysmans, had come to:
that everyday life is full of ennui and emptiness; that the intellect
and the aesthetic sensibility are incapable of creating happiness;
and that scientific objectivity is worthless as a moral system. The
transformation that Kishimoto (Tōson) undergoes in Haute
Vienne is one that takes him beyond the egotistical objectivity of
the Naturalists to a level where he is aware of his emotions and
senses and capable of self-acceptance and peace.

The passage that marks Kishimoto's transformation is one of
the most beautiful pieces of sustained lyricism in the novel. The
scene is pervaded by the traditional Japanese feeling of *aware*, in
which the individual self is fused or united for the duration of a
poetic moment with the divine in the form of nature:

> It seemed to Kishimoto that he had found rest, real rest, for the first
> time since he had come to France, here on the banks of the Vienne.
>
> When he had lived almost two months in the peaceful village, not
> only his affairs since he had come to Europe but even those from the
> time when he had left home had somehow become ordered in his
> mind. He thought to himself: If humanity were to judge him and he
> were forced to defend himself, would he be able to relate fully all that
> had happened inside of himself, using some kind of psychological ex-
> planation as a shield? And the fact that he had come up against a
> crisis situation in his life, one in which he had had to live, even
> though it meant sacrificing someone else—how could he talk about

---

Tōkyō no sanjūnen, p. 377. Itō Kazuo discusses Baudelaire's influence on Tōson at
this time in *Shimazaki Tōson kenkyū*, pp. 577-580. It is noteworthy that later on
in *Shinsei* Tōson has Kishimoto look back on his solitary, emotionally and
spiritually stagnant life prior to his affair with Setsuko, as decadent (he uses the
French word *décadence*). *Shinsei*, pt. 2, *Zenshū*, 6: 362-363 (chap. 72). It appears,
then, that Tōson realized after the publication of *Ie* that his artistic method had
become almost completely aesthetic under the influence of Naturalist objectivity. The period of the affair with Komako (1913-1919) can be seen as a time
when Tōson recovered a more vital and spiritual view of art, of the sort that he
had had when he wrote *Hakai*. It is this view that informs *Shinsei*.

this in a clear, logical, noncontradictory, and rational way? Fears
which arose in his mind as if he were attacked by long, endless
nightmares; suspicion of his relatives and friends that he could not
suppress; his soul trembling before the power of an unseen persecution; the crests of waves hurrying toward him as if in a dream; the
unspeakable sorrow of going among unknown people—what horrible
eyes he had encountered! What feelings of panic he had experienced!
What a failure his life had been! Sometimes the deep impressions
seemed to become more vivid with time—they weren't the sort that
faded away. However, the agitation of violent feelings that he had
felt temporarily had gradually left him. The only thing left now was
his feeling toward his unfortunate niece. Before, he had looked back
serenely on his deed. He now came to feel, he who had wanted to
bury the crime committed only because he had somehow wanted to
live, that even though it meant suffering temporarily, he wanted to
try to do something about the deep wound he had once inflicted on
his niece as well as the blot which remained on his own life. The more
he tortured himself, the sadder he became.

In the midst of his thoughts, Kishimoto went into the vegetable
garden in the enclosure of the farm house. He walked down a small
path in the center of the garden; on both sides of the path were
planted numerous fruit trees. This was the place where he and
Makino had often come to rest, where they had picked ripe peaches
right off the branch and tasted them, and where they had walked
around breathing in the fragrance of the earth. The last days of October were here. Not only had the French green pears turned slightly
red on their branches and many of them hung down, but the ripe
fruits swayed occasionally in the autumn wind, some of them falling
on the ground, like stones, in front of him.

On one side, the field adjoined a narrow bypath on the edge of the
village; on the other, it opened into the garden of the neighboring
house, which had the typical village-style red tiled roof. From the
byway, he could hear the sound of people passing in wooden shoes; on
the other side, from the garden, he heard the sound of hoes hitting
the earth. Kishimoto walked between the peach and pear trees,
breathing in the fragrance of the new fruits, just as if he wanted to
accept, with all his heart, the life of the ripened trees into himself.

The autumn in Haute Vienne aroused mellow feelings in Kishi-

moto. He even recovered his interest in life, an interest that had been
quite lost for long months and years. Even though his sin still seemed
to live on inside of him, with his softened feelings he came to be able
to face it.[24]

In the atmosphere of emotional and sensual relaxation of rural
France, Kishimoto has become conscious of his primary motive
for escaping from Japan. The words "a crisis situation in his life,
one in which he had had to live, even if it meant sacrificing someone else" are an indication that Kishimoto recognizes that he had
left Japan chiefly because he had desired freedom from an unbearable situation. Instead of condemning himself for having had
such a desire, he is now able to accept its validity and to take
responsibility for it.

It is clear from Kishimoto's realizations in this passage that his
guilt toward Setsuko is not the primary focus of his moral problem. The main focus is his own moral stagnation, which had
existed even before Setsuko came on the scene. Setsuko's revelation of her pregnancy, then, had merely shocked him into an
awareness of his moral situation. When Kishimoto allows himself
to relax in silence and in peaceful rural surroundings, free from
everyday family obligations, his tension leaves him and he can see
his situation clearly. It is only after he faces his own moral stagnation that he is able to think of Setsuko and the wrong he has done
her. Finally, his willingness to accept the fact that he has done
real harm to Setsuko through his insistence on having his own
freedom signifies a rejection of shame and secrecy and an acceptance of responsibility for his deed. It is the same kind of change
that Tōson's character Ushimatsu underwent in *Hakai*, under the
influence of Inoko, when he decided to stop being ashamed of his
origins and reveal them proudly.

The ideals of responsibility for oneself and honesty toward the
outside world were ideals of Kitamura Tōkoku that had inspired
Tōson (Kishimoto) as a youth, but he had forgotten them during

[24] *Shinsei*, pt. 1, *Zenshū*, 6: 185-186 (chap. 98).

the period after his wife's death. In this passage, the awareness that Kishimoto gains of his old desire for freedom is an indication of the reemergence of the spirit of his youth, and the lonely, premature middle age that he had accepted in despair is replaced by a spirit of youthful idealism. Once Kishimoto recovers the spirit of his youth, he begins to despise his solitariness, and his dishonesty, and eventually he decides to return to Japan. He talks of freeing himself from his self-torturing loneliness, and thinks about remarrying as well as arranging a marriage for Setsuko. Life in a rural atmosphere has the effect of relaxing him, of making him open to the perceptions of his senses and aware of his dynamic moral nature. It is no accident that it is in nature that he dares to pose the question for the first time of whether he should confess everything.

The rebirth scene of Kishimoto was possibly influenced by Tolstoy's *Resurrection*, which Tōson had read with enthusiasm in 1904. *Resurrection* deals with a man who in his youth seduced a servant girl, but later in his life becomes conscious of the crime he has committed against her. He sets out to atone for his action by helping her, and in so doing learns to live again in peace and happiness. Nekhludov clearly sees the rebirth of his moral nature, which had been dead during his years of cynical aristocratic life, as a new life, and he uses the words "new life" when he discusses this experience in his journal. Both Tōson and Tolstoy conceive of the spiritual rebirth of their characters as somehow related to childhood, youth, and the natural, uncorrupted countryside, and in this they are true disciples of Rousseau. For example, just before Nekhludov leaves for Siberia to help Maslova, he spends several days on the old estate where he had first met her, and where he had lived in the innocence of childhood:

> Nekhludov sat beside the window, looking into the garden and listening. A fresh spring breeze wafted the scent of newly turned soil across the window sill, all scarred with marks of a knife. It lifted the hair from his moist forehead and rustled the papers that lay on the

sill. He heard the swift regular patter of the wooden paddles which the women used to beat the clothes they were washing, as it echoed over the glittering sunlit surface of the mill stream, the rhythmical sound of the water rushing over the wheel, and the loud buzzing of a startled fly.

And suddenly he remembered hearing these very sounds many years ago, when he was young and innocent . . . ; it was not exactly that he remembered himself as a boy of eighteen, but he seemed to feel himself the same as he was then; he felt the freshness, the purity, the great possibilities, and all the aspirations of his youth; and yet, like one in a dream, he knew that all this could be no more, and he felt very sad.[25]

As in Tōson's *Hakai* and *Shinsei*, man's ability to enjoy or feel unity with nature is linked to childhood and innocence. Consequently, a recovery of this ability, for Nekhludov, would mean a recovery of the innocence he has lost.[26]

At the end of part one, just before Kishimoto returns to Japan, he thinks back on the twenty years that have passed since the death of his mentor Aoki (Tōkoku) and comes to a resolution:

[25] Leo Tolstoy, *Resurrection*, trans. Vera Traill, New York, 1961, p. 205.

[26] A passage in *Shinsei* that occurs on p. 188, shortly after the long passage I quoted on Kishimoto's rebirth in Haute Vienne, reminds of the above passage from *Resurrection*. Describing Kishimoto's favorite walking place in Haute Vienne, Tōson notes that Kishimoto likes to stand on a bridge overlooking the river and watch the women washing clothes in the river, and remarks that "The sound of washing sticks beating on the stones reverberated on the quiet water." Since the sound of washing sticks being whacked against stones (or the similar sound of fulling sticks beating on cloth) is probably a sound that Tōson had heard as a child in rural Magome, and since the scene where Kishimoto hears it occurs after his rebirth in the fruit garden, Tōson probably intends to show that Kishimoto, as he hears the sound, is once more enfolded in the atmosphere of his childhood innocence. In both works the sound of the beating of washing sticks is heard at a crucial moment in the inner life of the character, and in both works it evokes memories of childhood and innocence. Yet where Kishimoto has recovered his innocence, Tolstoy's Nekhludov is aware only of the great distance that separates his present self from his childlike, innocent self of long ago.

Up to that day (when Aoki died) he had acted only according to the youthful spirit he had been born with. But somehow that spirit had been lost.

"That's it. I must return to that youthful spirit, before anything else."[27]

Under the influence of the spirit of his youth that he has now regained, Kishimoto reviews his attitudes toward love and women. He recalls his love for Katsuko (Sukeko in real life), a student of his, twenty years before. She was promised to another man even before he had fallen in love with her, but Kishimoto had kept the feelings of bitterness and resentment over his loss of her all this time. He now realizes the effect that the disappointment over the loss of Katsuko had had on the relationship with his wife:

'Father, trust me—trust me—.'

These words of Sonoko, which she had spoken, crying, her head buried in his arm, twelve years after they were married, were the most heartfelt, the most difficult words he had ever heard his wife say. In taking love terribly seriously, he had lived a miserable life. Attempting to recover the one he had lost, he had lost the one he had. When Sonoko had died from loss of blood after childbirth, with hardly the time to say good-bye to her children, he could only dazedly find fault with women. If he had only been able to believe in love, he would not be unfree, a bachelor, saddled with the children. Perhaps he should simply have listened to the suggestions of relatives and friends, and remarried. He had fallen into the deep abyss of mistrust, and as a result, he had piled up disappointment after disappointment. From mistrust stemmed his solitariness and boredom. The way in which he viewed women had been deformed by it as well.[28]

Kishimoto feels that if he readopts the spirit of youthful idealism and openness with a consciousness of the destructiveness of his former attitudes toward women, he will be able to love and trust

27 *Zenshū*, 6: 234 (chap. 128).
28 Ibid., p. 232 (chap. 127).

them. For the first time he speaks of Heloise and Abelard as symbols of a new type of love that includes trust and loyalty. Kishimoto had often visited the graves of the twelfth-century lovers in Père Lachaise Cemetery: "The graves of Abelard and Heloise remained distinctly before Kishimoto's eyes. It was not only that the famous monk of the Middle Ages had shared a love until death with the nun who was both his disciple and his lover, but even after death they slept in the same old, blackened tomb, sharing the same pillow. They were a symbol of a world of deep ecstasy. They were a symbol of an almost unfathomable trust between man and woman."[29] These two figures provide an example of an idealistic love, a kind of love that Kishimoto eventually learns to accept and that contributes toward his resurrection and the "new life" of the title.

Now that Kishimoto has freed himself from the specter of his past misery with women, he is able to look more rationally at a problem that will face him when he returns to Japan: his future relationship with Setsuko. Kishimoto is quite aware of the awkwardness of his relationship with Setsuko, and thinks that the best way to clarify his position toward her would be for him to remarry and arrange a marriage for her as well. As the narrator remarks, "Only with the idea of leaving behind the bachelor's life and marrying a second time could he face Setsuko again."[30] Kishimoto's intention to remarry also represents his conscious desire not to fall back into the same sort of relationship with Setsuko as before. Indeed, now that he views her with compassion, he is much more aware of the crime that further exploitation of her would mean. Complex feelings such as these cause Kishimoto to treat Setsuko warily at first, but seeing the condition she is in inevitably arouses his pity. During his absence she had contracted a skin disease that affected her hands, and she was in very low spirits. When Yoshio, her father, tells Kishimoto how miserable

[29] Ibid., p. 233 (chap. 128).
[30] *Shinsei*, pt. 2, *Zenshū*, 6: 251 (chap. 8).

and sick she had been while he was abroad, Kishimoto thinks guiltily to himself: "You made her that way."[31] Furthermore, Kishimoto sees that Setsuko has suffered mental torture while he was abroad. Since Yoshio was unable to vent his resentment of Kishimoto's actions on his brother himself, who besides being out of reach was actually his benefactor at the time, he had treated his daughter harshly instead. Kishimoto soon notices that it is only in his presence that she seems lively and happy: "The way her eyes brightened that day and the way her lips were silent testified to the misery of the life inside her, which seemed to want to expand and be free but couldn't."[32] He begins to see Setsuko as a human being with the same irrepressible desire to live that he had discovered in himself while in France. His compassion for her, then, stems not only from his awareness of the suffering he himself had inflicted on her, but from his seeing in her an individual seeking freedom from a hostile and uncomprehending family.

Kishimoto's natural sympathy, awakened through his suffering, draws him toward her, and Setsuko herself is in the awkward position of depending upon Kishimoto as her only source of earthly affection and support. It is not surprising, then, that the two very soon resume the affair. I think that it is fair to say that Kishimoto's resolve to stay away from Setsuko and do disinterested good by her was genuine, as was his pity for her. Yet, as before, his unconscious need for feminine contact and her need of him as a combination father, friend, and lover were real psychological needs that could not be put out of the way by resolutions of the conscious mind. It would have taken Kishimoto's full resolve to avoid emotional involvement with Setsuko, in the manner of a monk's vow to avoid women, in order for him to have changed the course of events. Besides, Kishimoto's experience in France had if anything softened his feelings toward involvement. As it is, the two were once again living in the same house, and spending several hours of each day in one another's company.

[31] Ibid., p. 288 (chap. 29).   [32] Ibid., p. 299 (chap. 35).

Setsuko's appeals for affection and kindness spoke to Kishimoto like a fate that could not be avoided. In a passage quoted
earlier there was the phrase: "Again he reminded himself how
deep were the roots of the bond between man and woman, a bond
he had thought was so easy to leave behind and forget." If anything, the bond between him and Setsuko was now stronger, for
Kishimoto was much more conscious than before of his indebtedness to her and was now willing to respect the demands of the
bond between them. It would have been much easier on the respectability of the family, of course, if Kishimoto had been able
to avoid the compassion for Setsuko and the bond between them
that it furthered. Yet in following the demands of his attachment
to Setsuko, Kishimoto was following the demands of his heart.
These demands were to lead him eventually to defy his family
more openly.

One would expect the old Puritanism to have reasserted itself
when Kishimoto resumed the affair with Setsuko. However, the
conflicts of his youth had been tempered by the crisis Kishimoto
underwent in France. He was now tired of self-imposed loneliness
and separation from women. As the narrator remarks:

> He who had once experienced a horrible burn was now, once more,
> being swallowed up by fire. Kishimoto thought of his relationship
> with Setsuko as exactly like this. But he was no longer the same
> Kishimoto as before. He was not the man who had despised and
> hated women so much that he had considered bachelorhood as a kind
> of revenge against them. He was not the Kishimoto of the past who
> refused to remarry, . . . who wanted to pursue his own willful, un-
> natural path alone in a boundless human desert. . . .
> A deep compassion overflowed in Kishimoto's breast. The feeling
> overwhelmed him that he wanted to save not only Setsuko, but him-
> self as well.[33]

It is clear by now that the resurrection or "new life" of the title
will involve Kishimoto's relationship with Setsuko. The fact that
Kishimoto will direct his compassion toward himself as well as

[33] Ibid., p. 302 (chap. 37).

toward Setsuko is a sign that he will now submit to his feelings in a natural way and not cover himself with guilt, as he had done during the three years in France. The perspective on his past life that he has gained through suffering and the acceptance of his guilt now, paradoxically, free him to accept the relationship with Setsuko. It seems cynical, then, in light of these considerations, to consider Kishimoto's resumption of his affair with Setsuko as merely the outcome of his inability to control his lust, as some critics have seen it, and it seems even more cynical when it becomes clear just what Kishimoto gains from this relationship.

The next period of Kishimoto's life sees him coming to a gradual understanding of what Setsuko is like as a person, as she visits and works for him regularly. At one point, he makes the odd remark to her that she had become better through her suffering, and that he likes her now, whereas before he hadn't.[34] This remark is a good example of the unconscious callousness of Kishimoto's behavior toward Setsuko that critics have noted. Yet it seems he has just begun to realize what Setsuko means to him, beyond the means of satisfying his emotional and sexual needs. Consequently, no matter how much it may shock the reader, it is doubtless a true expression of the author's feelings at the time. Soon after Kishimoto and Setsuko resume their relationship, Aiko (a niece of Kishimoto's from the family home at Negishi) informs him that she has someone in mind as a possible marriage partner for him. Kishimoto postpones his decision on remarriage, however, because he is gradually favoring the idea of helping Setsuko to make her way in life. At the same time, Kishimoto is beginning to see their relationship as degenerate, for he realizes that no matter how much it benefits them, as long as they cannot make it public in the form of a marriage, the relationship will appear, both to themselves and to others, to be a sordid, illicit affair. Kishimoto is bothered already by the lack of honesty in his behavior, and he decides to try to break off the physical aspect of the relationship.

[34] Ibid., p. 307 (chap. 40).

Kishimoto's brother, probably also out of a desire to end the relationship, finally moves out of Kishimoto's house, taking Setsuko with him. Now that she is gone, Kishimoto realizes that his feelings toward her have changed: "Though Kishimoto had lived in the same house with Setsuko only a short four months, his feelings had changed considerably. He used to be afraid of her, as he had been afraid of other women, but now she no longer called up any fear in him. Since he had been approaching her with compassion instead of awkwardly avoiding her, he realized that his heart had become light."[35] After her departure he feels the lack of her presence: "Just as the winter came stealing secretly from Musashi Moor into the garden of his house in Takanawa, before long the loneliness that Setsuko had left behind was inside and outside of him."[36] He gradually feels that the barrier he had set up between the compassionate one (himself) and the pitied one (Setsuko) is now artificial, and, as the narrator puts it, "he began to feel a passion that he wanted somehow to communicate to her."[37] Now that she is no longer there with him, he becomes aware of what Setsuko has come to mean to him: "The nights like this when he found it difficult to sleep continued. During the past three years when he had continually been tormented by suffering for his crime, Kishimoto's soul had frequently called out to the unfortunate Setsuko. That was the first time he had become conscious of his loyalty to her. The long anxiety, the melancholy, the enduring, the lonely exile abroad all seemed to him to have occurred in order to make him realize this. More and more the desire grew in him to continue the relationship."[38]

A few pages later Kishimoto reflects that he, who had thought that he could never love again, is in love with Setsuko: "He could still love. When he thought of it, he was overwhelmed by a feeling of deep happiness and astonishment."[39] The love that he feels for Setsuko now acts as a kind of purification of his past sins and

[35] Ibid., p. 325 (chap. 50). [36] Ibid., p. 331 (chap. 53).
[37] Ibid., p. 331 (chap. 53). [38] Ibid., pp. 331-332 (chap. 53).
[39] Ibid., p. 334 (chap. 55).

sorrows: "From that time on, Kishimoto realized that he had
been forgiven by Setsuko, regardless of whether he had been forgiven by anyone else. The more he became conscious of his loyalty toward Setsuko, the more he was able to extricate himself
from the long suffering for his crime and not only that—the more
he was able to change the life of defeat and shame, the immorality
which had made him want to kill himself and his ego, into something with a completely different meaning."[40] His love for
Setsuko is described as a "new world," and thus it can be seen as
the beginning of the "new life" of the title: "A new world of love
had opened up before Kishimoto. It gave courage to Kishimoto's
spirit to see that honesty of this sort could be dipped from the
bottom of an illicit relationship. He had thought he would never
finish being ashamed of this relationship, yet he had gained from
it a kind of strength that he had never before experienced."[41]
What Kishimoto had thought would be the most shameful event
of his life has turned out to be the event that reopens the door to
life that he had closed during the period of his moral stagnation.

After Kishimoto's discovery that he is once more able to love,
he realizes also that he has recovered the youthful spirit he had
vowed to regain while still in Paris:

> Kishimoto's past had been a succession of days of almost unbeliev-
> able suffering. On top of that, he had stubbornly closed off his emo-
> tions to an excessive degree because of the conflict within him. He
> recalled the thought he had had in his Paris boarding house that more
> than anything else, he must return to the spirit of his youth. But
> somehow the return to this spirit had not been granted to him.
> Whether it was the long years and months he had spent as a suffering
> spectator of the world, so that, standing in front of the iron door of
> the crematorium, he was unable to shed a tear when he looked at the
> ashes of his dead wife, or the three-year journey abroad when he had
> cold-heartedly faced the stone wall of his boarding house room—
> what he had continuously thought about was actually the truth con-
> tained in the following words:

[40] Ibid., p. 334 (chap. 55).   [41] Ibid., p. 340 (chap. 58).

"I am a pitiful laborer for art. Why is it that the freedoms given easily to ordinary men are not granted to me? That is just. Ordinary people have hearts [Tōson uses the English word *"haato"*—heart]. In the last analysis, someone like me has no heart. . . ."

A gradual change was occurring day by day in the Kishimoto who had thought those things. He became aware of the fact that the day had come when he was able to return to the spirit of his youth. When the time came, he discovered that there existed someone to whom he could give his love. He discovered the happiness of that giving. . . . He began to immerse himself in this new happiness, thinking that it was a gift bestowed on a traveler like himself by nature. . . .

Feelings now freed, which he would never have suspected in himself, began to pour from Kishimoto's heart. For almost a month he was unable to sleep at night.[42]

Kishimoto sees now that in the period before his encounter with Setsuko, he had existed as a spectator of life, as a person outside of the normal, everyday life of the emotions. One could almost say, then, that Kishimoto, in his forties, has rediscovered the Romantic self of his twenties, which had been buried under the unemotional, Naturalist-influenced spirit that had dominated his thirties. In giving him love, nature had given him back the vital, sensual self of his youth as well, and Kishimoto seems almost to fear this youthful spirit that now wells up in him with more force than he had ever experienced before: "Kishimoto, who had forgotten about food and sleep for a month now, began to consider what people would think if they saw him in this distracted and absent-minded condition. He was shocked that he hadn't slept for a month. Even in his younger days, when his feelings were turbulent and wild because of his young blood, he had never missed more than seven nights in a row. He wondered if he would be able to stand such emotional turbulence if he were twenty years younger. Finally he began to be afraid of his passion."[43] Kishimoto is also unable to write during this period. It is as if the new life that is welling up from below, from the un-

---

[42] Ibid., pp. 340-342 (chap. 59).   [43] Ibid., p. 343 (chap. 60).

conscious, takes all his strength to assimilate. As Tōson describes it, Kishimoto is suffering the traumatic effects of a rebirth. The relationship with Setsuko has now changed definitively. A few pages before the preceding passage, Kishimoto had broken off the engagement that his niece Aiko had arranged for him, feeling that he could not honestly enter into a marriage relationship while he was devoting himself physically and emotionally to Setsuko. However, by rejecting a marriage tie that would have regularized his life in the eyes of his family, he has accepted the incestuous love affair with his niece as his own individual choice. From this point on, the love relationship between Kishimoto and Setsuko comes in conflict with the family and, indirectly, with society. The conflict occurs because Kishimoto feels more and more dissatisfied with his own secrecy in regard to a relationship that has meant his rebirth. Traditionally, such a relationship would have been considered illicit and would have had to be concealed. However, this relationship enters so much into the emotional and moral life of Kishimoto that he can only conceal it by being dishonest to himself and to others. It should be no surprise to the reader, then, that honesty and sincerity become increasingly important to Kishimoto, for they are a part of the youthful spirit that Kishimoto had regained through his love for Setsuko. In a passage in part one, in which Kishimoto (Tōson) was discussing his mentor, Tōkoku, with a friend in Paris, he quoted some words of Tōkoku that have direct relevance to Kishimoto's own idea of sincerity. Tōkoku had said: "Of all the things in this world, there is not one which does not pass away. In this world, I would at least like to preserve my honesty."[44] In the context of Tōkoku's life, this statement probably meant something like the following: "When all other ideals fail—love, individual freedom in the world, access to God—this one alone is left." It is a statement of an individual driven into a corner, with no other way of proving his dignity. Kishimoto will likewise be attracted to Tō-

---

[44] *Shinsei*, pt. 1, *Zenshū*, 6: 229 (chap. 126).

koku's ideal of sincerity, but only when he has no other means of action.

Kishimoto gradually comes to see himself as a prisoner of moral norms set up by tradition and enforced within his family by his older brother Yoshio. At this point he cannot bring himself to tell his brother the real reason why he does not want to remarry, but it is clear that when he does so Yoshio will be opposed to the kind of relationship that he and Setsuko now have. Kishimoto is forced to rethink his attitude toward love and toward their relationship:

> He had come to realize that the newly discovered feelings between himself and Setsuko, and the truth contained in them, were incompatible with the old morality that had caused him such suffering for a long time. Human life is vast. It is a thing difficult to fulfill in this world, yet there is much truth in it. Such deep thoughts directed Kishimoto. He felt intensely that he had set out on a path different from Yoshio, who concealed his own defeats for the sake of the honor of the family. He decided not to reject Setsuko, even if it meant turning his back on his brother's feelings.[45]

Kishimoto realizes that it will be impossible to explain to his brother that he owed the rebirth of his desire to live to a love affair regarded by the outside world as illicit. He also guesses—correctly, as it turns out—that his brother will be unable to understand Kishimoto's desire to devote himself to Setsuko when he has the opportunity to marry someone else. It is clear to Kishimoto that for his brother, rejecting Setsuko will mean saving the family honor, whereas for Kishimoto himself, it will mean canceling his responsibility toward a human being who has given him his happiness and his freedom from guilt. Kishimoto foresees that he and Setsuko will have to face eventual separation; yet he decides here that he will support her morally and psychologically, whatever happens.

Some time later, Kishimoto considers telling Yoshio directly

---

[45] *Shinsei*, pt. 2, *Zenshū*, 6: 351-352 (chap. 65).

about the kind of relationship he and Setsuko have, but he knows
that his brother will not understand:

> There was no one besides Setsuko who knew the deeper reasons why
> he had willingly begun this life. He had resolved several times to re-
> veal to Yoshio how he had found his way to that boarding house—the
> whole relationship between him and Setsuko.
> "Aren't you uncle and niece? Isn't what you're doing, finally, a
> continuation of your immorality?"
> When he imagined his brother's reply, it finished with these
> words. Every time he thought of this, Kishimoto sighed and returned
> to his customary silence.[46]

From this time on, the two see each other much less. Knowing
that he and Setsuko could never hope to live together, Kishimoto
had earlier suggested that they follow the example of the lovers
Abelard and Heloise—the lovers who, though forcibly separated
and living apart as monk and nun, continued their dialogue by
means of letters.

Yet at this point Kishimoto's love for Setsuko is hardly as
spiritualized as this remark would seem to indicate. In fact, it is
an attachment that is becoming more and more difficult to break:

> Kishimoto thought that he couldn't continue any longer the relation-
> ship with Setsuko the way it was now. . . . The time had come to
> change the basis of the relationship. He considered their present situ-
> ation. The situation was such that, in fact, it was impossible for him
> and Setsuko to be together but neither could he part with her. The
> more he loved Setsuko, the more deeply he felt about this. In the
> long run, there was no hope that they would be able to be together.
> In that case, they could observe a strict isolation from one another
> and resign themselves to a platonic friendship, but his passion for her
> would not permit that. He doubted whether it made any difference

---

[46] Ibid., p. 391 (chap. 86). The "boarding house" refers to the place where
Tōson lived for a time after his return from Paris, and where his niece came to
help him with his work. Later, once they had renewed their relationship, it became the location of their clandestine meetings.

for him whether he somehow led Setsuko in a good direction or whether both of them took the path toward degeneracy.[47]

It is clear from this passage that Kishimoto does not want to give Setsuko up, yet he sees clearly that he will have to give her up. He could gradually help her to achieve her desire to enter the religious life. Or he could let the relationship drift until it becomes degenerate for both of them, and he foresees that a relationship without the freedom to develop into a marriage, a relationship that must be concealed, will inevitably become decadent. Neither solution takes into account Kishimoto's desire that the relationship be publicly acknowledged as a liberating love relationship. Thus, Kishimoto realizes that his freedom to love the way he wants will be curtailed, no matter what he does.

It is when Kishimoto's freedom to acknowledge his love as valid is cut off, then, that he for the first time seriously considers whether he should confess the whole story of his and Setsuko's relationship:

> Now Kishimoto had reached the stage where he felt he had to free himself from the prisonlike existence of confinement, restraint, and fear of giving offense that he had lived up to now, and to enter a wider, freer world.
>
> He had tried to conceal his secret for the past four years, but now he had reached a turning point. . . . He began to think: "Why not confess the whole thing in front of everyone?"[48]

His return to youthful idealism and openness, under the influence of Setsuko's love, now places a demand of sincerity on him that would have been quite unheard of only a year before. He conceives of the confession as a way of "opening the way to truth"[49] for both himself and Setsuko. It is doubtful whether one person can open the way to truth for another—in this, Kishimoto is naive—but there is no question that his words are meaningful for

[47] Ibid., p. 400 (chap. 91).   [48] Ibid., pp. 401-402 (chap. 92).
[49] Ibid., p. 401 (chap. 92).

himself. He considers himself in the role of confessor: "He would imitate the many people who had written confessions, and would confess to the world in the form of a trivial book. To write about 'that affair' was complete madness, seen from the viewpoint of the earlier Kishimoto, who couldn't bear to think about it and threw away or ripped up letters from Setsuko in order to avoid confronting the mention of it. What had led Kishimoto to this point was his deep love for Setsuko."[50] When Kishimoto says that his love for Setsuko has led him to make the decision to confess their affair, he is referring to the influence her love had had in restoring his confidence in himself, and in inspiring his desire to acknowledge the source of this confidence in self before the world.

Kishimoto is by no means unaware of the ambiguous effects such a confession might have on Setsuko. Setsuko had by this time indicated her desire to enter the religious life, and only after he heard this had Kishimoto asked for her permission to confess their affair. Yet Kishimoto still feels that he is responsible for the way her life has turned out. He has had the joy of seeing Setsuko turn into a much happier person through their relationship, at the same time as he is forced to realize that her affair with him has endangered her chances to lead what her family considers a "normal life," i.e., getting married. Kishimoto does not know to what extent Setsuko herself wants to lead this kind of normal life, and to what extent she has adopted the decision to enter the religious life in order to spare him guilt. Kishimoto is only too aware that their relationship is full of the corruption of everyday relationships, and yet he is aware of the spiritual dimension in it as well. Though he knows that the outside world is bound to see the relationship externally and therefore to misunderstand it, his confidence in its validity convinces him finally that it is necessary to reveal it.

Yet Kishimoto takes a long time to overcome his fear of the consequences of such a public confession, just as he had remained

[50] Ibid., pp. 402-403 (chap. 93).

for a long time in a state of fear before he finally left Japan for France several years before, and just as Ushimatsu had pondered a long while before confessing his secret in *Hakai*. Setsuko's confidence in the importance of confessing strengthens his resolve. However, the sickness of Setsuko's mother, Kayo (Asa in real life), is what ultimately precipitates the first stage of confession. Kayo had never been told that Kishimoto was the father of Setsuko's illegitimate child, though it was clear that she suspected the truth. Feeling that it is imperative that Kayo know the truth about him before she dies, Kishimoto writes her a letter confessing his relationship with Setsuko. He hears later that Kayo had read the letter before she died but requested her husband to burn it so that no one else would know about the matter. Kishimoto sees from her attitude that his confession, as it is published, will bring him up against his family's sense of honor, and Yoshio's actions also convince him of this. Apparently as a last-ditch attempt to save the family honor, Yoshio comes to see Kishimoto, hoping that he will persuade Setsuko to marry a certain Mr. Fuse. Kishimoto replies that he cannot, but does not explain why. Yoshio is unwilling to approach the subject of Kishimoto's affair with Setsuko directly. However, he reproaches Kishimoto indirectly for his failure to talk the problem over with him when it first began, indicating that he could have helped to "solve" it and could have prevented the outbreak of scandal that is now imminent. In the course of this angry conversation, it becomes clear how distant from one another the two brothers' conceptions of morality are.

Yoshio thinks that Setsuko's "mistake," as he calls it, is unimportant alongside the greater family honor, which must be saved at all costs, and he is willing to force Setsuko into a marriage now in order to save that honor, regardless of her desires. When Kishimoto admits that he had been so bothered about his crime against Setsuko several years before that he had considered committing suicide, Yoshio cannot understand such an attitude; he only blames Kishimoto for not telling him right away so that he could have devised a practical solution. Here Tōson points out a contrast between a traditional Japanese morality based on family honor and "face," and a morality based on the individual's assumption of responsibility for his actions. Yoshio, with his traditional rural morality, considers the relationship between Setsuko and Kishimoto—like the illicit love affair, the failed business venture, and the marital quarrel—as an event that is best concealed. Kishimoto, on the other hand, is bothered precisely by his concealment of an affair that is linked closely to his selfhood. He feels that to confess it will be proof of his honesty toward the public. Yet not only that—he intends his confession to be part of a process of public atonement for his original action of abandoning Setsuko. He writes Yoshio a letter explaining the reasons for his confession:

> He wrote: "You talked about being respectful to the family of Kishimoto, which has a long history, but burying my failure and enduring over a long period the suffering caused by my silence, for the sake of the family, finally became unbearable to me. The fact that such an immoral person as myself was born into the Kishimoto family, which possessed so many people of great virtue, has been the cause of disgrace to my ancestors, but I feel that having my immorality censured will, on the contrary, bespeak the virtue of my ancestors. . . . My confession to the public stems from my desire to flog myself."[51]

Yoshio replies to this letter in his own fashion: he forbids Kishimoto to see Setsuko again, and disowns him.

Kishimoto labors on alone on the confession, which is now beginning to appear in regular installments in the newspaper. The relationship has come to the only end that somewhat satisfies him. Setsuko will go to live with Kishimoto's eldest brother, Tamisuke (Hideo in real life), in Taiwan, where she will presumably pursue a religious life. Before they leave for Taiwan, this brother, on a visit to Japan, tries to effect a reconciliation be-

[51] Ibid., p. 448 (chap. 106).

tween Kishimoto and Yoshio. His attitude toward the affair is interesting, for though he does not agree with Kishimoto, he is genuinely sympathetic toward Kishimoto's side of the argument. He understands and respects Kishimoto's desire to save Setsuko, but wonders why there had to be the physical relationship along with it. Kishimoto replies: "You say 'relationship'—but isn't it true that if there weren't this element between a man and a woman, one wouldn't want to save the other person? There was a time when I, too, severely despised that kind of relationship. Because I'm the sort of person who has suffered from that attitude a great deal, I don't think I despise it now as much as my brothers."[52] In the arguments between Kishimoto and his two older brothers, Yoshio and Tamisuke, Tōson has presented a quarrel between a traditional and a modern Japanese view of the relationship between sexuality and love. Yoshio and Tamisuke (born in 1861 and 1858, respectively) still separate in their minds honorable sexuality (sexuality within marriage) and illicit sexuality, and can only consider the latter as trivial; the idea of love is incomprehensible to them. Kishimoto (born in 1872) refuses to accept this, to him, artificial division between moral and immoral sexuality, because his relationship with Setsuko proves that it is possible to have a relationship with a woman that is sexually based but nevertheless involves a real meeting of souls. Tōson had not known that such a relationship was possible in his adolescence, when he suffered from a conflict between his desires for both a sexual and a pure love of woman. That Kishimoto here is able to experience a love that is at the same time sensual and pure suggests that Tōson, through his relationship with his niece, had found a way of transcending his youthful conflict as well as the dualistic morality that underlay it.

Toward the end of the novel, Kishimoto feels humiliated and angry at being forced to adopt a solution to his life that is tantamount to bowing to the demands of society, particularly of his

---

[52] Ibid., pp. 479–480 (chap. 133).

family: "Kishimoto, who had renounced so much of what he wanted, had up to this point replied to his relatives in an extremely simple way. Yuriko (Setsuko's sister) had said at the time of his confession: 'Setchan won't be over to help you any more, so please accept it.' 'As you wish.' Yoshio had sent a letter with the following words: 'Please regard yourself as disowned.' 'As you wish.' Kishimoto even now had no other choice than to repeat this simple reply to Tamisuke. 'I've thought about it, and Setsuko will soon go far away from here with me.' 'As you wish.' "[53] The way in which the individual in Japan at the time was still subject to the will of the family, as represented by the decisions of the eldest son, is evident in the preceding passage, yet there are ways of wielding power even from a lower position in the hierarchy. For example, by not acting himself to end a relationship that he saw as degenerate since it could not develop into marriage, Kishimoto forces his family, particularly his elder brother Yoshio, to take steps to end it. These steps are Yoshio's actions of first forbidding him to see Setsuko, then disowning him, and finally, sending Setsuko away from him.

From the family's point of view, Kishimoto can say nothing but "as you wish" to all that they decide to do. He as an individual is by definition "wrong," while they as a family are by the same definition "right." Yet Kishimoto recovers a certain advantage by publishing the confession of all that has happened, and from his point of view. While he is prevented by the legal system from marrying Setsuko, and by his family from continuing the affair with her, he writes a confessional novel that speaks for the rights and desires of the individual. Thus, he has the last, and the longest word. The image of the individual that Shinsei communicates, then, is that of a person who emerges strong and victorious from a conflict that had threatened to plunge him into the depths of despair and self-hatred. After undergoing a long period of suffering, this person finally begins a new life, one in which he is

[53] Ibid., p. 487 (chap. 137).

able to act as an individual, taking responsibility for his actions before society and accepting aspects of himself that he had formerly considered evil. Finally, by writing his confession, Kishimoto (and Tōson himself) has symbolically destroyed the image of the powerless, suffering, thwarted individual that had existed in Japanese literature from the feudal period, for the device of confession is revealed here to be a stratagem of power.

Interestingly, the Kishimoto that emerges at the end of *Shinsei* resembles the figure of Abelard that had inspired him throughout the work—that Abelard who became a Western culture hero through his independence of mind, his outspokenness, and his individualist challenging of authority. Even Abelard's role in the love affair with Heloise can be seen from this point of view. Abelard was so eager to keep possession of Heloise that he was willing to risk the loss of his reputation as a scholar by marrying her. Furthermore, it was Abelard who determined the course of the relationship initially, it was he who forced Heloise to marry him against her wishes, and it was also he who forced her to enter a convent after his castration. Finally, the episodes of his ill-fated love, his castration, and his persecution at the hands of his enemies made Abelard a hero of his time, and out of them he made a confession. In this work, written in 1132 or 1133 and entitled *Historia Calamitatum*, Abelard defended himself as Rousseau was to do some six hundred years later. Like Rousseau and later writers of confessions, Abelard chose to circulate his literary self-defense, and ultimately his confession gained him sympathy, fame, and personal immortality. Like Tōson's confession in *Shinsei*, Abelard's confession remained as the source of truth about his life long after the criticisms of his contemporaries had been forgotten.

Yet Tōson often compares the love between Kishimoto and his niece, Setsuko, to that of Abelard and Heloise, and, given that the major theme of the novel is the resurrection of an individual through love, it is the twelfth-century lovers, not merely Abelard alone, that were the important inspirations behind *Shinsei*. Tōson

first stressed the "almost unfathomable trust" that united
Abelard and Heloise in life and even after death, a trust that
seemed to him to shine forth from the tomb of the lovers that he
visited in Père Lachaise Cemetery when he was in Paris. As the
book developed he depicted a similar trust growing between
Kishimoto and Setsuko. There are further similarities between
the two couples: in both relationships the lovers experience an initial sensual union. Then they decide to be faithful to an ideal of
eternal love, one that has nothing to do with the legal bond of
marriage, and in which the sexual element is not the most important one.[54] Finally, both couples are forced apart by circumstances but manage to derive solace from the thought that the
ideal relationship (if not the sensual one) will continue even after
their separation and, by implication, after death. It seems, then,
that Tōson used the love of Abelard and Heloise to express the
particular qualities of his love affair with his niece: a mingled sensual and idealistic love that ended in renunciation.[55]

The character of Setsuko in *Shinsei* is shadowy and ill-defined,
and, as Itō Kazuo put it, "the fact that the complicated secrets of
Setsuko's mind, her reproaches and sufferings are left out, is the
main thing which markedly lyricizes *Shinsei* as a novel, and makes
it lose the completeness of the novel form."[56] Basically, the

[54] Betty Radice notes that the love between Abelard and Heloise is con-
ditioned by their adherence to a contemporary "ethic of pure intention."
Heloise, relying on this ethic, argues against marriage to Abelard on the
grounds that "a lasting relationship should rest on the complete devotion of two
persons; this is true disinterested love. . . . *To such an ideal union a legal marriage
could add nothing, and the presence or absence of an erotic element is, in a sense, irrelevant. The intention toward the ideal relationship is all-important*" (my italics).
The Letters of Abelard and Heloise, Baltimore, 1974, p. 18.

[55] The idea of a love in which devotion and trust were paramount and the
erotic element was secondary but clearly valued was far indeed from the Christian Calvinist idea of love as either chaste or lewd that Tōson was exposed to at
the Meiji Gakuin. It is interesting that Tōson had to go back as far as the medieval West to find an ideal of love that reconciled flesh with spirit.

[56] Itō, *Shimazaki Tōson kenkyū*, p. 576. Itō calls *Shinsei* an iceberg, since one-
third of its truth is concealed, and Shimazaki Komako, Tōson's niece, gives her

structure of *Shinsei* is more lyrical than novelistic, for Tōson is interested in portraying a transformation of Kishimoto's personality, a transformation that unfolds poetically according to an internal emotional rhythm. In this sense, *Shinsei*, like Freedman's lyrical novel, subordinates all other characters to the main character, for Setsuko functions merely as the catalyst of Kishimoto's transformation. Indeed, Setsuko stands in relation to Kishimoto much as Sonya in Dostoevsky's *Crime and Punishment* stood in relation to Raskolnikov. Yet Setsuko is also similar to the figure of Beatrice in Dante's *La Vita Nuova*, the work after which Tōson named *Shinsei*: she is the female figure who leads the male hero through love and earthly sorrow to a "new life" of transcendent happiness. As Dante's Beatrice dies and ascends to heaven after her work is finished, Setsuko departs into the religious life once she has brought about Kishimoto's rebirth.[57]

Tōson's use of Dante's title suggests, then, that he intended

---

version of what happened between herself and her uncle in her *Higeki no jiden* (My Tragic Story, 1937), noting that "the novel records the facts but those parts that my uncle found unsuitable were suppressed" (cited in Itō, p. 575).

[57] Joan Ferrante argues that Dante's contribution to the Western medieval view of women was his validation of the spiritual role that woman played in man's salvation. She writes that in Dante, beginning with *La Vita Nuova*, "women have both a symbolic and an active function in the salvation of man. . . . As reflections of God, they draw out the good that is in man; as loving and compassionate beings, they bring the straying man back with their criticism, and help expiate his sins with their prayers." *Woman as Image in Medieval Literature from the Twelfth Century to Dante*, New York, 1975, pp. 130-131. Tōson describes Setsuko's salvation of Kishimoto from his dry self-hatred, and his moral and spiritual stagnation, in similar terms. It seems, then, that Tōson discovered, in his love for Komako, the spiritual, ennobling love between man and woman that Tōkoku had depicted in his essays, and that Dante had discovered and depicted in his *La Vita Nuova*. It is for this reason that figures from the period of Western medieval history that Colin Morris has called the period of the discovery of the individual—figures such as Abelard and Heloise and Dante—were so meaningful at the time he was writing *Shinsei*. For the discovery of love accompanies the discovery of self. See *The Discovery of the Individual, 1050-1200*, London, 1972.

the main theme of *Shinsei* to be the moral and spiritual transformation of Kishimoto through love. Several times Tōson has Kishimoto mention love in these terms. When he first realized that he loved Setsuko, Kishimoto realized also that "he had been forgiven by Setsuko," that his immorality had been transformed into "something with a completely different meaning." It was at this point in his life that a "new world of love opened before Kishimoto": a world that gave him back the vital self that had been buried under years of guilt. Toward the end of the novel Kishimoto thinks of Setsuko with a sense of wonder mingled with a sense of his fateful attachment to her:

> Every time he thought of his strange fate, the thought of Setsuko flashed through his mind: The fact that a woman like Setsuko had appeared to him in the midst of his solitary life not only seemed like a miracle to him, but her feeling of affection for him, her discovery in Kishimoto of the person she had long been seeking, also seemed miraculous. . . . She was the first woman he had seen that would go to the extent of waiting for him for the three years of his trip abroad. . . . On account of Setsuko, Kishimoto had suffered a great deal. On account of Setsuko, he had felt a great deal of compassion. The crime, the journey, and after that, the sadness of entrusting their lives to one another—all of these had occurred because of Setsuko.[58]

The love between Kishimoto and Setsuko is similar to that between Dante and his Beatrice, but it also includes an "almost unfathomable trust between man and woman," a trust that is firmly based on the physical relationship of "deep ecstasy" that Tōson saw in the lovers Abelard and Heloise. Thus, Tōson's idea of love transcended Tōkoku's ideal, in its reconciliation of the worlds of flesh and spirit in love.

Setsuko leaves Japan with Tamisuke for Taiwan on a cold, sunny November day. Before she leaves she sends Kishimoto a box containing the letters he had written and the gifts he had given her—everything that attests to their earthly relationship.

[58] *Shinsei*, pt. 2, *Zenshū*, 6: 437-438 (chap. 101).

Of things connected with Kishimoto she keeps only a rosary, which she will use in her future life. She also sends a note accompanied by four bulbs of a winter grass called *shūkaidō*, which puts out pale flowers late in winter. It is clear that Tōson means Setsuko to symbolize a principle of eternal life, for the memory of her will sustain Kishimoto in the future, just as the plant that she left behind will bear flowers even in the midst of the hard winter ahead:

> In the confusion over her departure, Kishimoto had planted the four bulbs in the garden, but he was worried that he might not have put them firmly in the ground. He couldn't help feeling that whether or not the roots took or didn't take was linked somehow to their destiny. When he dug them up to see, the four black bulbs of the *shūkaidō*, tumbled out of the soil, their roots springing out looking uncannily like hair. . . . Kishimoto buried the bulbs again so that they wouldn't be damaged by the frost which would be coming before long. Setsuko would remain not only in Kishimoto's heart—she would remain in the earth as well.[59]

[59] Ibid., p. 495 (chap. 140).

CHAPTER EIGHT

Shimazaki Tōson's Ideal of the Individual

Nagai Kafū wrote in 1914 that he still had the feeling that he was living in an era of feudalism, or rather, in "an inferior age of democracy which has eliminated the good points of feudalism and only preserves its evils." Kafū was probably referring to the climate of political repression that had emerged after the Kōtoku Incident of 1911, in which several anarchists were executed following an attempt to assassinate the emperor. Implied in his remark, however, is a criticism of a political system that maintained total autocratic control, and a lament for the possibility of a development of true individualism under such conditions. Kafū wrote often, at times nostalgically, at times critically and angrily, of the sadness and resignation that was at the heart of literature and music of the Edo period, and even of the Meiji period—a sadness and resignation that, in his opinion, were a consequence of the continued suppression of individual feeling in Japanese culture. In 1911 Kafū wrote that "if you want to get a powerful, vital art, you must nourish a spirit of bravery that will remove the terrible oppression of tradition."[1] He clearly did not see himself as possessing such a spirit, nor did Naturalists such as Katai, with their pessimistic world view, possess the heroic temperament that Kafū envisioned. Of all the Meiji and early Taishō (1912-1926) writers, Shimazaki Tōson came closest to achieving Kafū's ideal, for he alone provided a vision of the individual that

---

[1] Nagai Kafū, "Yatate no chibifude" (Thoughts from My Humble Inkhorn, 1914), *Zenshū*, 14: 274; "Nihon no niwa" (A Japanese Garden, 1911), *Zenshū*, 5: 316.

expressed confidence in his ability to define himself, and thereby to free himself from the "terrible oppression of tradition."

Kitamura Tōkoku had introduced the Japanese individual of the early 1890s to the private ideals of love, self-definition, and freedom. For Tōkoku, a child of early Meiji, the realization of the ideal of self-definition for every individual was the true purpose of the political, social, and philosophical revolution that had begun in 1868. Though only a few years younger than Tōkoku, Tōson had always looked on Tōkoku as his teacher; thus, Tōson in a sense belonged to a younger generation that lived on beyond Tōkoku's death and came to maturity with the goal of realizing Tōkoku's ideals. That Tōson saw this as his function already in the 1890s is evident from his depiction, in his novel *Haru*, of the thoughts he had had immediately after Tōkoku's death in 1894: "Kishimoto [Tōson] . . . thought of how he would pursue his path alone. There was territory before his eyes that was still uncultivated—wide, vast territory. Aoki [Tōkoku] had tried to colonize one part of it but he had died leaving behind his work unfinished. Inspired by this thought, Kishimoto decided to take his stand on the place where the bones of the sower were buried and continue his work."[2] A certain toughness of character, as well as an openness to emotional experience and an ability to stand great suffering in this area—qualities that were sharpened by a knowledge of scientific method and great skill in observation—enabled Tōson to explore in depth, and from the viewpoint of one individual, territory that Tōkoku had explored from a universal standpoint: the inner life of the modern Japanese individual. The task of the following pages will be to describe how Tōson made Tōkoku's ideals of love, self-definition, and freedom of spirit the basis of his own ideal of individualism, and then how he "cultivated a previously unexplored territory" of the self: literary confession. The discussion will attempt to clarify the nature and importance of Tōson's contribution to the Meiji novel's exploration of the self.

[2] Tōson, *Haru*, *Zenshū*, 4: 210.

Tōson's Ideals of Love, Self-Definition, and Freedom

The ideal of Tōkoku's that excited the most response at the time he wrote was unquestionably that of love. Tōkoku envisioned an ideal of love that, without excluding the sensual bond, posited a spiritual affinity between man and woman. He learned about this ideal of love through his association with Christians and through his reading of Western literature—in particular, English Romantic poetry. What attracted Tōkoku in the Western, Christian-influenced ideal of love was that it made possible a growth of the spirit in the individual. Just as the individual sought Christ's grace through his faith and devotion, he drew the loved one to himself through faith and love, and through the reciprocal gift of self, love was born. The ideal of love thus had the same dynamic quality as Tōkoku's ideals of self-definition and freedom: love was a force that transformed the base, sensual bond between man and woman into a relationship whose essence was spiritual and free. Yet Tōkoku's ideal of love was not only based on intuition, it was experienced, for Tōkoku had actually lived the ideal of love with his wife, Mina. That the ideal withered and died after the two were married does not deny the power of the ideal to transform the human personality; it merely demonstrates the inevitable limitations of an ideal when it is forced to conform to the demands of social reality.

The Meiji period was an age in which feelings that had formerly been expressed in the accepted channels of obligation were theoretically freed to go in any direction they wished. Thus the appeal of Tōkoku's "horizontal" ideal of love, which brought change, and above all, equality, into a relationship that had for centuries been one of vertical and hierarchical inequality. Furthermore, the bond between man and woman, which had been considered trivial under the Confucian moral system, was to be transformed, it seemed, into a Shelleyan thing of beauty and joy. This aspect of love surely appealed to the generation nourished on Romantic poetry. All of these implications of Tōkoku's ideal of love attracted the youthful Tōson, who himself had had a glimpse of the pure world of man-woman relationships during his years at the Meiji Gakuin. The ideal of love was associated already in Tōson's first poetry with that of freedom, for in his poem, *Okume* (1897), Tōson portrayed an individual who confidently and without pain defied social and religious laws in order to swim to meet her lover. In reality, love was not usually so simple, and Tōson knew it, for in the poem *Betsuri* (The Departure) the poet speaks of sin and emotional suffering in connection with love. It should be recalled also that Tōson's first experience of love in his late teens was accompanied by feelings of sin and guilt. Tōson's ideal of love, then, was mixed with impurities from the beginning, unlike Tōkoku's, yet these impurities turned out to be life-giving.

Tōson's poems in *Wakana-shū*, and even those in his later collections, expressed more than anything else his idealistic expectations of love and his disillusionment with it, not his understanding of it. His prose writings from the years 1899 to about 1910, the period of his marriage to Fuyuko, revealed, if anything, the disappointment in love and the jealousy and suspicion of women that characterized those years of his life. However, in his works of that period Tōson portrayed one love relationship that showed the influence of Tōkoku's ideal of love—a fact that seems almost fantastic when one considers the feelings of bitterness toward women that were typical of the Tōson of this time. That is the love relationship of Ushimatsu and Oshio, the daughter of a poor schoolteacher friend of Ushimatsu's, in *Hakai*. The hero thinks longingly of Oshio a few times during the story, more and more as he becomes increasingly tortured by his dishonesty in concealing his origins and needs a source of comfort. At the end of the novel she miraculously turns up at his side, ready to accompany him to America.

In *Hakai* Oshio undergoes severe hardship: after her drunkard father loses his job as a teacher, she becomes the foster daughter of a childless priest and his wife, but then is forced to flee the temple after the priest tries to seduce her. Oshio is hardly a character with realistic dimensions. She seems to be merely an unfortunate girl for whom Ushimatsu first has compassion, and with whom he gradually identifies as a social outcast. Yet she is a lover in Tōkoku's sense of the word, in that she is involved symbolically in the process of Ushimatsu's growth toward honesty. Though she symbolizes for him the world of the oppressed, the downtrodden, and the weak, she also increasingly comes to represent for him the selfhood that he has hidden for years, his *eta* nature, and thus his gradual concern and even love for her marks the progress of his self-love. When he takes the final step of self-revelation, he is free to face her, symbolically himself, and at this point he wins her in marriage, i.e., he gains his true identity. Oshio plays a role in Ushimatsu's transformation, but it is a small role in comparison to that of Inoko. Finally, the love relationship between Ushimatsu and Oshio exists only on the symbolic plane; of a flesh and blood relationship there is not a trace.

By 1910, the year of his wife's death, Tōson had lived through twelve years of the reality of marriage. In a sense, the ideal of love was rather far from his mind at this point, at least in the form that Tōkoku had expressed it or in the form that he had given to it himself as a youth. It had been crowded out of his mind by the pressures of everyday reality. Confronted with the difficulties of a day-to-day relationship, Tōson had consulted Havelock Ellis's book *Male and Female* some time during the writing of *Ie*, possibly because he was interested to know why man-woman relationships were so full of pain, jealousy, disappointment, and misunderstanding. Yet it may also have been because he still cherished the ideal of Tōkoku that Tōson was so eager to find out why his marriage was such a miserable failure. Eventually, however, toward the end of his marriage, Tōson was beginning to feel a deeper sexual and emotional intimacy with his wife, but then she suddenly died. After her death Tōson turned down several proposals of marriage made on his behalf, and it seems clear, from the depiction in *Shinsei*, that this was done out of a lingering suspicion of women. However, possibly another reason was his unwillingness to become involved again in the same kind of relationship on the sense plane, with children and everyday harassment, that he had had with Fuyuko. Or, disappointed that there had been no spiritual or intellectual relationship with his wife, he might have wished to avoid another such sterile union.

The relationship with his niece, Komako, though it brought him much pain, also paradoxically gave Tōson an opportunity to learn more about women, about the meaning of love, and the meaning of the bond between man and woman. For the relationship with Komako, unlike that with his wife, led him finally to realize the ideal of love that he had cherished as a youth but given up during the years of disappointment that were his married life. *Shinsei*, then, is a novel that depicts Tōson's coming to a mature realization of the meaning of love. Like *Hakai*, it depicts the transformation of an individual through love, but in *Shinsei* this theme is much more important. Setsuko plays a shadowy role in the novel since, as in *Hakai*, the woman is primarily the force that leads the man to self-knowledge. Unlike *Hakai*, however, *Shinsei* depicts a relationship between a man and a woman that is firmly anchored in reality. There is an affair, a child is born from it, and a bond between Kishimoto and his niece is formed on the sense plane, the strength of which amazes and in a sense terrifies him. The question immediately presents itself of why Tōson had not felt this deep bond with his own wife, for they had had seven children together. However, the nature of Tōson's relationship with his wife was determined by society and by law; it was conventional and thus unfree. What was different about his relationship with his niece, Komako, was its freedom. The relationship with Komako was brought about by chance; in the beginning it had the negative qualities of an accidental relationship, but later, with the passing of time, it became a union that was freely and consciously chosen. It is important to keep in mind that love, for Tōkoku, was an ideal linked to freedom; the love between Tōson and Komako existed in a state of freedom that was symbolized by its illicitness.

The relationship between Tōson and Komako, as it is described in *Shinsei*, is an ideal love, but it is not a pure love. It grows like a lotus from the depths of a muddy pond, for it is incestuous, the consequence of loneliness and misery in an empty house. It begins through an act of seduction, and the first reaction is to hide it. The first manifestation is physical, too: Setsuko's child, which is born illegitimate and given away in secrecy and shame. Much suffering is involved in the beginning for both partners, as long as the relationship between them is only seen as physical. All of this pain is transformed, however, as Kishimoto and Setsuko gradually develop what can be called a freely chosen love for one another. This love is offered first from Setsuko's side; gradually her love exerts pressure on Kishimoto, and *Shinsei*, particularly part two, is the story of the changes this pressure brings about in him. If it had been a merely platonic relationship, it would not have had to end. Yet because it exists partly in the realm of the senses, it is subject to the effects of time and to external circumstances, and in this sense it is not free. When Kishimoto realizes that their love has no future, his relationship with Setsuko is over. Yet the novel demonstrates that a deep feeling of relatedness to Setsuko remains, one that is on the sense level, for they are linked by a chance meeting that resulted in a child. Indeed, Kishimoto reminds himself twice in the novel of the deep roots of the bond between man and woman, and it is these roots Setsuko reminds Kishimoto of when she gives him as a farewell present a plant that brings forth flowers even in the cold season. The last scene shows Kishimoto digging up the plant to make sure the roots are properly planted in the dirt, and as he does so his thoughts drift toward Setsuko. One has the feeling that the physical bond between them will endure, since the memory of it will spring up with each blossoming of Setsuko's plant.

By emphasizing the physicality of the love between Kishimoto and Setsuko, and its natural expression in the creation of a child, Tōson is describing love in a traditional Japanese way, as a darkness of the heart (*kokoro no yami*). Buddhism in the Heian period emphasized the pain and, ultimately, the illusoriness of all human attachment, while the Heian poets stressed the poignancy and uniqueness of such attachments.[3] Love of a man for a woman, love of a parent for a child—these were the two forms of attachment that Buddhism saw as the most dangerous hindrances to the achievement of detachment from worldly things. Besides poetry, the Nō drama of the Muromachi period (1336-1573) portrayed men and women caught in the web of attachment. Many of them were saved by submitting to the teachings of the Buddha, after which they broke the cycle of birth and death; others, like the bereaved mother in *Sumidagawa* (The River Sumida), were left to pursue their object of attachment in intense and unrelieved suffering, caught in a seemingly eternal *kokoro no yami*. Tōson's depiction of love in *Shinsei* demonstrates the Heian awareness of the poignancy and beauty of passion without, however, the Muromachi condemnation of passion. For Tōson, the drama of attachment is one that, once the initial passion is over, lasts forever as a memory.

Yet Tōson depicted in *Shinsei* not only a love that was a "darkness of the heart"—he also depicted Tōkoku's *ren'ai*, or spiritual love, a psychic event that brought about change and growth in Kishimoto's personality. Tōson's *Shinsei* presents essentially the same process of development as did *Hakai*: that of the self-definition of an individual that is set in motion by a mediator, or savior figure, who loves him. In *Shinsei*, however, the steps of the transformation are more clearly shown. In the beginning of the

[3] Perhaps the most famous classical poem that uses the phrase *kokoro no yami* is that by the Heian courtier, Ariwara no Narihira (fl. ninth century): "Kakikurasu / Kokoro no yami ni / Madoiniki / Yume utsutsu to wa / Yohito sadame yo." ("Through the blackest shadow / Of the darkness of the heart I wander / In bewilderment— / You people of this twilight world, / Explain: is my love reality or dream?") For the translation, and for a discussion of this poem in the context of Heian culture, see Brower and Miner, *Japanese Court Poetry*, p. 217.

novel Kishimoto is in a mood of moral stagnation after his wife's death; under the influence of this mood he casually drifts into an affair with his niece. When he hears that she is pregnant he is thrown into a painful but dynamic situation of guilt that destroys his moral torpor and forces him to act. Yet his feelings of guilt and fear are so strong that they at first prevent him from acting constructively, and, instead of facing his crime, he flees abroad.

While Kishimoto is in France Setsuko's letters continually remind him of his guilt and, more importantly, make him aware of his victim as a person. After a period of two years spent in relative freedom from obligations, Kishimoto is ready to confront his crime. When he looks back on his motives at the time he sees clearly that though his act of abandoning Setsuko was unjustifiable by external moral standards, it was valid on the basis of his inner needs. The recognition of this fact allows Kishimoto for the first time to feel compassion for the person that he was when he left Japan, and for the self that he had hated since that time. Because he consciously accepts the guilt he had been trying to escape, he is able to take moral responsibility for himself, and for the first time he feels a strong sense of responsibility for Setsuko as well. Kishimoto sees clearly that Setsuko's continued concern for him, expressed in her letters, is the true source of his changed feeling about himself. Under her influence he has developed a new sense of life that makes him wish to recover his lost youthful innocence and stimulates him to atone for his crime.

Yet when Kishimoto returns to Japan he again allows himself to drift into an affair with Setsuko. Though he feels that at bottom it is a relationship without a future and he tries to break it off, he is pulled in spite of himself into a passion so overwhelming that he cannot sleep for a month. It is here, in the depths of the experience of a physical passion that he knows will be degenerate in the long run, that Kishimoto feels a new world of love has opened up for him, one that is characterized by absolute honesty and freedom from guilt. As the earlier platonic relationship with Setsuko across the miles had awakened his compassion for himself, and for Setsuko, the sensual love that Kishimoto finds with Setsuko after his return to Japan makes him aware of his ability to love. As the novel presents it, this realization is less important for his future relationship with Setsuko than it is for his development of self-confidence and, ultimately, for his definition of self.

At about this time Kishimoto refuses an offer of marriage, for he has decided to devote himself to furthering the prospects of the woman who has reawakened his sense of self. Yet he still feels the ambiguity of continuing a relationship that has no future. The worst problem for Kishimoto, however, is that his own brother continually degrades a relationship to which Kishimoto feels he owes his present sense of self-worth. As the relationship drags on and Kishimoto is being increasingly harassed by his brother, he decides to confess publicly in a literary work what the relationship to Setsuko has meant to him, as well as his original crime of seducing her. Ushimatsu in *Hakai* had finally made his confession when the secrecy and falsehood of his position became more painful to him than his fear of public disdain. Similarly, Kishimoto, finding the hypocrisy of his position unbearable, begins to publish a novel that will reveal his guilt as well as his transformation through Setsuko's love. Once she is taken away from him, Setsuko lives on in Kishimoto as the spirit of youth, freedom, and honesty that had inspired him first to pride in self and then to confession.[4]

Tōkoku saw love primarily in its spiritual sense, as the key that unlocks man's humanity, as a power that gives freedom to man. His ideal of *ren'ai* was influenced by Emerson, who in turn was influenced by the tradition of love as an ennobling force that had been handed down from Plato's *Symposium* via the troubadours, the Florentine *stilnovisti* of the thirteenth century, and Dante's *La*

[4] Not every reader would necessarily agree that Kishimoto's sacrifice of life to art was an ethically satisfactory solution. Indeed, balancing the critics who praised Tōson's sincerity in writing *Shinsei* were those who criticized his hypocrisy, such as Hirano Ken, in his *Shimazaki Tōson*, and Satō Yasumasa, in his "*Shinsei*," in *Shimazaki Tōson hikkei*, ed. Miyoshi Yukio, Tokyo, 1967.

Vita Nuova.[5] It is this tradition of viewing love that Tōson turned
to directly when he depicted his transformation by the love of
Setsuko in *Shinsei*, his personal "Vita Nuova." However, Tōson
depicted love as an illicit passion as well, in the sense of the passion of the Western lovers Abelard and Heloise—a kind of love
that is fraught with ambiguity because of its intensely individualistic and antisocial nature. His preoccupation with the tension
between love of the flesh and love of the spirit took him beyond
his own culture, beyond the ideals of Tōkoku, and back to a period of Western culture when the Provençal troubadours, Abelard
and Heloise, and Dante were discovering the spiritual significance of love between man and woman. Furthermore, the fact
that Tōson was moved by Nekhludov's painful struggle between
spiritual and sensual love in Tolstoy's *Resurrection*, and by Raskolnikov's salvation from his guilt through the love of Sonya, in
Crime and Punishment, demonstrates that he felt an intense sympathy for the modern, Western ideal of a love that is linked
dynamically to man's sensual, moral, and spiritual selfhood.

Shinsei is the only novel of its time to explore the nature of love
in such depth, and the only novel that depicts the moral transformation of an individual through love. Futabatei Shimei in his
Ukigumo had depicted what could be called a spiritual love on the
part of Bunzō for Osei, but Osei gives Bunzō only pain in return
for his love, a pain that shocks the timid Bunzō but fails to stimulate him to growth. Tayama Katai, in his *Futon*, saw love not as a
dynamic force leading Tokio to free expression of his selfhood but
rather as a source of energy that, because he lacked the courage to
act, turned into self-hatred and envy. Though Tokio's desire for
Yoshiko was clearly a mixture of lust and a desire to regain his
youth, he did not have the self-confidence and self-love to throw
himself on life, to sin, and to be reborn. Natsume Sōseki was
more interested in the relationship of two individuals in marriage
than in the growth of love in one partner or the other. His last

⁵ See Valency, *In Praise of Love*, for an illuminating discussion of this tradition.

and perhaps his greatest novel, the unfinished *Meian* (Light and Darkness, 1916), depicts a married couple who suffer from the fact that they are enmeshed in a legal and therefore unfree bond, and here the emphasis of his scrutiny is the blind egotism of the characters and the power that each, in his blindness, desires to gain over the other.

Sōseki's interest in marriage rather than love suggests that by temperament he preferred a Buddhist view of life, which sees human relationships as unfree attachments, to a Western-influenced view, which emphasizes the growth of the lover through the liberating influence of love. *Meian* suggests that if the male hero, Tsuda, had been willing to give up his egotism he might have been transformed by the love of a woman who had rejected him as a suitor years before, and the novel ends tantalizingly with him meeting this woman by chance at a health resort. Yet this is the only ray of light shed on the egotism of the characters in Sōseki's novel. In the last analysis, then, Tōson's ideal of love was the only one of his time that overcame the traditional Buddhist view of love as a degrading attachment to the world of the flesh. In a sense, too, it was the only one that continued the idea, expressed in Chikamatsu's plays, of love as a force that ennobles lovers and leads them to heroic action.[6] However, where

[6] Another attitude toward love in traditional Japanese culture is exemplified by the story of Saikaku entitled "Chūdan ni miru koyomiya monogatari" (The Almanac Maker's Tale in the Middle Section), which is one of five stories in his collection *Kōshoku gonin onna* (Five Amorous Women, 1686). Here a married woman of the merchant class, compromised with one of her husband's employees, decides to run off with him. The two feign suicide in order to put the husband off their trail, then lead a short, intense life devoted to passion, in a distant town. After their inevitable discovery they are brought back and executed publicly as examples of lewdness and lawlessness. From the viewpoint of the psychology of love, it is significant that the heroine, Osan, cannot admit to herself that she is attracted to her husband's steward, Moemon, and has to contrive to be accidentally seduced by him in order to achieve her desires. Once she has compromised herself with him, however, she gives herself wholeheartedly to her passion with an absence of guilt feelings that stems from the fact that she feels no responsibility for her love. Whereas Kishimoto became conscious of his guilt

Chikamatsu's Jihei and Koharu had to commit suicide to gain their freedom to love, Tōson's Kishimoto lives on, his selfhood transformed and restored by love. Yet Kishimoto remains alone at the end of *Shinsei*, as if overcoming the degradation attached to the relationship between man and woman meant overcoming the relationship itself. Ultimately, then, Tōson subordinated his ideal of love to that of self-definition.

For Tōkoku life (*seimei*) was a state of spiritual freedom that man had to work hard to achieve; it was a state of mind that came naturally after he had done the necessary work of self-definition. Sin was an idea that Tōkoku had written virtually nothing about, for his philosophy of man, ideally at least, transcended such basic realities in the interest of emphasizing the mystical inner transformation of the individual. Due to his personal experience, however, Tōson was forced to realize that in defining oneself in the world the individual sometimes created suffering for others, and thus his mature conception of self-definition included the experience of sin. For Tōson sin was the important experience that, if it were honestly confronted, would cause man to define himself and eventually to attain life. Thus, Ushimatsu in *Hakai* acquires a sense of guilt and Kishimoto in *Shinsei* commits a crime; both are led by someone who loves them to face this crime; both, when the crime is confronted and confessed, reacquire peace of mind; and both finally are reborn into a new life of innocence.

The origins of the pattern of sin that is followed by severe moral and spiritual suffering and issues in rebirth, are to be found in Tōson's adolescence at the Meiji Gakuin, when he was sud-

---

toward Setsuko and then took responsibility for his love, defending it against charges of illicitness and immorality, Osan and Moemon accept society's verdict that a love between two people of different classes is illicit, and do nothing to prevent the punishment that the law prescribes for it: death. They merely attempt to postpone this punishment, and their love is all the more intense because it is forced to exist in the brief interval between the revelation of desire and its inevitable end in death. Their love is a brief passion that does not contribute to the development of their personalities, while Kishimoto's love gains its freedom from the fact that it has time to change him.

denly confronted with the problem of sin. The consciousness of his own evilness weighed on him for over a year until he attended a summer camp at which he heard a lecture about the meaning of sin in Christianity. Here the awareness of sin was revealed as a natural consequence of man's striving for a world of the spirit; sin could be interpreted, then, as a dynamic moral process whose natural end was its transformation into something else, i.e., purity or innocence. (Note that in *Shinsei* Kishimoto realizes that through the love of Setsuko "the immorality which had made him want to kill himself . . . [was changed] into something with a completely different meaning.") For a time Tōson tried to force himself into that state of purity by leading a puritanical life, but he was unsuccessful. He knew at this point in his life what the opposite of sin was—a state of innocence that sin had interrupted and destroyed—but he did not yet know how to achieve it. Already during his summer at the camp, however, Tōson had accidentally discovered a way of attaining this coveted state of innocence, for he wrote later that while watching a sunset one evening he suddenly "awoke to his existence." Apparently, the Wordsworthian experience of nature's sublimity and beauty had aroused his vital self, which, deadened by sin, suddenly awoke to new life.

By the time Tōson wrote *Shinsei* the pattern of sin followed by moral suffering and culminating in rebirth, had evolved into a world view. In fact, the scene that is the heart of *Shinsei*—the scene where Kishimoto rethinks his crime in Haute Vienne—evokes the experience of rebirth that Tōson had had in 1890, as an adolescent: as Kishimoto walks among the trees in the orchard, his heart heavy with guilt, he suddenly begins to feel relief pouring into him, and his vital senses reawaken. As his feelings are softened, he is able to confront his sin for the first time. Thus, in this experience, as in Tōson's youthful experience at the summer camp, relief from guilt came not from a conscious decision to lead a pure life but from a submission of self to nature. According to Tōkoku, Christ was the power that led man to his inner *kokoro*;

for Tōson, however, it was life itself that led man to a state of innocence, and "life" meant experience in its most vital and free form in nature. It is clear, then, why he placed such importance on nature in his works, especially in the novels *Hakai* and *Shinsei*. Nature was destined to be the location of man's rebirth, for it had been the site of man's existence in a presocial, prerational state of innocence.

Tōson's tendency to view nature as innocence or the spirit of youth regained was linked also to the way he viewed his childhood. In later years, long after he had left behind the mountains of his home town, Magome, he often looked back with nostalgia at the innocent stage of his life before he had gone to the capital to acquire Western knowledge, and before he had achieved his complicated individuality. In addition, his intuition that nature was linked with a world of innocence that the thoughtful and careworn adult could only fleetingly, and with difficulty, recapture, might have been encouraged by his reading of Wordsworth's "Tintern Abbey" and "Ode. Intimations of Immortality." He could have found nature and the rebirth of the self linked also in Rousseau's *Confessions* and Tolstoy's *Resurrection*. Finally, he could have found the spiritual self of man linked to nature in his favorite Japanese poet, Bashō, for whom submission to the transitoriness of nature was a means of transcending the bondage of the ego. Tōson's view of guilt as a valuable energy that, through the experience of suffering and the inspiration of love, can be transformed into innocence, is a way of viewing man's spiritual struggle that can be found both in the East and the West. In Tōson's ideal of the new life, then, there is much that recalls the Blakean goal of a stage beyond experience that is innocence regained, and much that reminds also of the Shinto and Zen Buddhist stage of existence beyond adulthood and egotism that is compared to a childlike innocence and spontaneity.

Tōkoku viewed man as living essentially in the outer *kokoro* but striving to define the mystical inner *kokoro*. With Tōson life becomes an eternal process of moral transformation: man exists in a state of numbness, forgetful of his real nature and his spirit of youthful honesty, until sin or sorrow jolts him into a state of awareness. From that point, life takes him beyond suffering into a state of innocence. Based on his autobiographical fiction it is clear that Tōson saw his own life, at least through the period of his mid-forties, in these terms: as several periods of moral darkness, each of which ended in his regaining the innocent spirit of his youth. Thus, Tōson's view of man is a hopeful one, for if man relies on life, no matter how deep his suffering or how deep his guilt, he will emerge from his suffering into a new stage of innocence. This does not mean that he will be happy, for a person is often scarred very deeply by suffering. Rather, it means that he will find a peace like that of Ushimatsu at the end of *Hakai*, who, though he had lost any chance for social validation in Japan, nevertheless had regained his selfhood. *Hakai* was permeated by a New Testament spirit of optimism, as Inoko's Christlike sacrifice brought about the resurrection of Ushimatsu. In *Shinsei*, however, the atmosphere is down-to-earth and realistic, and Kishimoto's new life is brought about through the love of an ordinary mortal, as Raskolnikov's was in *Crime and Punishment*.

Man emerges as the center of *Shinsei*. Man is valuable in and through his struggles, it seems to say, and, like Tōkoku's fighter for truth, whether he wins or loses visibly, he has won inwardly. In *Shinsei* and *Hakai* nature aids in the individual's rebirth, but the important thing is that man is reborn. Finally, the endings of both novels point toward a future that contains new opportunities for growth. Man was the center of *Ukigumo* also, but he was hardly heroic. Futabatei's view of man was wistful or ironic; like Chekhov, he expected little of man—though at moments Bunzō does shine gloriously, at least in his thoughts. Katai's character Tokio, a cowardly nature, was also at the center of the pessimistic universe depicted in *Futon*. He was not brave enough to take the step into immorality, however, and hence he had no chance of being reborn. Through lack of imagination he never realized there was an opportunity for self-definition, so he suffered not for himself, but unreally, and for nothing. He ended, significantly, by clutching a tired fragment of the past.

Natsume Sōseki was the only other major writer of Tōson's time who had what can be called an ideal of individualism or self-definition. His mature concept of individualism (*kojinshugi*) was most succinctly expressed in a remark he made in a lecture given in 1914, two years before his death: "If you intend to pursue individuality for yourself, you must also, at the same time, respect the individuality of others."[7] It is clear that Sōseki's ideal of individualism was one that precluded egotism, yet in his novels he depicted the people he saw around him: people who were unable to admit the validity of other selves, with their troublesome demands as well as their offerings of trust and love. That man was not the center of life for Sōseki became evident when, in the last few years of his life, he advocated the ideal of "following Heaven and forsaking the ego" (*sokuten-kyoshi*). Sōseki's last two novels, *Michikusa* (Grass on the Wayside, 1915) and *Meian* (Light and Darkness), present an essentially comic vision of man, in that the author looks at his characters with a pragmatic sense of how they diminish themselves through their egotism. Yet Sōseki's attitude toward his characters is not the self-disparaging and self-pitying attitude of Katai, for he believes in the possibility of attaining a state of mind beyond egotism. Thus, while suffering for Katai's characters was merely pitiful, in Sōseki's novels the suffering of the characters is rational or at least understandable as the logical outcome of their egotism. *Meian* in particular implies that if the characters only had insight into their blindness they could transform suffering into happiness, and darkness into light.[8]

---

[7] From "Watakushi no kojinshugi" (My Individualism), cited in Komashaku Kimi, *Sōseki: sono jiko-hon'i to rentai to*, Tokyo, 1970, p. 203.

[8] See the discussion of Sōseki's last two novels in my dissertation, "The East-West Context of Shimazaki Tōson's *Shinsei* (The New Life)," Harvard University, 1974, pp. 164-179.

Tōson and Sōseki are similar, then, in that their view of man looks into the future—though Tōson sees man's goal as continual self-definition while Sōseki looks forward to man's continual progression toward selflessness. Neither approved of the self-seeking egotism that was the mark of the Meiji *seikō-seinen* ("success-seeking youth"), though Tōson's view of individualism at times seemed to justify the right of the individual to trespass on the rights of others. Sōseki was looking ahead to a time when the egotism unleashed by the Meiji atmosphere of expansion and unlimited opportunity could be transcended, and, compared to his view, Tōson's ideal of the individual seems lacking in farsightedness. It also seems naive in its assumption that the process of self-definition will ultimately lead the individual to a state of happiness and harmony with the universe. Yet Tōson's view of man, moreso than Sōseki's, reflected a stage in the cultural enlightenment of the individual that it was possible for Western-educated, middle-class people of his time to achieve. For individuals caught up in the Meiji longing for self-definition and self-expression, Tōson's confessional poems and novels presented an inspiring vision of an individual who valued his selfhood and who had the confidence to remove himself from the bondage of tradition and the family. Finally, for those who feared that by defining themselves they would cut themselves off from the cultural matrix, Tōson provided a reassuring model of how to find the way back to their rightful state of innocence and harmony with the universe.

One of Tōkoku's most cherished hopes was that modern Japanese would develop a quality that he called freedom of spirit. Tōkoku felt that the way of life proper to modern people was not to base their existence on scriptures or on blind faith in a deity or on tradition, but to make their inner *kokoro* or selfhood the basis of their lives. The process of making one's inner *kokoro* the basis of one's life Tōkoku conceptualized as a battle in man between "God's nature and man's nature." God's nature can be interpreted as those aspects of the spirit in man that lead him to a higher level of freedom, i.e., toward freedom of spirit, while human nature is that which keeps him enslaved on a purely material level. If there were no struggle between the two natures man would remain on a material level; nevertheless, struggle was meant to end eventually, though for each individual the cessation of struggle, or the peace of self-definition, occurred at his own, proper time. Finally, it was the possession of hope and faith in life itself that enabled an individual to define himself and thereby to transcend the purely material level of existence.

Tōson's novels *Hakai* and *Shinsei* show the influence of Tōkoku's ideal of freedom of spirit in that both heroes are depicted as undergoing a struggle between God's nature, or the spirit of freedom, and man's nature, or the spirit of reified tradition. In his struggle to make his inner *kokoro* the basis for his life Ushimatsu found himself pulled between his father, who represented life on the material plane, and Inoko, who symbolized the possibility of attaining freedom of spirit. By *material plane* I mean the father's acceptance of traditional assumptions about the nature of *eta*, assumptions that denied their existence as free beings. Ushimatsu's father had made the choice of living by the "scripture" of tradition and submerging his inner *kokoro*, yet it must be said in his favor that he conveyed to Ushimatsu his frustration at not having defined himself, as well as his strong desire that Ushimatsu define himself somehow, no matter what the cost. Ushimatsu underwent a process of self-definition that involved severe emotional suffering, but his struggle ended when Inoko's death stimulated him for the first time to feel hope toward the future. This hope gave him the strength to make the final step in the process of defining the inner *kokoro* and, given the fact that Ushimatsu's transformation had been inspired by Inoko's ideal of honesty, it was natural that he manifested his changed selfhood in the form of a confession. Finally, by confessing his crime, Ushimatsu broke through the old material world of silence and lack of self-definition, and helped to make a new world that rested on the ideals of honesty and full definition of self.

Kishimoto's transformation began in an act of unconscious rebellion at his stagnant life, an act that society and his family interpreted as a gesture of rebellion against the social order. For Kishimoto, however, the issue was not the antisocial or illegal nature of his act but rather his concealment of it. As he was gradually transformed by Setsuko's love, he felt that he must be totally honest with himself and others. Also, as he defended his relationship with Setsuko against his brother's attacks, his freedom of spirit was strengthened, with the result that the confession that was the manifestation in society of his new selfhood, unlike his earlier act of unconscious rebellion, was a conscious attack on the traditional morality of self-concealment.

While Tōkoku's battle between God's nature and man's nature seemed to take place in the private spiritual world of the individual, Tōson gave Tōkoku's ideal a social dimension by interpreting the latter's battle of the spirit against the material sphere of life as the struggle of liberating ideas against the rigid world of outmoded social prejudices. Also, where Tōkoku envisioned freedom of spirit as the peace attained by him who had achieved self-definition, Tōson saw freedom of spirit as the peace that followed upon the act of self-revelation through words, or confession. In both *Hakai* and *Shinsei* the confession of the hero becomes an act that juxtaposes the living sincerity and private truth of the individual to a stagnant and reified social world. Rather than as the last refuge of the passive and antisocial artist who is unable to play a role in the society at large, confession in Tōson's novels should be seen as a criticism of that society in that it stimulates readers to rethink the bases of traditional morality.[9] That Ushimatsu's confession has such an effect on its witnesses, his class of schoolchildren, is evident in the fact that, though raised to believe that *eta* are not human beings, they are moved by the per-

[9] For a view that, contrary to mine, considers Tōson and Katai as writers who took pride in the honesty of their confessions, but failed to criticize society in any meaningful way, see Tatsuo Arima, *The Failure of Freedom: A Portrait of Modern Japanese Intellectuals*, Cambridge, Mass., 1969, pp. 70-98.

sonal sincerity and humanity of their *eta* teacher to defend his rights. In this scene Tōson revealed his hopes for the development of freedom of spirit in Japan.

Tōson and Literary Confession

Tōkoku's ideals of self-definition and freedom of spirit undoubtedly lay behind Tōson's conception of self-expression as a necessary step in the process of defining the self. Yet Tōkoku himself wrote no strictly confessional works, other than letters, and it is consequently difficult to see him as anything more than an indirect inspiration for Tōson's decision to use literature as a means of confession. Far more important in this respect was Rousseau, the Rousseau of the *Confessions* that Tōson first became acquainted with in his early twenties. It was most likely Rousseau who influenced Tōson to value the moral, and the immoral, self and to see his personal life as having greater than personal value. Yet Dostoevsky was an important inspiration too, for Tōson was admittedly so impressed with the scene in *Crime and Punishment* where Raskolnikov kneels down in the marketplace to confess his crime, that he modeled Ushimatsu's confession scene in *Hakai* after it.[10] Literary confession was probably Tōson's most important innovation, and his most lasting contribution to Meiji literature. In order to evaluate that contribution, however, it is necessary to understand the context in which Tōson made his experiments in literary confession.

Before the Meiji period it was unheard of for a person to write his confessions for general public scrutiny, as Rousseau had done

[10] Itō, *Shimazaki Tōson kenkyū*, pp. 386-387. Possibly Tōson's sympathetic response to the scene in the Haymarket is due to his remembrance of scenes from his childhood where persons who had committed a crime would confess in front of the whole village. In any case, Tōson certainly ignored the ludicrous aspects of the Dostoevsky scene when he recreated it in *Hakai*. For while Raskolnikov's kissing of the earth was greeted by jeers and catcalls on the part of the unsympathetic passersby, Ushimatsu's abject bowing in front of his pupils clearly moves them, and the scene as a whole conveys an impression of utter seriousness.

and as Tōson did in *Shinsei*. It is not that honesty toward oneself and others was not valued in traditional Japan—the dominant samurai ethic did indeed stress sincerity and honesty, but it was a sincerity of actions, not of words.[11] The samurai attempted to live up to an ideal of behavior that he had not personally evolved but in which he believed. If he failed to live up to this ideal, he did not wait for the verdict of others; he knew immediately that he had failed. His main task was to restore his lost honor, and since ritual suicide was the established means of doing this, he usually committed suicide. *Seppuku*, or ritualized suicide, then, was the samurai form of sincerity, a form that was spontaneous (in that it required no lengthy moral self-questioning), clean, and above all, final. The samurai who committed *seppuku* to restore his honor had no division of consciousness as to whether his action was wrong or right,[12] and by committing suicide he effectively cut off any possibility of further dishonor.

[11] This is not to say that there was no literary sincerity in traditional Japan—see, for example, the memoirs of Kumazawa Banzan (1619-1691), a philosopher of the Wang Yang-ming school. Yet Kumazawa narrated the story of his life not in order to impress upon his readers the uniqueness, or the innocence, of his selfhood but rather in order to give an example of how to unite self-understanding and self-discipline in the service of action. There was no question in his mind that political action was the ultimate goal of self-scrutiny. For other vivid examples of samurai sincerity in action see Ivan Morris, *The Nobility of Failure: Tragic Heroes in the History of Japan*, New York, 1975, especially the chapters on Kusunoki Masashige and Saigō Takamori.

[12] Lionel Trilling argues that the ethics of the European nobility originated in military ideals of behavior, and his description of the European noble at about the time of the beginning of the rise of the bourgeoisie reveals similarities to the Japanese samurai of the feudal era. Trilling writes of the noble self that acts on the basis of an approved code of behavior: "It stands before the world boldly defined, its purposes clearly conceived and openly avowed. In its consciousness there is no division, it is at one with itself." By contrast, middle-class sincerity shows a division of consciousness, according to Trilling, and the same can be claimed of the sincerity of middle-class Japanese individuals of the Meiji period such as Tōson. See *Sincerity and Authenticity*, Cambridge, Mass., 1972, pp. 26-52.

Tōson's sincerity clearly rested on the traditional samurai assumption that a man must maintain his honor before himself and others—in other words, sincerity, for Tōson, was a form of moral action.[13] However, Tōson evolved his attitude of sincerity in a period when a respect for individual morality was gradually developing in the subculture of intellectuals to which he belonged. For the middle-class individual educated according to Western liberal ideals, the ideal of truth was the one to which he owed his loyalty, but where the samurai concept of honor had been an objective concept, this truth was subjective and relative. Consequently, when the Meiji middle-class individual such as Tōson attempted to live up to his own ideal of honor, he was often unsure of how to evaluate his actions. Unlike the samurai, he had to look to others for judgment and sympathy. Tōson's practice of literary confession was clearly influenced by the lack of clear-cut moral assumptions of the Meiji period. Before acting to restore his honor he deliberated a long time, unsure of the sincerity of his motives and fearing the opprobrium of his peers. Finally, his act of confession, far from removing him from the possibility of further dishonor, merely paved the way (from the samurai point of view) for further corruption, for what was to stop him from making a second, and a third confession? The sincerity of Tōson and his contemporaries was of decidedly human proportions, the product of an age when a heroic ideal of behavior befitting the superior man was being replaced by an ideal that validated the morality of the average individual. The new kind of confessor saw his judges as equal to himself or, as Rousseau put it, at least no

[13] In Kishimoto's letter to his brother (in *Shinsei*) explaining why he had decided to confess the secret of his affair, Tōson expressed his own rationale for writing *Shinsei*: "The fact that such an immoral person as myself was born into the Kishimoto family, which possessed so many people of great virtue, has been a cause of disgrace to my ancestors, but I feel that having my immorality censured will, on the contrary, bespeak the virtue of my ancestors." *Shinsei*, pt. 2, *Zenshū*, 6: 448 (chap. 106). In this passage can be seen the loyalty to family or clan honor, coupled with the desire to restore one's honor by means of a heroic gesture, that were typical of the traditional samurai.

better than himself. For whereas individuals differ greatly in their capacity for heroism of the samurai variety, everyone can be an individualist hero and everyone can carry out the act of confession, as has been proved in the two hundred years since Rousseau inaugurated the modern form of literary confession.[14]

Like Goethe in *Die Leiden des jungen Werther* and Alfred de Musset in *La Confession d'un enfant du siècle*, Tōson wrote confessional literature in order to relieve as well as to transcend the emotional and moral torment that was brought on by painful experiences in his life.[15] Throughout his life Tōson was engaged in a continuous process of self-definition, a process that reached a crisis point at those times when he felt that his independence was threatened by the external world. In his teens he felt threatened by a strict moral system, in his twenties by his family. Later, after he had defined himself as a writer, the pressures came increasingly from the inside. In each situation Tōson struggled to

[14] The practice of literary confession has always generated criticism in the West among those who are skeptical of mortal man's capacity to be sincere. One should not be surprised, then, that a suspicion of sincerity through confession of the sort that Tōson introduced existed in the minds of many of Tōson's contemporaries who were still under the sway of the stoic and austere samurai ethic. Perhaps the most famous example of contemporary criticism of Tōson, as well as of Rousseau, is the following remark of Akutagawa Ryūnosuke (1892-1927) in his nonconfessional poetic autobiography, *Aru ahō no isshō* (The Life of a Certain Fool, 1927): "Coldly grinning at his own spiritual collapse (fully aware of all his weaknesses and vices) he went on reading book after book. But even Rousseau's *Confessions* was stuffed full of heroic lies. Worse yet was Tōson's *A New Life*. In it he encountered a hero more slyly hypocritical than any." *A Fool's Life*, trans. Will Petersen, New York, 1970, p. 121. For the Japanese text see *Akutagawa Ryūnosuke zenshū*, Tokyo, 1956, 8: 135.

[15] Goethe has left a lucid explanation of his frame of mind while writing *Werther* in *Aus Meinem Leben: Dichtung und Wahrheit, Goethes Werke*, vol. 9, Hamburg, 1967, bk. 12, pp. 540-546; bk. 13, pp. 574-594. For the facts behind Musset's writing of *La Confession* as well as for speculations as to his motives, see Louis Evrard, *George Sand et Alfred de Musset*, Monaco, 1956, and Claude Duchet's preface in Alfred de Musset, *La Confession d'un enfant du siècle*, Paris, 1968.

find a means of saving his vital self, and from the Sendai period on, the means was literary confession. In each case the confession of his sufferings that he made indirectly through a literary work appears to have played the role of challenging the outside world that he saw as threatening to stifle his sense of self. At the same time, literary confession gave him a chance to juxtapose his own subjective truth to the facts of his oppression and to reaffirm his sense of self publicly. That his confessions had the effect of validating his selfhood is clear from the fact that the publication of at least three of his confessional works—*Wakana-shū*, *Hakai*, and *Shinsei*—resulted in a sudden enthusiasm for or a renewed interest in Tōson the individual and writer. It is also possible, however, to interpret his audience's sudden enthusiasm for him—in particular, the enthusiasm after the publication of *Shinsei*—as a voyeuristic fascination with the thoughts and deeds that he had revealed.

In writing *La Confession d'un enfant du siècle* Musset was apparently motivated at least partially by a desire to confess, and thereby to atone for, his reprehensible behavior in the love affair with George Sand. The work, in fact, contains several elements of a real religious confession: there is a scene in which the hero undergoes an *examen de conscience* that ends dramatically in his confession, carried out next to the bed of his sleeping mistress, of the wrongs he has done her. Furthermore, the novel ends with an equally melodramatic scene in which the hero, Octave, his moral self reborn after his confession, selflessly turns the mistresss he has mistreated over to a new lover![16] The novel uses a Christian pattern of confession followed by salvation from sin in order to convince the reader of the author's sincerity, though this sincerity is jeopardized by the tone of mixed self-pity and self-aggrandizement. In *Hakai* Tōson depicted an individual whose dramatic confession was motivated by his guilt at having concealed the truth about his origins from the people around him, and though

---

[16] Musset, *La Confession*, pp. 312-315, 315-320.

the confession issued in his moral and spiritual rebirth, in a Christian sense, it was also a means of restoring his honor and baring his shame in a traditional manner.[17] *Shinsei* contains no dramatic confession scene, but two motives for Kishimoto's confession are given. His decision to "imitate the many people who had written confessions"[18] suggests that he felt a Western-influenced longing to validate his personal sense of truth, whereas in another passage he speaks of the desire to have his immorality censured. Yet Kishimoto's deed was known for certain only by Setsuko and her father, and from the viewpoint of the family no one else would have had to know about it. Kishimoto's decision in 1918 to reveal his crime, then, stemmed less from a desire to restore a lost sense of honor than to regain a sense of personal honesty that he had lost six years before.

When Tōson began to write *Shinsei* he was forty-six years old, a well-known writer for whom the public had a special, enduring affection. He hesitated a long time before beginning the confession for he knew that he might destroy his relationship with that public, a relationship on which his future career as a writer depended. The practice of a writer's depicting incidents from his own life as well as from the lives of his family and close friends was quite widespread in Japanese fiction by this time, so that Tōson's personal revelations per se would not have seemed overly shocking.[19] However, the incident that Tōson wished to depict

---

[17] As Ushimatsu decides to confess on the night of Inoko's murder, he speaks of confession in terms of a "new world" of self-pride that Inoko has led him into. Yet immediately after, he notes that he will confess in order to avoid causing trouble to his class and colleagues (*narubeku hito ni meiwaku o kakenai yō ni*). He also begs his father's forgiveness mentally for having disobeyed him. *Zenshū*, 3: 290-291 (chap. 20). For an insightful discussion of the traditional Japanese trait of desiring not to cause injury to others see Takie Sugiyama Lebra, *Japanese Patterns of Behavior*, Honolulu, 1976, pp. 41-42.

[18] *Shinsei*, pt. 2, *Zenshū*, 6: 402 (chap. 92).

[19] An interesting discussion of this typically Japanese fictional practice may be found in Itō Sei, "L'Ecrivain et sa vie privée," in *Conférence internationale P.E.N.*, Paris, 1959, pp. 66-69. The confession of unflattering circumstances

in *Shinsei* was one that was especially unflattering to his image of self: namely, how he, a mature man, had been so unaware of his feelings that he seduced a girl though he did not want to get involved with women; then, like any frightened youth in the same position, attempted to escape responsibility for his act by fleeing. Tōson knew that the way he presented the facts would shape people's perception of them and therefore their evaluation of his behavior. Somehow he had to find a way of presenting his thoughts and actions so that they made a positive impression of sincerity on the reader, yet he did not wish to conceal the truly unflattering details of his conduct. In order to fulfill these contradictory obligations, he used a mode of third-person narration that allowed him to stand poised between identification with his character and distance from him.[20]

In his pose as the Romantic young man alternating between cynicism and rapture, Musset had relied on the Romantic first person, the mere use of which in his time created an appealing impression of spontaneous frankness and even lucidity.[21] Tōson, however, was a person whose samurai training and rural origins guaranteed that he would accustom himself only slowly, and with difficulty, to the volubility and easy frankness of the city. Consequently, he had used the first person only with diffidence in his poetry and sketches, and not at all in his early autobiographical novel, *Haru*. A certain shyness kept him in *Shinsei* also from

---

in the writer's life, and in the lives of those intimate with him, was a special prerogative of the I-novelist.

[20] Though *Shinsei* is technically an autobiographical novel, Tōson's position vis-à-vis *Shinsei* is similar to that of the author in a third-person autobiography. According to Philippe Lejeune, in a third-person autobiography, "the third person figures provide a range of solutions in which distancing is more prominent, though always used to express an articulated connection (a tension) between identity and difference." "Autobiography in the Third Person," *New Literary History* 9 (1977): 32.

[21] For a discussion of the impression of sincerity conveyed by a writer writing in the first person in the Romantic period see André Wurmser, "Je, romancier," *Journal de Psychologie Normale et Pathologique* 44 (1951): 335-343.

using the first person to narrate a subject that was so potentially revealing of his moral self. Then, too, the fact that Tōson had done his literary apprenticeship as a writer of fiction under the aegis of Naturalism probably influenced him to adopt an objective, third-person point of view. But Tōson chose not to use a first-person point of view for another important reason: as a conscious artist he feared that using the first person would make it impossible for him to reveal certain aspects of his character that the reader would have to know about, and understand, before he could reach a fair evaluation of Kishimoto's behavior.[22] If Tōson had narrated the changing feelings of his character in the first person, Kishimoto would have seemed sentimental and perhaps even unstable to the reader, and would most likely have failed to gain his sympathy and understanding. By using the third person to narrate the potentially shocking behavior of Kishimoto, whom his audience would identify with himself, Tōson succeeded in blunting the effect of that behavior. Kishimoto thus gives the impression of being a serious-minded individual with a sober samurai temperament that makes him understandable to his audience. Also, the use of a sober third-person point of view guaranteed that when Tōson mentioned his lovers in connection with Abelard and Heloise and Dante and Beatrice, the reader would be able to imagine Kishimoto and Setsuko in a broader, more universal context than that afforded by the scandalous events themselves.

The use of the first-person point of view in autobiographical writing generally gives the illusion of directness. That Tōson did not use the first person suggests that he wished to "proclaim his indirectness," and to take a position vis-à-vis his material that

---

[22] Bertil Romberg notes in this context that because the first-person narrator cannot look at himself from the outside, it is difficult for an author using such a narrator to create a picture of the character's objective behavior. For Tōson, however, it is crucial to show Kishimoto's (his own) actions from the outside. *Studies in the Narrative Technique of the First-Person Novel*, Stockholm, 1962, p. 59. See also the section entitled "Who Narrates the First-Person Novel?"

was ambivalent. By using "he" instead of "I" he was able to say to the reader, "The 'he' that I use conveys something about me, but it is not me."[23] Even the genre of *Shinsei* shows ambivalence: it appears to be fiction but in fact (and his audience knew this) it is virtually autobiography. The reader of *Shinsei* is shown the actions of Kishimoto by the narrator, who by and large narrates objectively. Yet here and there the reader becomes conscious of another point of view that is not objective like the narrator's but that seems to identify with Kishimoto. Thus, behind the ostensible third-person narrator stands a concealed first-person narrator. For example, Kishimoto thinks the following thoughts while in Haute Vienne: "If humanity were to judge him and he were forced to defend himself, would he be able to relate fully all that had happened inside of himself, using some kind of psychological explanation as a shield? And the fact that he had come up against a crisis situation in his life, one in which he had had to live even though it meant sacrificing someone else—how could he talk about this in a clear, logical, noncontradictory, and rational way?"[24] Though these thoughts are presented in third-person indirect statement, they give the impression of first-person utterances. By having someone besides himself, but not too distant from himself, i.e., the narrator, reveal the one acceptable justification for Kishimoto's abandonment of Setsuko, Tōson succeeds in having his motives laid before the reader in the most favorable light, yet without risking making the impression that he is excusing his behavior. At the same time he has been able to speak to the reader almost in his own voice, in a personal plea for sympathy, understanding, and forgiveness.

Tōson sometimes allows his sympathy for Kishimoto to filter through the objective narration of the official narrator, as in the previous episode. Yet at times he expresses his condemnation as well—for example, by having the narrator present Kishimoto's behavior toward his niece as both tactless and cruel. At a point

[23] Lejeune, "Autobiography in the Third Person," pp. 32, 29.
[24] *Shinsei*, pt. 1, *Zenshū*, 6: 185 (chap. 98).

early in the novel Kishimoto visits a friend who, when he hears that Kishimoto has made his niece pregnant, jokingly suggests that he relieve his obvious depression by making a lengthy tour of Europe. Kishimoto returns home that night in the attitude of someone who has found a way to escape from a difficult situation:

> Kishimoto returned home to his familiar quarter. Though it was a district where there was activity until rather late at night, it was now midnight, and the cries of chickens in their roosts could be faintly heard nearby. In his house, too, everyone appeared to be asleep and, assuming this, Kishimoto knocked on the gate.
>
> "Is that you, Uncle?" Setsuko's voice could be heard and, before long, the sound of the latch being unfastened from the inside. Kishimoto was still drunk.
>
> "Oh, you look strange," said Setsuko, frightened, looking at Kishimoto.
>
> Even after Kishimoto had gone to his own room he was unable to suppress the feelings which bubbled up inside him. Just then, Setsuko brought some cold water for her inebriated uncle. Kishimoto couldn't help but share his feelings even if it meant sharing them with his niece, who was unaware of what had happened.
>
> "Poor girl." He said this involuntarily and embraced Setsuko heavily, she who had been injured like a little bird by him.
>
> "I've got good news. I'll tell you about it tomorrow."
>
> When she heard this Setsuko, as if her heart were suddenly full, stood with her face pressed against the wall. The dark tears she could not restrain penetrated the ears of the drunken Kishimoto.[25]

It would have been impossible to have written this passage in the first person without making Kishimoto (Tōson) sound extraordinarily cruel and setting him beyond the sympathy of the reader. As it is, the narrator is anything but objective toward Kishimoto here. In this passage, then, Tōson assumes momentarily a pose of quasi-identity with his character in order to condemn himself and elicit the reader's disapproval.

Another way in which Tōson confesses indirectly in *Shinsei* is

[25] Ibid., pp. 68-69 (chap. 28).

through the scenes that present Kishimoto's deepest feelings in a natural setting. For example, in the long passage quoted in the preceding chapter where Kishimoto finds peace in Haute Vienne, Kishimoto is at first depicted in the midst of tortuous and painful self-analysis. Toward the end of the paragraph, however, he seems to be nearing a resolution and his thoughts break off abruptly as he steps into the orchard. Then, after the torrent of involved, complicated thoughts that reason has failed to solve comes a description of the sights, sounds, and smells of the orchard as Kishimoto walks through it. All thought, all mental torture is laid aside as various rural phenomena, both natural and man-made, assault and stimulate his senses. As his dulled senses slowly awaken his mind gradually achieves peace; it is literally "softened," as Tōson puts it, by Kishimoto's immersion of self in the nature of Haute Vienne. Here, as in the other two passages, Tōson temporarily steps forward from his concealed position behind the narrator to identify with Kishimoto, this time not in order to make the reader either forgive or condemn his behavior or motives but rather to make him identify with Kishimoto. Judgment implies separation of reader and character, while what Tōson aims at here is a lyrical fusion of the two.

Tōson's idea of literary confession, then, was similar to that of European Romantics in that it allowed him to use literature in order to relive painful feelings that he was unable or unwilling to confront otherwise. Tōson used confession, as did Rousseau and his numerous followers, as a subtle way of justifying his actions. Yet he also employed it to obtain the judgment of his peers, even if, similarly to Rousseau, he was fearful of the form that judgment might take. Tōson's practice of literary confession, however, was quite unlike that of Rousseau in its rejection of detailed analysis of motivation in favor of a solipsistic recollection and even sanctification of personal experience.[26] Tōson's unusual use

---

[26] Rousseau's influence on Tōson's practice of literary confession seems to have been in his inspiring Tōson to confess; *how* Tōson confessed was shaped by Tōson's own culture, particularly by the traditional concept of feeling. The idea

of the third person in his confessional novels seems, retrospective-
ly, to have been a successful strategy born out of his desire to remain faithful to his goal of self-expression, as a modern follower
of Rousseau, as well as to the traditional attitudes of reticence and
self-concealment. It was probably Tōson's combination of openness and shyness that enabled him to gain the sympathy of the
readers of his time who, like himself, had been educated to respect and value a self that was sincere but reticent.

Tōson's practice of literary confession had more than a literary
significance—it was intimately related to his personal attempt to
live out the existence of the modern self (*kindaiteki jiga*). For
Tōson's two quasi-fictional heroes, Ushimatsu and Kishimoto,
the act of confession already took on such dimensions, as it criticized the traditional moral system that, in its insistence on the
suppression and concealment of the self, had created an inhuman
society. Yet Tōson's personal act of confession—his publication
of the novel *Shinsei*—can be seen in a similar light. When Tōson
began to write *Shinsei* he probably felt, alongside his fear of an
unfavorable verdict on his actions, an excitement generated by
the nature of his act, for by publishing such intimate details of
his life in the newspaper he was challenging traditional attitudes
toward self-exposure. It became clear, however, by the time the
last episode of part one had appeared that his public was generally
sympathetic to his gesture. At this point Tōson could have
stopped his novel, since he had achieved his original goal (as
stated in *Shinsei*) of ending the falsehood and secrecy that had tor-

of one modern critic, in which I concur, is that the concept of feeling that dominates the I-novel is closer to the traditional *aware*, a process of experiencing the
unity of events and perceiver, than to Rousseau's *sentiment*: a self-assertive, aggressive process of psychological analysis. Thus, for Tōson and the confessional
novelists who followed him, confession was primarily a solemn or ecstatic, but
above all, a lyrical reexperiencing of feelings in their momentary contexts pervaded by *aware* rather than an analysis and critique of emotion. An example of
aware in *Shinsei* is the scene where Kishimoto awakes to himself in the orchard in
Haute Vienne, and *Hakai* has several such scenes. Yasuoka Shōtarō, *Shiga Naoya
shiron*, Tokyo, 1968, pp. 199-204.

tured him ever since he had abandoned his niece several years earlier.

If Tōson had ended *Shinsei* with what is known as part one, he
would have written another *Hakai*, for part one closes with a rebirth of the hero stemming from his awareness of his crime, as
well as a decision to recover the spirit of his youth—a decision
that parallels Ushimatsu's recovery of his sincerity through confession. The act of publishing part one of *Shinsei* had validated
Tōson's morality vis-à-vis society, the obstacle that society had
posed to his morality having been overcome. Yet by the time part
one was finished a new obstacle to Tōson's self-validation had
arisen: his own family. One must consider here that the immediate effect of Tōson's publication of the novel in the newspaper was
to bring the intimate affairs of the Shimazaki family to the attention of thousands of unknown readers. By the time Tōson had
completed part one of the novel his family was becoming increasingly disturbed by his continued meetings with Komako. His
brother was unhappy about the appearance of *Shinsei*, but he was
even more worried about the future scandal that could result from
the continuation of the affair. It became gradually and painfully
clear to Tōson that his brother considered his present relationship
with his niece to be in fact a crime—a crime worse than the relationship with her years before that had issued in an illegitimate
child. The subject matter of part two, then, was this new crime
of Tōson's relationship with Komako.

The important theme in part two is Kishimoto's validation of
his relationship with Setsuko through the act of confession.
Tōson makes his brother a representative of the traditional attitude of self-concealment when he has him disapprove of the affair and the confession that attempts to defend it. On the other
hand, Tōson makes himself, through the character of Kishimoto,
an advocate of modern, Western-style self-revelation—and there
is no confusion as to where his sympathy lies.[27] It is in the nature

[27] Tōson often seems to believe that the act of confession will naturally lead
his character to a state of purity and innocence. In *Shinsei*, for example, Kishi-

of confessional writing that Kishimoto in the novel gained the readers' sympathy as a victim of his brother's authoritarian decisions. Yet Tōson also personally gained the sympathy of his readers through his publication of *Shinsei*, a novel that revealed the old morality of secrecy and self-concealment in an unfavorable light. Tōson's publication of part two of *Shinsei* in particular can be seen as his successful attempt to expose the family-based morality that suppressed individual freedom in the name of tradition. As the schoolchildren in *Hakai* were the new advocates of a modern spirit that allowed for individual freedom, the numerous readers that Tōson addressed in *Shinsei* were the potential advocates of a modern attitude of openness and pride in self.

Futabatei Shimei and Tayama Katai had written, like Tōson, out of a need to pursue and make valid a private truth, yet neither of them succeeded in validating the self and its actions through literary confession. Katai's indirect confession in *Futon* was made by a fearful and self-pitying penitent who had no hope whatever of overcoming the oppression of his vital self. Futabatei's only confessional novel, *Heibon* (Mediocrity, 1907), depicted a man who saw himself as a fool and for whom confession was merely an occasion for self-revilement, though his insights into his moral nature were often acute. Natsume Sōseki wrote no confessional novels—yet one of his novels, *Kokoro* (Human Feeling, 1914), contains a lengthy confession written by its hero, a man known only as "Sensei" (a title of respect). Sensei is a man who, after

moto was faced with a difficult moral dilemma: either he could continue his relationship with Setsuko and see it vilified, though tolerated, by his family, or he could reveal its true nature—a step he must have known would end it as well as expose Setsuko to unwanted publicity. The moral dilemma is insoluble because by keeping silent Kishimoto will become a victim of his family's morality, yet by confessing he will become an unintentional oppressor of Setsuko. Tōson presents Kishimoto's confession as a genuine ethical solution to this dilemma. Yet in spite of his suggestion that Kishimoto, by confessing, can somehow escape his moral dilemma, the reader cannot help feeling that in this respect, at least, Tōson is either insincere or naive, for what Kishimoto achieves at the end of *Shinsei* is more a state of irresponsibility than innocence.

suffering for years from guilt over a secret crime, commits suicide. His suicide is in a sense a samurai gesture made to restore his honor, but it is an unusually lonely one, in that no peer group knows of his crime. Yet just before he dies he breaks out of his loneliness by confessing to an outsider, a young man of another generation who sincerely wishes to know the truth of Sensei's life. [28]

In *Kokoro* suicide made no sense in traditional samurai terms, yet confession, a modern gesture uniting the individual with the broader community, also failed to overcome the essential loneliness of the human being. For Tōson, however, confession was a sober concern for the fate of the moral self that rested on his belief in the continued existence of a community that valued sincerity in the samurai sense. Yet Tōson was unique among novelists of the self of his time in his acceptance of Rousseau's attitude of pride in self as well as Rousseau's ideal of literary confession before an unknown public. Through his joining of two ethical traditions—the modern Western tradition of self-pride and public confession and the samurai tradition of sincerity and public defense of honor—Tōson created a form of literary confession that, in its defense of individual morality against the traditional moral system, spoke strongly to Meiji readers who were struggling to define themselves in an age of rapid modernization.

Tōson and the Autobiographical Novel

Along with the European writers of *romans personnels*, Goethe, Musset, Gottfried Keller, Strindberg, and Tolstoy, Shimazaki Tōson can be seen as an heir of Rousseau in the matter of his use of literary confession. [29] It is just this preoccupation with confes-

---

[28] For a discussion of the significance of Sensei's confession in *Kokoro* see my dissertation, "The East-West Context of Shimazaki Tōson's *Shinsei*," pp. 362-367.

[29] On this topic see Mark J. Temmer's essays on Rousseau's influence on Goethe and Keller in *Art and Influence of Jean-Jacques Rousseau*, Chapel Hill,

sion as an act of moral self-validation and self-judgment, in fact, that differentiates Tōson's novels of the individual from the I-novels, or *shishōsetsu*, of his time. Yet Tōson's novels also differ from the I-novel in their length, for where I-novels of the time were seldom more than one hundred pages, Tōson's *Hakai* is 291 pages, *Haru*, 246 pages, and *Shinsei*, 495 pages. The length of his novels alone suggests that Tōson had a larger purpose in mind than the depiction of a small slice of individual life. Furthermore, the systematic depiction of his life up to about age fifty-five, in a series of autobiographical novels that is comparable to August Strindberg's series in the West, implies that Tōson saw his life as an important *document humain* of his age.[30] The I-novelist lacked a philosophical or spiritual ideal by which he could measure his hero's development, and consequently he had no means of depicting change or growth—only experience as it unrolled in a series of events. But Tōson was able to present a vision of the development of an individual that included the future and the past, as well as the present, because he could measure his hero's progress or development against Tōkoku's ideal of self-definition. As he wrote each of his novels Tōson looked back on the process of

---

N.C., 1973; Elie Poulenard, *Strindberg et Rousseau*, Paris, 1959; and the preface to Musset's *La Confession*, p. vii.

[30] Tōson's series of autobiographical novels includes *Haru* (Spring, 1908), a record of the years between 1892, when he became associated with Kitamura Tōkoku and the *Bungakkai* group, and 1896, when he left to teach in Sendai; *Ie* (The Family, 1911), which treats the years of his marriage to Hata Fuyuko and the years in Komoro; *Osanaki hi* (My Childhood Days, 1913), which covers the period from Tōson's birth through his arrival in Tokyo in 1881; *Sakura no mi no juku-suru toki* (When the Cherries Ripen, 1918), which goes back to Tōson's years as a student at the Meiji Gakuin and a teacher at the Meiji Jogakkō (1887-1893); *Shinsei* (1919), which deals with the period of Tōson's liaison with his niece and his trip to France (1912-1919); and the short story, *Arashi* (The Tempest, 1927), which describes Tōson's life with his children in the politically turbulent 1920s. However, many other short works in the *zuihitsu* ("random notes") form treat aspects of Tōson's life. See my comparison of Tōson's and Strindberg's series of Naturalist-inspired autobiographical novels in "The East-West Context of Shimazaki Tōson's *Shinsei*," pp. 432-438.

self-definition that he had been undergoing at the time and, without attempting to give an analytical overview of his progress—as, for example, Goethe does in *Dichtung und Wahrheit*—suggested the nature and importance of his struggle. The epic quality of these novels that deal, paradoxically, with only one individual, emerges precisely from the fact that Tōson succeeded in imbuing the struggles of this individual with great meaning.

The plot of the novels is the same: the internal pattern of the reawakening of the individual's vital self. The development that Tōson's Kishimoto undergoes in the course of each separate novel that together make up one big *roman-fleuve* of his life is not a development of character, for character is the individual seen in his interactions with others. Rather, Tōson's novels depict a development of the individual that is moral, but not in the sense of an external, social morality. For Tōson immorality is the individual's neglect of his vital self, which, containing the instinct for life and freedom, is essentially pure and therefore cannot be considered in terms of an external good or evil. Morality, then, is allowing the vital self to flourish. Thus, rather than being concerned with the individual's connection with the world, Tōson is interested in his connection to his vital self, viewing the vital self as essentially related to nature rather than to society—though, when consciousness and manifestation of this self are required, the individual affirms himself before others in the act of confession.

Tōson's subjective novels, then, are not I-novels but novels depicting the process of self-definition. They see man, not as the I-novelists did—as immersed in the present and deprived of a future—but as the inheritor of a future of free selfhood that he has struggled consciously to achieve. In contrast to the pessimistic I-novel, they present a vast, man-centered view of life. As the I-novel is similar, in its limited focus, its fragmentary vision of life, and its size, to the French *roman personnel*, Tōson's large novels, especially *Shinsei*, are comparable to the German form of the *Bildungsroman*. The latter genre has been defined as the "representation of the interactions between the self and the world, with special reference to the process of the education of the self"—as a spiritual autobiography.[31] The stages of the education of the self are internal ones, and in such novels action occurs only as material for the use of the self.

There are obvious similarities between the two novel forms. Both concentrate on inner processes of growth, or the awakening of the self. Other similarities are the extreme length, and the origin of both forms in the context of the development, in the respective cultures, of an individualist morality.[32] The *Bildungsroman*, a development largely of the eighteenth and nineteenth centuries, flourished, like Tōson's novels, in a culture where the individual strove to define himself spiritually and socially in a political situation of lingering feudalism. Often the German individual yearned to find his place in society, whereas Tōson's Kishimoto struggles to define himself in relation to life. However, at least two *Bildungsromane*—Gottfried Keller's *Der grüne Heinrich* (1855) and Adalbert Stifter's *Der Nachsommer* (1857)— presented the individual in nature in many passages, as if the relationship of the individual to nature, in its meaning of external landscape as well as of the internal state of innocence and purity, were also of great importance. Normally the *Bildungsroman* de-

[31] François Jost, "The 'Bildungsroman' in Germany, England, and France," in *Introduction to Comparative Literature*, New York, 1974, p. 136.

[32] Martin Swales sees the *Bildungsroman* as having developed in a period (eighteenth-century Germany) when the bourgeois humanistic ideal of "humanity" (*Humanität*) was a central concern for German writers. He defines it as a "novel form that is animated by a concern for the whole man unfolding organically in all his complexity and richness." *The German Bildungsroman from Wieland to Hesse*, Princeton, 1978, pp. 14-15. For a discussion of the origins of the term *Bildungsroman* and its ideological and social context, see also Fritz Martini, "Der Bildungsroman: Zur Geschichte des Wortes und der Theorie," *Deutsche Vierteljahrsschrift für Literaturwissenschaft und Geistesgeschichte*, 31 (1961): 44-63. See W. H. Bruford, *The German Tradition of Self-Cultivation*, Cambridge, 1975, for a discussion of the evolution of the concept of *Bildung* in Germany in the nineteenth and twentieth centuries.

picted an adolescent or a youth in the important formative period of life, and this betrays an emphasis on character. Tōson's interest is rather in the vital self at all periods of life, for the vital self, like the seasons, sometimes declines and sometimes flourishes; it may undergo a hard winter but it knows that it can expect to reawaken in the spring. In fact, Tōson's particular contribution to the ideal of individualism in the Meiji period was his intuition that the development of the individual even in social terms proceeds in harmony with his deepest attachment, which is an attachment not to other human beings but to pure and vital nature. His series of epic novels depicted the unfolding of the individual's inner self in relation to this vital nature, as if to say that this process was the true education of the Meiji individual.

After Tōson completed *Shinsei* in 1919 he wrote no more confessional novels. It is possible that, as he entered his fifties, he felt that he had brought to completion a process of self-definition that he had begun in his late adolescence, for he had learned the meaning of *ren'ai*, he had tested his independence from the family and tradition and found it strong, and he had seen his inner moral life respected by his peers. For whatever reason, however, Tōson in the 1920s turned away from the self-exalting form of confession and began to devote himself to the world beyond the sphere of the lonely individual. At the height of the influence of the Naturalist movement, he had been sustained in his autobiographical efforts by the sincere conviction that by writing about the life of one Meiji individual who was attempting to lead a modern life, he was pursuing a truth that had wider implications for the society at large. Furthermore, he could work at developing his individual morality with the confidence that he was helping Japan to fulfill the Naturalist goal of breaking away from the anti-individualistic, feudal morality of the past. Yet the decline of Naturalism by the mid-teens of the twentieth century deprived him of this support. *Shinsei* (1919), for example, was a work written in the Naturalist ambience that Tōson carried with him to France in

1913 and brought home again in 1916. It was the last work that he could write according to the ideology of Naturalism.

Yet if Tōson himself gave up the I-novel or confessional form, the 1920s saw it reach its height of popularity, in the hands of writers such as Shiga Naoya (1883-1971). In 1921 there appeared the first half of Shiga's lengthy autobiographical novel, An'ya kōro (Long Journey through the Dark Night), followed by most of the second part in 1922 and 1923. Shiga, born in a later age that assumed the validity of the self, was less interested than Tōson in defining the self, and directed his attention rather to the traditionally aristocratic areas of perception, dream, fantasy, and sensation.[33] Yet Shiga, trained, like Tōson, as a Christian in his youth, felt a similar ambivalence toward rigid morality and, like Tōson, he was preoccupied with the affirmation and validation of the vital self. In a sense, then, Shiga continued the scrutiny of the asocial, essentially innocent self that Tōson, and the I-novelists, had begun in the last decade of Meiji. Like Tōson, Shiga advocated an antitragic view of man that emphasized the necessity of following one's inner self, a selfhood that was revealed at its most essential level in nature. Yet where the development of Tōson's individual was always linked to social change, Shiga's self expanded to fill the whole world in his vast, introspective novel. Finally, the concern for political and social freedom that underlay Tōson's novels was replaced, in Shiga, by a concern for the freedom of the privatistic, aristocratic self.

The people of the Meiji period, influenced by nineteenth-century Western political and social philosophies, tended to view individualism in terms of the idea of progress—as the steady, continuous development of individual freedom in time. Thus, Fukuzawa saw independence as an inevitable development of a cultured nation, and Tōkoku viewed the definition of each individual's inner kokoro as the inevitable result of the cultivation of

---

[33] William F. Sibley gives an excellent account of this aspect of Shiga in his dissertation, "The Shiga Hero," University of Chicago, 1971.

freedom of spirit. Tōson's view of the individual who sins but is eventually reborn into innocence also shows the influence of the ideal of progress, as well as the optimistic ideal of a "new life in Christ" that was disseminated by Protestant Christian missionaries. In fact, it is the middle-class individual engaged in a continuous process of development in the socially free world of the Meiji period that Tōson depicts in his novels through *Shinsei*. The ideal of progress, however, is an ideal of youth, an ideal proper to a youthful stage of development; it was in the optimistic context of early Meiji, after all, that Tōson's "spirit of youth" had its roots. Those who followed the writers of the first generation of Meiji in depicting the individual lost the social idealism of individualism in its Meiji form, though writers such as Shiga brought to their task a renewed awareness of traditional ways of viewing the self. But that is a story that remains to be told.

Works Consulted

Akutagawa Ryūnosuke 芥川龍之介. *Aru ahō no isshō* 或阿呆の一生 [The Life of a Certain Fool]. *Akutagawa Ryūnosuke zenshū* [Complete Works]. Vol. 8. Tokyo: Iwanami Shoten, 1965, pp. 117–138.

————. *A Fool's Life.* Translated by Will Petersen. New York: Grossman, 1970.

Anesaki, Masaharu. *History of Japanese Religion.* London: Kegan Paul, Trench, Trubner, 1963.

Ara Masahito 荒正人. "Shishōsetsu ron" 私小説論 [On the I-Novel]. *Bungakkai* 6 (September 1952): 23–30.

Arima, Tatsuo. *The Failure of Freedom: A Portrait of Modern Japanese Intellectuals.* Cambridge: Harvard University Press, 1969.

Beasley, W. G. *The Meiji Restoration.* Stanford: Stanford University Press, 1972.

————. *The Modern History of Japan.* New York: Praeger, 1963.

Bellah, Robert N. *Tokugawa Religion: The Values of Pre-industrial Japan.* Glencoe, Ill.: The Free Press, 1957.

Benl, Oscar. *Flüchtiges Leben.* Berlin-Schöneberg: Landsmann Verlag, 1942.

Best, Ernest E. *Christian Faith and Cultural Crisis: The Japanese Case.* Leiden: E. J. Brill, 1966.

Blacker, Carmen. *The Japanese Enlightenment: A Study of the Writings of Fukuzawa Yukichi.* Cambridge: At the University Press, 1964.

Booth, Wayne. *The Rhetoric of Fiction.* Chicago: University of Chicago Press, 1961.

Brower, Robert H., and Miner, Earl. *Japanese Court Poetry.* Stanford: Stanford University Press, 1961.

Bruford, W. H. *The German Tradition of Self-Cultivation: "Bildung" from Humboldt to Thomas Mann.* Cambridge: At the University Press, 1975.

Cheng, Ching-mao. "Nagai Kafū and Chinese Tradition." Ph.D. dissertation, Princeton University, 1970.

Craig, Albert M. "Fukuzawa Yukichi: The Philosophical Origins of Meiji Nationalism." In *Political Development in Modern Japan,* edited by Robert E. Ward. Princeton: Princeton University Press, 1968, pp. 99–148.

De Vos, George, and Wagatsuma, Hiroshi. *Japan's Invisible Race: Caste in Culture and Personality*. Berkeley and Los Angeles: University of California Press, 1972.

Dilworth, David A., and Hirano, Umeyo, trans. and introd. *Fukuzawa Yukichi's "An Encouragement of Learning."* Tokyo: Sophia University, 1969.

Doi Takeo 土居健郎. *Amae no kōzō* 甘えの構造 [The Structure of *Amae*]. Tokyo: Kōbundō, 1971.

———. *The Anatomy of Dependence*. Translated by John Bester. Tokyo: Kōdansha, 1977.

Dostoevsky, Feodor. *Crime and Punishment*. Translated by Jessie Coulson. Edited by George Gibian. New York: Norton, 1964.

Dumoulin, Heinrich. "The Consciousness of Guilt and the Practice of Confession in Japanese Buddhism." In *Studies in Mysticism and Religion Presented to Gershom G. Scholem*, edited by E. E. Urbach, R. J. Zwi Werblowsky, and C. Wirszubski. Jerusalem: Magnes Press, The Hebrew University, 1967, pp. 117–129.

Etō, Jun. "An Undercurrent in Modern Japanese Literature." *Journal of Asian Studies* 23 (May 1964): 433–445.

Evrard, Louis. *George Sand et Alfred de Musset: Correspondance; Journal intime de George Sand (1834); nombreux documents, annexes et lettres inédits*. Monaco: du Rocher, 1956.

Fairbank, John K.; Reischauer, Edwin O.; and Craig, Albert M. *East Asia: The Modern Transformation*. Boston: Houghton Mifflin, 1965.

Feldman, Horace Z. "The Meiji Political Novel: A Brief Survey." *Far Eastern Quarterly* 9 (May 1950): 245–255.

Freedman, Ralph. *The Lyrical Novel: Studies in Hermann Hesse, André Gide, and Virginia Woolf*. Princeton: Princeton University Press, 1971.

Fukuzawa Yukichi 福澤諭吉. Gakumon no susume 学問のすすめ [An Encouragement of Learning]. *Fukuzawa Yukichi zenshū* [Complete Works]. Vol. 3. Tokyo: Iwanami Shoten, 1960, pp. 21–144.

Futabatei Shimei 二葉亭四迷. *Mediocrity*. Translated by Glenn W. Shaw. Tokyo: Hokuseido, 1927.

———. *Ukigumo* 浮雲 [Floating Clouds]. *Futabatei Shimei zenshū*

[Complete Works]. Vol. 1. Tokyo: Iwanami Shoten, 1953–1954, pp. 3–153.

————. "Yo no aidoku sho" 予の愛讀書 [My Favorite Books]. *Zenshū*, 15: 180–182.

Goethe, Johann Wolfgang von. *Aus meinem Leben Dichtung und Wahrheit. Goethes Werke.* Hamburger Ausgabe. Hamburg: Christian Wegner Verlag, 1967. Vol. 9, *Autobiographische Schriften.*

Goldin, Frederick, trans. *Lyrics of the Troubadours and Trouvères: An Anthology and a History.* Garden City, N.Y.: Doubleday, Anchor Books, 1973.

Goodheart, Eugene. *The Cult of the Ego: The Self in Modern Literature.* Chicago: University of Chicago Press, 1968.

Grimsley, Ronald. *Jean-Jacques Rousseau: A Study in Self-Awareness.* Cardiff: University of Wales Press, 1969.

Halpern, Manfred. "Four Contrasting Repertories of Human Relations in Islam." In *Psychological Dimensions of Near Eastern Studies,* edited by L. Carl Brown and Norman Itzkowitz. Princeton: Darwin Press, 1977, pp. 60–102.

Hasegawa Izumi 長谷川泉. "Shishōsetsu sanjūgosen" 私小説三十五選 [Thirty-five Selected I-Novels]. *Kokubungaku Kaishaku to Kanshō* 27 (no. 14): 77–91.

Hauser, Arnold. *Naturalism, Impressionism, and the Film Age.* Vol. 4 of *The Social History of Art.* New York: Random House, Vintage Books, n. d.

Hayashi Isamu 林勇. *Komoro naru kojō no hotori: Shimazaki Tōson to Komoro* 小諸なる古城のほとり—島崎藤村と小諸 [By the Old Castle of Komoro: Shimazaki Tōson and Komoro]. Komoro: Shiritsu Tōson Kinenkan, 1967.

Hemmings, F. W. J. *Emile Zola.* Oxford: Clarendon Press, 1966.

Henderson, Harold G. *An Introduction to Haiku.* Garden City, N.Y.: Doubleday, Anchor Books, 1958.

Hibbett, Howard S. *The Floating World in Japanese Fiction.* New York: Grove Press, 1960.

————. "The Portrait of the Artist in Japanese Fiction." *Far Eastern Quarterly* 14 (1955): 347–354.

————. "Sōseki and the Psychological Novel." In *Tradition and Modernization in Japanese Culture,* edited by Donald H. Shively. Princeton: Princeton University Press, 1971, pp. 305–346.

Hirano Ken 平野謙. *Shimazaki Tōson* 島崎藤村 [Shimazaki Tōson]. Tokyo: Satsuki Shobō, 1957.

Hirschmeier, Johannes, "Shibusawa Eiichi: Industrial Pioneer." In *The State and Economic Enterprise in Japan: Essays in the Political Economy of Growth*, edited by William W. Lockwood. Princeton: Princeton University Press, 1965, pp. 209–247.

Hytier, Jean. *Le Roman de l'individu*. Paris: Les Arts et Le Livre, 1928.

Ihara, Saikaku. *Five Women Who Loved Love*. Translated by William Theodore de Bary. Rutland, Vt.: Charles E. Tuttle, 1956.

———. *The Life of an Amorous Woman and Other Writings*. Translated and edited by Ivan Morris. New York: New Directions, 1963.

Ishibashi Ningetsu 石橋忍月. "*Ukigumo* no homeotoshi" 浮雲の褒貶 [Praise and Criticism of *Ukigumo*]. In *Gendai bungakuron taikei*. Vol. 1, *Meiji jidai* 現代文学論体系・第一・明治時代 [Outline of Contemporary Comments on Literature. Vol. 1, The Meiji Period]. Tokyo: Kawade Shobō, 1955, pp. 44–51.

Itō Kazuo 伊東一夫. *Shimazaki Tōson jiten* 島崎藤村事典 [Shimazaki Tōson Dictionary]. Tokyo: Meiji Shoin, 1972.

———. *Shimazaki Tōson kenkyū* 島崎藤村研究 [Research on Shimazaki Tōson]. Tokyo: Meiji Shoin, 1969.

Itō, Sei. "L'Ecrivain et sa vie privée." In *Conférence internationale P.E.N.: Septembre 1958 à Paris*. Paris: Julliard, 1959, pp. 64–72.

Iwamoto, Yoshio. "Suehiro Tetchō: A Meiji Political Novelist." In *Japan's Modern Century:* A Special Edition of *Monumenta Nipponica* Prepared in Celebration of the Centennial of the Meiji Restoration. Edited by Edmund Skrzypczak. Tokyo: Sophia University, 1968, pp. 83–114.

Jansen, Marius B., ed. *Changing Japanese Attitudes Toward Modernization*. Princeton: Princeton University Press, 1965.

Jones, P. Mansell. *French Introspectives from Montaigne to André Gide*. Cambridge: At the University Press. 1937.

Josephson, Matthew. *Jean-Jacques Rousseau*. New York: Russell and Russell, 1959.

Jost, François. "The 'Bildungsroman' in Germany, England, and France." In his *Introduction to Comparative Literature*. New York: Bobbs-Merrill, 1974, pp. 134–150.

Jung, Carl Gustav. *Aion: Researches into the Phenomenology of the Self*. Princeton: Princeton University Press, 1959.

————. *Psychological Types*. Princeton: Princeton University Press, 1971.

Kahler, Erich. *The Inward Turn of Narrative*. Translated by Richard and Clara Winston. Foreword by Joseph Frank. Princeton: Princeton University Press, 1965.

Kataoka Ryōichi 片岡良一. *Kindai nihon no sakka to sakuhin* 近代日本の作家と作品 [Modern Japanese Writers and Works]. Tokyo: Iwanami Shoten, 1954.

————. *Shizenshugi kenkyū* 自然主義研究 [Studies in Japanese Naturalism]. Tokyo: Chikuma Shobō, 1957.

Keene, Donald, trans. *Essays in Idleness: The "Tsurezure-gusa" of Kenkō*. New York: Columbia University Press, 1967.

————. trans. *Major Plays of Chikamatsu*. New York: Columbia University Press, 1962.

————. *World Within Walls: Japanese Literature of the Pre-modern Era, 1600–1867*. New York: Holt, Rinehart, and Winston, 1976.

Kinmonth, Earl H. "The Self-Made Man in Meiji Japanese Thought." Ph.D. dissertation, University of Wisconsin, 1974.

Kipling, Rudyard. *Rudyard Kipling's Verse*. Inclusive Edition. 1885–1926. Garden City: Doubleday, Doran, 1928.

Kisimoto, Hideo, ed. *Japanese Religion in the Meiji Era*. Translated and adapted by John F. Howes. Tokyo: Tōyō Bunko, 1969.

Kitagawa, Joseph M. *Religion in Japanese History*. New York: Columbia University Press, 1966.

Kitamura Tōkoku 北村透谷. *Emaruson* エマルソン [Emerson]. In *Tōkoku zenshū* [Complete Works]. Vol. 3. Tokyo: Iwanami Shoten, 1960, pp. 1–122.

————. *Ensei shika to josei* 厭世詩家と女性 [The World-Weary Poet and Woman]. *Zenshū*, 1: 254–264.

————. *Jinsei ni aiwataru to wa nan no ii zo* 人生に相歩るとは何の————. 謂ぞ [What Does It Mean "To Benefit Mankind"?]. *Zenshū*, 2: 113–126.

————. *Jōnetsu* 情熱 [Romantic Ardor]. *Zenshū*, 2: 297–303.

————. *Kakujin shinkyūnai no hikyū* 各人心宮内の秘宮 [The Heart, a Holy of Holies]. *Zenshū*, 2: 3–15.

————. *"Ka'nenbutsu" o yomite* 「歌念仏」を読みて [On Reading *"Ka'nenbutsu"*]. *Zenshū*, 1: 345–353.

Kitamura Tokoku. *Naibu seimei ron* 内部生命論 [On the Inner Life].
Zenshū, 2: 238–250.

———. *Netsui* 熱意 [Romantic Ardor]. *Zenshū*, 2: 255–259.

———. *Ninomiya Sontoku Ō* 二宮尊徳翁 [Ninomiya Sontoku].
Zenshū, 1: 251–254.

———. *Saigo no shōrisha wa dare zo* 最後の勝利者は誰ぞ [Who Will
be the Final Victor?]. *Zenshū*, 1: 316–321.

———. *Seishin no jiyū* 精神の自由 [Freedom of Spirit]. *Zenshū*, 2:
159–167.

———. *Shinki myōhen o ronzu* 心機妙変を論ず [On Mystical
Metamorphoses]. *Zenshū*, 2: 15–25.

———. *Takai ni kansuru kannen* 他界に対する観念 [The Idea of
Another World]. *Zenshū*, 2: 35–45.

———. Letter to Ishizaka Mina, August 18, 1887. *Zenshū*, 3:
160–169.

———. Letter to Ishizaka Mina, January 21, 1888. *Zenshū*, 3:
198–202.

Kobayashi Hideo 小林秀雄 "Shishōsetsu ron" 私小説論 [On the I-
Novel]. *Kobayashi Hideo zenshū* [Complete Works]. Vol. 3. Tokyo:
Shinchōsha, 1968, pp. 119–145.

Komashaku Kimi 駒尺喜美. *Sōseki: sono jiko-hon'i to rentai to*
漱石・その自己本位と連帯と [Sōseki: His Egotism and His Idea
of Solidarity]. Tokyo: Yagi Shoten, 1970.

Konrad, Nikolai I. *West-East: Inseparable Twain*. Moscow: Central
Department of Oriental Literature, 1967.

Kōsaka, Masaaki. *Japanese Thought in the Meiji Era*. Tokyo: Tōyō
Bunko, 1969.

Kume Masao 久米正雄. "Shi-shōsetsu to shinkyō-shōsetsu"
私小説と心境小説 [The I-Novel and the Contemplative Novel].
In *Gendai bungakuron taikei*. Vol. 3, *Taishō jidai* 現代文学論
体系・第三・大正時代 [Outline of Contemporary Comments on
Literature]. Tokyo: Kawade Shobō, 1955, pp. 286–293.

LaFleur, William R. "Saigyō and the Buddhist Value of Nature."
History of Religions 13, no. 2 (November 1973): 93–128; 13, no. 3
(February 1974): 227–248.

Lane, Richard. "The Beginnings of the Modern Japanese Novel:
Kanazōshi, 1600–1682." *Harvard Journal of Asiatic Studies* 20 (1957):
644–701.

Lebra, Takie Sugiyama. *Japanese Patterns of Behavior*. Honolulu: University Press of Hawaii, 1976.

Lee, Leo Ou-fan. *The Romantic Generation of Modern Chinese Writers*. Cambridge: Harvard University Press, 1973.

Lejeune, Philippe. "Autobiography in the Third Person." Translated by Annette and Edward Tomarken. *New Literary History* 9 (Autumn 1977): 27–50.

Levin, Harry. *The Gates of Horn: A Study of Five French Realists*. New York: Oxford University Press, 1966.

Lowenthal, Leo. *Literature and the Image of Man: Studies of the European Drama and Novel, 1600–1900*. Boston: Beacon Press, 1957.

Martini, Fritz. "Der Bildungsroman: Zur Geschichte des Wortes und der Theorie." *Deutsche Vierteljahrsschrift für Literaturwissenschaft und Geistesgeschichte* 31 (1961): 44–63.

Maruyama Masao 丸山真男. "From Carnal Literature to Carnal Politics." Translated by Barbara Ruch. In *Thought and Behavior in Modern Japanese Politics*, edited by Ivan Morris. London: Oxford University Press, 1963, pp. 245–267.

―――. *Gendai seiji no shisō to kōdō* 現代政治の思想と行動 [Thought and Behavior in Contemporary Japanese Politics]. 2 vols. Tokyo: Miraisha, 1961.

―――. "Nationalism in Japan: Its Theoretical Background and Prospects." Translated by David Titus. In *Thought and Behavior in Modern Japanese Politics*. pp. 135–156.

Mathewson, Rufus W., Jr. *The Positive Hero in Russian Literature*. New York: Columbia University Press, 1958.

Mathy, Francis. "Kitamura Tōkoku: The Early Years." *Monumenta Nipponica* 18 (1963): 1–44.

―――. "Kitamura Tōkoku: Essays on the Inner Life." *Monumenta Nipponica* 19 (1964): 66–110.

―――. "Kitamura Tōkoku: Final Essays." *Monumenta Nipponica* 20 (1965): 41–63.

Matsumoto, Shigeru. *Motoori Norinaga: 1730–1801*. Cambridge: Harvard University Press, 1970.

McClellan, Edwin. "Tōson and the Autobiographical Novel." In *Tradition and Modernization in Japanese Culture*, edited by Donald H. Shively. Princeton: Princeton University Press, 1971, pp. 347–378.

————. *Two Japanese Novelists: Sōseki and Tōson.* Chicago: University of Chicago Press, 1969.

McCullough, Helen Craig, trans. *Gikeiki. Yoshitsune: a Fifteenth-Century Japanese Chronicle.* Stanford: Stanford University Press, 1966.

————, trans. *Tales of Ise.* Stanford: Stanford University Press, 1968.

Merlant, Joachim. *Le Roman personnel de Rousseau à Fromentin.* Paris: Hachette, 1905.

Miner, Earl. *The Japanese Tradition in British and American Literature.* Princeton: Princeton University Press, 1958.

Miyoshi, Masao. *Accomplices of Silence: The Modern Japanese Novel.* Berkeley and Los Angeles: University of California Press, 1974.

Miyoshi Yukio 三好行雄. *Shimazaki Tōson ron* 島崎藤村論 [On Shimazaki Tōson]. Tokyo: Shibundō, 1966.

Moore, Charles A., ed., with the assistance of Aldyth V. Morris. *The Japanese Mind: Essentials of Japanese Philosophy and Culture.* Honolulu: University Press of Hawaii, East-West Center Press, 1967.

Morita, James R. "Shimazaki Tōson's Four Collections of Poems." *Monumenta Nipponica* 25 (1970): 325–369.

Morris, Colin. *The Discovery of the Individual, 1050–1200.* London: Published for the Church Historical Society by S.P.C.K., 1972.

Morris, Ivan. *The Nobility of Failure: Tragic Heroes in the History of Japan.* New York: New American Library, Meridian Books, 1976.

Murasaki Shikibu 紫式部. *Genji monogatari* 源氏物語 [The Tale of Genji]. Edited by Yamagishi Tokuhei 山岸徳平. In *Nihon Koten Bungaku Taikei.* Vol. 15. Tokyo: Iwanami Shoten, 1975.

————. *The Tale of Genji.* Translated by Edward G. Seidensticker. 2 vols. New York: Alfred A. Knopf, 1976.

Musset, Alfred de. *La Confession d'un enfant du siècle.* Paris: Garnier, 1968.

Naff, William E. "Shimazaki Tōson: A Critical Biography." Ph.D. dissertation, University of Washington, 1965.

Nagai Kafū 永井荷風. "Nihon no niwa" 日本の庭 [A Japanese Garden]. In his *Kafū zenshū* [Complete Works]. Vol. 5. Tokyo: Iwanami Shoten, 1964, pp. 309–321.

————. *Reishō* 冷笑 [Sneers]. *Zenshū,* 4: 249–465.

————. "*Reishō* ni tsukite" 「冷笑」につきて [On *Sneers*]. *Zenshū,* 13: 41–44.

————. "Yatate no chibifude" 矢立のちび筆 [Thoughts from My Humble Inkhorn]. *Zenshū*, 14: 273–278.

————. "Yahazu-gusa" 矢筈ぐさ [Notes of an Arrow-Notch]. *Zenshū*, 14: 247–272.

Nakamura Mitsuo 中村光夫. *Futabatei Shimei* 二葉亭四迷 [Futabatei Shimei]. In his *Sakkaron-shū* 作家論集 [Collected Essays on Writers]. Vol. 3. Tokyo: Kōdansha, 1968, pp. 6–131.

————. *Fūzoku shōsetsu ron: kindai riarizumu no hihan* 風俗 小説論—近代リアリズムの批判 [On the Novel of Customs and Manners: Comments on Modern Japanese Realism]. In *Nakamura Mitsuo zenshū* [Complete Works]. Vol. 7. Tokyo: Chikuma Shobō, 1973, pp. 525–615.

————. *Meiji bungakushi* 明治文学史 [History of Meiji Literature]. Tokyo: Chikuma Shobō, 1963.

————. *Modern Japanese Fiction: 1868–1926*. Tokyo: Kokusai Bunka Shinkokai, 1968.

————. *Nihon no kindaika to bungaku* 日本の近代化と文学 [Modernization and Literature in Japan]. *Zenshū*, 8: 548–575.

————. *Nihon no kindaishōsetsu* 日本の近代小説 [Modern Japanese Fiction]. *Zenshū*, 11: 307–441.

————. *Tayama Katai* 田山花袋 [Tayama Katai]. In his *Sakkaron-shū*, vol. 1. Tokyo: Kōdansha, 1968, pp. 134–180.

Natsume Sōseki 夏目漱石. *Grass on the Wayside* 道草 [Michikusa]. Translated by Edwin McClellan. Chicago: University of Chicago Press, 1969.

————. *Kokoro* こころ [Kokoro]. Translated by Edwin McClelland. Chicago: Henry Regnery, 1957.

————. *Light and Darkness* 明暗 [Meian]. Translated by Valdo H. Viglielmo. Honolulu: University of Hawaii Press, 1971.

The New Testament in Modern English. Translated by J. B. Phillips. New York: Macmillan, 1958.

Odagiri Hideo 小田切秀雄. *Kitamura Tōkoku ron* 北村透谷論 [On Kitamura Tōkoku]. Tokyo: Yagi Shoten, 1970.

Okamura Kazuo 岡松和夫. "Kindaiteki jiga o meguru kansō" 「近代的自我」をめぐる感想 [Impressions of the "Modern Self"]. *Koten to Gendai* 1968 (no. 7): 8–14.

Okazaki, Yoshie. *Japanese Literature in the Meiji Era*. Translated by Valdo H. Viglielmo. Tokyo: Ōbunsha, 1955.

Oketani Shūshō 桶谷秀昭. "Kindaiteki jiga to kojinshugi"

近代的自我と個人主義 [The "Modern Self" and Individualism]. *Kokubungaku Kaishaku to Kanshō* 36 (1971): 16–23.

Pascal, Roy. *Design and Truth in Autobiography.* Cambridge: Harvard University Press, 1960.

Peyre, Henri. *Literature and Sincerity.* New Haven: Yale University Press, 1963.

Poulenard, Elie. *Strindberg et Rousseau.* Paris: Presses Universitaires de France, 1959.

Průšek, Jaroslav. "Subjectivism and Individualism in Modern Chinese Literature." *Archiv Orientální* 25 (1957): 261–286.

———. *Three Sketches of Chinese Literature.* Prague: Academia, 1969.

Pyle, Kenneth B. *The New Generation in Meiji Japan: Problems of Cultural Identity, 1885–1895.* Stanford: Stanford University Press, 1969.

Radice, Betty, trans. *The Letters of Abelard and Heloise.* Baltimore: Penguin Books, 1974.

Rekho, K. "Dostoevskii i yaponskii realisticheskii roman kontsa XIX veka" [Dostoevsky and the Japanese Realistic Novel at the End of the Nineteenth Century]. *Narody Azii i Afriki* 1 (1972): 117–127.

Rimer, J. Thomas. *Mori Ōgai.* Twayne's World Authors Series. Boston: G. K. Hall, 1975.

Roggendorf, Joseph, "Shimazaki Tōson, A Maker of the Modern Japanese Novel." *Monumenta Nipponica* 7 (January 1951): 40–66.

Romberg, Bertil. *Studies in the Narrative Technique of the First-Person Novel.* Stockholm: Almqvist & Wiksell, 1962.

Roske-cho, Wha Seon. *Das Japanische Selbstverständnis im Modernisierungsprozess bei Natsume Sōseki.* Wiesbaden: Otto Harrassowitz, 1973.

Rougemont, Denis de. *L'Amour et l'occident.* Paris: Plon, 1939.

———. *Les Mythes de l'amour.* Paris: Gallimard, 1967.

Rousseau, Jean-Jacques. *Les Confessions.* Paris: Garnier, 1964.

Ryan, Marleigh Grayer. *The Development of Realism in the Fiction of Tsubouchi Shōyō.* Seattle: University of Washington Press, 1975.

———. *Japan's First Modern Novel: "Ukigumo" of Futabatei Shimei.* New York: Columbia University Press, 1967.

Sansom, George B. *The Western World and Japan: A Study in the*

Interaction of European and Asiatic Cultures. New York, Alfred A. Knopf, 1962.

Sasabuchi Tomoichi 笹淵友一. *Bungakkai to sono jidai* 「文学界」とその時代 [*Bungakkai* and Its Era]. 2 vols. Tokyo: Meiji Shoin, 1961.

Satō Yasumasa 佐藤泰正. *"Shinsei"* 「新生」 [*Shinsei*]. In *Shimazaki Tōson hikkei* 島崎藤村必携 [A Shimazaki Tōson Handbook], edited by Miyoshi Yukio 三好行雄. Tokyo: Gakutōsha, 1967, pp. 138-149.

Scholes, Robert, and Kellogg, Robert. *The Nature of Narrative.* New York: Oxford University Press, 1966.

Schwantes, Robert S. "Christianity *versus* Science: A Conflict of Ideas in Meiji Japan." *Far Eastern Quarterly* 22, no. 2 (February 1953). Reprinted in *Japan: Enduring Scholarship Selected from the "Far Eastern Quarterly"—The "Journal of Asian Studies," 1941-1971.* Edited by John A. Harrison. Tucson: University of Arizona Press, 1972, pp. 37-46.

Sei Shōnagon. *The Pillow Book of Sei Shōnagon.* Translated by Ivan Morris. 2 vols. New York: Columbia University Press, 1967.

Seigle, Cecilia Segawa. "An Integral Translation with an Introduction of *Ie* (The Family) by Shimazaki Tōson (1872-1943)." Ph.D. dissertation University of Pennsylvania, 1971.

Senuma Shigeki 瀬沼茂樹. *Hyōden. Shimazaki Tōson* 評伝・島崎藤村 [Critical Biography of Shimazaki Tōson]. Tokyo: Jitsugyō no Nihonsha, 1959.

――――. *Kindai nihonbungaku no kōzō.* Vol. 1, *Meiji no bungaku* 近代日本文学の構造・第一・明治の文学 [The Structure of Modern Japanese Literature. Vol. 1, Meiji Literature]. Tokyo: Shūeisha, 1963).

――――. *Kindai nihonbungaku no naritachi* 近代日本文学の成り立ち [The Origins of Modern Japanese Literature]. Tokyo: Kadokawa Bunko, 1962.

Shiga Naoya 志賀直哉. *A Dark Night's Passing* 暗夜行路 [An'ya kōro]. Translated by Edwin McClellan. Tokyo: Kōdansha, 1976.

――――. "Kuniko" 邦子 [Kuniko]. In *Shiga Naoya shū* [Collected Works]. *Gendai nihonbungaku zenshū,* vol. 20. Tokyo: Chikuma Shobō, 1959, pp. 345-359.

Shimazaki Tōson 島崎藤村. "Bashō no Isshō" 芭蕉の一生 [Life of

Bashō]. *Shimazaki Tōson zenshū* [Complete Works]. Vol. 14. Tokyo: Shinchōsha, 1948–1952, pp. 123–124.

———. *The Broken Commandment* 破戒 [*Hakai*]. Translated by Kenneth Strong. Tokyo: University of Tokyo Press, 1974.

———. *Chikumagawa no suketchi* 千曲川のスケッチ [Sketches of the Chikuma River]. *Zenshū*, 3: 297–446.

———. *The Family* 家 [*Ie*]. Translated by Cecilia Segawa Seigle. Tokyo: University of Tokyo Press, 1976.

———. *Hakai* 破戒 [Breaking the Commandment]. *Zenshū*, 3: 3–293.

———. *Haru* 春 [Spring]. *Zenshū*, 4: 3–248.

———. "*Haru* to *Ryūdokai*" 「春」と「龍土会」 [*Haru* and the *Dragon Earth Society*]. *Zenshū*, 17: 323–324.

———. *Ie* 家 [The Family]. *Zenshū*, 5: 1–441.

———. "Inshōshugi to sakubutsu" 印象主義と作物 [Impressionism and the Literary Work]. *Zenshū*, 14: 35–37.

———. "Kisotani nikki" 木曽谿日記 [Diary of the Kiso River Valley]. *Zenshū*, 2: 173–194.

———. "Meiji Gakuin no gakusō" 明治学院の学窓 [The Meiji Gakuin]. *Zenshū*, 14: 91–94.

———. *Nōfu* 農夫 [The Farmer]. *Zenshū*, 2: 236–271.

———. *Osanaki hi* 幼日 [My Childhood Days]. *Zenshū*, 10: 367–420.

———. "Rūsō no *Zange*-chū ni miidashitaru jiko" ルウソオの「懺悔」中に見出したる自己 [The Self that I Discovered in Rousseau's *Confessions*]. *Zenshū*, 14: 13–15.

———. *Sakura no mi no juku-suru toki* 桜の実の熟する時 [When the Cherries Ripen]. *Zenshū*, 4: 249–409.

———. "Seika yokō" 西花餘香 [Lingering Fragrance of Western Flowers]. *Zenshū*, 2: 166–172.

———. "Shasei" 写生 [Sketching from Life]. *Zenshū*, 14: 37–39.

———. *Shinsei* 新生 [The New Life]. *Zenshū*, 6: 1–495.

———. *Wakana-shū* 若菜集 [Collection of Young Shoots]. *Zenshū*, 2: 5–96.

———, Letter to Tayama Katai. January 23, 1904. *Tōson zenshū* 藤村全集 [Complete Works of Tōson]. Vol. 17. Tokyo: Chikuma Shobō, 1966–1971, pp. 77–78.

Sibley, William F. "Naturalism in Japanese Literature." *Harvard Journal of Asiatic Studies* 28 (1968): 157–169.

————. "The Shiga Hero." Ph.D. dissertation, University of Chicago, 1971.

Starobinski, Jean. *Jean-Jacques Rousseau. La Transparence et l'obstacle*. Paris: Plon, 1957.

————. *L'Oeil vivant*. Paris: Gallimard, 1961.

Strong, Kenneth L. C. "Downgrading the 'Kindai Jiga': Reflections on Tōson's *Hakai* and Subsequent Trends in Modern Literature." In *Nihon bunka kenkyū kokusai kaigi—gijiroku* 日本文化研究国際会議—議事録 [Proceedings of the International Conference on Japanese Studies]. Vol. 1. Tokyo: Nihon P.E.N. Kurabu, 1973, pp. 406–411.

Suzuki, Daisetz T. *Zen and Japanese Culture*. New York: Pantheon Books, for the Bollingen Foundation, 1959.

Swales, Martin. *The German Bildungsroman from Wieland to Hesse*. Princeton Essays in Literature. Princeton: Princeton University Press, 1978.

Taine, Hippolyte. *Philosophie de l'art*. Textes réunis et présentés par Jean-François Revel. Paris: Hermann, 1961.

Takahama Kyoshi 高濱虚子 "Shaseibun no yurai to sono igi" 写生文の由来とその意義 [*Shaseibun*: Its Origins and Significance]. In *Gendai bungakuron taikei*. *Vol. 2, Shizenshugi to han-shizenshugi* 現代文学論体系・第二・自然主義と反自然主義 [Outline of Contemporary Comments on Literature. Vol. 2, Naturalism and Anti-naturalism]. Tokyo: Kawade Shobō, 1955, pp. 324–327.

Tayama Katai 田山花袋. *Futon* 蒲団 [The Quilt]. In *Tayama Katai shū* [Collected Works]. *Gendai nihonbungaku zenshū*. Vol 9. Tokyo: Chikuma Shobō, 1955, pp. 31–58.

————. *Tōkyō no sanjūnen* 東京の三十年 [Thirty Years in Tokyo]. In *Gendai nihonbungaku zenshū*, Vol. 97, *Bungakuteki kaisōshū* 文学的回想集 [Collection of Literary Reminiscences]. Tokyo: Chikuma Shobō, 1959, pp. 278–383.

Temmer, Mark J. *Art and Influence of Jean-Jacques Rousseau: The Pastoral, Goethe, Gottfried Keller, and Other Essays*. Studies in Comparative Literature, no. 56. Chapel Hill: University of North Carolina Press, 1973.

Tokutomi Roka 徳富蘆花 [Kenjirō] 健次郎. "Indoyō" 印度羊

[The Indian Ocean]. In *Tokutomi Roka shū* [Collected Works]. *Gendai nihonbungaku zenshū*. Vol. 12. Tokyo: Kaijōsha, 1928, p. 552.

Tokutomi Sohō 徳富蘇峰 [Iichirō] 猪一郎. *Taishō seinen to teikoku no zento* 大正青年と帝国の前途 [Taishō Youth and the Future of the Empire]. Tokyo: Minyūsha, 1916.

Tolstoy, Leo. *Resurrection.* Translated by Vera Traill. New York: New American Library, Signet Classics, 1961.

Trilling, Lionel. *Sincerity and Authenticity.* Cambridge: Harvard University Press, 1972.

Tsubouchi Shōyō 坪内逍遥. "Futabatei no koto" 二葉亭の事 [On Futabatei]. In *Kaki no heta* 柿の蔕 [The Calyx of the Persimmon]. *Gendai nihonbungaku zenshū*, Vol. 97, *Bungakuteki kaisōshū* (Collection of Literary Reminiscences). Tokyo: Chikuma Shobō, 1959, pp. 7–48.

―――. *Shōsetsu shinzui* 小説神髄 [The Essence of the Novel]. *Nihon gendaibungaku zenshū*. Vol. 4. Tokyo: Kōdansha, 1962, pp. 150–205.

Tsuda Sōkichi 津田左右吉. *Bungaku ni arawaretaru kokumin shisō no kenkyū*. Vol. 4, pt. 2, *Heimin bungaku no teisai jidai* 文学に現はれたる国民思想の研究・Ⅳ・2：平民文学の停滞時代 [An Inquiry into the Japanese Mind as Mirrored in Literature. Vol. 4, pt. 2, The Stagnation Period of Popular Literature]. *Tsuda Sōkichi zenshū* [Complete Works]. Vol. 7. Tokyo: Iwanami Shoten, 1964.

―――. *An Inquiry into the Japanese Mind as Mirrored in Literature: The Flowering Period of Common People* [sic] *Literature.* Translated by Fukumatsu Matsuda. Tokyo: Japan Society for the Promotion of Science, 1970.

Tsuruta, Kinya. "Akutagawa Ryūnosuke and I-Novelists." *Monumenta Nipponica* 25 (1970): 13–27.

Ueda, Makoto. *Literary and Art Theories in Japan.* Cleveland: Western Reserve University Press, 1967.

―――. *Modern Japanese Writers and the Nature of Literature.* Stanford: Stanford University Press, 1976.

Valency, Maurice. *In Praise of Love: An Introduction to the Love-Poetry of the Renaissance.* New York: Macmillan, 1961.

Wada Kingo 和田謹吾. *Shizenshugi bungaku* 自然主義文学 [Japanese Naturalist Literature]. Tokyo: Shibundō, 1966.

Walker, Janet A. "The East-West Context of Shimazaki Tōson's

Shinsei (The New Life): A study in the Modern Confessional Novel." Ph.D. dissertation, Harvard University, 1974.

Watt, Ian. *The Rise of the Novel: Studies in Defoe, Richardson and Fielding.* Berkeley and Los Angeles: University of California Press, 1957.

Wurmser, André. "Je, romancier." *Journal de Psychologie Normale et Pathologique* 44 (1951): 335–343.

Yamamori, Tetsunao. *Church Growth in Japan: A Study in the Development of Eight Denominations 1859–1939.* South Pasadena: William Carey Library, 1974.

Yasuoka Shōtarō 安岡章太郎. *Shiga Naoya shiron* 志賀直哉私論 [A Personal Essay on Shiga Naoya]. Tokyo: Bungei Shunshu, 1968.

Yosano Akiko 與謝野晶子. *Midare-gami* みだれ髪 (Tangled Hair]. In *Yosano Akiko zenshū* [Complete Works]. Vol. 1. Tokyo: Bunsendō, 1976, pp. 3–70.

———. *Tangled Hair: Selected Tanka from "Midaregami" by Akiko Yosano.* Translated by Sanford Goldstein and Seishi Shinoda. Lafayette: Purdue University Studies, 1971.

Yoshida Seiichi 吉田精一. *Gendai bungaku to koten* 現代文学と古典 [Contemporary Japanese Literature and the Classics]. Tokyo: Shibundō, 1962.

———. *Shizenshugi no kenkyū* 自然主義の研究 [Studies in Japanese Naturalism]. 2 vols. Tokyo: Tōkyōdō, 1955.

———. *Zuihitsu nyūmon* 随筆入門 [Introduction to the *Zuihitsu*]. Tokyo: Kawade Shobō, 1961.

Zola, Emile. *Le Roman expérimental. Oeuvres Complètes.* Vol. 41. Paris: Bernouard, 1928.

Index

Abelard, Peter, 239; *Historia Calamitatum*, 239
Abelard and Heloise: and Tōson's *Shinsei* (The New Life), 223, 232, 239-40, 241n, 242, 254, 271
"aesthetic-emotional values" (Bellah): in Tokugawa period, 8-9; in *Ukigumo* (The Floating Clouds), 57-60. *See also* aristocratic values, individual, image of
Aikoku Kōtō (Public Party of Patriots), 20
Akutagawa Ryūnosuke: on Tōson's sincerity, 267n
Ara Masahito, 102n
Arima Tatsuo, 263n
aristocratic values, 4-5; in *Ukigumo* (The Floating Clouds), 58-60. *See also* "aesthetic-emotional values," individual, image of
Ariwara no Narihira, *see* Narihira
As You Like It, 143
Asahi Shimbun (Asahi Newspaper), 201, 202
aware (pathos), 217; in Tōson, 275n

Baba Kochō, 135, 188n
Balzac, Honoré de, 61, 95, 162
Bashō, *see* Matsuo Bashō
Baudelaire, Charles, 216-17
Bellah, Robert N., 8n, 49n, 74n
Benkei and Yoshitsune, 6
Benl, Oscar, 107n
Bentham, Jeremy, 21
Best, Ernest E., 65n

Bildungsroman, 3; Tōson's novels compared to, 280-82
Blacker, Carmen, 17n, 20n, 36n, 37n
Blake, William, 258
Brower, Robert H., 88n, 91n, 251n
Bruford, W. H., 281n
Buckle, Henry Thomas, 17, 62
Buddhism, 172; Pure Land sect, 5; Nichiren sect, 5; *ukiyo* (floating world) of, in Saikaku, 10; and Kitamura Tōkoku, 71, 73-74, 78n, 84; view of love, 86, 255; and Tōson, 86, 89, 131; concept of self, 96, 98; and Naturalist concept of self, 97-98; and individualist morality, 117; view of man, 166-67, 172; and confession, 149n. *See also* Zen Buddhism
bundan (literary world), 107; as refuge of Meiji writer, 60. *See also* Meiji writer
Bungakkai (Literary World, magazine), 75, 76, 80, 136, 139, 144, 188, 195, 279n
Bunzō (character), 62, 76; as samurai, 41; and *amae* (indulgence), 44n; as introvert, 41, 42-46, 56; as carrier of dream of lost social harmony, 46-48; compared to Goncharov's Oblomov, 47-48, 55-56; as superfluous man, 55. *See also* Futabatei Shimei, Noboru, *Ukigumo* (The Floating Clouds)
Burns, Robert, 133
Byron, (George Gordon), Lord, 81n;

Byron (cont.)
The Prisoner of Chillon, 68; Manfred,
68, 146; and Kitamura Tōkoku,
68, 76, 77; and Tōson, 133, 134,
142, 145; Childe Harold (character), 152

Carlyle, Thomas, 94; On Heroes, Hero
Worship, and the Heroic in History, 3
Chateaubriand, François, Vicomte de:
René, 104; René (character), 152
Chekhov, Anton, 259
Chikamatsu Monzaemon, 12; Shinjū-
ten no Amijima (The Love Suicides at
Amijima), 11, 15, 82; character
depiction in, 40; view of love, 82,
255-56. See also freedom, love
Christ, 75; role of, in Kitamura Tōkoku's thought, 70, 73; Tōson's
idea of, 130-31
Christian higher schools, 113, 114,
127-28. See also Meiji Gakuin
Christian Socialism, 171, 172, 175
Christianity, 124, 283; and ideal of
individualism, 63, 284; political
role of, 63-65; and higher education, 63, 64, 65; importance of, to
Japanese, 63-64, 128; and People's
Rights movement, 64; and ideal of
freedom, 64, 72-73; and Kitamura
Tōkoku, 66, 68, 70-71, 72-75,
78n, 246; and Tōson, 85, 128-33,
134, 135, 137, 140-42, 147, 155,
187, 189, 284; concept of self, 97;
view of sin, 257; view of love, 240;
view of rebirth or new life, 184-86,
269
Chu Hsi, 36n
confession, ideal of: in Rousseau, 99,
147, 148, 274, 275n; in Tayama
Katai's Futon (The Quilt), 119,

277; and Tōson, 147-49, 150,
153-54, 155, 194, 253, 262-63,
264-78, 280; in Tōson's Hakai
(Breaking the Commandment),
174, 176, 180, 183, 184, 187,
253, 262, 263-64, 268-69, 276; in
Tōson's Shinsei (The New Life),
233-36, 238-39, 253, 263, 265,
266n, 267n, 268, 269-70, 276n-
77n, 278-79; in Dostoevsky's Crime
and Punishment, 264; in Musset's La
Confession d'un enfant du siècle, 268-
69; in Futabatei Shimei's Heibon
(Mediocrity), 277; in Natsume
Sōseki's Kokoro (Human Feeling),
277-78
Confucian moral system: and chōnin
(townsman) class, 10-11; influence
of, in Tokugawa period, 12; and
idea of role (mei), 39; role of fiction
under, 39; influence of, on fiction
of Meiji period, 56-57; and Kitamura Tōkoku, 71, 73; view of love
12-13, 81-82, 85, 199, 246; and
Tōson, 85, 153; concept of self,
97, 98, 100; and Naturalism, 98;
and individualist morality, 117;
view of sin, 140
Constant, Benjamin: Adolphe, 104
Craig, Albert M., 20n, 22n, 24n,
98n

Dante, 131n; and Tōson, 133, 145,
271; La Vita Nuova and Tōson's
Shinsei (The New Life), 241-42,
253-54
Darwin, Charles, 23, 162; doctrine of
survival of the fittest, 23, 67
decadence, 216n, 217n
Defoe, Daniel: Robinson Crusoe, 50
De Vos, George, 172n

Diderot, Denis, 95
Dilworth, David A., 18n
Doi Takeo, 44n
Dostoevsky, Fyodor, 56, 145, 176;
and Futabatei Shimei, 38, 41;
Crime and Punishment and
Futabatei's *Ukigumo* (The Floating
Clouds), 38; *Crime and Punishment*
and Tōson, 183-86, 193, 215,
241, 254, 259, 264. *See also* confes-
sion, individualism, rebirth, self-
definition, sin
Dream of the Red Chamber (Hung Lou
Meng), 139
Dumoulin, Heinrich, 149n

Ellis, Havelock: *Male and Female*, 248
Emerson, Ralph Waldo: and Kitamura Tōkoku, 66, 69, 79, 253
eta (outcast), 172ff
European fiction: and validation of individual, 116
European Romantic poetry, 105, 246;
and Kitamura Tōkoku, 68, 77;
love in, 85; and Tōson, 131, 133,
142-43, 149, 154. *See also* Burns,
Byron, Goethe, Heine, Shelley,
Wordsworth
European Romanticism, 270, 274;
and Tōson, 198
Evrard, Louis, 267n

Fairbank, John K., 20n, 22n, 24n,
98n
Faust (character), 146, 147n
Feldman, Horace Z., 51n
Ferrante, Joan, 241n
Fielding, Henry, 12
Flaubert, Gustave, 37, 95, 96, 101,
162
Freedman, Ralph, 103n, 104n, 241

freedom, ideal of: and Saikaku, 9-10,
117; and Tokugawa *chōnin*
(townsman), 11; and Chikamatsu,
15, 82; as political ideal in 1880s,
50-52, 53; and Christianity, 64,
72-73; and Kitamura Tōkoku,
71-73; and Tōson, 84-86, 261-64,
277; and Yosano Akiko, 88-91; in
late Meiji period, 99; and Rousseau, 99, 152; and Naturalism,
101; in traditional Japan, 106n; in
Tayama Katai's *Futon* (The Quilt),
112-14; in Tōson's *Shinsei* (The
New Life), 249; in Tōson's *Hakai*
(Breaking the Commandment),
262
Fukuzawa Yukichi, 35, 69, 93, 123,
283; *Gakumon no susume* (An Encouragement of Learning), 17-19,
26, 71; ideal of independence in
1870s, 17-21, 26, 62, 78; *Tsūzoku
minken-ron* (A Simple Account of
People's Rights), 21; view of independence in 1880s, 22-24; concept
of rights, 38, 50, 53; and Christianity, 64
Furukawa Tesshi, 22n
Futabatei Shimei, 21, 29, 67, 97,
145, 147; education, 30-31; and
Dostoevsky, 38, 41; on *Crime and
Punishment*, 38n; and Turgenev,
41, 56, 145, 168; as introvert,
41-42; as critic of Meiji society,
54-55; as defender of individualist
morality, 58-61; later career, 59n.
See also Bunzō, *Heibon* (Mediocrity),
Noboru, *Ukigumo* (The Floating
Clouds)
Futon [The Quilt] (Tayama Katai),
123, 193, 196, 200; as Naturalist
novel, 108; and individualist mo-

Futon (*cont.*)
rality, 108-15, 119-20; as I-novel, 110; and Hauptmann's *Einsame Menschen*, 111-12; and Turgenev's *Diary of a Superfluous Man*, 111-12; psychological analysis in, 118; as confession of author, 119-20; sin in, 112, 259; confession in, 119, 277; love in, 254; self-definition in, 259-60. *See also* Tayama Katai

Gaigo Gakkō (Foreign Language School), 31
Genji monogatari (The Tale of Genji), 5, 58, 139, 167. *See also* Murasaki Shikibu, nature, self
Goethe, Johann Wolfgang von, 80n, 87, 131, 133, 145, 149, 151; *Die Leiden des jungen Werther*, 12, 267; *Dichtung und Wahrheit*, 267n, 280
Goldin, Frederick, 137n
Goldstein, Sanford, 88n, 91n
Goncharov, Ivan, 56, 145; *Oblomov* and Futabatei Shimei's *Ukigumo* (The Floating Clouds), 41, 47-48, 55-56
Goncourt, Edmond and Jules de, 95, 96, 162
Goodheart, Eugene, 148n
Guizot, François, 17

Hagakure (Hidden under the Leaves), 7-8
Haijin Buson [The *Haiku* Poet Buson] (Masaoka Shiki), 161
haikai, see haiku
haiku, 75, 76, 158, 160, 161, 167, 169
Hakai [Breaking the Commandment] (Shimazaki Tōson), 124, 148, 155, 156, 194, 195, 196, 197, 204,

206, 209, 215n, 217n, 219, 221, 235, 253, 275n, 277, 279; and Tolstoy, 171; as realistic social novel, 172, 174-75; self-definition in, 175-80, 184, 249, 251, 262; concept of self in, 175-83; and Dostoevsky's *Crime and Punishment*, 176, 183-86, 193; and Kitamura Tōkoku, 176, 177-80, 183, 186-87, 247-48; and Rousseau's *Confessions*, 176, 183, 186; autobiographical elements in, 187-93. *See also* confession, freedom, inner life, love, nature, rebirth, sin
Halpern, Manfred, 27n
hammon-seinen (anguished youth), 94
Hata Fuyuko, *see* Shimazaki Fuyuko
Hauptmann, Gerhart, 101; *Einsame Menschen*, 111
Hayashi Isamu, 157n
Hazlitt, William: *Liber Amoris*, 206n
Heibon [Mediocrity] (Futabatei Shimei), 107; confession in, 277
Heine, Heinrich, 80n, 149, 151
Heiwa (Peace, magazine), 69, 72
Hesse, Hermann: *Demian*, 131
Hibbett, Howard S., 1on, 102n
Hirano Ken, 175n, 203n, 253n
Hirano, Umeyo, 18n
Hirose Yoshiko, 138, 139
Hirschmeier, Johannes, 28n
Howes, John F., 63n
Hugo, Victor, 67
Huysmans, Joris Karl, 216, 217
Hytier, Jean, 104n

Ibsen, Henrik, 101, 162
Ihara Saikaku, 72; *Kōshoku ichidai onna* (The Life of a Woman Who Loved Love), 9-10, 117; view of man, 167, 168; *Kōshoku gonin onna*

(Five Women Who Loved Love), 255n-56n. *See also* freedom, love, nature, self, sin

impressionism, 162-63, 166n

impressionist novel, 163

independence, ideal of, 17-21, 51, 60, 62; internalization of, in 1890s, 25-28; in Tōson's *Nōfu* (The Farmer), 152. *See also* individual, individualism, individualist morality, inner life, self, self-definition

individual, image of: modern, middle-class, 3, 4, 16, 92, 238-39; aristocratic, 4; samurai, 4, 5, 6; *chōnin* (townsman), 4, 8-11. *See also* "aesthetic-emotional values," aristocratic values, Saikaku, samurai values

individualism, ideal of, 116n, 124, 194; definition, 3; Western, post-Renaissance, 6; and concept of rights, 19-20; in *Crime and Punishment*, 38n; in 1890s, 62, 63, 94; materialistic, 79-81; and Naturalism, 98; in *roman personnel*, 104-05; and I-novel, 107; and rise of European bourgeoisie, 116; and Tōson, 148; Nagai Kafū on, 244; and Natsume Sōseki, 260-61. *See also* independence, individual, individualist morality, inner life, self, self-definition

individualist morality, 26, 80, 281; obstacles to, in Meiji period, 26-29; in Futabatei Shimei's *Ukigumo* (The Floating Clouds), 60, 61; beginnings of, in Meiji period, 61; and Naturalism, 94, 107; in Tayama Katai's *Futon* (The Quilt), 108-15, 119-20; in late Meiji period, 117; and Buddhism,

117; and Confucian moral system, 117; and Tōson, 133, 144, 148, 204; and Rousseau, 146-48, 152. *See also* independence, individualism, inner self, self, self-definition

inner life, ideal of (Kitamura Tō-koku), 65, 69, 70-72, 73-75, 76n, 77n, 78; in Tōson's *Hakai* (Breaking the Commandment), 176, 177-80, 183, 186-87, 192. *See also* independence, individualism, individualist morality, self, self-definition

I-novel (*shishōsetsu*), 16, 58, 76, 92, 94, 107, 110, 123, 196, 197, 279, 280, 283; characteristics of, 102-03; concept of self, 102, 103; compared to *roman personnel*, 104-05, 116-17; and validation of individual, 115-16; and revelation of individual, 115-18. *See also* Japanese Naturalism, Japanese Naturalist fiction

Ise monogatari (Tales of Ise), 85

Ishibashi Ningetsu: on Futabatei Shimei's *Ukigumo* (The Floating Clouds), 49

Ishizaka Mina, *see* Kitamura Mina

Itagaki Taisuke, 20-21

Itō Hirobumi, 22

Itō Kazuo, 129n, 135n, 136n, 170n, 171n, 184n, 187n, 202n, 217n, 240n-41n, 264n

Itō Sei, 269n

Iwamoto Yoshiharu, 134, 199

Iwamoto, Yoshio, 52n, 57n

Izumi Shikibu, 87, 88

Japanese fiction: faults of traditional, 32, 40; Futabatei Shimei's innova-

Japanese Fiction (*cont.*)
tions in, 34, 49; role of, under
Confucian moral system, 39; and
decline of Confucian moral system,
39; role of political novels (*seiji-
shōsetsu*) in development of, 52;
function of, according to Murasaki
Shikibu, 58n; lack of fully
socialized characters in, 61; role of,
according to Tsubouchi Shōyō, 96;
Naturalism and development of,
97, 107; development of, compared to that of European, 116-17.
See also Genji monogatari, Ihara
Saikaku, *kana-zōshi*, Motoori
Norinaga, *ninjō-bon, Shōsetsu shinzui*, Takizawa Bakin, Tamenaga
Shunsui
Japanese Naturalism, 37, 92, 105,
123, 124, 162, 194, 196, 197,
198n, 216n, 217, 229, 271, 279n,
282, 283; and individualist morality, 94, 97, 98, 107; and modernization, 96-99; as ideology,
95-101, 107, 117-18; as literary
movement, 101-02; concept of nature, 99-100, 145-46; concept of
self, 100-01, 107; concept of freedom, 101; and psychological
analysis, 117-18; and Tōson, 123n,
165-66. *See also* Japanese Naturalist
fiction, Zola
Japanese Naturalist fiction: theme of
sensual awakening, 99, 101, 102,
107-08; Zolaesque novel, 101-02,
123n; and psychological analysis,
101; and freedom, 101; I-novel,
102-03; and Tsubouchi Shōyō, 115;
and Kitamura Tōkoku, 115. *See
also* Shimazaki Tōson, Tayama
Katai, Zola

Japanese Romanticism, 101, 124;
ideals of, 80-81. *See also* European
Romantic poetry, European
Romanticism
Jogaku Zasshi (Magazine for the Edu-
cation of Women), 134, 135, 139
Jost, François, 281n
Jung, Carl Gustav, 41n

Kafū, *see* Nagai Kafū
kana-zōshi (writings in the *kana* syllabary), 9
Katai, *see* Tayama Katai
Kataoka Ryōichi, 123n, 175n
Keene, Donald, 39n
keimō (enlightenment) movement, 17;
and logical thinking, 35
Keller, Gottfried, 278; *Der grüne
Heinrich*, 281
Kimura Yūji, 128, 129, 130, 149,
157
kindaiteki jiga (modern selfhood),
175-76; and Tōson, 192, 275. *See
also* independence, individual, individualism, individualist morality, inner life, self, self-definition
Kitagawa, Joseph M., 19n
Kitamura Mina (wife of Kitamura
Tōkoku), 67n, 68, 83, 246
Kitamura Tōkoku, 21, 93, 97, 98,
115, 123, 137, 138, 144, 145,
146, 148, 152, 188, 197, 219,
221, 230-31, 241n, 283; and
Christianity, 66, 68, 70-71,
72-75, 78, 80; education, 66-67;
and Quakers, 68-69, 71; and Byron, 68, 76, 77; anti-materialism,
70-71, 75-78; ideal of freedom of
spirit, 70-73; ideal of inner life,
70-72, 73-74, 94, 96, 106; ideal of
love, 71, 81-84, 89, 91; ideal of

self-definition, 75; and Buddhism,
71, 73-74, 78, 84; and Confucian
moral system, 71-72, 73, 74; ideal
of poet, 75-78; and Romanticism,
80-81, 84, 89, 91; and Tōson, 84,
89, 135-36, 139, 171, (inner life)
176-80, 183, 186, 192, (love)
245, 246-49, 251-54, (self-
definition) 256, 257-58, 258-59,
279, (freedom of spirit) 261-63,
(confession) 264; and Yosano
Akiko, 91; and concept of spontaneous self, 100; as Inoko Rentarō
in Tōson's *Hakai* (Breaking the
Commandment), 186-87
   WORKS:
   Emaruson (Emerson), 79
   Ensei shika to josei (The World-
   Weary Poet and Woman), 82, 83,
   84, 135
   Hōrai-kyoku (A Tale of Mount
   Horai), 68, 139
   Jinsei ni aiwataru towa nan no ii zo
   (What Does It Mean "To Benefit
   Mankind?"), 76, 77n
   Jōnetsu (Romantic Ardor), 77,
   78n
   Kakujin shinkyūnai no hikyū (The
   Heart, A Holy of Holies), 70,
   72-73, 75
   "Ka'nenbutsu" o yomite (On
   Reading *Ka'nenbutsu*), 83
   Naibu seimei ron (On the Inner
   Life), 71-72, 77, 78n
   Netsui (Romantic Ardor), 77
   Ninomiya Sontoku Ō (Ninomiya
   Sontoku), 74-75
   Saigo no shōrisha wa dare zo (Who
   Will Be the Final Victor?), 70
   Seishin no jiyū (Freedom of
   Spirit), 71, 72

Shinki myōhen o ronzu (On Mysti-
cal Metamorphoses), 73, 76
Soshū no shi (The Poem of the
Prisoner), 68
Takai ni kansuru kannen (The
Concept of Another World), 77
Kobayashi Hideo, 102n
kokoro no yami (darkness of the heart),
250-51
Kokugaku (National Learning), 187n
Kokumin Shimbun (The Nation's
Newspaper), 94n
Kokumin no Tomo (The Nation's
Friend, magazine), 189
kokutai (national polity), 61n, 93,
98n
Komachi, 87, 88n, 91
Konrad, Nikolai I., 12n
Kōsaka Masaaki, 5n, 94n, 96n
Kumazawa Banzam, 265n
Kume Masao, 102n
Kusunoki Masashige, 265n

LaFleur, William R., 143n
Lamartine, Alphonse de: *Méditations*,
87
Lane, Richard, 9n
Lebra, Takie Sugiyama, 269n
Lejeune, Philippe, 270n, 272n
Le Sage, Alan René: *Gil Blas*, 12
love, ideal of: and *chōnin* (townsman),
11; under Confucian moral system,
12-13, 81-82, 85, 199, 246; in
eighteenth-century European
novel, 12; and Kitamura Tōkoku,
71, 81-82, 83-84, 89, 91; and
Chikamatsu, 82, 255-56; in West,
82-83, 84, 254; in Heian poetry,
85, 87-88; in European Romantic
poetry, 85; in Tōson, 85-86, 91,
129, 136-39, 150-52, 155, 199,

love, ideal of (*cont.*)
   247-56; under Buddhism, 86, 255;
   and Yosano Akiko, 87-89, 90-91;
   and Rousseau, 151; in Futabatei
   Shimei's *Ukigumo* (The Floating
   Clouds), 254; in Tayama Katai's
   Futon (The Quilt), 254; and Nat-
   sume Sōseki, 254-55; in Saikaku's
   Kōshoku gonin onna (Five Women
   Who Loved Love), 255n-56n
Lyrical Ballads, The (Wordsworth and
   Coleridge), 87
lyrical novel (Freedman), 241; com-
   pared to I-novel, 103-04

Madame Bovary (Flaubert), 165n
Mallarmé, Stéphane, 216n
Mann, Thomas: *Buddenbrooks*, 198n
Marivaux, Pierre de, 12
Martini, Fritz, 281n
Maruyama Banka, 160
Maruyama Masao, 26n, 54n, 61n
Masaoka Shiki, 161, 162, 169, 170.
   See also nature, self
Mathewson, Rufus W., Jr., 57n
Mathy, Francis, 67n, 70n, 76n
Matsumoto, Shigeru, 13n
Matsuo Bashō, 75, 77n, 145, 152;
   and Tokugawa individualism, 7;
   and Tōson, 131n, 138, 142, 143,
   158-60, 165, 170, 171, 186, 258;
   Sarashina kikō (A Visit to
   Sarashina), 159; *Oku no hosomichi*
   (Narrow Road to the Interior),
   159n-60n, 161; *haiku* of, 161-62,
   167. *See also* nature, self
Maupassant, Guy de, 96, 101, 162,
   163, 166n
McClellan, Edwin, 193n, 207n-08n
Meiji Gakuin (Meiji College), 127,

   128, 129n, 130, 132, 133, 134,
   135, 136, 137, 138, 139, 140,
   142, 143, 147, 188, 195, 199,
   202, 211, 241n, 247, 256
Meiji Jogakkō (Meiji Girl's School),
   128, 129, 134, 138, 144, 199,
   200, 211
Meiji writer: as similar to the Tokugawa *chōnin* (townsman), 27-28;
   position of, 58-60, 78
Merezhkowski, Dmitri: *Tolstoi as Man
   and Artist*, 171
Merlant, Joachim, 104n, 105n
Midare-gami [Tangled Hair] (Yosano
   Akiko), 87, 88n, 89n
Mill, John Stuart, 62, 65; *On Liberty*,
   17
Milton, John, 133
Miner, Earl, 88n, 91n, 251n
Miyake Katsumi, 160
modernization, 27n; and Natu-
   ralism, 96-99
Monet, Claude, 162
mono no aware (the pathos of things),
   5. *See also* aware
Morley, John, viscount: *English Men of
   Letters*, 132
Morris, Colin, 241n
Morris, Ivan, 265n
Morse, Edward S., 23n
Motoori Norinaga: defense of feeling,
   13; and Tsubouchi Shōyō's theory
   of the novel, 31; *Genji monogatari
   tama no ogushi* (The Small Jeweled
   Comb: *The Tale of Genji*), 13
Murasaki Shikibu (Lady): definition of
   fiction, 58
Musset, Alfred de, 270, 278; *La Con-
   fession d'un enfant du siècle*, 104,
   267, 268
Myōjō (Bright Star, magazine), 87

Naff, William E., 125n
Nagai, Kafū: on *roman personnel* and Meiji subjective novel, 105-06; on failure of individualism in Meiji period, 105-06, 244
Nakazawa Rinsen, 201
Nakamura Hajime, 6n, 35n
Nakamura Mitsuo, 50n, 51n, 81n, 172n, 176n
Narihira, 251
Natsume Sōseki, 203, 208n; *Michikusa* (Grass By the Wayside), 107, 260; and love, 254-55; *Meian* (Light and Darkness), 255, 260; and individualism, 260-61; *Kokoro* (Human Feeling), 277-78; and confession, 277-78
Naturalism, *see* Japanese Naturalism
nature, concept of: in Rousseau, 96, 99-100, 152, 258; in Naturalism, 99-100, 145-46; in Shinto, 140-41, 142, 143n, 149n; in Tōson 140-43, 145-46, 149n, 152, 154-55, 257-58, 282; in Masaoka Shiki, 161; in Bashō, 161-62, 170, 258; in Tōson's *shaseibun* (sketches from life), 164-65; in *Genji monogatari* (The Tale of Genji), 167; in Saikaku, 167; in Futabatei Shimei's *Ukigumo* (The Floating Clouds), 167-69; in Tōson's *Hakai* (Breaking the Commandment), 180-83, 258; in Tōson's *Shinsei* (The New Life), 217-18, 221; in Wordsworth, 257, 258; in Tolstoy, 258; in Shiga Naoya, 283
Neo-Confucianism: and investigation of things, 35-37, 160
Nietzsche, Friedrich, 94

ninjō (human feeling), 11, 82; defense of, by Motoori Norinaga, 13
ninjō-bon (love books), 14, 82; validation of love, 16
Ninomiya Sontoku, 74-75
Noboru (character): as *seikō-seinen* (success-seeking youth), 54, 70, 114; and materialistic individualism, 79. *See also* Bunzō, Futabatei Shimei, *Ukigumo* (The Floating Clouds)

Oda Masanobu, 123n
Odagiri Hideo, 50n, 135n
Ōe Kenzaburō: *Kojinteki na taiken* (A Personal Matter), 116n
Ōhashi Totsuan, 36
Okamura Kazuo, 176n
Oketani Shūshō, 176n
Ōkuma Shigenobu, 50
Omokage (Likenesses), 80n
Ōnishi Hajime, 131
Ono no Komachi, *see* Komachi
Ozaki Kōyō: *Konjiki yasha* (The Gold Demon), 113

Paul, Saint, 138, 142, 155
People's Rights movement, 21-22, 28, 51, 60, 62, 63, 67-68, 72, 98, 124, 128; decline of, in 1890s, 25-26; and Christianity, 64
Plato: *Symposium*, 253
political novel (*seiji-shōsetsu*), 21, 50-53; role of, in development of modern novel, 52. *See also* I-novel, Japanese fiction, Japanese Naturalist fiction
Poulenard, Elie, 279n
Princesse de Clèves, La, 116
Protestantism: and ideal of freedom,

Protestantism (*cont.*)
72-73. *See also* Christianity,
Kitamura Tōkoku
psychological analysis: as goal of Meiji
novel, 32; in Futabatei Shimei's
Ukigumo (The Floating Clouds),
34-38, 42-48; and logical thinking, 35-37; and Chikamatsu,
40-41; and Naturalism, 117; in
Tayama Katai's *Futon* (The Quilt),
118; in Tōson's *Shinsei* (The New
Life), 269-75
Pyle, Kenneth B., 189n

Radice, Betty, 240n
rebirth, ideal of: in Tōson, 140-42,
148-49, 149-50, 154-55, 194,
256-59; in Tōson's *Hakai* (Breaking the Commandment), 179, 183,
184-86, 187, 259, 269; in Christianity, 184-86, 269; in Dostoevsky's *Crime and Punishment*, 184,
185-86, 193; in Tōson's *Shinsei*
(The New Life), 215, 225, 228,
229-30; in Tayama Katai's *Futon*
(The Quilt), 259
Reischauer, Edwin O., 20n, 22n,
24n, 98n
Rekho, K., 55n
ren'ai (love) (Kitamura Tōkoku), 81,
83-84, 137, 138, 139
Richardson, Samuel: *Pamela*, 12
risshin-shusse (success and achievement
in life), ideal of: 18-19, 54
roman personnel (Merlant), 278, 280;
compared to I-novel, 104-06; validation of individual, 116
Romans, Book of, 138, 185-86
Romantic poetry, *see* European
Romantic poetry
Romanticism, *see* European Romanti-

cism, Japanese Romanticism
Romberg, Bertil, 271n
Rougemont, Denis de, 82n
Rousseau, Jean-Jacques, 62, 95, 171,
220, 239, 266, 279n; *Julie, ou la
nouvelle Héloïse*, 12; *Confessions* and
Tōson, 96, 97, 99-100, 105,
144-48, 149n, 150, 151, 152,
153, 156, 165, 176, 183, 186,
258, 264, 274-75, 278. *See also*
confession, freedom, individual
morality, love, nature, self, self-
definition, sin
Rudel, Jaufré, 137n
Ruskin, John, 160
Ryan, Marleigh Grayer, 30n, 31n,
32n, 34n, 41n, 42n, 43n, 44n,
45n, 46n, 47n, 55n, 59n, 168n

Saigō Takamori, 30, 56, 265n
Saigyō, 76, 131n, 138, 142n, 143,
152
Saikaku, *see* Ihara Saikaku
Sainte-Beuve, Charles: *Volupté*, 104
samurai values, 22; in Tokugawa period, 7-9; in Meiji period, 49-50;
decline of, in 1880s, 54-55, 63-64;
and Tōson, 89, 266, 278; and Tōson's family, 125, 126; sincerity of
action, 265-66; and Natsume
Sōseki, 278. *See also* individual
(samurai)
Sansom, G. B., 25n, 52n
Sasabuchi Tomoichi, 81n, 131n,
133n, 135n, 141n, 142n
Satō Sukeko, 135, 136-37, 138, 139,
144, 150, 211, 222
Satō Yasumasa, 253n
Schiller, Johann Christoph Friedrich
von, 11n, 80n; *Wilhelm Tell*, 51;
ideal of *schöne Seele*, 116

Schubert, Franz: *Die Winterreise*, 152
Schwantes, Robert S., 23n, 64n
Sei Shōnagon, 162, 163, 165; *Makura no sōshi* (The Pillow Book), 163, 169
seikō-seinen (success-seeking youth), 54, 94; Tanaka of Tayama Katai's *Futon* (The Quilt) as, 114-15; attitude of Tōson and Natsume Sōseki toward, 261. *See also* Noboru
self, concept of: under Confucian moral system, 97, 98, 100; in Naturalism, 100-01, 107; in I-novel, 102, 103; in Shinto, 140-41, 142, 149n; in Tōson, 140-42, 145-47, 154-55, 158-60, 165-66, 171, 175-84, 187-93; in Rousseau, 145-46, 258; in Bashō, 161-62, 165; in *Genji monogatari* (The Tale of Genji), 167; in Saikaku, 167; in Futabatei Shimei's *Ukigumo* (The Floating Clouds), 167-69; in Masaoka Shiki, 169-70; in Tolstoy, 171; in Tōson's *Hakai* (Breaking the Commandment), 175-83
self-definition, ideal of, 123; and Kitamura Tōkoku, 75; and Tōson, 91, 197, 251-53, 254, 256-61, 267-68, 280; in early 1900s, 93-94; in Naturalist novel, 115; in Rousseau, 146, 148; in Dostoevsky's *Crime and Punishment*, 193; in Tōson's *Shinsei* (The New Life), 194, 256-64; in Tōson's *Hakai* (Breaking the Commandment), 249, 251, 262; in Futabatei Shimei's *Ukigumo* (The Floating Clouds), 259; in Tayama Katai's *Futon* (The Quilt), 259-60. *See also* individualism, individualist morality, inner self

Self-Help (Samuel Smiles), 17, 49-50
Senancour, Etienne Pivert de: *Obermann*, 104
Senuma Shigeki, 60n, 61n, 125n, 135n, 143n, 176n, 191n, 200n
Shakespeare, William, 76, 131, 133, 139, 143
shasei (sketching from life), 160-61, 162, 163-65, 169-70. *See also* impressionism
Shelley, Percy Bysshe, 81n
Shiba Shirō, 51-53, 56; *Kajin no kigū* (Strange Encounters with Elegant Ladies), 51-53
Shibusawa Eiichi, 28n, 50
Shiga Naoya, 275n, 283, 284; *An'ya kōro* (Long Journey in the Dark Night), 103, 283; on Tōson's *Hakai* (Breaking the Commandment), 191. *See also* nature
Shiki, *see* Masaoka Shiki
Shimazaki Asa (Komako's mother), 235
Shimazaki Fuyuki (Tōson's wife), 157, 198-200, 208, 247, 249
Shimazaki Hideo (Tōson's eldest brother), 125, 144, 157, 198, 203, 236
Shimazaki Hirosuke (Tōson's second-eldest brother), 200, 202, 203, 205
Shimazaki Komako (Tōson's niece), 201, 202, 203, 205, 217n, 240n-41n, 249, 250, 276; *Higeki no jiden* (My Tragic Story), 241n
Shimazaki Masaki (Tōson's father), 125, 126-27, 187
Shimazaki Tomoya (Tōson's younger brother), 126
Shimazaki Tōson, 21, 66, 84; childhood, 124-27; experiences at Meiji Gakuin, 127-34; moral conflict in

Shimazaki Tōson (*cont.*)
adolescence, 129-34, 137, 140-42;
and Christianity, 85, 128-33, 134,
135, 137, 140-42, 147, 155, 187,
189, 284; early efforts as writer,
133-34, 136, 139; friendship with
Kitamura Tōkoku, 135-36, 144;
and Satō Sukeko, 136-37, 138,
139, 144; moral conflict in early
twenties, 136-39, 142; travels
around Japan, 137-38; stay in Sendai, 136, 149; stay in Komoro,
157-58, 187-91; experiments with
shasei (sketching from life), 160,
162, 163-65, 166n; evolution of
fictional method, 195-97, 204-05;
marriage, 198-200; liaison with
niece, 201, 202; stay in France,
201-02; writing of *Shinsei* (The
New Life), 202-03; and European
Romantic poetry, 131, 133, 142-
43, 149, 154; and Sei Shōnagon,
162-63, 165; and impressionism,
162-63; and French Naturalist fiction, 165n-66n, 198n; and autobiographical novel, 278-82; and
Confucian moral system, 85, 153;
and Buddhism, 86, 89, 131; and
samurai values, 89, 266, 278; and
Shinto, 140-42, 143n; and *kindaiteki jiga* (modern selfhood), 192,
275; and Kitamura Tōkoku, 84,
89, 135-36, 139, 171, (inner life)
176, 177-80, 183, 186-87, 192,
(love) 245, 246-49, 251-54, (self-
definition) 256, 257-58, 258-59,
279, (freedom) 261-63, (confession) 264; and Rousseau, 96, 97,
99-100, 105, 144-48, 149n, 150,
151, 152, 153, 156, 165, 176,
183, 186, 258, 264, 274-75, 278;
and Bashō, 131n, 138, 142, 143,
158-60, 165, 170, 171, 186, 258;
and Tolstoy, 170-71, 183, 186,
220-21; and Dostoevsky, 183-86,
193, 215, 241, 254, 259, 264
WORKS:
"Bashō no isshō" (Life of Bashō),
159
Betsuri (Parting), 150-51, 247
Biwa hōshi (The Biwa Priest),
139, 153
Chikumagawa no suketchi
(Sketches of the Chikuma River),
163-65
Hakai (Breaking the Commandment), *see* separate entry
Haru (Spring), 135-36, 195,
196, 197, 198n, 245, 270, 279
Ie (The Family), 191, 194,
195-96, 197, 198-200, 216,
217n, 248, 279n
"Inshōshugi to sakubutsu" (Im-
pressionism and the Literary
Work), 162-63
"Kisotani nikki" (Diary of the
Kiso River Valley), 159
Nōfu (The Farmer), 151-55, 158
Okume (Okume), 84-86, 247
Osanaki hi (My Childhood Days),
125-26, 127n, 279n
Otsuta (Otsuta), 89
"Rūsō no *Zange*-chū ni
miidashitaru jiko" (The Self That I
Discovered in Rousseau's *Confes-
sions*), 145-46
Sakura no mi no juku-suru toki
(When the Cherries Ripen), 128,
130, 132, 133, 202, 279n
"Shasei" (Sketching from Life),
162
Shinsei (The New Life), *see* sepa-
rate entry
Wakana-shū (Collection of

Young Shoots), 85, 87, 89, 90, 91, 149-51, 153, 154, 157, 158, 175, 179, 190, 193, 197, 247, 268

Yoake-mae (Before the Dawn), 127, 195, 202, 203. *See also* confession, love, freedom, independence, individualism, individualist morality, inner life, nature, rebirth, self, self-definition, sin, Byron, Wordsworth

Shin Shōsetsu (New Fiction, magazine), 166n

Shinoda, Seishi, 88n, 91n

Shinsei [The New Life] (Shimazaki Tōson), 124, 148, 155, 248; narrative method, 204-05; moral conflict, 207-39; compared to Dostoevsky's *Crime and Punishment*, 215, 241; and Christianity, 216; and Huysmans, 216-17; compared to Tolstoy's *Resurrection*, 220-21; and Abelard and Heloise, 223, 232, 239-40, 241n, 242, 254, 271; and Dante's *La Vita Nuova*, 241-42, 253-54; psychological analysis in, 269-75; point of view in, 270-75; as autobiography, 272; as confession of Tōson, 275-77; as *Bildungsroman* (novel of education), 280-82; sin, 214, 228, 242; rebirth, ideal of, 215, 225, 228, 229-30; nature, 217-18, 221; love, ideal of, 223, 227-30, 237, 240, 242, 249-56; confession, ideal of, 233-36, 238-39, 253, 263, 265, 266n, 267n, 268, 269-70, 278-79; freedom, ideal of, 249. *See also* Shimazaki Tōson

Shinto, 166; concept of nature, 140-41, 142, 143n, 149n; concept of self, 140-41, 142, 149n

Shōsetsu shinzui [The Essence of the Novel] (Tsubouchi Shōyō), 31-32; character depiction, 39-40; purpose of the novel, 57. *See also* Tsubouchi Shōyō

Sibley, William F., 283n

sin: in Tayama Katai's *Futon* (The Quilt), 112, 259; (lack of) in Saikaku, 117; in Tōson, 131-33, 142, 148, 155, 190, 193, 256-59; in Confucian moral system, 140; in Rousseau, 147-48; in Tōson's *Hakai* (Breaking the Commandment), 184, 187, 193, 256; in Dostoevsky's *Crime and Punishment*, 184, 193; in Tōson's *Shinsei* (The New Life), 194, 214, 228, 242; in Christianity, 257

sincerity: samurai, 265; of middle-class individual in West, 265n; in Tōson, 266-68

Sisley, Alfred, 162

Smollett, Tobias, 12

Sōseki, *see* Natsume Sōseki

Spencer, Herbert, 17, 62, 65

Starobinski, Jean, 147n

Stendhal, pseud. (Beyle, Marie Henri), 95

stilnovisti, 253

Strindberg, August, 278, 279

Strong, Kenneth L. C., 176n, 181n, 182n, 183n

Suehiro Tetchō, 51-53, 56; *Setchūbai* (Plum Blossoms in the Snow), 51, 52, 56-57

Sugii, Mutsuro, 129n

Sumidagawa (The River Sumida—Nō play), 251

Suzuki, Daisetz T., 8n

Swales, Martin, 281n

Tachibana Itoe, 157, 199

Taine, Hippolyte, 3n, 61, 147n; *History of English Literature*, 134
Takahama Kyoshi, 169n
Takayama Chogyū, 80, 101; *Biteki seikatsu o ronzu* (On the Aesthetic Life), 94
Takizawa Bakin, 32, 76; *Hakkenden* (Biography of Eight Dogs), 39-40
Tamenaga Shunsui, 14, 15
tanka, 86; and Yosano Akiko, 87-90; of Ono no Komachi, 87, 91; of Izumi Shikibu, 88; of Ariwara no Narihira, 251n
Tayama Katai, 107ff, 244, 263n; *Tōkyō no sanjūnen* (Thirty Years in Tokyo), 188n, 196n, 216n-17n; on Tōson, 188, 196n, 203, 216n-17n. *See also Futon* (The Quilt), Japanese Naturalism, Japanese Naturalist fiction
Temmer, Mark J., 278n
Togawa Shūkotsu, 135, 188n
Tokuda Shūsei: *Kabi* (Mold), 107
Tokutomi Roka, 118; reaction to *Ukigumo* (The Floating Clouds), 37
Tokutomi Soho, 94n, 189
Tolstoy, Leo, 37n, 101; and Tōson, 170-71, 183, 186, 220-21; *Resurrection*, 171, 220, 221, 254, 258; *The Kreutzer Sonata*, 200n. *See also* nature, self
Trilling, Lionel, 265n
Tōson, *see* Shimazaki Tōson
Tsubouchi Shōyō, 31-32, 96, 115; description of Futabatei Shimei, 41-42; and Murasaki Shikibu's theory of fiction, 58. *See also Shōsetsu shinzui* (The Essence of the Novel)
Tsuda Sōkichi, 11n, 14n
Tsunajima Ryōsen, 94

Tsuruta, Kinya, 102n
Turgenev, Ivan, 101; and Futabatei Shimei, 41, 56, 145; *The Diary of a Superfluous Man* and Tayama Katai's *Futon* (The Quilt), 111; *A Sportsman's Sketches* and Tōson's *Chikumagawa no suketchi* (Sketches of the Chikuma River), 163n, 164; *Aibiki* (Futabatei's translation of Turgenev's *The Rendezvous*), 168

Ukigumo [The Floating Clouds] (Futabatei Shimei), 29, 114, 123, 193; as novel of individual, 34-35, 41, 48, 57; psychological analysis in, 34-35, 117-18; reaction of Tokutomi Roka, 37; and Dostoevsky's *Crime and Punishment*, 38; and Goncharov's *Oblomov*, 41, 47-48, 55-56; reviewed by Ishibashi Ningetsu, 49; as descendant of political novels (*seiji-shōsetsu*), 53; as fulfillment of Tsubouchi Shōyō's ideal of novel, 57, 58; depiction of man and nature in, 167-69; love in, 254; self-definition in, 259. *See also* Bunzō, Futabatei Shimei, Noboru

Valency, Maurice, 82n-83n, 254n
Verlaine, Paul, 216n

Wada Kingo, 175n
Wagatsuma, Hiroshi, 172n
Walker, Janet A., 260n, 278n, 279n
Wang Yang-ming School, 265n
Warens, Madame de, 100
Watt, Ian, 12n
Westernization, 106n
Whistler, James A. M., 163

Wordsworth, William, 76, 81n, 139; and Tōson, 131, 133, 134, 139, 142-43. *See also* nature

Wurmser, André, 270n

Yamaji Aizan, 75-76
Yamamori, Tetsunao, 65n, 129n
Yasuoka Shōtarō, 275n
Yosa Buson, 161
Yosano Akiko: use of *tanka* form, 87-90; and *Myōjō* (Bright Star), 87; *Midare-gami* (Tangled Hair), 87, 88n, 89n, 90-91; freedom, ideal of, 88-91; love, ideal of, 88-91
Yosano Tekkan, 87, 88
Yoshida Kenkō, 7; *Tsurezure-gusa*

(Grasses of Idleness), 5, 209; similarity to Meiji writers, 60
Yoshida Seiichi, 102n, 103n, 159n, 161n, 169n

Zen Buddhism, 7, 74, 101, 162, 166n, 258; concept of self, 5-6. *See also* Buddhism
Zola, Emile, 198n, 216; definition of Naturalism, 95-96, 97, 99; Zolaesque novel in Japan, 101-02, 123n, 165, 166n. *See also* Japanese Naturalism, Japanese Naturalist fiction
zuihitsu (random notes), 279n; and I-novel, 103; of Sei Shōnagon, 162, 163n

Library of Congress Cataloging in Publication Data

Walker, Janet A   1942-
   The Japanese novel of the Meiji period and the
ideal of individualism.

   Includes bibliographical references and index.
   1.   Japanese fiction—Meiji period, 1868-1912—
History and criticism.   2.   Individualism in literature.
3.   Shimazaki, Tōson, 1872-1943—Criticism and interpretation.   I.   Title.
PL747.6.W34   895.6'303   79-4501
ISBN 0-691-06400-8